A PROMISED LAND,
A PERILOUS JOURNEY

A PROMISED LAND,

A PERILOUS JOURNEY

Theological Perspectives on Migration

Edited by DANIEL G. GROODY

and GIOACCHINO CAMPESE

University of Notre Dame Press
Notre Dame, Indiana

Copyright © 2008 by University of Notre Dame

Notre Dame, Indiana 46556

www.undpress.nd.edu

All Rights Reserved

Designed by Wendy McMillen

Set in 10.6/13.9 Bembo by Four Star Books

Printed on 55# Natures Natural (50% PCR) by Thomson-Shore, Inc.

Reprinted in 2009, 2010

Library of Congress Cataloging-in-Publication Data

A promised land, a perilous journey : theological perspectives on migration /
edited by Daniel G. Groody and Gioacchino Campese.

p.   cm.

Includes bibliographical references and index.

ISBN-13: 978-0-268-02973-9 (pbk. : alk. paper)

ISBN-10: 0-268-02973-3 (pbk. : alk. paper)

1. Emigration and immigration—Religious aspects—Christianity.
2. United States—Emigration and immigration.   3. Mexico—Emigration and
immigration.   I. Groody, Daniel G., 1964–   II. Campese, Gioacchino, 1967–

BV2695.E4P76   2007

277.2'1086912—dc22

2007043189

To the thousands of immigrants

who are dying at the U.S.-Mexico border

in search of more dignified lives

Contents

CONTENTS

CONTENTS

A Witness to Hope

Migration and Human Solidarity

OSCAR ANDRÉS CARDINAL RODRÍGUEZ

The fact that thousands of migrants have died along the U.S.-Mexico border, and many more die each day, challenges all of us to ask why so many people suffer such injustice today.[1] History shows that people have trouble accepting those who they consider to be fundamentally "other" than themselves. While it took the United States centuries to officially acknowledge the dignity of Native Americans and African Americans, we still encounter the problem of discrimination in many different ways. The influx of immigrants from Latin America and other regions has continued this troubling dynamic, and it pushes us to ask the question: How is it that nearly twenty-one centuries after Jesus Christ, we still fail to see the migrant as our neighbor?

Sadly, the U.S.-Mexico border is not the only international border where migrants suffer indignities. Governments across Latin America are approving policies that directly or indirectly endanger the life of the migrant. For instance, in Honduras, migrants from Ecuador, Peru, and Colombia are encountering tougher and increasingly inhumane immigration policies. In many cases, immigration authorities in Mexico and Guatemala are becoming even more inhumane than those of the United States.[2] Why? What is happening to our humanity? Perhaps the problem lies in our failure to be the migrant's neighbor and our inability to work towards, as Pope John Paul II noted, "a globalization of solidarity."[3]

As they witnessed to the power of the risen Lord, the apostles urged the first Christian communities not to forget the poor among them.[4] This message is as relevant today as ever, and it has a special urgency, especially for us in Latin America because in most of our nations it is the poor—the migrant poor—who are supporting our economies. The remittances they send tend to be the most important and the most reliable income sources for our economies, especially in countries like El Salvador, Nicaragua, Guatemala, Mexico, and Honduras.[5]

Still, not everyone realizes the challenges involved in migration, neither in the migrant's homeland nor in the migrant's new country. In particular, the greatest difficulties are the suffering migrants experience when they decide to leave their loved ones, when they find their way north through dangerous lands, and when they finally face the daunting task of settling into a new place. Their suffering usually involves a process of letting go, of displacement and loss, and even mourning in various ways.

Migration and the Challenge of Mourning

We usually think of mourning when a loved one dies. But mourning is also experienced in many other situations. For instance, we mourn after a relationship breaks up, after losing a long-term job, or leaving a phase of life behind. In the case of the migrant, there is the deep mourning they feel when leaving their country of birth. Leaving friends and family is among the most painful moments in the life of the migrant. It means the disintegration of their emotional world, as well as the weakening, if not the disappearance, of a support system. Many migrants experience this isolation acutely when they are away from home and fall ill for the first time. For various reasons, sometimes they are unable to build a new basic support system in time of need, although sometimes such struggles also open for them the opportunity of discovering new friends and loved ones.

The migrant also mourns the inability to use his native language on a daily basis. Readjusting to a country where another language is spoken can be difficult and even traumatic since ideas, thoughts, perceptions, feelings, and knowledge are communicated through the medium of a shared language and a shared culture. Leaving one's culture behind is more than just leaving a geographical location because culture shapes one's identity and sense of place in the world. But perhaps for most Latin American immigrants, it is the loss of one's footing in their homelands that is most painful. The affective relationship with the land is powerful in our culture because through the land our ancestors are made present. To the migrants, the land is the *Madre Tierra,* the *Pacha Mama,* or Mother Earth.

According to psychologists, the geographical displacement migrants undergo is not insignificant because of this cultural mourning. The changes in scenery and weather and the movement from a rural to an urban setting take a toll on the psyche of migrants. Cultural coordinates, such as using public transportation, learning how to read basic street signals, and many other challenges, can become complex hurdles when migrants enter a new land. In their home countries, people may orient themselves by sights and sounds, by the colors of neighbors' homes, or even by plants and trees. The experience of learning street names, metro stations, fixed schedules, bus numbers, and such in the new country only increases the stress, anxiety, and suffering of migrants. Unfortunately, if they are unable to overcome these challenges, they begin to close themselves off to their new surroundings while at the same they romanticize their home culture.[6] Migrants may also experience sorrow for the loss of daily contact with their ethnic groups. It is there where race, culture, language, values, and beliefs take shape and permeate daily life. But if the migrants do not overcome such loss, they may fall prey to a type of ethnic fundamentalism or cultural absolutism.

Many people in receiving countries associate immigrants with people who are poor and uneducated. There are a number of immigrants with a college education or even a professional background, but when they become migrants, they must start their life anew in jobs of lower social status. This entails a certain professional mourning. Whereas some worked previously as lawyers or accountants, they are forced now to work as dishwashers and taxi drivers. As a consequence migrants end up interiorizing a sense of inferiority, yet their situation is greatly influenced by labor market factors and immigration policies.

Beyond the physical and professional challenges, migrants also suffer from various health problems including depression or even migraines and ulcers. All this helps us understand why the migrants mourn the loss of their own health. From the moment they leave their home countries, migrants become exposed to innumerable risks from malnutrition to exposure to infectious diseases. These risks rob migrants of their opportunity to achieve the full use of their God-given gifts along with their potential to serve the community at large according to their possibilities.

So is it hard to migrate? It is clear at this point that migrating is a difficult experience undertaken by strong people. It takes a strong character, body, mind, and soul to undertake this journey, which some have compared to a way of the cross.[7] In addition, we see in the journey of the migrants a troubling contradiction: although they sustain much of the infrastructure of the U.S. economy, they are forced to live as foreigners and outsiders. And although the United States is a country of immigrants, those who come to this country today from foreign lands are still marginalized and excluded. This happens not only in the United States but is a problematic pattern we see in other parts of the world as well. And while globalization has opened borders to capital and commerce, people are being left out.[8] This state of affairs cannot continue. The world must change.

Migration and the Challenge of Hope

Awareness of the migrants' plight and of the current state of the world is useless if such understanding is not placed at the service of hope. Hope is our strength because we are a people of faith. Therefore we may not become embittered because of so much suffering. We must share the good news through the sweet taste of the gospel. We need to remember basic evangelical attitudes if we are to become the migrant's neighbor: *accompaniment, encouragement,* and *generosity.* Sharing the journey with the migrants as companions entails remaining in love (Jn 15:1–11). Consider the enduring love of Jesus toward his apostles, to whom he gave the new commandment to love one another: "As I have loved you, so you also should love one another" (Jn 13:34). The one who truly shares the journey is the person who remains in love. Accompanying the migrant, though, also means doing so through the path of suffering, of pain, of depression, and of carrying their crosses with them. And so the road that leads to spiritual brotherhood and sisterhood is precisely that of sharing in their suffering.

In addition, there is no charity in justice without tears flowing from the eyes and the heart. Encouraging the migrants along the way—to animate them, to put life back into them—is also an important attitude we must learn from Jesus. Time and again throughout the Gospels our Lord animates, gives life and strength to those who in their suffering approach him. The Lord's concern for Peter and the apostles comes across even though he knew Peter and Judas would respectively deny and betray him. He tells Peter: "I have prayed that your own faith may not fail; and once you have turned back, you must strengthen your brothers" (Lk 22:32). As for generosity, we must not forget that our Lord identifies himself with the least among us: "For I was hungry and you gave me food, I was thirsty and you gave me drink, a stranger and you welcomed me, naked and you clothed me, ill and you cared for me, in prison and you visited me. . . . Amen, I say to you, whatever you did for one of these least brothers of mine, you did for me" (Mt 25:35–40). We must share our resources accordingly.

Those who accompany, encourage, and share generously with migrants must remember hope. We must hope against hope. We are called to do so especially within a hopeless humanity that is more and more paralyzed by fear. There is a fear, not without reason, that terrorists are everywhere. But fear is useless, and instead we must look for love far and wide. In this climate of fear, hope is difficult because it is not seen. Hope is not evident because it is only found when one looks for it. Hope is as fragile, small, and gentle as the little child that was born in Bethlehem. Therefore we must take care not to lose hope because, although it is as vulnerable as the Christmas baby, it is also as strong as the Easter resurrection. And our people, especially migrants, know this. They celebrate hope in our liturgy with joy even amidst the most painful suffering. Migrants know this, and we must it learn from them.

We have unfinished business, however. Many of the migrants who come to the United States are also migrating out of the Catholic Church and joining other churches. Why? Perhaps it is because we have abandoned them. Perhaps it is because they have not found a welcoming church, a friendly church. Perhaps they just do not know where the church is. This is a great challenge for the church in Latin America and the United States.[9] Perhaps it is because we are not missionary enough with our own people when they leave for the United States. We are not being shepherds in a way we are called to be, and we carry that burden in our conscience.

During the Santo Domingo Conference of Latin American Bishops in 1992, a proposal was made for the dioceses of Latin America to pay the expenses of priests and religious and other pastoral animators to carry on the mission of the church. When immigrants in the last two centuries came from Europe, they frequently brought their own chaplains that helped them establish faith communities in this country. If the bishops in Latin America and the whole of the church do not take more responsibility to evangelize migrants and respond to their needs, many may simply lose their faith or leave the church altogether.

Finally, I am very concerned about the second and third generation of the Latin American immigrant community. When good schools and health services are inaccessible, when even driver's licenses are beyond the reach of migrants, the children of migrants have few choices except to look for their options on the streets. If there is no home, no family, no love, where are these children going to grow up? The streets await them. Easy money earned through selling drugs awaits them. And sadly, prison may also await them. The biggest problem is not terrorism but organized drug trafficking. Drug traffickers and drug dealers are the ones supporting arms trafficking, gangs, and the kidnapping industry. If this trend continues, our people will only become increasingly marginalized and will be looked upon as criminals. We cannot ask migrants to stop having children, nor may we prevent them from uniting with their families. Are these children going to be the true victims in the future? We need responsible and creative answers. We need to accompany the migrants even to the point of suffering with them. And yet, we must hope against all hope, even and especially in the face of enormous challenges. This is our calling. We are called to see in our migrant brothers and sisters a common humanity and work together for a common solidarity, that is, a community of love and fellowship reflective of the reign of God.

NOTES

1. For statistics on the deaths of immigrants at the U.S.-Mexico border and more information on the U.S. southern border strategy see www.stopgatekeeper .org. This border strategy has also been denounced by the joint document of the Mexican Catholic Bishops' Conference and the United States Conference of

Catholic Bishops, *Strangers No Longer: Together on the Journey of Hope* (Washington, DC: United States Conference of Catholic Bishops, 2003), 86–89. This document can be downloaded from www.usccb.org.

2. On the process of constructing "fortress continents" in the Americas (following the example of the European Community) see Naomi Klein, "The Rise of the Fortress Continent," www.thenation.com, February 3, 2003.

3. John Paul II, *Ecclesia in America*, 55 (available at http://www.vatican.va).

4. In Gal 2:10 Paul says that when he went to Jerusalem the apostles James, Cephas (Peter), and John "asked only one thing, that we remember the poor, which was actually what I was eager to do."

5. For more information on the size and impact of remittances by immigrants from the USA see Kevin O'Neil, "Remittances from the United States in Context," www.migrationinformation.org, June 1, 2003.

6. For a discussion of the diverse and multiple implications of the process of migration for the mental health of immigrants see Alejandro Portes and Rubén G. Rumbaut, *Immigrant America: A Portrait*, rev. ed. (Berkeley: University of California Press, 1996), 155–91.

7. Gioacchino Campese and Flor María Rigoni, "Hacer Teología desde el Migrante: Diario de un Camino," in *Migration, Religious Experience, and Globalization*, ed. Gioacchino Campese and Pietro Ciallella (New York: Center for Migration Studies, 2003), 184. See also Daniel Groody, *Border of Death, Valley of Life: An Immigrant Journey of Heart and Spirit* (Lanham, MD: Rowman and Littlefield, 2002).

8. This stark contradiction between economic integration promoted by the North American Free Trade Agreement (NAFTA) and the U.S. refusal to deal with the immigration issue is repeatedly denounced by Douglas S. Massey, Jorge Durand, and Nolan J. Malone, *Beyond Smoke and Mirrors: Mexican Immigration in an Era of Economic Integration* (New York: Russell Sage Foundation, 2002).

9. This issue has been underlined in the document by the U.S. Catholic Bishops, *Encuentro and Mission* (Washington, D.C., 2002), 64–66. This document can be downloaded at www.usccb.org. See also Allan Figueroa Deck, "A Latino Practical Theology: Mapping the Road Ahead," *Theological Studies* 65, no. 2 (2004): 291–92.

Preface

This book is the fruit of a common journey of faith, a common mission, and a friendship that began developing across borders. We (Gioacchino Campese and Daniel Groody) first met at a conference on "Migration, Religious Experience, and Globalization," which took place on January 24–27, 2002, in Tijuana, Mexico, just across the line from California. This conference was organized by the Scalabrinian missionaries in the United States and the Transborder Institute of the University of San Diego, California.[1] It was a first attempt to promote theological reflection on the experience of international migration, with a particular emphasis on undocumented, Mexican immigrants coming to the United States. At the same time it became an opportunity for human rights activists, religious leaders, scholars, and others involved in the issue of migration to establish relationships and to share ideas, experiences, and common concerns. This conference was the beginning of many important relationships that gave birth to many significant projects, including this one.

Following the conference we met again at Casa del Migrante in Tijuana, a shelter for immigrants run by the Scalabrinian missionaries, where Gioacchino had been working for seven years. On the other side of the border, Daniel had been working with immigrants in Coachella, California, while pursuing his doctoral studies.[2] During our conversations we realized that foremost in our hearts and minds was our pastoral interest in the plight of immigrants, who were suffering and dying in alarming numbers at the U.S.-Mexico border. At the same time, we wanted to do more serious theological reflection that emerged precisely out of this painful context. Not only was there an urgent need for this reflection, but also we felt it was long overdue. In the months and years that followed, others in church and academic circles reiterated the urgency of this issue and the hunger for a more solid conceptual grounding of theology and migration.

Over a breakfast in Casa del Migrante, we wanted to explore other ways to continue this important conversation. On September 19–22, 2004, we organized an international conference on migration and theology at the University of Notre Dame. The interest and participation in this event was much greater than we anticipated, which confirmed our sense that we were on the right track, speaking to an important need and addressing a very relevant issue. After this conference we asked various other scholars to submit articles for this present volume.

As a complement to the scholarly issues in this volume, we recognized that more work had to be done in reshaping the imagination of people in regards to who these immigrants are, where they come from, and what they go through in coming to the United States, mostly to work at jobs that no one else wants. We felt one of the best ways to do this was through a video production. We wanted to portray the human face of these immigrants, the face of Christ that became evident to us (Mt 25:35), and the profound, but often hidden, theological dimension of their perilous journey toward the "promised land." Frequently we have likened this journey to the way of the cross, and one of the central theological challenges has been deciphering and discerning the dimensions of death and resurrection in this journey. For three years we worked on the production of a DVD called *Dying to Live*. We interviewed leading scholars in the field, border patrol agents, smugglers, pastoral workers, and immigrants, and they helped shape both the socioeconomic, political, and above all theological contours of this issue. Since its release in the fall of 2005, *Dying to Live* has been used in various educational settings ranging from parishes to colleges around the world. It has been accepted to various international film festivals, won numerous awards, and has aired on various television stations, including PBS. More information about the film can be found at www.dyingtolive.nd.edu. This film offers an important supplement to this volume precisely because many of the scholars in the film also have essays in this work.

Migration today, perhaps more than in any other era in human history, is a worldwide phenomenon that is integrally related to the dynamics of globalization.[3] This book, in fact, precipitated a more systematic reflection on the relationship not only of theology to immigration but also of theology to globalization.[4] While all the essays are written with these global dimensions in mind, our focus will be on how this phenomenon is experienced particularly at the U.S.-Mexico border, which is closest to our context, our experience, and our hearts.

At the same time, we also believe that what is happening at this particular border has important universal implications. The border reveals, perhaps more than any other context, the controversial nature of migration, the misunderstandings and ignorance that surround it, and the political interests that criminalize and dehumanize the immigrants themselves. Images and metaphors fanning fears of invasions, borders out of control, criminality, drug smuggling, and—especially since the tragic events of 9/11—threats of national security abound in virtually any debate about immigration in the United States. Much of the mass media, instead of helping to sort out this issue, unfortunately adds to and promotes this negative anti-immigrant rhetoric. During these debates many so-called experts and pundits reveal a simplistic and politically charged understanding of immigration, which often leads them to the conclusion that it is only by getting tougher at the border and criminalizing all "illegal aliens" that the "problem" will be solved. These people, willingly or unwillingly, tend to forget and ignore that immigration is a complex issue that has no easy solutions because it has become an integral part of the globalization process, which demands not only movements of ideas and products but also of people. Our reflection then is not only about the border where the United States meets Mexico but about the border between national security and human insecurity, sovereign rights and human rights, citizenship and discipleship. We believe a serious reflection on the theological dimensions of immigration helps us go beyond inflammatory debates and consider in a deeper way what it means to be human before God and what it means to live together as a human community.

A serious intellectual debate on immigration requires listening to all sides of the conversation in order to understand the concerns that all constituencies bring to the table. Many of the issues that surface are legitimate and need to be considered, no matter how extreme, but too often the concerns of the central protagonists—namely, the immigrants and their families—go completely unheard, unrecognized, and unheeded. Whenever the voices of the immigrants are left out of the debate, our capacity to see the fundamental human dignity of these people is diminished, which paves the way to various kinds of injustices. As people created in the image and likeness of God, this same dignity is the foundation from which to build a Christian interpretation of the immigrant reality.

In recent decades, U.S. Hispanic theologians, especially the pioneering work of Virgilio Elizondo, Orlando Espín, Roberto Goizueta, and others, have made important contributions to our contextualized understanding of Latinos in the United States.[5] More recently, various Latina theologians, such as María Pilar Aquino, Jeanette Rodríguez, Daisy Machado, Carmen Nanko, Michelle Gonzalez, Nancy Piñeda and others, have looked at the unique experience of women and their struggles for dignity, empowerment, and human liberation.[6] A Christian theological interpretation of the border reality, however, has been one of the most neglected areas of immigration research.[7] While recently social scientists have been rediscovering the importance of religion in the journey of immigrants in the United States, theologians have not yet fully explored the theological implications of the reality of migration. It is precisely the theological dimension of the phenomenon of migration—beginning with the humanity of the immigrant—that we consider the foremost contribution of this volume.

Building on the methodology of other praxis-based theologies, one of our central goals is to propose a theology of immigration based on the experience of immigrants and the reality of immigration. The essays contained in this volume are divided into four parts. The first three parts examine the reality of immigration, the theological tradition and political context that affect our interpretation of that reality, and the pastoral practice that in turn shapes our theological reflection. The final part does not offer a definitive theology of immigration but offers some initial ways through which such a theology can begin to be developed and articulated.

In the first part the authors provide the foundations of a theology of migration. The first article by Jacqueline Hagan is a description of religion, and particularly popular religion, as an essential resource in the difficult journey of undocumented migrants. Her social-scientific perspective adds to our understanding of popular religion as an important *locus theologicus* in the context of migration and is an invitation to theologians to join in fruitful dialogue with social scientists on the topic of the faith of immigrants. Donald Senior offers in his essay some important biblical perspectives on the subject of migration and summarizes the main motifs that the New Testament texts attach to the experience of social dislocation. Peter C. Phan deals with the era immediately following the New Testament communities and writings, also known as the patristic era, and provides historical and theological overviews of the importance of the theme of migration during this influential period of church and world history. Drawing on personal experience, as well as the experience of mystics, poets, and other writers throughout the ancient tradition and contemporary times, Alex Nava discusses the metaphor of the desert, and examines the challenge of finding the mystery of the divine presence amidst the death of many at the border. Gustavo Gutiérrez approaches the issue from a more systematic perspective, and particularly from the optic of the option for the poor, one of the essential theological themes of contemporary Christian theology.

The second part deals with the issue of mission and ministry to the migrants both in theoretical and practical terms. Stephen Bevans lays out the missiological and ecclesiological principles of ministry to the immigrants and of the immigrants, and in this way reminds the church that these people are not just a preferential target of our ministry but that they are also the protagonists of the *Missio Dei*. Robert Schreiter underlines the significance of the ministry of reconciliation in the context of migration, and describes the steps that must be taken to address the challenges that the migrants have to confront in the different stages of the migration process. Giovanni Graziano Tassello traces the trajectory of the Scalabrinian tradition of ministry among migrants, which is one of the most extensive outreaches to immigrants around the world, and looks at how this tradition can help us face the challenges ahead. The last two essays of this section narrate and reflect on two particular experiences of direct ministry to the migrants in two different geographical contexts in the United States. Patrick Murphy reflects on his ministerial experience among the growing population of Hispanic immigrants in Kansas City, Kansas, and enumerates the challenges that such a ministry poses to the Catholic Church in the United States. Robin Hoover gives an account of an ecumenical and civic initiative, the organization Humane Borders, which aids undocumented immigrants at the U.S.-Mexico border, and whose goals include not only saving the lives of these human beings but also influencing the political process that leads to the formulation of U.S. immigrations laws.

The third part treats the issues of global ethics, human rights, and gender. Here the authors formulate some of the ethical and philosophical principles that should guide the policy and politics of migration. In a context in which immigration is seen from a moral and legal perspective, which tends to emphasize solely the fact that immigrants are breaking the "law of the land," these essays bring challenging and refreshing insights to the table. Graziano Battistella shows the advantages and limitations of a human rights approach to migration, which leads him to a meaningful discussion of the ethical bases of migration policies. The ethics of inclusion proposed by the social teachings of the Catholic Church provide a solid foundation for migration policies and are a powerful reminder of more fundamental human and Christian values. Donald Kerwin indicates how the debate about immigration policies unfolds in the United States. He affirms that the actual immigration legislation does not reflect the natural rights of immigrants, and shows how the Catholic tradition helps clarify what these rights are and how they are to be promoted in a post-9/11 United States. Raúl Fornet-Betancourt talks about the dynamics of intercultural interaction, which is a constitutive part of the collective transformation of a society. The last paper of this part deals with the issue of gender, which has been until very recently one of the most neglected dimensions in the study of migration. In a revealing essay Olivia Ruiz Marrujo explains the numerous risks associated with the journey of immigrant women, underlining perhaps one of the most painful and less talked about aspect of their immigration experience, that is, sexual violence.[8]

The fourth and last part of this volume offers three different theological interpretations of the reality of the U.S.-Mexico border seen from the optic of migration. Jorge E. Castillo Guerra proposes an intercultural methodology for theologizing about the reality of migration. Gioacchino Campese employs the metaphor of the crucified people, coined by Ignacio Ellacuría and later developed by Jon Sobrino, to explain how especially undocumented immigrants live and experience the reality of the U.S.-Mexico border. In his essay he underlines both the prophetic and grace-filled dimensions of this "crucified" reality. Daniel Groody relates the reality of the U.S.-Mexico border to the theology of the Eucharist, and shows how the experience and witness of immigrants can give us a new way of understanding God's presence through the encounter with Christ in the migrant and the encounter with Christ in this sacrament. In this encounter we can begin to see Christ in the eyes of the immigrant and begin to see the immigrant with the eyes of Christ.

This volume would not have been possible without the commitment, collaboration, and friendship of many people. First of all we thank our religious communities, the Congregation of Holy Cross and the Missionaries of St. Charles (Scalabrinians), for their unwavering support of this project. Secondly, our gratitude and recognition goes to the people who organized the "Migration and Theology" conference and made it possible with their dedication and hard work: John Cavadini, Gilbert Cardenas, Allert Brown-Gort, Terry Garza, Claudia Ramirez, Virgilio Elizondo, Anthony Suarez, Joseph Fugolo, Claudio Holzer, Edward Malloy, and Gustavo Gutiérrez. Victor Carmona also was of great assistance in transcribing and translating much of the material that contributed to the essays of Gustavo Gutiérrez and Oscar Cardinal Rodríguez. Special thanks also to Raquel Ferrer, Larry Cunningham, Mark Roche, Gretchen Reydams-Schils, Julia Braungart-Rieker, Carolyn Woo, Tim Matovina, Bill Seetch, Maribel Rodriguez, Zoe Samora, Caroline Domingo, Cheryl Kelly, Doug Franson, Nathan Hatch, Brett Keck, and Marisa Marquez. Mary J. Miller in particular has provided detailed and careful editorial feedback, frequently going above and beyond the call of duty, which has been invaluable in the preparation of this volume. Our gratitude goes also to the following institutions and departments of the University of Notre Dame: the Office of the President, the Department of Theology, the Institute for Latino Studies, the Graduate School, the Center for Civil and Human Rights, the Center for Social Concerns, the College of Arts and Letters, the Institute for Scholarship in the Liberal Arts, the Kellogg Institute for International Studies, the Mendoza College of Business, the Henkels Lecture Series, and the Center for Continuing Education. We are also thankful to the two Scalabrinian North American Provinces, St. John the Baptist and St. Charles Borromeo, the Scalabrini International Migration Institute, and the Center for Migration Studies. Finally we acknowledge the support of the Catholic Relief Services, the Secretariat for the Church in Latin America, and Migration and Refugee Services of the United States Conference of Catholic Bishops.

Through the efforts of this book, we hope to create a space where the voice of the powerless can be heard so that we can work together for a more just, peaceful, and humane world that is reflective of the reign of God. Above all, we dedicate this book to those who have died in the deserts of the American Southwest, particularly the nameless multitudes who have perished without a trace, yet whose lives are known to God alone.

NOTES

1. Most of the papers presented at that conference have been published in Gioacchino Campese and Pietro Ciallella, eds., *Migration, Religious Experience, and Globalization* (New York: Center for Migration Studies, 2003).

2. One of the outcomes of this period of ministry and research has been the publication of Daniel G. Groody, *Border of Death, Valley of Life: An Immigrant Journey of Heart and Spirit* (Lanham, MD: Rowman and Littlefield, 2002).

3. See Stephen Castles and Mark J. Miller, *The Age of Migration: International Population Movements in the Modern World*, 3rd ed. (New York: Guilford Press, 2003).

4. For more on the issue of globalization and theology, see Daniel G. Groody, *Globalization, Spirituality, and Justice: Navigating the Path to Peace* (Maryknoll: Orbis Books, 2007).

5. Virgilio P. Elizondo, *Galilean Journey: The Mexican-American Promise* (Maryknoll, NY: Orbis, 1983); Orlando O. Espín, "Immigration, Territory, and Globalization: Theological Reflections," *Journal of Hispanic/Latino Theology* 7, no. 3 (2000): 46–59, and *The Faith of the People: Theological Reflections of the People* (Maryknoll, NY: Orbis, 1997); Roberto Goizueta, *Caminemos Con Jesús: Toward a Hispanic/Latino Theology of Accompaniment* (Maryknoll, NY: Orbis, 1995); Timothy Matovina, ed., *Beyond Borders: Writings of Virgilio Elizondo and Friends* (Maryknoll, NY: Orbis, 2000).

6. Daisy L. Machado, "The Unnamed Woman: Justice, Feminists, and the Undocumented Woman," in *A Reader in Latina Feminist Theology*, ed. María Pilar Aquino, Daisy L. Machado, Jeanette Rodríguez, 161–76 (Austin: University of Texas Press, 2002); Carmen Marie Nanko, "Justice Crosses the Border: The Preferential Option for the Poor in the United States," in Aquino et al., *A Reader in Latina Feminist Theology*, 177–203.

7. Among the many studies in this field, see Robert A. Orsi, *The Madonna of 115th Street: Faith and Community in Italian Harlem, 1880–1950* (New Haven: Yale University Press, 1985); Jorge Durand and Douglas S. Massey, *Miracles on the Border: Retablos of Mexican Migrants to the United States* (Tucson: University of Arizona Press, 1995); R. Stephen Warner and Judith G. Wittner, eds., *Gatherings in Diaspora: Religious Communities and the New Immigration* (Philadelphia: Temple University Press, 1998); R. Stephen Warner, "Religion and New (Post-1965) Immigrants: Some Principles Drawn from Field Research," *American Studies* 41, nos. 2–3 (2000): 267–86, and "Coming to America," *Christian Century*, Feb. 10, 2004, 20; Helen R. Ebaugh and Janet S. Chafetz, eds., *Religion and the New Immigrants: Continuities and Adaptations in Immigrant Congregations* (Walnut Creek, CA: AltaMira Press, 2000), and *Religion Across Borders: Transnational Immigrant Networks* (Walnut Creek, CA: AltaMira Press, 2002); Jacqueline Hagan and Helen R. Ebaugh, "Calling Upon the Sacred: Migrants' Use of Religion in the Migration Process," *International Migration Review* 37,

no. 4 (2003): 1145–62; Pierrette Hondagneu-Sotelo et. al., "'There is a Spirit that Transcends the Border': Faith, Ritual, and Postnational Protest at the U.S.-Mexico Border," *Sociological Perspectives* 47, no. 2 (2004): 133–59; Pierrette Hondagneu-Sotelo, ed., *Religion and Social Justice for Immigrants* (New Brunswick, NJ: Rutgers University Press, 2006).

8. On the issue of gender and immigration in the United States see also Pierrette Hondagneu-Sotelo, ed., *Gender and U.S. Immigration: Contemporary Trends* (Berkeley: University of California Press, 2003).

PART ONE

Foundations of a Theology
of Migration

CHAPTER ONE

Faith for the Journey

Religion as a Resource for Migrants

JACQUELINE HAGAN

When Celia traveled to the United States from her hometown of Puebla, Mexico, in 1991, she was nineteen years of age. Unable to pay for the training she needed to pursue a career as a medical technician, and with little hope of securing a meaningful job in Mexico, she decided to follow the path taken by many of her friends and head north to the U.S. She, her sister, and her brother-in-law flew to the Mexican border city of Tijuana, where they met a *coyote* they knew and trusted, who, for a fee of $500 per person, accompanied them across the border into California. Before embarking on what she suspected would be a dangerous journey and uncertain future, they performed a series of religious rituals at home. Celia's mother purchased a bouquet of flowers and two *veladora* of the Virgin of Guadalupe (a candle in a glass container that is adorned with the image of the Virgin) with which she "cleaned" (rubbed over) the bodies of her two daughters. Once this domestic ritual was completed, they went to their local church and asked the priest to bless the girls, the flowers, and the candles. The priest anointed Celia and her sister with holy water while performing his blessing, gave a holy card of the Virgin of Guadalupe to carry with them and wished them good fortune and safety on their trip. He urged them to "work hard and to send money home to their parents and sisters." The day of their departure from Puebla, their mother lit the candles and placed them, along with the flowers, next to a statue of the Virgin of Guadalupe on a home-made altar in the main room of their home. The candles stayed lit until Celia called her mother the next day from San Isidro, California, to let her know they had arrived safely. Recalling the experience brought Celia to tears.

Celia is one of many young and poor undocumented migrants from Latin America who are forced to migrate because of deteriorating economic conditions and opportunities in their home communities. Prospective migrants, who rarely traveled beyond the villages and towns in which they spent their whole lives, are now forced to contemplate a trip to a strange land with a foreign culture. Husbands leave behind wives, not knowing when they will see them again. Mothers, fearing for the safety and future of their children, leave them behind in the care of trusted relatives. Increasingly, even adolescent boys and girls, lacking any educational or economic prospects in their home communities, have no recourse but to bid farewell to their families and head north in search of some small glimmer of opportunity. The more fortunate can pay for a *coyote* to help them travel to the United States. However, as the dangers of crossing have escalated in recent years because of increased enforcement efforts along the Mexico-Guatemala and U.S.-Mexico borders, so too have the *coyote* fees, which, for migrants traveling from Central America, can reach as high as $8,000 per person. To pay the *coyote,* migrant families often put up their homes or land for collateral. Even with the protection of a *coyote,* a successful journey is not guaranteed. The journey is long and arduous. Migrants from Guatemala, for example, must endure the dangers of traveling across two heavily guarded international borders and a thousand miles of treacherous terrain. Even if they manage to cross successfully into the United States, the potential perils continue. The unforgiving heat of the Texas and Arizona deserts and blistering cold of the California mountains place them in harm's way. During the long trek, migrants fall prey to local bandits, corrupt border officials, and reckless *coyotes* using dangerous tactics. Robbery, assaults, accidents, and even deaths along the journey are increasingly common for undocumented Latin Americans traveling north to the United States.[1]

To cope with these perceived hardships, many prospective migrants do what Celia did: they turn to that which they hold sacred—their religious icons—and to those they know and trust—their families and local clergy. Drawing on the migration experiences of several hundred recent migrants from Mexico and Central America, in this essay I discuss how undocumented migrants—Catholics and Protestant, frequent and rare church-goers, men and women—draw on sacred images and local clergy to prepare for the hardships and uncertainty of the migration journey.[2]

My approach to the migration process departs from that of most research about the origins of poor labor migration from Latin America. In general, migration scholars focus either on the economic factors that drive poor migrants from Latin America to the United States or on the social processes that sustain it. Theories that attempt to explain why migrants make the decision to leave their home communities usually depend on some mix of economic variables operating at different levels of analysis.[3] To explain the persistence of flows, scholars usually focus on conditions that arise during the course of migration, such as migrants' personal networks, which reduce the cost for subsequent migrants from the home community, along with the development of institutions that support international migration.[4] What has been largely neglected in scholarship is the inclusion of the cultural context of the migration experience, specifically, the spiritual resources that religion contributes to the migration process. For many prospective migrants, religion reinforces their decision to migrate and fortifies them psychologically and spiritually to prepare for the hardships of the journey. It also sanctions what is otherwise defined as an illegal act by the state.

This gap in the literature is striking when we consider that poor and working-class Latin Americans share a long historical tradition of turning to religion for solace and guidance in times of personal crisis, such as illness or job loss. Lacking the economic resources to change their precarious situations or to realize their aspirations, many religious poor seek divine intervention. The hundreds of thousands of daily petitions that pilgrims leave at shrines and churches throughout Latin America testify to people's reliance on their church, its saints, and holy images when faced with personal problems or formidable challenges. When marginalized from the church, the poor and the downtrodden in some areas of Latin America, including the U.S.-Mexico border region, have created their own folk saints and holy images for psychological sustenance.[5]

Preliminary field evidence from other studies suggests that religious ministries in migrant-sending communities are not only well aware of the spiritual needs of prospective migrants, but they cater to them. In an earlier study of a Maya transnational community that encompasses one municipality in the Totonicapan department of the highlands of Guatemala, and several neighborhoods of settlement in Houston, Texas, we showed how evangelical pastors provided for migrant needs in their ministries by incorporating migration counseling into their services.[6] In another study of Pentecostalism and migration, Rijk Van Dijk found that departing migrants turn to healing and deliverance rituals at prayer camps in Ghana for spiritual counsel and protection in their travel.[7] From this research and my own, it is clear that many migrants draw on religious and spiritual resources to help them prepare for the journey, especially if the journey is perceived as a dangerous one, as it is for the lion's share of departing undocumented migrants from Latin America.

The Financial and Human Costs of Departure

Uprooting oneself from family and community, and fortifying oneself for a journey of hardship and an uncertain length of stay in a foreign land, involves a host of practical and religious preparations, most of which have enormous financial and psychological consequences for migrants and their families. Many migrants had to scrape together their meager earnings and sell their only assets to cover the cost of the journey—perhaps a *coyote*'s fees—and initial settlement in the United States. Some drew on savings, while others borrowed from family and friends. Others were forced to make enormous sacrifices and take large financial risks. Armando, a forty-two-year-old Catholic, left his hometown in Honduras for the United States in 2001. In Honduras, he and his brothers were struggling to hold on to their coffee fields, but the collapse of coffee prices was making their livelihood increasingly precarious. To pay for his trip to the United States, he sold his portion of the family land, his house, his truck, and his animals. En route to the United States, he was assaulted and robbed of most of his belongings. He made it across the border with the help of some companions he met along the way. They wandered for days in Texas ranchland before arriving by foot in Houston. He worked as a day laborer and stayed at a Houston shelter for several months, until he earned enough money to move into an apartment with other migrants. Several years after his arrival, he was earning only $600 a month working part-time as a janitor in a movie theater. He has been unable to recoup his losses. As Armando explained, "I expected to make enough money in several months to help my family back home.

I have not yet been really able to help them. I have no working papers so I can't find better work. I have nothing here, but I gave up everything at home so how can I return?"

In addition to sacrificing all they own to cover the costs of travel and settlement—without any assurance of a successful outcome—prospective migrants also face the heartbreaking chore of burdening family and friends with the care of loved ones, including children, that they leave behind. Not knowing how long they will be separated from family members, this task takes its toll on departing migrants, but some find refuge and comfort in religion. Daniela, a devout Pentecostal and wife and mother, left her home in Oaxaca, Mexico, for the United States in the late 1990s. For some time she struggled with the decision to join her husband in Texas because it meant leaving her children in Mexico. "I didn't want to come here. My husband sent money to my nephew to get a *coyote* to take me to him." As much as she missed her husband and wanted to see him, she refused to leave her three young daughters. Only when her husband sent her a substantial sum of money to give to her mother to provide for the long-term care of her children did she decide to leave. Even then, she was tormented: "I prayed and I fasted and asked God to give me the strength and peace I needed to leave my children. I prayed that my children would not cry when I left; they didn't. That was a sign from God that I could go." Sadly, many young mothers in the sample who traveled to the United States for work left one or more of their children behind. Fearful of taking their children, especially the young and the female, along with them on the dangerous journey north, they had no choice but to leave them in the care of female relatives. Concern for the long-term well-being of their children dominated their prayers.

Calling Upon the Sacred

Burdened by these overwhelming financial, emotional, and psychological concerns, prospective migrants—like Daniela—turn to religion for fortitude and spiritual sustenance as they prepare for the journey north. Among the sub sample of 202 departing undocumented migrants, more than three-quarters (78 percent) turned to God to help them with the decision to migrate. Moreover, four out of five members of the sample—women and men, Protestants and Catholics, Central Americans and Mexicans alike—prayed to God, a saint, a religious icon, or sought counsel from trusted local clergy within several days prior to embarking on their journey. Calling upon the sacred during the preparation stage of migration manifested itself in numerous ways.

Most Catholics and Protestants prayed in solitude or with family members. Central American and Mexican Catholics alone, however, sought guidance from the Virgin Mary and other holy images, many of which are popular religious icons in their home communities. With their long tradition of venerating sacred images of Christ and the Virgin, Mexicans also turned to other holy icons as they prepared for their journey north, the most called upon of which was the Virgin of Guadalupe, the patroness of Mexico. Migrants from the well-established sending communities of western Mexico—a region long recognized for its faith and devotion—called upon the area's many religious images for spiritual guidance in preparing for the journey. Among those icons were the Virgin of San Juan of Los Lagos, the Virgin of Zapopan, the baby Christ (Santo Niño de Atocha), and San Toribio, the latter two of which are known among their followers for the miracles they grant travelers in danger, including journeying migrants. Catholics from Central America also called upon their popular icons of Christ and the Virgin for guidance and protection when preparing for the journey. A number of Catholic Hondurans and Guatemalans prayed to the Black Christ (El Cristo Negro), an image with whom many indigenous Maya Catholics identify and who is located in the sanctuary of Nuestro Señor de Esquipulas in Eastern Guatemala, several miles from the Honduran border. Several of the migrants from Honduras also prayed to the patroness of their country, the Virgin of Suyapa (Nuestra Señora de Suyapa). Among the Salvadoran migrants, that country's spiritual protector, Our Lady of Peace (Nuestra Señora de la Paz), provided a major source of guidance to prospective migrants.

The prayers departing migrants made reflected the practical concerns of those leaving behind the only life they have known and embarking on a journey of uncertainty. When praying to God, the Virgin, or a religious image, individuals generally requested guidance and help in securing a *coyote* and travel funds, protection on the journey, care for family members left behind, and assistance during initial settlement in the United States. Several days before leaving his hometown of Morelia, in Michoacan, Mexico, Carlos, a devout Catholic, began to pray in earnest. "I prayed many times each day. I prayed for protection from evil forces I might see on the journey north,

I prayed for the protection of my wife and children who stayed home, and I prayed to God and to the Virgen de Guadalupe to let me enter safely into the United States so that I could find work to feed and house my family." Carlos's general plea to God was a prayer echoed by many departing migrants.

By a large margin, the most important concern that departing undocumented migrants expressed through private prayer was protection on the journey. More than two-thirds (68 percent) requested protection on the journey; in particular, they prayed for their personal safety and security. Carla, a Catholic and wife and mother, prayed to the Virgin Mary on a constant basis before leaving her home in La Union, in El Salvador, with her two-year-old daughter. "My husband sent us $6,000 to get a *coyote* and a letter with instructions for traveling, but I was scared. I went to church the day before we left and prayed to God and to the Virgin Mary. I said the rosary and I fasted for twenty-four hours. I prayed to the Virgin Mary to protect me and my daughter on the trip and to let us arrive safely to the home of my husband."

Among the undocumented sample, nearly half (42 percent)—Catholics and Protestants—also made one or more *special religious preparations* before leaving their hometowns. These preparations included receiving final blessings by clergy, visiting sacred shrines to make petitions, and purchasing religious items to accompany them on their trip. The most widespread religious practice that departing migrants and their families undertook was consultation with clergy. During these private consultations, migrants presented and discussed their hopes and fears, but most of all they sought final blessings from their spiritual leaders. These blessings provide comfort to prospective migrants and the family they leave behind.

Catholic religious workers in Mexico and Central America spoke often of the frequency and the importance of these blessings and other last minute religious preparations for departing migrants. A Scalabrinian sister who is a Brazilian woman and who runs a shelter for displaced women in Tijuana, Mexico, explained that she often receives requests for blessings from departing migrants before they leave to cross the border.[8] Although she feels somewhat awkward about providing blessings because she is not an ordained priest, she nonetheless complies. As she explains, "How can I refuse them? Their faith is too strong to resist. They truly believe that God will help them endure the migration. Without God they have nothing." An evangelical lay worker, a young woman, who works closely with her father who is pastor of an evangelical church and director of a Salvation Army shelter in

Tijuana, expressed similar sentiments. "We always bless them," she explained. "Although we do not encourage their departure, we recognize how important a blessing is for them on the long and hard journey."

Even when the blessings fail to protect the migrants on their journey, their faith in God does not waiver. An Argentinean priest and Scalabrinian missionary, who works with migrants in Juarez, Mexico, reported that it was not uncommon for him to provide final blessings to several departing migrants each day. On one occasion, a group of five migrants—three Hondurans and two Mexicans—approached him for a blessing before crossing the U.S.-Mexico border. He complied with their requests, but less than three weeks later, they called him from a Mexican border city about eight hours from Juarez and explained that they had been apprehended by U.S. Border Patrol agents and sent back to Mexico. They now wanted to come to see the priest to receive another blessing before attempting the trip again. Once the migrants arrived, the young priest asked them, with a touch of irony, "So the blessing didn't help you that much, did it? Why would you want another one?" As he explains, they responded with pure faith and conviction: "Father, forgive me if I contradict you, but with that blessing we arrived as far as Houston, if we had not had your blessing, who knows how far we might have gone, probably not even to the border." This steadfast belief in the power of these blessings was a constant theme.

Migrants receive many of these blessings at shrines they visit prior to departure. The most popular pilgrimage site in Mexico, the Basilica de Guadalupe in Mexico City, is home to the country's most revered religious image, the Virgin of Guadalupe. Among the many pilgrims who throng to the basilica on a daily basis are departing or journeying migrants. Some come to be blessed by the priest who holds court in a small glass room just outside the church store. The priest, who blesses hundreds of pilgrims a day, explained that in the months of May and June, the hottest and deadliest crossing months for migrants, he is often approached for requests for final blessings from young men and women who are preparing for the journey to the United States. Departing migrants also visit the massive retail store in the basilica, which is crammed with religious items commemorating the "Queen of Mexico," ranging from prayer books to T-shirts to medallions. According to staff at the store, the most popular item purchased by departing migrants is the *Devocionario del Migrante* (*Migrants Prayer Book*), which is published by the Catholic Diocese of Mexico City and the Scalabrinian congregation, the Italian Catholic congregation that provides pastoral care for migrants throughout the world. The fifty-six-page prayer book, which is provided to migrants by clergy throughout Mexico, contains numerous prayers for migrants to recite on their journey north.

Pilgrims also flock to numerous shrines in the devoutly Catholic Mexican states of Guanuato, Jalisco, and San Luis Potosi, which house some of the most honored holy images in the regions, including La Virgen de San Juan de los Lagos, La Virgen de Zapopan, El Señor de la Misericordia, and San Toribio Romo, who is better known, because of his many miracles performed for journeying migrants, as the "Patron Saint of Migrants." Since many of the more established migrant-sending communities in the country are located in these states, it is not surprising to learn that many of the pilgrims to these sites are migrants. Indeed, in their fascinating analysis of *retablos* (hand-painted drawings on sheets of tin) fashioned by migrants to the United States, Jorge Durand and Doug Massey have illustrated the importance of these particular shrines for returning migrants, who visit them to leave *retablos* as offerings of thanks for the miracle of a successful journey.[9]

In Central America, the most visited pilgrim sites are in Guatemala. The most popular religious image in the region, El Cristo Negro (the Black Christ), reclines on a marble altar in the Basilica of Esquipulas, in eastern Guatemala. Situated in a mountain valley in the far Eastern corner of Guatemala, the town of Esquipulas serves as a principal border town to both Honduras and El Salvador. Its proximity to two unregulated international borders draws scores of departing and journeying migrants daily to Esquipulas for material assistance and religious counsel. According to one of the priests at the basilica, about forty to fifty migrants visit the shrine each day. Some are journeying migrants, who stop primarily for material assistance, such as a meal and a fresh change of clothes. Most, however, are departing migrants, who make the pilgrimage to Esquipulas to muster up the spiritual strength necessary to endure the hardships of the journey north. "They come to be blessed," explained the attending priest. "Some pass by the feet of El Cristo and pray, but most go to the confessionary or the atrium where we bless them. At these blessings, which are often group blessings, we anoint them with holy water, pray together for their safety, and counsel them on the family they are leaving behind." He explained, "The blessings are very important to them. Sometimes, if time allows, they also share the Eucharist with us, but since many who stop here are not practicing Catholics, all they really want is a final blessing to protect them before they go on their way." At the request of migrants, the young priest reported that at times he provides them with a cross or prayer book to take with them on the journey. "It is very important for the migrants to have something religious to carry with them," he elaborated. "You see, it represents the presence of God with them, which they never seem to doubt. The presence of God is certain with the migrants, compared to the others who think, in contrast, 'Is God with me?'"

Miguel, a nineteen-year-old nonpracticing Catholic from the Honduran city of San Pedro Sula, traveled to the United States without papers in 2001. Unable to afford a *coyote,* he traversed the two-thousand-mile distance by bus and by foot. Upon leaving his hometown, he traveled by bus to the border of Guatemala and Honduras and proceeded on foot for six miles before arriving in Esquipulas. He went to the basilica, received a final blessing from the attending priest, and then made his way to the little store, where he purchased several religious items to take with him on his trip: a medallion of the Black Christ, which he has never removed from his neck, and an international phone card with the image of the Virgin of Guadalupe on one side of it. He credits his safe arrival in the United States to the miraculous powers of El Cristo Negro and El Virgin de Guadalupe.

Protestants typically eschew icons and Catholic shrines on their journey north. Their practices are more diverse, reflecting the differences among Protestants. In some evangelical communities in the rural highlands of Guatemala, where religion is often a mix of evangelical beliefs and local indigenous practices, departing migrants seek counsel from traditional prayer makers and soothsayers at *ayunos,* or fasting and prayer services, before departing. Mayan people attend *ayunos* at sacred sites, including hilltops and mountain summits, where they go to appeal directly to God to fulfill numerous needs and where they may also convey their needs through a religious mediator who is usually an evangelical pastor with an independent ministry. Attendees believe that if they fast before an *ayuno* their requests have a greater chance of being heard. The *ayuno* opens with a period of devout prayer and sermon, followed by individual petitions. In general, the petitions reflect the needs of the poor and the destitute, who remain marginalized from the larger society and have no other recourse but to turn to religion for help and guidance. Some come requesting recovery from a sickness; others, a job sorely needed; still others, reunification with a deserted spouse. Increasingly, persons come to seek guidance before leaving and request protection on the journey north. Pastors who preside over these *ayuna* estimate that on any given day, they counsel up to ten departing migrants or their family members.

At an *ayuno* held at the summit of a mountain in the highlands of western Guatemala, participants stepped forward with a number of migration requests. One father requested protection for his son, who was en route to the United States. Another attendee sought information on the status of her husband, who had left some months ago, but had not been heard from. The pastor delivered the message that the journeying migrants were safe. At another *ayuno,* held around an altar in a private home, a group of about one hundred persons gathered with their petitions. After the initial prayer, a group of young men sought prayer and guidance in preparation for their travels to the United States. They asked the pastor and others attending the service to pray over their tightly bound bundles of traveling clothes for safe passage across two international borders. She prayed for the young men and over their clothes, told them that she anticipated a safe journey for them, and asked them to send pictures to her upon their arrival in the United States. Later, the pastor explained her views of the role of the *ayuno* in the migration of those in her ministry: "Their goal is to go, to go and work to feed their families, but it's not good for them to go without God's prayers. . . . [T]hey will need Him in the days ahead."

The Fundamental Importance of Religious Resources for Migrants

How do migrants cope with leaving home and prepare for the dangerous journey north to the United States? First, they rely on counsel from those whom they know and trust: local clergy, the anchors of their communities. The functions of the priests, pastors, and in some cases soothsayers are twofold. Many clergy provide important sources of information to prospective migrants: migrants learn about the dangers of crossing international borders and, in some cases, are directed to alternative and safer routes than they would otherwise adopt. For example, priests often provide prospective migrants with prayer books to accompany them on the trip, which also include a directory of shelters and legal services that migrants can draw on if

necessary during their journey. Second, clergy also provide religious sanction for the migration, a kind of spiritual travel-permit that has huge symbolic value. The degree to which clergy sanction the migration varies by
religion. Most ministers of Protestant churches in Guatemala and Mexico
reluctantly endorse the migration of their members. Recognizing the devastating effects migration can have on family left behind, and also the financial loss to an independent church itself, evangelical pastors often attempt to discourage the migration of their members before ultimately
granting approval. Catholic priests, on the other hand, counsel the potential migrant on the consequences of family separation, but rarely discourage the migration itself, recognizing that the need to migrate in order to
feed and provide for one's family is a fundamental human right. Faith tradition also plays a role in how clerics sanction the migration. On sacred
grounds in indigenous communities in the highlands of Guatemala, pastors
act as mediators between departing migrants and God. Upon the advice of
God, a pastor may or may not sanction the migration of one of her or his
followers.

In Catholic communities throughout Latin America, migrants also often
cope with leaving by approaching saints at shrines. Before leaving their families and communities, migrants frequently make a pilgrimage to popular
shrines where they deposit petitions in which they request safety during
their trip and well-being for the family they leave behind. In addition, before leaving the shrines, migrants take with them mementos—medals, de-
votionals, scapulars—to comfort them on their long trek north. What has
been most striking to me, however, is the consistent evidence that regardless
of the particular religious faith or even the level of individual religiosity, undocumented Latin American migrants preparing for the journey north to
the United States permeate their leave-taking with spirituality and the search
for religious support.

APPENDIX

Research Design and Study Sample

The data for this chapter come from a larger project on religion and migration that explores the ways in which migrants have access to and draw upon

religious resources during various stages of the migration process, including (1) decision making, (2) preparation, (3) the journey, and (4) the arrival.[10]
I designed the larger project to explore how migrants interpret and create
everyday religious practices to derive meaning for the decision to migrate,
and to seek spiritual guidance and protection during the process of international travel. I administered a religion and migration survey to 312 recently
arrived Mexican, Guatemalan, Salvadoran, and Honduran immigrants: Catholics and Protestants, women and men, frequent and rare church-goers, legal
and undocumented. The respondents were interviewed in 2001 and 2002 in
religious and nonreligious settings in Houston, Texas. The diversified sample
was designed to provide data on the various ways in which different sub-
populations express or engage in religious rituals and practices related to
the migration experience.

The migrants often spoke of religious places, shrines, and sacred locations that they had visited prior to departure to pray to a holy image for
protection. Part of the subsequent fieldwork involved travel to a sample
of the shrines and holy places that migrants described in their interviews.
These sites included Catholic shrines, folk shrines, and sacred places in
Mexico, Guatemala, and along the U.S.-Mexico border. I also visited Maya
sacred grounds in the highlands of Guatemala, which are now used by Pentecostal pastors and their followers. In Mexico and Guatemala, holy icons
housed in Catholic shrines reflect popular images of Christ and the Virgin,
such as La Virgen de Guadalupe in Mexico City, La Virgen de San Juan de
los Lagos in Jalisco, Mexico, and El Cristo Negro in Esquipulas, Guatemala.
At these various shrines and religious places, I have interviewed migrant
pilgrims, along with the pastors who oversee the shrines and the curators
and employees who maintain them.

In this essay I draw on interviews with religious workers, observations at
sacred places that departing migrants visit, and preliminary survey findings
from a subsample of 202 migrants, focusing only on the undocumented in
order to explore the ways in which migrants use religious resources during the preparation for the journey, which is one stage of the larger migration process. As table 1 shows, close to two-thirds of the undocumented
sample are Mexican, a percentage we targeted when designing the sample
in order to reflect the larger number of Mexicans in the United States. The
predominance of men in this sample of undocumented migrants reflects
their slight predominance in undocumented streams. Both Protestants and

Catholics were interviewed to capture any possible differences in them. The larger percentage of Catholics reflects the distributions of Mexicans and Central Americans in the total sample; Mexicans identified themselves primarily as Catholics, while Central Americans often self-identified as Evangelical or Pentecostal, as well as Catholic. The sample is a fairly religious one, with two-thirds of the respondents reporting that they attended church at least once a week.

Table 1. Profile of Undocumented Study Sample

Characteristic	*Percentage (n)*
Region of Origin	
Mexico	61 (123)
Central America[1]	39 (79)
Sex	
Female	39 (78)
Male	61 (124)
Religion when traveling[2]	
Protestant[3]	25 (50)
Catholic[4]	74 (147)
Church attendance before migrating[5]	
Several times a week	27 (54)
About once a week	40 (80)
Several times a month	12 (24)
Several times a year	13 (27)
Did not attend	8 (16)

N = 202

[1] The Central American respondents consisted primarily of Salvadorans (41%), Guatemalans (32%), and Hondurans (24%). Nicaraguans and Costa Ricans constituted less than 3% of the total sample.

[2] The N = 197, not 202, because four of the respondents identified themselves as Christians only. A fifth respondent reported an affiliation with the Mormon Church.

[3] The Protestant respondents included Pentecostal, Evangelical, Apostolic, Jehovah's Witness, or Baptist; none claimed to be affiliated with more mainstream Protestant churches, such as the Episcopal or Presbyterian.

[4] The Catholic respondents include a small percentage (5%) of Charismatic Catholics.

[5] The N = 201 because one of the respondents did not report church attendance.

NOTES

1. There is a burgeoning literature on the increasing dangers associated with contemporary undocumented travel from Latin America. Karl Eschbach, Jacqueline Hagan, and Nestor Rodriguez, "Deaths during Undocumented Migration: Trends and Policy Implications in the New Era of Homeland Security," in *In Defense of the Alien,* vol. 26 (New York: Center for Migration Studies, 2003), document deaths incurred by migrants while trying to cross the heavily guarded U.S.-Mexico border. George W. Grayson, "Mexico's Southern Flank: A Crime-ridden 'Third U.S. Border,'" *Hemisphere Focus* 11, no. 32 (December 22, 2003). Cecilia Menjivar, *Fragmented Ties: Salvadoran Immigrant Networks in America* (Berkeley: University of California Press, 2000), focuses on the dangers experienced by undocumented Central American migrants during the journey north. Ximena Urrutia-Rojas and Nestor Rodriguez, "Potentially Traumatic Events among Unaccompanied Migrant Children from Central America," in *Health and Social Services among International Labor Migrants. A Comparative Perspective,* ed. Antonio Ugalde and Gilberto Cardenas (Austin, TX: CMAS Books, The Center for Mexican American Studies, University of Texas Austin, 1997), focuses on the particular perils confronting young unaccompanied migrants. Jacqueline Hagan and Nestor Rodriguez, "Church vs. the State: Borders, Migrants and Human Rights," (Paper presented at the annual meetings of the American Sociological Association, San Francisco, August 2004). Nestor Rodriguez, "Crossing the Mexican Gauntlet: Trials and Challenges of Central American Migration to the United States" (Presented at the Latin American Conference on "The Other Latinos," Harvard University, April 2002), provides preliminary comparisons of the comparative risks of Central Americans and Mexicans. Leo Chavez, *Shadowed Lives: Undocumented Immigrants in American Society* (Orlando: Harcourt Brace Jovanovich, 1992), writes about the undocumented experience in general, including the perilous journey. Jacqueline Hagan looks at how the dangerous crossing varies by national origin, gender, and mode of crossing in *Migration Miracle: Faith, Hope, and the Undocumented Journey* (Cambridge, MA: Harvard University Press, forthcoming).

2. Several institutions and individual scholars helped bring this research to fruition. Funds for the initial case study and immigrant survey on which this research is based was funded by the Pew Charitable Trust's RENIR project. RENIR was directed by Helen Rose Ebaugh, who, from the beginning and with great intellectual and financial generosity, encouraged and supported the development of this project. I would also like to thank the University of Houston, which provided initial support for fieldwork in Mexico, and the Ford Foundation, which provided additional funds to travel to other regions in Mexico and to Central America to visit shrines and interview journeying migrants and religious workers who provide services for them. A warm thanks also goes to my dear friend and longtime editor, Janet Chafetz.

3. See, for example, neoclassical theories in Michael P. Todaro, *Internal Migration in Developing Countries* (Geneva: International Labor Office, 1976); the new economics of migration in Oded Stark and David E. Bloom, "The New Economics of Labor Migration," *American Economic Review* 75, no. 2 (Papers and Proceedings, ninety-seventh annual meeting of the American Economic Association, May 1985): 173–78, and J. Edward Taylor, "Differential Migration, Networks, Information and Risk," in *Research in Human Capital and Development,* vol. 4 of *Migration, Human Capital and Development,* ed. Oded Stark, 147–71 (Greenwich, CT: JAI Press, 1986); dual labor market theory in Michael J. Piore, *Birds of Passage: Migrant Labor in Industrial Societies* (Cambridge: Cambridge University Press, 1979). For a comprehensive overview of theories of migration, see Douglas S. Massey et al., "Theories of International Migration: A Review and Appraisal," *Population and Development Review* 19 (1993): 431–66.

4. Numerous studies have demonstrated that the conditions that sustain migration are different from those that trigger it. See for example, Douglas S. Massey, Rafael Alarcon, Jorge Durand, and Humberto Gonzalez, *Return to Aztlan: The Social Process of International Migration from Western Mexico* (Berkeley: University of California Press, 1987); Jacqueline Hagan, *Deciding to Be Legal: A Maya Community in Houston* (Philadelphia: Temple University Press, 1994); John S. MacDonald and Leatrice D. MacDonald, "Chain Migration, Ethnic Neighborhood Formation, and Social Networks," in *An Urban World,* ed. Charles Tilly (Boston: Little, Brown, 1974); Larissa Lomnitz, *Networks and Marginality: Life in a Mexican Shantytown* (New York: Academic Press, 1977); Bryan R. Roberts, "The Interrelation of Cities and Provinces in Peru and Guatemala," in *Latin American Urban Research IV,* ed. Wayne A. Cornelius and Felicity M. Trueblood (Beverly Hills: Sage Publications, 1974). For a recent overview of the role of everyday practices and institutions, including religion, that support transnational migration, see Peggy Levitt, Josh DeWind, and Steven Vertovec, "International Perspectives on Transnational Migration: An Introduction," *International Migration Review* 37, no. 3 (2003); Jose Casanova, "Globalizing Catholicism and the Return to a 'Universal' Church," in *Transnational Religion and Fading States,* ed. S. H. Rudolph and J. Piscatori (Boulder, CO: Westview Press, 1997); Helen Rose Ebaugh and Janet Saltzman Chafetz, *Religion and the New Immigrants: Continuities and Adaptations in Immigrant Congregations* (Walnut Creek, CA: AltaMira Press, 2000); Peggy Levitt, *The Transnational Villagers* (Berkeley: University of California Press, 2001).

5. Across Latin America, people have historically turned to folk religion because they felt ignored or excluded by the church. Along the U.S.-Mexico border, numerous shrines have been erected that house statues or framed pictures of poor heroes believed to have been victims of an unjust society. Two of the most popular shrines are located in the Tijuana area and house Jesus Malverde, a Robin Hood–style outlaw from the Pacific coast state of Sonora, and Juan Soldado (G. I. Joe), a young soldier in the Mexican Army who is believed by his followers to have been unjustly tried and killed for the alleged rape and murder of a young girl in

1938. Today, he is worshiped by many on both sides of the border, some of whom believe he grants miracles to migrants and their families.

6. Jacqueline Hagan and Helen Rose Ebaugh, "Calling upon the Sacred: Migrants' Use of Religion in the Migration Process," *International Migration Review* 37, no. 4 (2003); Jacqueline Hagan, "Religion and the Process of Migration: A Case Study of a Maya Transnational Community," in *Religion across Borders: Transnational Religious Networks,* ed. Helen Rose Ebaugh and Janet Chafetz (Walnut Creek, CA: AltaMira Press, 2002). See also Hagan, *Migration Miracle.*

7. Rijk A. Van Dijik, "From Camp to Encompassment: Discourses on Trans-subjectivity in the Ghanaian Pentecostal Diaspora," *Journal of Religion in Africa* 27 (1997): 135–59.

8. The Scalabrinian Missionaries, or Missionaries of St. Charles, is a Catholic religious community made up of priests, brothers, and sisters who respond to the special needs of migrants. The priests and brothers were founded in 1887 by Bishop John Baptist Scalabrini, and the sisters in 1895 by Bishop Scalabrini, Fr. Giuseppe Marchetti, and Assunta Marchetti. In most countries in the world, including the United States, the Missionaries of St. Charles assist in the settlement of migrants and their families. In Guatemala and Mexico, however, its mission also includes pastoral and humanitarian care for the journeying migrant.

9. Jorge Durand and Douglas S. Massey, *Miracles on the Border: Retablos of Mexican Migrants to the United States* (Tucson: The University of Arizona Press, 1995).

10. See Hagan, *Migration Miracle.*

CHAPTER TWO

"Beloved Aliens and Exiles"

New Testament Perspectives on Migration

DONALD SENIOR

Whenever one reflects on the scriptures through the lens of a profound human experience, one discovers a deeper understanding of the biblical text and its meaning, while at the same time bringing the illumination of the scriptures to our human experience. Fired by the Spirit of God the biblical story yet remains a human saga, drenched in human experience and human history. Surely migration, the displacement of peoples, the suffering and longing it creates, and the complex web of causes that produce it, make it a profound human experience. Migration, along with the human and spiritual issues it raises, has been an intimate part of the biblical saga from the beginning.[1]

Old Testament Perspectives on Migration

From the remotest origins of the patriarchal period, migration of peoples was a backdrop for the unfolding biblical story. Genesis 11 tells us that Terah, the father of Abraham, takes his clan from Ur of the Chaldeans to the land of Canaan and so begins a long story of migration that in many ways would never end. God sanctions this journey for Abraham: "Go from your country and your kindred and your father's house to the land that I will show you" (Gn 12:1).

Down through biblical history the deepest experiences of Israel are marked by migration. The tortured journey of Jacob and his sons to Egypt in search of food in a time of famine is a migration experience, as is the defining experience of the Exodus—a migration of peoples seeking escape from oppression and the promise of a new land and new future.[2] Recent historical probes into the background of the Exodus assert that in fact the Exodus was probably not a single mass migration as dramatically portrayed in the Bible. The emergence of Israel in the land of Canaan was more gradual and episodic and involved the merger over time of indigenous peoples with the waves of immigrants.[3] So be it—the complex weave of history and theological reflection that makes up the biblical account only makes the Exodus more akin to the complex experiences of migration and border crossing in our world today. In any case, the Bible views the Exodus as a definitive revelation: portraying God as a liberator who hears the cries of the poor; portraying Israel as people who began as landless migrants dependent only on God and for whom the land was a gift not a birthright—an origin the scriptures do not want Israel to forget.

Other experiences of migration were equally searing. The deportation of the northern tribes by Assyria in the seventh century ended the kingdom of Israel and forcibly scattered a people and assimilated them into an alien culture to the point where their own identity no longer existed.[4] And then came the Babylonian exile a century or more later, a violent destruction of the people and institutions of Judah by a world power with the people transplanted into a strange land. In this case, though, assimilation was less thorough, and the Jewish people in exile retained their cultural and religious identity, living through several generations with a memory of a homeland they might never see. The aching lament of Psalm 137 still touches us:

> By the rivers of Babylon there we sat down and there we wept when we remembered Zion. On the willows there we hung up our harps. For there our captors asked us for songs, and our tormentors asked for mirth, saying, "Sing us one of the songs of Zion!" How could we sing the Lord's song in a foreign land? If I forget you, O Jerusalem, let my right hand wither! (Ps 137:1–3)

With the later Babylonian exile, and with subsequent mass dispersions under the Greeks and the Romans, a new entity would be born. Now woven into Israel's history and becoming part of the biblical story was the Diaspora or dispersion—colonies of Jewish people living in communities throughout the Mediterranean world—eventually their numbers exceeding those who were able to return and build a new community in the homeland of Israel. Strangely, even when political conditions allowed the Diaspora Jews to return to the homeland of their dreams, then as now, many would not or could not return for a variety of practical economic and social reasons. Yet even though rooted deeply in the Hellenistic cultures of Asia Minor or Greece or Egypt or Syria, the Jewish people of the Diaspora still felt the tug of going home and still prayed and longed for a return to Jerusalem—a deep, unsettling desire stoked by pilgrimage and a religious literature that portrayed Zion as the center of the world and as the ultimate meeting place with God.

These markers in the biblical saga—the wanderings of the patriarchs, the Exodus, the exile, the dispersion, and the return—became embedded in the consciousness of the people of Israel and helped define their character as a people and the nature of their relationship to God.[5] For a people who longed for a land of their own, the biblical story had sharp reminders that one's claim on the land was relative—vulnerable to the threat of powerful outside forces who would covet it, and to the seductions of their own failings as a people who would squander their ideals and violate the land and its bounty through injustice.[6] For the New Testament, too, these experiences of migration and the biblical reflection upon them would be an integral part of their understanding of Jesus and the Christian life. And to these we now turn.

New Testament Perspectives on Migration

If one can correctly affirm that the history of Israel is rooted in migration, a similar case can be made for Jesus and the early Christian community, a community that obviously emerged from and remained steeped in the experience of Judaism.

The Gospels of Matthew and Luke attempt to wrap the origins of Jesus himself in the experience of a displaced people. In Luke's Gospel the birth of Jesus takes place at a time when his parents must return to their ancestral home for a census imposed by a world ruler (Lk 2:1–7). Jesus is born on the road, as it were. In Matthew's Gospel the origins of Jesus are even more radically affected by the experience of migration. Shortly after his birth Joseph is warned in a dream to take Mary and the child to Egypt to flee the deadly violence of Herod and the threat of genocide in Bethlehem (Mt 2:13–23). Jesus and his family recapitulate the migration of Jacob and an earlier Joseph to find refuge in an alien land. And then, too, God calls them out of Egypt—evoking the memory of the Exodus—only to find that they cannot go home to Bethlehem, once more because of threat from a despot (Archaelaus) and have to settle in the north, in Nazareth. Matthew portrays Jesus and his family as recapitulating the migrant experience of Israel. Jesus begins his earthly journey as a migrant and a displaced person—Jesus who in this same gospel would radically identify with the "least" and make hospitality to the stranger a criterion of judgment (Mt 25:35).

In the same vein, all of the Gospels portray the adult Jesus as an itinerant, one who has nowhere to lay his head (Lk 9:58), who leaves behind family and lands and possessions (Mk 10:28–31), whose entire ministry is characterized in the synoptic Gospels as a journey to a homeland beyond Jerusalem (Lk 9:51). In John's Gospel, the Jewish crowds speculate that when he speaks of going to a place they cannot come, he means to go to the Diaspora and join the ranks of the Jews permanently away from home (Jn 7:32–36). For the synoptic Gospels of Matthew, Mark, and Luke, the journey of Jesus is enacted on the way from Galilee to Jerusalem, a geographical movement that finds its ultimate meaning in the journey of Jesus from death to life in the Paschal experience that awaits him at journey's end in Jerusalem (Mk 10:32–34 and parallels). In the prologue of John's Gospel the journey becomes a cosmic movement—the beginning of the journey is in the primal and timeless movement of the Word as an articulation of God—a Word spoken by God and so eloquent and complete it fully expresses God, indeed, is God. This divine Word arcs down into the created world, taking flesh and becoming embodied in the human journey of Jesus (Jn 1:1–18). The endpoint of this migration is not just the cross in Jerusalem but, through that cross, a lifting up back through the cosmos into the bosom of God, a moment of ultimate return home, a communion in which all humanity can follow (Jn 17:20–21). In the letter to the Hebrews, the earthly journey of Jesus is merely a reflection of the heavenly journey in which Jesus, the Son of God and the forerunner of our salvation, leads the people through the veil of the heavenly sanctuary and into the living presence of God (Heb 10:19–20).[7]

This experience of Jesus in its human and theological dimensions is recapitulated in the experience of the early community. The Acts of the Apostles portrays the early Christians as a beleaguered people, often scattered through violent persecution. Chapter 8 of Acts notes that in the wake of Stephen's martyrdom, a deadly persecution broke out in Jerusalem, scattering the apostles and members of the church throughout Judea and Samaria, bringing the gospel to Samaria itself (Acts 8:1–8). Later the shock waves of the persecution also propelled Jewish Christians to Phoenicia and Cyprus (Acts 11:19–21). And some of the Greek-speaking Jewish Christians who were dispersed took the gospel to Antioch and on out into the Mediterranean world, an inadvertent pastoral plan for the early Christians but, from Luke's perspective, a providential stratagem of the Spirit of Jesus who can bring life from death. Indeed, one of the scourges of the early Christians who attempted to scatter and destroy the church, Paul himself, became God's "chosen instrument" (Acts 9:15–16), one who would bring the gospel beyond the boundaries of Israel. The God-intended movement of the Christian community "from Judea, Samaria, and to the ends of the earth" (Acts 1:8; see also Lk 24:47) was, according to Luke's theology, part of the mysterious plan of God for the "salvation of all flesh" (Lk 3:6). And the inherently mobile and rootless Christian community, Acts tells us, would first be known as the people of the "way" (or "journey") (Acts 18:25–26; 19:23; 22:4; 24:14, 22).[8]

This theological narrative of Acts has its firm historical roots: Christianity did move out rapidly from its Judean and Galilean origins, and often, we know, the development of early Christianity was marked with tensions, no doubt some of them violent, between Jewish Christians and other Jewish groups in a period of great stress for all versions of Judaism. The increasingly oppressive Roman occupation and the eruption of the Jewish revolt in AD 66, with the subsequent destruction of Jerusalem in AD 70, would bring profound and wrenching changes to all factions of Judaism and to Jewish Christianity itself.

One footnote in all this is the so-called Pella legend, the site on the east bank of the Jordan River valley where the Jerusalem Christians are reported by later traditions to have fled at the time of the Roman siege of Jerusalem. These traditions have a good deal of historical probability. In the first century AD, Pella was a prosperous Roman and Hellenistic city of the Decapolis with a sizeable Jewish population. Favorably located some thirty miles south of the Sea of Galilee and far enough from the chaos of Jerusalem, it would have been a good choice as a city of refuge.[9] If true, it means that the heart of the Christian world at that time—the apostolic Jerusalem church with its Jewish Christian leadership—would also have experienced first hand the wrenching reality of forced migration under the threat of violence. Many Johannine scholars suggest that the references to expulsion from the synagogue in chapter 9 of the Gospel and the cryptic reference to Jesus's going to the Diaspora (Jn 7:35–36) may be hints, among others in the Gospel, that during this same chaotic period the Johannine community itself left its origins in Palestinian Judaism and migrated to Asia Minor or some other part of the Mediterranean world outside of Israel.[10]

Although we are unsure of the precise circumstances and extent of the disruption, we know from Roman sources that the Emperor Claudius expelled some Jews and Christians from Rome around AD 40. According to the contemporary Roman historian Suetonius, this was provoked by riots stirred up by a slave "Chrestus," more than likely a mistaken reference to Christ. Tensions between Christian and Jewish factions may have been the source of the clashes that resulted in Claudius's action. This is corroborated in Acts 18:1–3, where Luke describes Paul's first encounter with the Jewish Christian couple Aquila and Priscilla, who had left Rome and come to Corinth because of Claudius's edict. In an ironic and providential pattern typical of Acts, their dislocated presence in Corinth—caused by their expulsion from Rome—provided an essential base of support for Paul's evangelization in that key city.

The author of the first letter of Peter addresses the scattered Christian communities of northern and central Asia Minor as resident aliens (*paroikia*) and exiles. Some contemporary commentators on this exquisite early Christian letter believe the designation as resident aliens and exiles is not simply used as a spiritual metaphor but is an indication of the social and ethnic status of these Christians as migrant workers who were socially and ethnically estranged to these regions as well as experiencing spiritual isolation and harassment because of their Christian allegiance.[11]

Likewise, the author of James addresses his pastoral letter to the "twelve tribes in the Dispersion" (1:1), a designation that obviously appropriates a symbolic and theological concept from Jewish tradition and applies it to a Christian audience. But this designation, too, may also reflect the social experience of these communities and their history, as they attempted to live as Christian communities in the midst of a dominant, uncomprehending, and often hostile society.

Thus in the highly mobile and interconnected Mediterranean world of the first century AD the early Christians were not strangers to the experience of dislocation caused by violence and persecution. There is little doubt that they reflected on this same experience in the light of Jesus's own life and that of the history of God's people. The whiplash experiences of longing to be at peace and at rest coupled with forced dislocation and the vulnerability of being strangers in the land were not only a cause of suffering and discontinuity but, paradoxically, also yielded profound insight into the meaning of the gospel and the experience of faith.

Theological Dimensions: Migration as Symbol and Expression of the Christian Experience

In this final section I would like to summarize a few of the theological motifs that the New Testament attaches to the experiences of migration and social dislocation. I will concentrate on three.

Solidarity with the Poor and Oppressed

The portrayal of Jesus as itinerant and homeless is part of a larger portrait in the gospel literature of Jesus as in solidarity with the poor and suffering. The fact that Jesus himself was born in dislocated circumstances, to a family either on a forced journey because of Roman legislation or, even more dire in Matthew's account, because they are being hunted down to be destroyed, aligns Jesus from the beginning with the poor and vulnerable. At the same time, it recapitulates in Jesus's own experience the experience of Israel that from its origins and throughout its history suffered from threat and forced migration.

I do not have to make the case in detail here, but clearly the gospel literature portrays Jesus in solidarity with the poor and suffering. Luke's Gospel, for example, begins Jesus's ministry in the synagogue of Nazareth with a
keynote quote of Isaiah 61 (Lk 4:16–19). The prophetic Jesus will proclaim
liberty and justice to the oppressed. Many of Luke's parables challenge the
rich to be aware of the poor, such as vivid stories of the rich man and his
barns (Lk 12:16–21) or that of Dives (the name traditionally given to the
unnamed rich man in this parable) and Lazarus (Lk 16:19–31). The same is
true in Matthew where Jesus explicitly identifies with the "little ones" (Mt
18:6–14)[12] and the "least" (Mt 25:40, 45); divine judgment will be attentive
to how the strong treat the weak. Likewise in Matthew's classic parable of the
sheep and the goats, the reign of God belongs to those who feed the hungry, clothe the naked, and welcome the stranger (Mt 25:31–46).

The itinerancy of Jesus is also in part meant as evidence that Jesus himself lived poorly, without land or possessions. "The foxes have their lairs, the
birds of the air have their nests, but the Son of Man has nowhere to lay his
head" (Lk 9:58). In the healing stories of Mark's Gospel—a major preoc-
cupation of this Gospel—Jesus has compassion on the crowds who themselves have nowhere to go for nourishment and would faint on the way, a
point not grasped by Jesus's obtuse disciples (Mk 8:1–4). In inviting the disciples to also put behind their attachments to family, land and possessions
and to follow him in this life on the road, Jesus offers his followers the opportunity to have the same freedom as he did to now live in solidarity with
and in awareness of the needs of the poor and the vulnerable.[13]

Thus the gospels leave little doubt: Jesus does not live securely in one
stable place but walks in solidarity with those who are forced to wander aim-
lessly like sheep without a shepherd (Mk 6: 34).

Seeking a True Homeland

The attachment of the Christian experience to the experience of migration, of having left home and familiarity behind, is also used by a variety
of New Testament traditions as a critique of false values and false security.
Contrary to human wisdom, those who are comfortable in place, fortified
with the security of land and possessions and food, are also in danger of
delusion about ultimate reality. In the overall landscape of the gospel stories,

the rich and powerful are often "in place"—reclining at table, calculating their harvest, standing comfortably in the front of the sanctuary, or seated on the judgment seat passing judgment on the crimes of others. The poor, on the other hand, are often mobile or rootless: the sick coming from the four corners of the compass seeking healing; the crowds desperate to hear Jesus, roaming lost and hungry; the leper crouched outside the door of Dives. No story is more explicit on this point than Luke's story of the rich man and his barns (12:16–21). Faced with a bountiful harvest the landed farmer pulls down his old barns and builds bigger ones, comforting himself with false security: "Soul, you have ample goods laid up for many years: relax, eat, drink, be merry. But God said to him. 'You fool! This very night your life is being demanded of you. And the things you have prepared, whose will they be?'"

The notion of the Christian as living in exile in this world, longing for one's true and heavenly home, is a classic spiritual motif with roots in the New Testament itself. In reflecting on the migration of Abraham and the patriarchs, the author of the letter to the Hebrews observes, "They confessed that they were strangers and foreigners on the earth, for people who speak in this way make it clear that they are seeking a homeland. If they had been thinking of the land that they had left behind, they would have had opportunity to return. But as it is, they desire a better country, that is, a heavenly one" (Heb 11:13–15). It is possible that an overemphasis on this motif can devalue the gift of life in this world and rob the Christian conscience of responsibility for the work of justice in this life and for human responsibility for the environment. The overenthusiastic attention some Christians gave to the timing of the final judgment and the advent of the next world is already a problem for the Gospel of Mark which labels as "false prophets" those who attempt to foreshorten the end time and take attention from the responsibility of proclaiming the gospel to the ends of the earth (Mk 13:5–10, 21–23).

But, properly understood in concert with the entirety of the Christian vision, the notion of being in exile or a spiritual migrant or stranger (i.e., the Greek terms *parepidemos* [stranger, alien] and *paroikia* [literally, one not at home]) can be salutary and not world denying.[14] The human reality of the migrant challenges the experience of those who falsely assume they have absolute control of their own land and their own destiny. The mobility of migrant peoples, their experience of having to leave behind family and land and possession to avoid death and to seek new life, their legitimate claim to refuge and hospitality, to the opportunity for work and respect in their new homeland, challenges the experience of those who feel absolutely stable and secure in their own situations. This ensemble of conditions and experiences reveal a profound dimension of all of human existence whether migrant or not. These experiences challenge the false ideologies of unlimited resources, the myth of unchecked progress, the idolatry of unconditional national sovereignty, and the absolute claim to individual satisfaction that so plague our contemporary world and choke its spiritual capacity.

The exhortation of the first letter of Peter written to a series of Christian communities in northern Asia Minor is instructive. It is clear from the letter that these communities were experiencing isolation and some harassment for refusing to conform to the values of the dominant society. This extraordinary letter is not content to condemn this surrounding society but calls on the Christians to lead lives of virtue as a witness of life that might win over their pagan neighbors. "Beloved," the author writes, "I urge you as aliens and exiles to abstain from the desires of the flesh that wage war against the soul. Conduct yourselves honorably among the Gentiles, so that, though they malign you as evildoers, they may see your honorable deeds and glorify God when he comes to judge" (1 Pt 2:11–12). The integrity and transparent values of the socially vulnerable Christians in these communities, including the respect they showed to their non-Christian neighbors, could serve as antidote to the false values of the dominant society.

Welcoming the Stranger

The New Testament also couples the experience of migration with the biblical virtue of hospitality.[15] Welcoming the stranger or alien is a traditional biblical injunction. Deuteronomy warns Israel that "the Lord your God is God of gods and Lord of lords, the great God, mighty and awesome, who is not partial and takes no bribe, who executes justice for the orphan and the widow, and who loves the strangers, providing them food and clothing" (Dt 10:17–18). Israel's care for the stranger was to be guided by God's command and their own experience: "You shall also love the stranger, for you were strangers in the land of Egypt" (Dt 10:12).

The Pastoral Epistles list being hospitable as one of the virtues required for the office of *episkopos* or overseer (1 Tm 3:2; Ti 1:8) as well as the sign of a "real" widow (1 Tm 5:10). The first letter of Peter also urges the Christians "to be hospitable to one another without complaining" (1 Pt 4:9). The author of Hebrews evokes the famous story of Abraham and Sarah's hospitality to the three mysterious visitors to Mamre in Genesis 18: "Do not neglect to show hospitality to strangers, for by doing that some have entertained angels without knowing it" (Heb 13:2). Matthew's Gospel, strongly attuned to the covenantal injunctions of the Torah, includes in Jesus's famous parable of the sheep and the goats the call to welcome the foreigner or stranger (*xenos*), making it a criteria for righteousness: "I was a stranger and you welcomed me" (Mt 25:35, 38, 43, 44).

Jesus's explanatory words to the righteous and the unjust, "whatever you did to the least of my brethren you did to me," takes the call to welcome the stranger to yet a deeper level within the theological vision of the New Testament. Welcoming the stranger is not simply an act of kindness and solidarity, or doing unto others as you would have them do unto you. The stranger who migrates across one's borders is also a sign of the full scope of the human family, a scope that, within the New Testament vision, transcends bloodlines and national boundaries.

Here one taps into a fundamental perspective of the New Testament and early Christian experience. Luke's portrayal of the Christian community in Acts shows the slow dawning of its consciousness that God's word of salvation was to extend beyond the boundaries of Judea and Samaria even to the ends of the earth. The poignant encounter of Peter with Cornelius, his first Gentile convert, an incident to which Luke gives major attention, describes in detail the apostle's attempt to come to grips with this wider vision of the human family. Faced with the Spirit's descent on Cornelius and his household, Peter exclaims: "I begin to see that God shows no partiality, but in every nation anyone who fears him and does what is right is acceptable to him" (Acts 10:34). This intuition would drive the universality of the gospel. The key, as Peter himself confesses, is being able to recognize the other as sacred and as part of God's human family: "God has shown me that I should not call anyone profane or unclean" (Acts 10:28). Peter's transforming encounter with the Gentile Cornelius at Caesarea Maritima is one dramatic implementation of a vision already anticipated at Pentecost.

Representatives of the Jewish Diaspora gathered in Jerusalem from across the Mediterranean world are able through the power of the Spirit to hear the gospel in their own language (Acts 2:11). Through the ministry of Paul and Barnabas (Acts 13:2–3) and the host of men and women named in Acts, that same Spirit would welcome Gentiles from virtually all of the known world into the community of Israel fashioned by the Crucified and Risen Christ.

Luke's expansive vision of the church is echoed in different ways in other major New Testament writings. Matthew's Gospel traces the unfolding of the Christian mission from its initial stage where Jesus concentrates exclusively on the "lost sheep of the house of Israel" during his earthly ministry (Mt 10:4; 15:24) to a dramatic turning to the nations authorized by the risen Christ in the final scene of the Gospel on a mountain top in Galilee (Mt 28:16–20). This movement no doubt reflects the fact that the universality of the Christian mission, embracing Gentiles as well as Jews, dawned on the early community only gradually. Yet even during Jesus's lifetime, Matthew's Gospel shows, there were harbingers of the universality of God's redemptive embrace in the response of Jesus to outsiders and strangers. Stargazers from the east came to worship the newborn messiah while those in power failed to recognize his presence (Mt 2:1–12). Struck by the faith of the centurion in Capernaum, Jesus saw a vision of an inclusive future: "I tell you many will come from east and west and eat with Abraham and Isaac and Jacob in the kingdom of heaven" (Mt 8:11). Similarly, the story of the Canaanite woman in Matthew 15 is a remarkable example of the role of the stranger and alien who brings a new consciousness even to Jesus himself. The woman's pleas on behalf of her desperately ill daughter are ignored and even rebuffed by Jesus because she is not within the scope of his mission to Israel. Undeterred she forces herself, on behalf of her daughter, into Jesus's consciousness. Ultimately Jesus proclaims this stranger to be an exemplar of authentic faith (Mt 15:21–28). Jesus—who was characterized by his opponents as one "who welcomes sinners and eats with them" (Lk 15:2) and "as a wine bibber and a glutton, a lover of tax collectors and those outside the law" (Mt 11:19)—would be recognized by the Christian community as the revealer of God whose words and deeds pointed the way to God's salvation.

Paul, of course, is more explicit about this than any of the New Testament writers. In an important autobiographical passage in Galatians, Paul rests his tenacious defense of the mission to the Gentiles on his inaugural experience of the risen Christ. Echoing the words of Isaiah and Jeremiah, he affirms that even before the first moment of his existence, before he had been knit together in his mother's womb, God had called him to be a chosen instrument to bring salvation to the Gentiles (Gal 1:15–16; see Is 49:1; Jer 1:4, 11). The God of Israel, Paul insisted, was also the God of the Gentiles (Rom 3:29). Christ died for all, Jew and Gentile alike (2 Cor 5:15; see also Rom 2:10). And therefore the Gentiles had every right of access to God's grace.

Here one arrives at the bedrock of the Christian vision. "There is no longer Jew or Greek, no longer slave or free, no longer male or female—all are one in Christ Jesus" (Gal 3:28). This does not erode the elect status of Israel as God's people, or by extension the unique role of the church, but puts the particularity of salvation history into a broader and inclusive framework. God's embrace reaches to the ends of the earth and all its peoples. Here is the ultimate bond that ties the human family together. Before God all are one. Here is the bulwark against an ideology of racial superiority, here is the challenge to the absolute claims of national or cultural boundaries, here is the basis for all human dignity, including the dignity of the stranger in the land—the right of the migrant to cross borders, whether in fleeing danger or seeking opportunity; the obligation to welcome the stranger and to provide refuge and respect. For the Christian all of these commitments flow ultimately from the biblical vision of the human family as one before God.

The God of Israel and the God of all Nations

Much of the Bible is pulled by the tension between the particular and universal: between Israel's sense of its election as God's chosen people and the fact that God is also the God of the nations, between covenant obligations to one's own people and land and the haunting reminder about their migrant origins and the need to care for the stranger. The same tension is found in the New Testament as well: the tension between the obligation to build up the community and the call to carry the gospel to the dispersed people of the Mediterranean world, the tension between caring for the lost sheep of the house of Israel and the insistent claim of the Canaanite woman, the tension between a mission of justice in the world and the longing to be free of the body and to be at home with the Lord.

Ultimately, the Bible and our Christian tradition refuse to choose between the poles of this tension but attempt to embrace both. The reality of the migrant raises this same issue in an acute way and holds us accountable to the full scope of the gospel vision. The suffering of those forced to migrate reminds us of the relativity of national boundaries and our obligations of justice that transcend bloodlines and family ties and the loyalty claims of our nationality. The face of the migrant also reminds us that God's beauty embraces all of the human family and that the word of God is directed to the world, not simply to the family or church. And the reality of the continual migration of peoples, the unsettled immigrant and alien status imposed on so many, is also a prophetic challenge to a false vision of human destiny that can only imagine this world and this life and therefore underestimates the unfathomable transforming power of God.

NOTES

1. Frank Crüsemann, "'You Know the Heart of a Stranger' (Exodus 23.9): A Recollection of the Torah in the Face of New Nationalism and Xenophobia," in *Migrants and Refugees,* ed. D. Mieth and L. S. Cahill (London: SCM Press, 1993), 96: "Indeed, from Abraham's departure—and fundamentally even from Cain—to the child in the manger, in its main lines the Bible is a story of people who depart, set out in search of bread, land and protection, wander about and return."

2. Genesis 42–50.

3. See Norbert F. Lohfink, *Option for the Poor: The Basic Principle of Liberation Theology in the Light of the Bible* (N. Richland Hills, TX: BIBAL Press, 1987), 39–41; Anthony R. Ceresko, *Introduction to the Old Testament: A Liberation Perspective* (Maryknoll, NY: Orbis Books, 1992), 72–79.

4. 2 Kings 17:5–41. Interestingly, the descendants of the Northern tribes, the Samaritans, are referred to as "foreigner(s)" by Jesus in Luke 17:18. These "foreigners," the Samaritans, are portrayed as exemplary figures in Luke's Gospel (10:25–37; 17:11–19) and in John's Gospel (4:1–42).

5. For further reflections on the role of immigrants and immigration in the Old Testament see Dianne Bergant, "Ruth: The Migrant who Saved the People," in *Migration, Religious Experience, and Globalization,* ed. Gioacchino Campese and Pietro Ciallella, 49–61 (New York: Center for Migration Studies, 2003); José E. Ramírez

Kidd, "Inmigrantes en el Antiguo Testamento: Realidad, Problema y Misterio," *Vida y Pensamiento* 24, no. 1 (2004): 51–68.

6. On the subject of the land in the Bible see Walter Brueggemann, *The Land: Place as Gift, Promise, and Challenge in Biblical Faith,* 2nd ed. (Minneapolis: Fortress Press, 2002).

7. Joseph A. Mindling, "Chosen People in Foreign Lands: Scriptural Reflections on Immigration and the Uprooted," *New Theology Review* 12, no. 1 (1999): 11–12 speaks of an "immigrant Christology."

8. For an insightful missionary reading of the Acts of the Apostles see Stephen B. Bevans and Roger P. Schroeder, *Constants in Context: A Theology of Mission for Today* (Maryknoll, NY: Orbis Books, 2004), 10–31; also Donald Senior and Carroll Stuhlmueller, *Biblical Foundations for Mission* (Maryknoll, NY: Orbis Books, 1983), 255–79.

9. See Robert Huston Smith, "Pella," in *The Anchor Bible Dictionary* (New York: Doubleday, 1992), 5:219–21.

10. See Raymond E. Brown, *The Community of the Beloved Disciple* (New York: Paulist Press, 1979), 55–58; Sandra M. Schneiders, *Written That You May Believe: Encountering Jesus in the Fourth Gospel* (New York: Crossroad, 1999), 37–47.

11. This interpretation has been championed particularly by John H. Elliott, *A Home for the Homeless: A Social-Scientific Criticism of 1 Peter, its Situation and Strategy,* With a New Introduction (Minneapolis: Fortress Press, 1990). More likely the reference in 1 Peter is metaphorical, referring to the social alienation experienced by the Christians because they adhered to different values than the majority culture; see Donald Senior, *1 Peter,* Sacra Pagina 15 (Collegeville, MN: Liturgical Press, 2003), 8–10.

12. The Greek term *mikroi* does not refer to children (*paidioi*) but to those vulnerable to threat and force from the strong.

13. See, for example, the story of the rich young man in Matthew 19:16–22.

14. These two terms are analyzed in Elliott, *Home for the Homeless,* 21–58.

15. On the theme of hospitality in the Bible and its missiological implications see Christine D. Pohl, "Biblical Issues in Mission and Migration," in *Missiology* 31, no. 1 (2003): 3–15.

CHAPTER THREE

Migration in the Patristic Era

History and Theology

PETER C. PHAN

My essay draws from two disciplines, history and theology, to study a social phenomenon—migration—in the period of church history commonly referred to as the "patristic era." The age of the "fathers of the church" conventionally designates the first six centuries AD, to Gregory the Great (d. 604) in the West and to John of Damascus (d. 749) in the East. There is however no unanimity among scholars regarding what is meant by migration and what constitutes a migrant, and part of the task of this essay is to explore to what extent the modern concepts of migration and migrant are applicable to the migratory movements and the migratory people during the patristic era. I begin with introductory remarks on contemporary scholarship on migration and the migrant. I then survey forms and movements of population shifts during the first seven centuries of the Christian era. I next present the thought of some early Christian writers on migration, mainly in its ethical and theological dimensions. I will conclude with reflections on the relevance of patristic thought for our contemporary understanding of migration and the migrant.

Migration, Emigration, Immigration

Interestingly, practically all contemporary studies on migration date this phenomenon to the beginning of the modern era, even though it is recognized

that from the very origins of our human species, extensive migratory movements did occur as large groups of our ancestors left Africa to populate the
rest of the world, and continued to take place regularly in the subsequent
millennia.[1] *The Cambridge Survey of World Migration,* an authoritative and
comprehensive study of the subject, despite acknowledging that there was
a variety of forms of migration in the premodern era, deems it "sensible to
begin a survey of world migration in the 'modern' period." This historical
periodization is predicated upon Immanuel Wallenstein's claim that modernity was "marked by the flourishing of long-distance trade and the opening
up of global lines of communication."[2] It is argued that the European world
mercantilism that emerged in the late fifteenth and early sixteenth century,
in distinction from the previous empire-building world economies of China,
Persia, and Rome, brought about the hitherto largest process of forced
migration—the shipment of ten million slaves from western Africa to the
New World. After considering this forced African emigration, the historical
account of world migration would move on to chronicle the successive
waves of population movements: (1) the voluntary, often state-sponsored,
settlement of Europeans in their colonies (e.g., Britain, the Netherlands,
Spain, France, Portugal, Germany, and Italy); (2) the massive emigration from
Europe to the U.S., Canada, and South America in 1850–1933; (3) the in-
dentured labor migration, especially from China, India, and Japan, to the U.S.
and the victorious Allied states after the Second World War; and finally,
(4) the current post–Cold War global movements of displaced peoples and
refugees on a scale not seen since the end of the Second World War.[3] One
common conclusion of surveys of world migration is that slavery and inden-
tured labor, which fueled migration, are intrinsic parts of the evolution of
capitalism on the global scale

Whatever the scholarly merits for dating the beginning of world migration to the modern period, it offers a comprehensive and helpful description of migration, emigration, immigration, and the migrant. Thus, on the
basis of population movements since the rise of modernity, it is common
to classify forms of migration as follows:

- internal versus intercontinental/international migration
- forced versus free migration
- settler versus labor migration
- temporary versus permanent migration

- illegal versus legal migration
- planned versus flight/refugee migration[4]

Of course, these six binaries are not mutually exclusive antinomies. On the contrary, often each side of these dyads merges with its opposite. They are, as Robin Cohen suggests, rather "more akin to Weber's 'ideal types,' which can be briefly defined as archetypes for analytical, evaluative and comparative purposes."[5] To what extent they are helpful signposts for understanding the migrations during the patristic era will be examined in the next part of the essay.

For the moment, it is important to note that thanks to continuous migrations there were, long before the advent of Christianity, constant mutual fertilizations among the four principal civilizations of the ancient world. The Greco-Roman civilization, sustained by a common Greek language and culture and bolstered by the imperial rule of the city of Rome, flourished in the Mediterranean basin. The Persian civilization, whose political center was located in the region now known as Iran and whose dominant religion was Zoroastrianism, extended from the Euphrates River to the Himalaya Mountains. The Indian civilization, whose main religions included Hinduism and Buddhism, prospered in the Indian subcontinent and sections of Southeast Asia. Lastly, the Chinese civilization, which was dominated by Confucianism, spread from China westward into Central Asia, eastward into Korea and Japan, and southward into Vietnam.

While these regions and civilizations were kept separated from one another by natural barriers such as mountains, deserts, and seas, they were constantly brought together by two frequent human enterprises, namely, war and trade. Emperors and kings often forced or paid different peoples to fight wars against other countries and sponsored colonization to expand their power and territories. At times they transplanted the entire conquered population to distant lands to prevent insurgency. Soldiers returning from foreign campaigns and prisoners of war taken as slaves brought new cultures and languages back to the victors' homes. In these and other ways, elements of various cultures—Egyptian, Ethiopian, Greek, Jewish, Roman, Persian, Indian, Chinese—were mixed together and were found everywhere in the world of late antiquity.

More important than the migration of armies and peoples through warfare was the migration of merchants through trade, which established long-lasting interregional and cross-cultural exchanges of goods, ideas, and peoples. The most important trade route of the ancient world was the Silk Road, which stretched westward from the Great Wall of China through Central Asia and India to the Mediterranean coast. At the eastern end of the Silk Road in Syria and Arabia, caravans regularly crossed the deserts and carried goods among the cities and to the seacoasts. In addition, ships plied the Mediterranean Sea, the Red Sea, the Arabian Sea, the Indian Ocean, and parts of the Pacific to bring goods from China and India to markets in Alexandria, Antioch, Carthage, and Rome and the other way round.

In addition to the four major civilizations mentioned above, in which cities played a central role, there were in the north a large number of nomadic tribes scattered from Siberia across Central Asia into modern Russia and northwestern Europe. They were grouped into several families of distinct cultural and ethnic identity: Celtic, Germanic, Slavic, Turkish, and Mongolian. Migration was their way of life, and by the first century AD, they reached the Mediterranean world and changed its urban civilization. South of the Mediterranean, on the African continent, there were also numerous migratory tribes and peoples who, also through warfare and trade, moved along the Nile River and by the first century AD came into contact with the urban civilization in the north. Further south, also in about the first century AD, several major waves of migration took place among the Bantu-speaking peoples along the Congo River.

Finally, from Asia, and possibly from northern Europe and even Africa, tribal peoples had crossed the seas to the Americas, north and south, many millennia earlier. At about the same time, there were a series of migrations by sea from Southeast Asia to present-day Oceania. Some fifty thousand years ago, another wave of migrants came to Australia, Tasmania, and New Guinea. Some ten thousand years ago, agriculturalist peoples migrated to Melanesia and Micronesia, and later to Polynesia. Clearly, migrations during the patristic era were no rare and isolated events but were part of a frequent and established pattern of humanity's attempts to survive and expand across seas and continents.

Migratory Movements in the Patristic Era

Even though migration seems to be rooted in the human instinct to wonder and wander in search of better opportunities and new horizons, it has often been triggered throughout the centuries by, *inter alia,* population increase, natural disasters, poverty and famine, civil disturbances, international wars, political oppression, religious persecution, and human trafficking. No doubt these phenomena were present in various degrees during the first seven centuries of the Christian era, and each contributed in its own way to migratory movements during this period. These movements affected both the peoples making up the Roman and Persian Empires at large and Christians in particular. In what follows, the focus will be on how these migrations impacted early Christianity.[6]

The Jewish Diaspora

One of the most extensive and well-documented migrations in antiquity is no doubt the Jewish Diaspora. Begun in the Assyrian and Babylonian deportations (c. 721 and c. 597 BC), then expanding into the eastern Mediterranean (especially in Syria, Asia Minor, and Egypt) during the Hellenistic period, and later to the west and Italy (especially Rome) in the mid-second century BC, and after the three insurrection wars against the Romans in Palestine between AD 66 and 132, the Diaspora was one of the largest migrations with which early Christians were quite familiar.[7] By the fourth century BC, there were already more Jews living outside than inside the land of Israel.[8] By New Testament times, according to Philo, there were more than one million Jews in Alexandria, the Egyptian city famous for the most important community of Diaspora Jews, with a splendid synagogue and a highly creative intellectual life, which produced among other things the Septuagint. Also in Egypt, at the southern city of Elephantine, there was a sizable Jewish garrison and even a Jewish temple.

The Acts of the Apostles testifies to the prominence of Jewish communities with their synagogues in most of the cities of the eastern Mediterranean. In Antioch, the Jewish community traced its origins back to the founding of the city by the Seleucids in 300 BC. In the first century AD, Antiochene Jews numbered in the tens of thousands. At the ancient city of Dura Europos in Syria, halfway between Aleppo and Baghdad, the Jews' synagogue was much more impressive than the Christians' modest house-church. In Rome there were, in the second to the fourth centuries AD, eleven synagogues. Jews in Sardis boasted a massive, oft-renovated synagogue adjoined to the city's main bath complexes.

In general, in the Roman Empire, Judaism was considered a *religio licita* on account of its antiquity. Its basic practices such as male circumcision, observance of the Sabbath and dietary restrictions, payment of the Temple tax, and pilgrimage to Jerusalem were officially allowed. Diaspora Jews adapted well to their various environments, using Greek as their common language, and not a few of them held important political positions, for example, in Berenice in Cyrene. By the first century, there was a small but symbolically significant class of proselytes to Judaism from among the Gentiles in the Greco-Roman and the Persian worlds. Within the Hellenistic world, there were many whom Jews called "God-fearers," that is, those who attended synagogue services but did not convert to Judaism on account of the requirement of circumcision.

This tolerance and even sympathy for Judaism does not mean that Jews were not at times subjected to discrimination and violent attacks. In Alexandria, anti-Semitic literature was produced in the Hellenistic period, and in AD 38, during Marcus Iulius Agrippa I's visit to the city, synagogues were burnt, shops looted, and the Jews herded into a ghetto. Under emperor Gaius Caligula, around AD 40, a riot against Jews broke out in Antioch, with a high number of casualties and the destruction of several synagogues. Jews were expelled three times from Rome, in 139 BC, in AD 19 by Tiberius, and under Claudius in AD 41–54.

The destruction of the Second Temple in AD 70 and the subsequent massive migration of Jews out of Israel introduced radical changes to Judaism worldwide. Religious leadership shifted decisively from the priesthood to the rabbinate; piety no longer focused on sacrifices but on the study and observance of the Torah; synagogues assumed greater importance as centers of worship rather than the Temple; and the land of Israel became known by its Roman name, Palestine.

The Diaspora also played an important role in the spread of Christianity in the first centuries of the Christian era. It is repeatedly reported in Acts that Paul, wherever he went, preached first to the Jews, most often in their synagogues, and that even though his mission to the Jews was a failure as a whole, the first important converts and leaders of the early church (e.g., Titus, Timothy, Apollo, Priscilla and Aquila, Barnabas, and many other men and women) came from Diaspora Judaism. What the early Christians thought of the Diaspora will be discussed when we treat the patristic theology of migration and exile.

Migration and the Spread of Christianity

The destruction of the Temple in AD 70 and the subsequent events surrounding the Jewish revolts of 115–17 and 132–35 caused extensive migration not only of Jews but also of Christians. Prior to the crushing of the revolt of the Judeans by the Roman general Titus, Jewish Christians, or more precisely, Greek-speaking Jewish Christians (the "Hellenists") had already migrated from Jerusalem after Stephen's martyrdom (c. 35) and the killing of James, the brother of John, by Herod Agrippa I in 44. As the result of this migration, Christian mission, as Acts reports (11:19), was extended not only to Jews in the Diaspora but also to Gentiles throughout Judea and Samaria and even as far as Phoenicia, Cyprus, and Antioch.

Following on the heels of this first migration was another, much more extensive, exodus of the Christian community out of Jerusalem and Palestine. After James, "the brother of the Lord" and the leader of the Jerusalem church, had been executed by order of the Sanhedrin (c. 62) and especially after Titus destroyed Jerusalem and razed the Temple in 70, it is highly likely that most of the Jewish Christians emigrated from Jerusalem. Their departure coincided with the evangelizing activities of the church, symbolized theologically by the legend that the twelve apostles were assigned different parts of the world and that before leaving each composed one of the twelve articles of the Apostles' Creed. However, what actually occurred seems to be that the Christian community, numbering by that time in the thousands, emigrated en masse from Jerusalem, either by force or voluntarily, into different parts of the world.[9]

Five areas were the destination of this second Christian migration where eventually Christians built a great number of vibrant and mission-minded communities. The first was Mesopotamia and the Roman province of Syria, with its three major cities, namely, Antioch, Damascus, and Edessa. Antioch, the third largest city in the Mediterranean world, might be called the cradle of Christianity as a religious movement since it was there that the followers of Jesus were first called "Christians" (Acts 11:26). It was in Syria too that some of the originating documents of Christianity were composed or translated into Syriac such as the Gospel of Matthew, the *Didache,* the *Didascalia Apostolorum,* the *Diatesseron,* and several apocryphal writings such as the *Gospel of Thomas,* the *Acts of Thomas,* and the *Odes of Solomon.*

Syriac became the language of choice for Christians in eastern Syria, Mesopotamia, Persia, India, Mongolia, and China. In the three tiny protectorate kingdoms under the Parthian dynasty of the Persian Empire—Oshroene (with Edessa as capital), Adiabene (with Arbela as capital), and Armenia—Christians established vibrant communities with the help of not only evangelists but also of Jewish and Christian merchants, migrants, and slaves, so much so that around 301 Armenia officially declared itself Christian, the first nation to do so (perhaps Oshroene had done so earlier). As for church leaders and theologians, Syrian Christianity produced such luminaries as Addai (considered the founder of the Syrian Church), Ignatius of Antioch, Justin of Syria, Barbaisan of Edessa, Tatian the Assyrian, and Gregory the Illuminator (considered the founder of the Armenian Church).

The second area was Greece and Asia Minor. From the New Testament, especially from Paul's letters and Acts, names of cities such as Thessalonica, Corinth, Ephesus, Smyrna, Philadelphia, and many others, where there were Christian churches, are well known. First Peter is addressed to "the exiles of the Dispersion in Pontus, Galatia, Cappadocia, Asia, and Bithynia" (1:1). Even if the "exiles" of the Diaspora here are to be understood figuratively and spiritually, still there is no doubt that the migration of Christians from Jerusalem to these cities of Greece and Asia Minor contributed significantly to the establishment of strong Christian churches there by the beginning of the second century. Among church leaders we find Polycarp, bishop of Smyrna; Irenaeus (later bishop of Lyons); and Papias, bishop of Hierapolis in Phrygia. Most significantly, Christians in Asia Minor suffered persecution for their faith. From the letter of Pliny the Younger, the governor of Bithynia, to the emperor Trajan, we learn that Christians were required to invoke the Roman gods, to offer wine and incense to a statue of Trajan and images of Roman gods, and to curse Christ. Doubtless, many Christians were forced to flee and migrate for safety, and among those who were arrested and killed, Polycarp was the most famous.

The third destination was the western Mediterranean, including Italy, France, Spain, and North Africa. We do not know when and how the Christian movement arrived in the western end of the Mediterranean region, but there is little doubt that Christian migrants and merchants had a strong hand in establishing the churches there, certainly long before the arrival of Paul or any other apostle. To what extent Peter had a role in the founding

of the Roman church, we do not know, except that according to the tradition, he, together with Paul, was martyred there. However, from the fact
that the first Roman Christians spoke *koine* Greek rather than Latin, it is clear
that they were foreigners, hence, migrants, or members of a lower class.
We know for certain that by the mid-50s, when Paul wrote his letter to the
Roman Christians, there had been already groups of Christians among the
large Jewish community, which was estimated at fifty thousand. Furthermore, we also know that many of these Christians were migrants from Asia
Minor from the fact that they celebrated Easter on 14 Nisan, even if it fell
on a weekday, whereas others celebrated on the Sunday following 14 Nisan,
a difference that would involve Pope Victor in an unfortunate dispute with
the churches of Asia Minor in 189. We also know that the imperial capital attracted renowned Christian teachers from the East, such as Justin from
Syria, Marcion from Pontus, and Valentinus from Alexandria. Lyons in southern Gaul also enticed Christian migrants, the most famous of whom was
Irenaeus from Smyrna, later bishop of the city. In Roman North Africa,
Carthage, a heavily multicultural city where one could hear indigenous
African, Punic, Latin, and *koine* Greek languages spoken in the streets, was
a powerful magnet for Christian migrants. Persecutions also were respon-
sible for Christian migration: in Rome in 64 under Nero, in 95 under Do-
mitian, in 250 under Decius, in 257 under Valerian, and in 284–305 under
Diocletian; in Lyons in 177, when some fifty Christians lost their lives; in
Carthage in 203 a number of other Christians, among them Perpetua and
Felicitas, were killed. Christianity in the western Mediterranean also produced major church leaders and theologians: Clement of Rome; Hippoly-
tus, also of Rome and the author of the *Apostolic Tradition*; Irenaeus of Lyons;
Tertullian and Cyprian, both of Carthage; and of course, Ambrose, Augustine, Jerome, and many others in later centuries, when the church enjoyed
peace and prosperity.

The fourth destination of early Christian migration was Egypt, in particular Alexandria. As with the western Mediterranean, when and how Christians went to Alexandria is not known. But as the preeminent intellectual
center and the most cosmopolitan city of the ancient world, and with a
large Jewish contingent with their own political leadership and special rights
granted by the emperor, Alexandria was the destination of choice for Jewish
Christian migrants. Already Acts mentions Egypt as the country of origin of

some among the crowd present on the day of Pentecost (2:10), and Apollos is identified as an Alexandrian Jew who had become a follower of the Way (Acts 18:24–25). At any rate, by the middle of the second century, Christians, who most probably had migrated from Jerusalem, succeeded in establishing the most famous theological school in antiquity, with a distinct method of biblical interpretation and with a star-studded faculty including Pantaenus, Clement, and Origen. By the same token, Alexandria also hosted the most powerful heresy, that is, Gnosticism, with famous teachers such as Basilides and Valentinus.

The last destination of early Christian migration was East Asia, and more precisely, India. Unfortunately, this migration remains shrouded in mystery, since there is no incontrovertible historical evidence of the presence of a Christian community in India until the fourth century when one bishop by the name of John attending the council of Nicea (325) signed the document on behalf of all the churches of Persia and all India. However, according to the oral tradition, the apostle Thomas (or Bartholomew) was the first missionary to go to India. According to the apocryphal *Acts of Thomas,* the apostle Thomas accepted the invitation of an Indian king named Gudnaphar to build a palace in his country in northern India. Instead of building the palace, however, Thomas gave money to the poor and converted Indians by his preaching and miracles. The angry king condemned him to death, and tradition locates the site of his burial at a shrine in the southeastern city of Mylapore. On the other hand, according to a number of oral traditions and folk songs of the Indian churches, Thomas is said to have landed in 52 in south India along the Malabar coast, and not in the north. His preaching and conversions angered the Brahmins and when he refused to worship the goddess Kali he was put to death. Whatever the historical validity of these diverse traditions about Thomas's mission to India, it is certain that Christian migration to India did take place rather early. Some of these Christians were merchants, as trade between the Middle East and India was frequent and active, others were refugees from the Persian persecutions, and still others were missionaries. These Indian Christians used Syriac in their liturgy and rice cakes and palm wine in their Eucharist. They adapted well to their surroundings so that eventually they became a separate caste, a sign that they were granted social and political standing by the Indian rulers.

Migrations of "Barbarians" and Their Conversion to Christianity

The third major migratory movement during the patristic era was the migration of the Germanic tribes (*gentes*), which not only threatened the security of the Roman Empire but also posed severe challenges to the rapidly growing church. From Tacitus's *Germania* and *Agricola* and Caesar's *Commentaries* we learn that various groups of tribes inhabited northern Germany, southern Sweden, Denmark, and the shores of the Baltic, and were greatly feared for their barbarity and warlikeness. The chief Germanic tribes include the Vandals, the Goths, the Alemani, the Angles, the Saxons, the Burgundians, and the Lombards. By the first century, these tribes came into contact with the Romans, and in succeeding centuries, they became an increasing menace to the Roman Empire, both east and west. From the third through the sixth century, the most important migrations in European history took place as these tribes spread out in great movements southward, southeastward, and westward.

Early in the fifth century, in the West, the Vandals began a migration that eventually took them farther south than any other Germanic tribe. In 406 they invaded Gaul, and in 409 they crossed the Pyrenees into Spain. While in Spain, they fought against the Romans and the Visigoths, another Germanic tribe. In 429, under the leadership of Gaiseric, the Vandals crossed over into Africa and by 435 controlled most of the Roman province of North Africa, including Carthage. Though Arian Christians, the Vandals did not spare Christianity in North Africa and destroyed many churches, Donatist and Catholic alike. In 442, the emperor Valentinian III (419–55) recognized Gaiseric (d. 477) as an independent ruler, and the Vandal migration ceased.

In the third century AD, another important Germanic tribe, namely, the Goths, who had settled in the region west of the Black Sea, split into two groups, the Ostrogoths (East Goths) and Visigoths (West Goths), the former settling in the Ukraine, while the latter further west of them.[10] By the fourth century, the Visigoths were at the borders of the eastern Roman Empire. At the end of Constantine I's reign (d. 337), they had settled in Dacia as agriculturalists or served in the Roman army, and many had accepted (Arian) Christianity. About 364, a group of Visigoths ravaged Thrace, and again in 378 did the same. In 395, the Visigoth troops in Roman service elected Alaric as their king, and under his leadership, they attacked Italy and ransacked Rome in 410. Under Alaric's successor, Ataulf, they went into southern Gaul and northern Spain, and under Euric (466–84) completed the conquest of Spain. Toledo became the new capital of the Visigoths, and their history henceforth became essentially that of Spain. In c. 587–89, one of the Visigoth kings, Reccared (d. 601), converted to Catholic Christianity from Arianism, thus facilitating the fusion of the Visigothic and the Hispano-Roman populations.

The Ostrogoths, on the other hand, were made subject to the Huns until Attila's death (453) when they migrated to Pannonia (roughly modern Hungary) as allies of the Byzantine Empire. In 471, they chose Theodoric as king, who was commissioned by the Byzantine emperor Zeno to take Italy away from Odoacer. In 488, the Ostrogoths entered Italy, defeated Odoacer, and established the Ostrogothic kingdom with the capital at Ravenna. In 535, Byzantium destroyed the Ostrogothic kingdom, and subsequently the Ostrogoths disappeared as a national identity.

Another migration that is significant for early Christianity is that of the Angles, the Saxons, and the Jutes. The Angles, who seem to have come from what is now Schleswig, migrated to England in the fifth century, and founded the kingdoms of East Anglia, Mercia, and Northumbria. Their continental neighbors, the Saxons, also came to England in the late fifth century and laid the foundations for the later kingdoms of Sussex, Wessex, and Essex.

By the middle of the fifth century, there was a flood of immigrants pouring into the western Roman lands. The Vandals who crossed into North Africa were said to number more than 150,000, while the number of "barbarian" settlers in Gaul was said to reach 100,000. While it is true, as Peter Brown has shown, that "it is profoundly misleading to speak of the history of Western Europe in the fifth century as 'the Age of the Barbarian Invasions,'"[11] still there is no doubt that the migrations of these tribes posed great challenges for the early church. Before examining how the early church viewed and dealt with migration, its own and that of others, it would be helpful to summarize the main features of migration in the patristic era.

1. Christians experienced migration in great numbers at the very dawn of the church, especially after the destruction of Jerusalem in AD 70.

2. Christian migration coincided with and encouraged the church's missionary enterprise.

3. The reasons for migration in the early church were religious and political persecutions, but trade also played an important role, especially when Christians moved to the East. Thus, in contemporary categories, their migration was both forced and planned. In other words, Christians were both emigrants and refugees. Another significant reason for migration was evangelization. As pointed out above, Christian migration was intimately connected with Christian mission.

4. Christian migration was both, to use contemporary terminologies, internal, that is, within Palestine and within other countries, and intercontinental, that is, throughout the Roman and Persian Empires and outside them, especially to Asia.

5. Like most other migrants, Christians tended to settle in big cities such as Antioch, Damascus, Edessa, Alexandria, Rome, Lyons, Carthage, and the cities along the southern coast of India.

6. Like the Jews, Christians succeeded in forming vibrant and numerous communities in these cities. Christian migrants tended to be, in contemporary parlance, settlers rather than labor migrants, and permanent rather than temporary.

7. Differently from Jews, Christianity did not enjoy legitimacy as a *religio licita* in the Roman Empire because they had no homeland, no place of national origin, no common blood, no common language, and no common culture. In other words, early Christians were truly immigrants.

8. Like other migrants, early Christians adapted themselves quickly to the local cultures.

9. At the same time, like other migrants, they maintained distance from the surrounding societies, especially in their ethical and religious practices.

10. Lastly, Christian migration was not a unique phenomenon but was a part of a widespread and frequent pattern of population movements, such as the Diaspora and the migration of the Germanic tribes.

If migration was a common feature of life in the first seven centuries of the Christian era, something that most Christians shared with their neighbors, how did they view it? And how did they treat other migrants? To this we now turn.

Migration: Ethics and Theology

To grasp both what the early church understood by migration and the ethical behavior it urged toward the migrant, it is useful to remember that *migration* and *migrant* are modern categories whose sociological and political connotations cannot anachronistically be retrojected to the situation of late antiquity, even though, as shown above, the classification of migration resulting from contemporary studies proves helpful in highlighting the commonalities between migration in our times and that of the patristic age. On the other hand, the terms used by the Fathers to describe the condition of Christians and their meanings, different from those of today, may enlarge our contemporary understanding of migration and the migrant.[12]

In describing the Christian migrant, early Christian writers had at their disposal the three biblical terms of *stranger* (or *alien*), *foreigner*, and *sojourner*. Though these terms are often used interchangeably in English translations of the Bible, they denote three distinct categories of people in biblical times. A *stranger* (Hebrew *zār*, Greek *xenos*, Latin *hospes*) is one who does not belong to the house or community or nation in which he or she lives and is often considered an enemy (Is 1:7; Jer 5:19; 51:51; Ez 7:21; 28:7, 10; Ob 11). A *foreigner* (Hebrew *nokri*, Greek *allotrios*, Latin *alienus*) is one of another race, and because non-Jews were regarded as idolatrous, the term also designates someone worshiping idols. Hence, to prevent religious contamination, Jews were forbidden to marry a foreigner (Dt 7:1–6). A *sojourner* (Hebrew *gēr*, Greek *paroikos*, Latin *peregrinus*) is someone whose permanent residence is in another nation, in contrast to the foreigner whose stay is only temporary. Sojourners were protected by Jewish law. Jews must not oppress them (Ex 22:21); they must even love them (Dt 10:19). Sojourners are grouped with orphans and widows as defenseless people whom God protects, and God will judge their oppressors (Jer 7:6; 22:7, 29; Zec 7:10; Mal 3:5). On the other hand, sojourners must observe some of the provisions of the Law, such as observance of the Sabbath and the Day of Atonement (Ex 20:10; Lv 16:29), and abstention from eating blood (Lv 17:10, 13), immorality (Lv 18:26), idolatry (Lv 20:2), and blasphemy (Lv 24:16). The good news of Jesus is that those who were strangers [*apēllotri ōmenoi*] (Eph 2:12) from Israel, and so were "strangers and sojourners [*xenoi kai paroikoi*]" (Eph 2:19) have been made "fellow citizens [*sumpolitai*] with the saints and of the household of God [*oikeioi tou theou*]" (Eph 2:19).

It is most interesting that early Christian writers, while convinced that Christians were no longer "strangers and sojourners" but "fellow citizens" with regard to Israel and constituting the household of God, considered themselves as *paroikoi*—sojourners, displaced people without a home and a nation, migrants—by far the early Christians' favorite term to describe themselves. This self-consciousness as foreigners, strangers, and sojourners is found in Clement of Rome's letter to the Christians in Corinth (c. 96). It was sent from "the church of God which sojourns [*paroikousa*] in Rome" to "the church of God which sojourns [*paroikousei*] in Corinth." Polycarp, the bishop-martyr of Smyrna (d. 155), also addressed his letter to the Christians in Philippi: "To the church of God which resides as a stranger [*paroikousei*] at Philippi." Similarly, the *Martyrium Polycarpi* was sent "from the church of God which resides as a stranger [*paroikousa*] at Smyrna to the church of God residing as a stranger [*paroikousei*] at Philomelium and to all the communities of the holy and catholic church residing in any place [*paroikiais*]."

While this self-awareness as sojourners and foreigners may be given an eschatological and spiritual interpretation, it was quite likely exacerbated by the fact that Christians in these areas—Rome, Corinth, and Asia Minor—were mostly migrants, without full civic rights, and were subject to discrimination and persecution.

Ethics of Hospitality

Being themselves sojourners and migrants, how should Christians treat other migrants and sojourners? My focus is not on the early Christians' view of wealth and poverty and the duty of almsgiving nor on how they actually practiced charity in general.[13] Rather I will concentrate on what the early Christians taught about the duty of welcoming the stranger—the functional equivalent of today's migrant—and specifically the virtue of hospitality. It is interesting to note that the Latin *hostis* [enemy] originally means stranger [*hospes*] and that the dividing line between stranger and enemy was very thin, especially in closely knit communities, in which people were defined primarily by kinship through blood or marriage. In such communities, the outsider/stranger was often perceived as a threat, and what the stranger most urgently needed was welcome, material assistance, and acceptance as a full member of the community. Hence, the virtue most highly recommended to the community was *philoxenia,* literally, love of strangers or hospitality.

Needless to say, the early Christians were well schooled in the duty of hospitality, a practice which already figures prominently in the Old Testament, perhaps due to Israel's nomadic existence and reflecting the bedouin traditions. Hospitality is however more than a social custom. Rather, as the example of Abraham demonstrates, it is also an expression of gratitude and faithfulness to God who is Israel's generous host. Abraham's welcome toward the three strangers turned out to be hospitality extended to Yahweh himself (Gn 18:1–8). Indeed, throughout the Old Testament, God is depicted as entertaining Israel with abundant and endless banquets and as deeply concerned for the stranger, as the divine provision of cities of refuge (Nm 35:9–35; Jo 20:1–9) and care for the sojourner (Ex 22:21; Lv 19:10; Dt 10:19) make abundantly clear. Consequently, failure to provide for the stranger's physical needs is a serious offense, equivalent to breaching the covenant with God, and brings about God's punishment (Dt 23:3–4). Furthermore, the duties of the host also extend to securing the safety and welfare of the guests, as the stories of Lot (Gn 19:8) and the old man of Gibeah (Jgs 19:24–25) vividly illustrate.

For the early Christians, however, the most radical motive for and example of hospitality were Jesus's behavior and his teaching. Jesus often used images of food and drink and banquet to illustrate the kingdom of God he proclaimed. During his ministry he fed hungry people (Jn 6) and, as a "friend of tax collectors and sinners" (Mt 11:18), he shared table fellowship with them. He said that people would "inherit the kingdom" depending on whether they had fed the hungry, slaked the thirsty, clothed the naked, visited the sick and the imprisoned, and welcomed strangers: "I was a stranger and you welcomed me" [*xenos ēmēn kai suvēgagete*] (Mt 25:35). Given the importance of hospitality to strangers in Jesus's life and teaching, it is not surprising that his followers presented it as foundational to understanding the mission of the church. Indeed, Acts, which narrated the church's earliest missionary activities, may be read as a collection of guest and host stories played out among itinerant preachers such as Paul and the local communities. This reciprocal welcoming, preeminently at meals, was to become one of the main attractions to Christianity, and lack of it would be a powerful countersign to the nature of the church as *koinonia* (close mutual fellowship), as is made eloquently clear by Paul's reproaches to the Corinthian Christians for their abuses of the Lord's Supper in excluding and dishonoring the poor (1 Cor 11:17–34). First Peter, which is addressed to the "chosen sojourners of the Dispersion" [*ekklektois parepidēmois diasporas*] (1:1), strongly urges Christians "to be hospitable to one another without complaining" [*philoxenoi eis allēlous aneu goggusmou*] (4:9) since they themselves were all resident aliens and transient strangers [*paroikous kai parepidēmous*] (2:11). Hebrews adds another motive for the practice of hospitality, with implicit reference to Abraham: "Do not neglect to show hospitality to strangers [*philoxenia*], for by doing that some have entertained angels without knowing it" (13:2). In 3 John, the elder commends Gaius for practicing hospitality, treating as friends those who were strangers [*xenous*], condemns Diotrephes for failing to do so, and insists that Christians should support [*hupolambanein*] itinerant missionaries.[14]

Writers of the patristic era continue to insist on the practice of welcoming strangers, most of whom were migrants and missionaries. Hospitality for them was all the more necessary because inns were scarce, filthy, dangerous, and most often were nothing more than brothels.[15] Clement of Rome, writing in 96 to Corinthian Christians involved in a power struggle, recommended hospitality as a way to resolve the ecclesiastical crisis. He singled out the example of Abraham and Rahab as models of hospitality to the stranger, for which the former was granted a son in his old age and the latter was saved from death.[16] The second-century document *The Didache* urges Christians to welcome any orthodox teacher of the faith who came their way as well as everyone who came to them in the name of the Lord. Travelers must also be helped in any way possible, but they should not stay more than three days.[17] Tertullian (c. 160–c. 225), in his impassioned plea for the toleration of Christianity, pointed to the Christians' loving and generous care of the poor and the stranger:

Each person deposits a small amount on a certain day of the month or whenever he or she wishes, and only on condition that they are willing and able to do so. No one is forced; each makes a contribution voluntarily. These are, so to speak, the deposits of piety. The money there from is spent not for banquets or drinking parties or good-for-nothing eating houses, but for the support and burial of the poor, for children who are without parents and means of subsistence, for aged men who are confined to the house; likewise, for shipwrecked sailors, and for any in the mines, on islands or in prisons. Provided only it be for the sake of fellowship with God, they become entitled to loving and protective care for their confession. The practice of such a special love brands us in the eyes of some. "See," they say, "how they love one another;" for *they* hate one another, "and how ready they die for each other."[18]

Tertullian's fellow countryman and bishop of Carthage, Cyprian (c. 200–258), invoked Jesus's eschatological discourse in which he identified himself with the hungry, the thirsty, the stranger, the naked, the sick, and the imprisoned, and the bishop urged the Christians under his care to practice charity toward them.[19] In general, the fathers of the church reiterated Christ's identification with the strangers and those who suffer and require almsgiving as a form of sharing the earthly goods. Thus, Cyprian, after raising ransom money for the release of the Numidian Christians from their barbarian captors, said: "The captivity of our brethren must be reckoned as our captivity, and the grief of those who are endangered is to be thought of as our grief. . . . Christ is to be contemplated in our captive brethren."[20] Gregory of Nyssa reminded the rich that they must recognize Christ in the poor: "Do not despise these people in their abjection; do not think of them as of no account. Reflect what they are and you will understand their dignity; they have often taken upon themselves the person of our Savior."[21] John Chrysostom, whose fulminations against the rich and their greed are famous, said: "Do you really wish to pay homage to Christ's body? Then do not neglect him when he is naked. At the same time that you honor him here with hangings made of silk, do not ignore him outside when he perishes from cold and nakedness."[22] For Augustine, there is a hidden identity between Christ and the suffering Christians: "For consider, brethren, the love of our head. He is in heaven, yet he suffers here, as long as his church suffers here. Here Christ is hungry, here he is thirsty, is naked, is a stranger, is sick, is in prison. For whatever his body suffers here, he has said that he himself suffers."[23]

Matching deeds to words, the early church spent much of its material possessions to care for the strangers and the poor by means of charitable institutions. This social welfare work was supported by the individual community with the local bishop bearing responsibility for it. The direct administration was entrusted to a deacon, who had deaconesses and widows at his disposition for special services. Thus, in Caesarea of Cappadocia, Bishop Basil, along with his sister Macrina, had buildings constructed at the edge of the city to receive travelers and sick persons, especially lepers, and staffed them with qualified personnel. In Antioch, the Christian community possessed a rather large hospital and a special inn for strangers. The high esteem for hospitality by monasticism is testified by the presence of a guest house [*xenodochion*] in every cenobitic community. Works of social welfare were also sponsored by bishops such as Ambrose of Milan, Paulinus of Nola, Martin of Tours, Nicetius of Lyons, and Sidonius Apollinarius of Clermont. In Rome, under the vigilant care of popes such as Leo the Great, Gelasius, Symmachus, who founded three homes for the poor, and above all Gregory the Great, the practice of charity was extensive. For example, in 251, the Roman church took care of 1,500 widows, orphans, and destitute persons.

The early church's concern for the migrants was however not limited to providing material assistance. True to her spiritual mission, it devoted much of its energies and resources to the evangelization of the migrants, especially the various Germanic tribes. In this respect, care for the migrants went hand in hand with mission. Around 340, Eusebius, the Arian bishop of Nicomedia, ordained Ulfilas (c. 311–83) to the episcopacy to serve the Christians in the lands of the Goths. Through Ulfilas, who translated the Bible into the Gothic language (except the books of Kings so as not to encourage the Goths' bellicosity), the Arian form of Christianity was spread to the Germanic tribes.[24] Within decades the Goths converted en masse to Christianity, and by 400 the Vandals, the Burgundians, the Lombards, and others also embraced the Christian faith.[25]

Lest we form an idealistic picture of the early church's teaching on the migrant and the stranger and its social welfare for them, it is necessary to note, albeit only briefly, that its dealing with one group of migrants, namely, the Jews, was deplorable. As noted above, the migration of Christians from Jerusalem to other parts of the Roman and Persian Empires coincided largely with the Diaspora after AD 70, and Jewish and Christian migrants tended to settle in the same cities. In this coexistence the relationship between early Christians and Jews was highly complex and diverse, and here is not the place to enter into a detailed discussion of it. Suffice it to note that though the relationship between the two religious groups was marked by mutual hostility, it was by no means universally the same in the Roman and the Persian Empires where Christians and Jews were often treated differently by the authorities. On the other hand, groups of Christians and Jews continued to have friendly relations with one another, with Christians, including the clergy, participating in Jewish festivals and attending synagogue services, even as late as the fourth century. Nevertheless, from the end of the first century, there began among Christians an anti-Jewish attitude which was later embodied in the *Adversus Judaeos* tradition. Virulent forms of this tradition are found, for example, in Justin's *Dialogue with Trypho,* Melito of Sardis's *On the Passover,* and John Chrysostom's sermons at Antioch. Such anti-Judaism was stimulated by a mixture of political, economic, and religious considerations, and one of its oft-repeated themes was that the Diaspora was a divine punishment for the Jews' rejection of Jesus as the Christ and that the Jews were condemned by God to eternal migration for their faithlessness (the myth of the "Wandering Jew").[26] To this extent it may be argued that the care for migrants that the early Christians fervently urged was intended primarily for fellow believers and not for the members of other religions, especially Judaism, though of course assistance to people outside the Christian faith did certainly occur.

Theology of Migration: Christians as Strangers

As has been pointed out above, the early Christians, who believed that they were no longer "sojourners and strangers" but "fellow citizens" with Jews in God's household, paradoxically greeted one another as *paroikoi,* foreigners and migrants. Clearly, for them migration was an essential part of the Christian's permanent self-consciousness and theological—and not merely sociological—identity. No doubt this self-description had an eschatological and spiritual overtone insofar as Christians considered themselves to be the pilgrim people of God on the march toward the kingdom of God. At the same time, their social and political status as migrants and strangers, without a permanent residence and citizenship, as well as the persecutions they suffered, lent depth and poignancy to their theological reflections on their social condition.

Among early Christian writings there is arguably no more eloquent description of Christians as migrants than the anonymous letter known as the

Letter to Diognetus. Written in the second or third century by an unknown Christian to an equally unknown inquirer, it seeks to answer three questions concerning: "what God they [Christians] believe in and how they worship him," "the source of their loving affection that they have for each other," and "why this new race or way of life has appeared on earth now and not earlier."[27] In the course of answering these three queries, the author contrasts, in a string of striking antitheses, the Christians with their contemporaries. Given the beauty of the text, a lengthy quotation may be permitted:

> For Christians cannot be distinguished from the rest of the human race by country or language or customs. They do not live in cities of their own; they do not use a peculiar form of speech; they do not follow an eccentric manner of life. This doctrine of theirs has not been discovered by the ingenuity or deep thought of inquisitive men, nor do they put forward a merely human teaching, as some people do. Yet, although they live in Greek and barbarian cities alike, as each person's lot has been cast, and follow the customs of the country in clothing and food and other matters of daily living, at the same time they give proof of the remarkable and admittedly extraordinary constitution of their own commonwealth. They live in their own countries, but only as aliens [*paroikoi*]. They have a share in everything as citizens [*politai*], and endure everything as foreigners [*xenoi*]. Every foreign land is their fatherland, and yet for them every fatherland is a foreign land. They marry, like everyone else, and they beget children, but they do not cast out their offspring. They share their board with each other, but not their marriage bed. It is true that they are in the flesh, but they do not live according to the flesh. They busy themselves on earth, but their citizenship is in heaven. They obey the established laws, but in their own lives they go far beyond what the laws require. They love all, but by all are persecuted. They are unknown, and still they are condemned; they are put to death, and yet they are brought to life. They are poor, and yet they make many rich; they are completely destitute, and yet they enjoy complete abundance. They are dishonored, and in their very dishonor are glorified; they are defamed, and are vindicated. They are reviled, and yet they bless; when they are affronted, they still pay due respect. When they do good, they are punished as evildoers; undergoing punishment, they rejoice because they are brought to life. They are treated by the

Jews as foreigners [*allophuloi*], and are hunted down by the Greeks; and all the time those who hate them find it impossible to justify their enmity. To put it simply: What the soul is in the body, that Christians are in the world. The soul is dispersed through all the members of the body, and Christians are scattered through all the cities of the world. The soul dwells in the body, but does not belong to the body, and Christians dwell in the world, but do not belong to the world. . . . The soul, which is immortal, is housed in a mortal dwelling; while Christians are settled among corruptible things, to wait for the incorruptibility that will be theirs in heaven.[28]

Needless to say, the portrait of the Christians as drawn in this celebrated letter should not be taken as a historically accurate description of the behavior of each and every early Christian. Surely not all early Christians conducted themselves in as praiseworthy a manner as the letter claims. Rather than as factual description, the letter should be seen as presenting the ideal behavior of Christians. On the other hand, it should not be dismissed out of hand as a piece of self-serving propaganda either. Historical evidence, as reported above, tends to support many if not all of the letter's statements about early Christians. Whatever the historical validity of its claims about early Christianity and the value of its apologetics for the superiority of Christianity over pagan religions and Judaism, the letter's idealistic portrait of the Christian can certainly be viewed as an exceptionally rich and profound theology of migration. An extended commentary on this theology is not feasible here; suffice it to highlight its main points as significant contributions to a contemporary theology of the Christian as a migrant.

First, a Christian *qua* Christian does not possess a separate country, language, or customs. As Christians, migrants may therefore adopt any of these things as their own, wherever they live. Moreover, though strangers, they must do their best to contribute to the welfare of their new homeland.

Second, as best as they try to be inculturated into the new society and however much "every foreign land is their fatherland," as Christians, migrants will and must remain to a certain extent strangers to their adopted country, of course not in language and customs, which they share with others, but in their religious worldview and moral behavior: "They live in their own countries, but only as aliens. They have a share in everything as citizens, but endure everything as foreigners." The theology of migration must therefore be not only transcultural, contextual, and cross-cultural, but also countercultural by which the migrants can both incorporate and critique the surrounding cultures. Thus, migrants are people living-in-between two cultures. They do not belong fully to either; they are for example, neither fully Vietnamese nor fully American. Yet they are both Vietnamese and American. Furthermore, because they are neither-nor and both-and, they can go beyond both cultures and create something new, a "third race," as the early Christians sometimes described themselves.

Third, because of their difference from the surrounding world, migrants, and especially Christian migrants, will inevitably experience discrimination and even persecution. They will be treated at times as "foreigners and enemies" by those to whom their beliefs and behaviors are incomprehensible, and perhaps even endure indirect reproach: "When they do good, they are punished as evildoers."

Fourth, even so, Christian migrants should not retaliate with violence against those who oppress them. Rather, "they are poor, and yet they make many rich . . . they are reviled, and yet they bless; when they are affronted, they still pay due respect." Of course, this willingness to do good in spite of injustice is not a passive abdication of one's responsibilities for justice and fairness; rather, the migrants' nonviolent resistance and doing good to those who hate and persecute them are seen as the most effective ways to overcome hatred and injustice.

Fifth, the motivation for such behavior of returning good for evil is hope, which is the virtue par excellence of migrants. This hope is not for material remuneration but for "the incorruptibility that will be theirs in heaven." Eschatology is then an intrinsic part of any theology of migration that sees it not only as a personal and societal curse—which it certainly is—but also as an urgent call for self-transcendence and for a collective action to overcome structural evils.

Sixth and finally, migration is a permanent feature of the church, and not just a historical phenomenon of the early church or of any other period of church history. Like unity, catholicity, holiness, and apostolicity, "migrantness," to coin a new word, is a note of the true church because only a church that is conscious of being an institutional migrant and caring for all the migrants of the world can truly practice faith, hope, and love, in obedience to Jesus' command.

The theology of migration as proposed by the *Letter to Diognetus,* centers, I suggest, on the theology of the migrant's life as *imitatio Christi.* After all, Jesus is the paradigmatic migrant who dwelt between the borders of two worlds. Through the incarnation, ontologically, he stood between divinity and humanity and embodied both. Already as a child, he experienced migration to Egypt. As an adult, politically, he lived between colony and empire; culturally, between Roman and barbarian; linguistically, between Aramaic and Greek; religiously, between the Chosen People and the *goyim* (other, Gentile nations). During his ministry, he was itinerant and homeless, having nowhere to lay his head, unlike foxes that have holes and birds that have nests (Lk 9:58). As a migrant, Jesus was a "marginal Jew," to use the title of John Meier's multivolume work on the historical Jesus.[29] His migration carried him over all kinds of borders, both geographical and conventional: Palestine and the pagan territories, Jews and non-Jews, men and women, the young and the old, the rich and the poor, the Sadducees and the Pharisees, the powerful and the weak, the healthy and the sick, the clean and the unclean, the righteous and the sinners. Because his multiple border-crossings were a threat to those who occupied the economic, political, and religious centers of power, he was hung upon the cross, between heaven and earth, between the two cosmic borders, a migrant until the end.[30] That is why he could truly say that whoever welcomes a migrant/stranger, welcomes him: "I was a stranger [*xenos*] and you welcomed me" (Mt 25:35). A contemporary theology of migration that fails to see Jesus as identified with the migrant and to view migration as an essential note of the church would not do justice to both the migratory experiences of the early church and its theology of the migrant.

NOTES

1. In his *Guns, Germs, and Steel: The Fates of Human Societies* (New York: Norton, 1999), Jared Diamond gives an overview of human migration from the *homo australopithecus* and the *homo erectus* (seven million years ago) through the *homo sapiens* (one million years ago) to the last major migrations in ancient times, when Polynesians sailed to Hawaii in AD 100 and when Polynesians sailed to New

Zealand in AD 1000. Diamond shows that these global migrations have produced profound and irreversible changes for both the human species and the ecology.

2. Robin Cohen, ed., *The Cambridge Survey of World Migration* (Cambridge: Cambridge University Press, 1995), 1. The quotation from Immanuel Wallenstein is taken from his *The Modern World System: Capitalist Agriculture and the Origin of European World-Economy in the Sixteenth Century* (New York: Academic Press, 1974), 15. See also Kenneth Pomeranz and Steven Topik, *The World that Trade Created: Culture, Society and the World, 1400 to the Present* (Armonk, NY: M. E. Sharpe, 1999).

3. For a survey of recent migration in the United States, Europe, Asia, Australia, and Africa, see Leonore Loeb Adler and Uwe P. Giellen, eds., *Migration: Immigration and Emigration in International Perspective* (Westport, CT: Praeger, 2003).

4. For these categorizations, see Cohen, *Cambridge Survey of World Migration,* 5–6. For a helpful discussion of various terms related to migration such as *migrant, immigrant, emigrant, migratory workers, international workers, aliens, illegal immigrants, asylum seekers, skilled transients, multinational transferees, capital assisted migrants,* and *refugees,* see Adler and Giellen, *Migration: Immigration and Emigration,* 10–13.

5. Cohen, *Cambridge Survey of World Migration,* 6.

6. The specific literature on migration during the patristic era is, as far as I can determine, practically nonexistent. This dearth of scholarly studies is of course due to the scarcity of extensive accurate historical and sociological data. What can be known about migration in general and migration of Christians in particular during this period is inferred from events reported in general histories of the Roman Empire and of early Christianity.

7. Helpful works on the Diaspora during the Greco-Roman period include: Menahem Stern, "The Jewish Diaspora," in *The Jewish People in the First Century: Historical Geography, Political History, Social, Cultural and Religious Life and Institutions,* ed. Shemuel Safari and Menahem Stern, 117–83 (Assen: Van Gorcum, 1974–76); Emil Schürer, *The History of the Jewish People in the Age of Jesus Christ (175 B.C.–A.D. 135),* trans. A. Burkill, rev. and ed. Geza Vermes and Fergus Miller (Edinburgh: Clark, 1973–87), 1–176; Tessa Rajak, *The Jewish Dialogue with Greece and Rome: Studies in Cultural and Social Interaction* (Leiden: Brill, 2001); and Erich S. Gruen, *Diaspora: Jews amidst Greeks and Romans* (Cambridge, MA: Harvard University Press, 2002).

8. See Arnold Ages, *The Diaspora Dimension* (The Hague: Martinus Nijhoff, 1973), 3–7.

9. Histories of the early church are of course legion. However, studies on migration as a social phenomenon during the patristic era are scarce. The most useful single-volume histories of the early church include: Henry Chadwick, *The Early Church* (London: Penguin Books, 1967), and *The Church in Ancient Society: From Galilee to Gregory the Great* (Oxford: Oxford University Press, 2001); W. H. C. Frend, *The Rise of Christianity* (Philadelphia: Fortress, 1984); and Peter Brown, *The Rise of Western Christendom,* 2nd ed. (Oxford: Blackwell, 2003). Multivolume histories include:

Kenneth Scott Latourette, *A History of the Expansion of Christianity,* rev. ed. (New York: Harper and Brothers, 1937–45); Hubert Jedin and John Dolan, eds., *History of the Church* (New York: Herder and Herder, 1965–81); Jean-Marie Mayeur, Charles et Luce Pietri, André Vauchez, Marc Venard, *Histoire du Christianisme des origins à nos jours* (Paris: Desclée, 1995). A helpful introduction to the various backgrounds of early Christianity is Everett Ferguson, *Backgrounds of Early Christianity* (Grand Rapids, MI: Eerdmans, 1987). One work that is highly useful for understanding Christianity as a world movement, with emphasis on the Christian expansion into Asia, is Dale Irwin and Scott W. Sunquist, *History of the World Christian Movement,* vol. 1, *Earliest Christianity to 1453* (Maryknoll, NY: Orbis Books, 2001); for what follows, see especially 57–97. For a history of Asian Christianity, see Samuel Hugh Moffett, *A History of Christianity in Asia,* vol. 1, *Beginnings to 1500* (Maryknoll, NY: Orbis Books, 1998).

10. See Walter A. Goffart, *Barbarians and Romans, A.D. 418–584: The Techniques of Accommodation* (Princeton: Princeton University Press, 1980); E. A. Thompson, *Romans and Barbarians: The Decline of the Western Empire* (Madison: University of Wisconsin Press, 1982); Thomas S. Burns, *A History of the Ostrogoths* (Bloomington: Indiana University Press, 1984).

11. Brown, *Rise of Western Christendom,* 104.

12. For a presentation of patristic theology, see the four-volume *Patrology,* the first three authored by Johannes Quasten (Utrecht/Antwerp: Spectrum, 1950–60) and the fourth edited by Angelo Di Berardino (Westminster, MD: Christian Classics, 1991).

13. On this, see the following works: L. William Countryman, *The Rich Christian in the Church of the Early Empire: Contradictions and Accommodations* (Toronto: Edwin Mellen Press, 1980); Justo L. González, *Faith and Wealth: A History of Early Christian Ideas on the Origin, Significance, and Use of Money* (San Francisco: Harper and Row, 1990); Martin Hengel, *Property and Riches in the Early Church* (Philadelphia: Fortress, 1974); Redmond Mullin, *The Wealth of Christians* (Maryknoll, NY: Orbis Books, 1984). For primary sources, see Peter C. Phan, *Social Thought: Message of the Fathers of the Church* (Wilmington, DE: Michael Glazier, 1984) and R. Sierra Bravo, *Doctrina social y economica de los padres de la Iglesia* (Madrid: COMPI, 1976).

14. See John Koenig, *New Testament Hospitality: Partnership with Strangers as Promise and Mission* (Philadelphia: Fortress, 1985).

15. See Ferguson, *Backgrounds of Early Christianity,* 67.

16. See Cyril Richardson, ed., *Early Christian Fathers* (New York: Macmillan, 1970), 48–49.

17. See Richardson, *Early Christian Fathers,* 176–77. Translation slightly emended.

18. See Charles J. Dollen, James K. McGowan, and James J. Megivern, eds., *The Catholic Tradition: Social Thought* (Wilmington, NC: McGrath Publishing Co., 1979), 1:85–86.

19. For a complete English text of Cyprian's *De opere et eleemosynis* [*On Works and Alsmgiving*], see C. Dollen, McGowan, and Megivern, *Catholic Tradition*, 1:97–114. For key excerpts of it, see Phan, *Social Thought*, 86–91.

20. Phan, *Social Thought*, 39.

21. Ibid., 132.

22. Ibid., 39.

23. Ibid.

24. See George W. S. Friedrichsen, *The Gothic Version of the Gospels: A Study of Its Style and Textual History* (London: Oxford University Press, 1926); Friedrichsen, *The Gothic Version of the Epistles: A Study of Its Style and Textual History* (London: Oxford University Press, 1939); and E. A. Thompson, *The Visigoths in the Time of Ulfila* (Oxford: Clarendon, 1966).

25. See Richard Fletcher, *The Barbarian Conversion: From Paganism to Christianity* (New York: Holt and Co., 1998), and Jocelyn N. Hillgarth, ed., *Christianity and Paganism: The Conversion of Western Europe* (Philadelphia: University of Pennsylvania Press, 1986).

26. The bibliography on Judaism and early Christianity is vast. The following deserve mentioning: A. Lukyn Williams, *Adversus Judaeos: A Bird's-eye View of Christian Apologiae until the Renaissance* (Cambridge: Cambridge University Press, 1935); Jacob Neusner, *Judaism and Christianity in the Age of Constantine* (Chicago: University of Chicago Press, 1987); Peter Richardson, ed., *Anti-Judaism in Early Christianity,* vol. 2, *Separation and Polemic* (Waterloo, Ontario: Wilfred Laurier University Press, 1986); James Parkes, *The Conflict of the Church and the Synagogue: A Study of the Origins of Antisemitism* (New York: Athenaeum, 1974); H. Schrenberg, *Die christlichen Adversus-Judaeos-Texte und ihr literarisches und historisches Umfeld (1-11Jh)* (Frankfurt: Lang, 1982); Robert L. Wilken, *John Chrysostom and the Jews: Rhetoric and Reality in the Late Fourth Century* (Berkeley: University of California Press, 1983); Graham Stanton and Guy G. Stroumsa, *Tolerance and Intolerance in Early Judaism and Christianity* (Cambridge: Cambridge University Press, 1988).

27. For the English text of this letter, see Richardson, *Early Christian Fathers,* 213–22.

28. Richardson, *Early Christian Fathers,* 217–18. Translation slightly emended.

29. John P. Meier, *A Marginal Jew: Rethinking the Historical Jesus,* 3 vols. (New York, NY: Doubleday, 1991); see especially vol. 1, *The Roots of the Problem and the Person.*

30. On Jesus as a border-crosser and migrant spirituality, see Peter C. Phan, *In Our Tongues: Perspectives from Asia on Mission and Inculturation* (Maryknoll, NY: Orbis Books, 2003), 13–50.

CHAPTER FOUR

God in the Desert

Searching for the Divine in the Midst of Death

ALEX NAVA

Although I was born and raised in the desert regions of the U.S. Southwest, in Tucson, Arizona, it was not until I lived elsewhere, especially in Chicago and Seattle for several years, that I began to notice the desert with new, more alert, and fresh eyes. I left Arizona to study religion at the University of Chicago and was immediately cognizant of the distinctiveness of my new surroundings. If it is the unique and incomparable Saguaro cacti that command one's attention in the deserts of Arizona, in Chicago it is the buildings and skyscrapers of the downtown skyline that evoke a feeling of awe. If the immensity of Lake Michigan reminds Chicagoans of their belonging to and dependence on nature, the vastness of the desert terrain does the same for Arizonans. As I look back at my time in Chicago, I am convinced that, besides preparing me for a life of study and teaching, the contrast of this great urban city with my desert experience in Arizona led me to reassess the desert and border regions of my upbringing. Perhaps, in addition to the substance of my theological learning, the distance from the Southwest gave me the perspective that I needed to understand and interpret the desert and border regions in a new light.

After graduation, and a couple years in Seattle, I returned to Tucson to teach at the University of Arizona. The passage from T. S. Eliot's "Little Gidding" kept returning to my mind: "the end of all our exploring / Will be to arrive where we started / And know the place for the first time." Everything was indeed new to me. The distinct, fragrant scent of the summer rains falling on the parched desert ground was more poignant than ever. The beauty and rarity of some of the cacti here—the Saguaros, the Organ Pipe, the Ocotillo—greeted me as if I were an explorer first entering this territory, a Cabeza de Vaca or Fr. Eusebio Kino. Indeed, I could see how surprising and unexpected some of this terrain might appear to someone who associates the idea of "desert" with Sahara-like desolation. The southern Arizona desert is amazingly verdant and mountainous. Here the deserts are pregnant with life, home to a great diversity of animal and bird species. If some of the ancient Egyptian monks described the desert as a wasteland, they also saw in it the seeds of a potential paradise, a "desert blooming with the flowers of Christ."[1] This vision of a desert in full bloom is easily understood by anyone who has visited the Sonoran desert regions of the U.S.-Mexico borderlands.

But there was something else happening in the desert that interrupted my contemplation of its surprising beauty: a growing number of migrant deaths. In the summer months the reports of women and men, children and infants dying in the desert is as endless and unforgiving as the heat of the sun. Almost inexplicably, every summer for the past several years seems to register a new record of deaths in the borderlands.

In my work with a couple of human rights groups, particularly Humane Borders and Borderlinks, I have come face-to-face with many immigrants beginning or in the midst of their journey to the north. In the small town of Sasabe, Mexico, over one thousand immigrants per day pass the town's doorstep with dreams that the ancient Israelites must have shared in their exodus from a land devoid of milk and honey. The first time I encountered a group of these pilgrims, besides being struck by the number of women and children, I could not help but recognize myself in their sunburnt faces, as every American with an immigrant past might understand. If the Statue of Liberty was the welcoming symbol of past generations of European immigrants, the desert of our southern border is now the symbol of new generations of the tired and poor, of the huddled masses.

It is easy for many Americans to repress memories of their immigrant past, however. Perhaps such memories conjure feelings of insecurity and anxiety that prove too frightening to summon again. Or perhaps we fear that the recognition of our past as strangers might shatter our confident and self-assured, at times arrogant, identity as Americans. Regardless, one thing seems quite clear: most of us North Americans have a profoundly short-term memory. Forgetfulness is our common malady. We need to be reminded, as the ancient Israelites were reminded, that we too were once strangers in the land (Dt 10:19).

While these reflections are motivated by the contemporary events along the border regions of the U.S. and Mexico, I would also like to consider in what follows some of the historical references to the desert in the Christian tradition as well as in some modern poets, before returning to the realities of death occurring in these regions today.

God in the Desert

It is not surprising that the geography of desert occupies a central place in the biblical imagination. The context of the Bible is indeed the stark, arid, desolate deserts of the ancient Near East. And it is in this difficult milieu that the ancient Jews experienced and interpreted the divine. To any careful reader, it is clear that the desert landscape influences and informs the way in which God was represented and symbolized in biblical times. It left its mark on theological language and beliefs among the ancient Jews and Christians. Indeed, one might see the desert as a major character in the biblical texts beginning with the narrative of Exodus. In Exodus, this character is frightening and untrustworthy. The desert wears the mask of death. "Was it for want of graves that you brought us out of the land of Egypt. . . . Why did you bring us out of Egypt, to kill us and our children and livestock with thirst?" (Ex 14:11; 17:3). The faith in the promised land that Moses sought to instill in the Israelites proved to be precarious and fragile when tested in the unforgiving and death-dealing environment of the desert. Even Moses's faith wavers: "Why have you treated your servant so badly? . . . Where am I to get meat to give to all this people? For they come weeping to me and say, 'Give us meat to eat.' . . . If this is the way you are going to treat me, put me to death at once." (Nm 11:10–15). And as we know, Moses died in the desert. He never made it to the promised land. Dr. Martin Luther King Jr. also invoked this narrative, fully aware that he too might share the fate of Moses, "I may not get to the promised land with you. . . ."

Anyone with experience in hot and arid desert regions will be able to understand the challenging and terrifying countenance of the desert. Inhospitable to human survival, impersonal and unrelenting to human needs and desires, the desert is a location where body and soul are easily wounded beyond recovery. Nothing seems to be in moderation here: the sun is fierce and excessive, deaf to the pleas of pilgrims seeking the refuge of shade. Any traveler to these regions will understand why clouds thus signal the presence of God to the wandering Jews in biblical times. Clouds not only hide the face of God (and hence are metaphors of divine incomprehensibility) but they also hide the severe face of the sun, providing an exiled people with respite from its damaging power. And clouds, of course, indicate rain. In the Sonoran desert, however, even the summer monsoon rains come with excess, announcing themselves with the suddenness of a flash flood, striking and pounding the earth with a violent force. Even the rains do not know gentleness. The desert terrain itself is immoderate, a parable of immensity, as vast as the sky. Surely to a migrant on foot the terrain seems endless, a kind of cruel, banal infinitude.

These experiences of desert living are recognizable to any careful reader of the Bible and inform the theology of biblical texts as well as the Jewish and Christian traditions. In his study of the symbols of desert in biblical and Christian thought, George Williams identifies at least four themes in the interpretation of desert: (1) the desert is a wasteland awaiting the blossoming of paradise, (2) the desert is a place of testing and punishment, (3) the desert is the location of God's nuptial union with Israel or the human soul, and (4) the desert is a place of refuge or contemplation.[2] Finally, as Bernard McGinn has explained with regard to the mystical traditions, the desert can become a symbol of the incomprehensible and inexpressible God (the God beyond God).[3] In this case, God's nature adopts desert-like characteristics. God is the "Divine Desert."

The Egyptian monks were among the first in the Christian tradition to take to the desert to encounter God (the Jewish community known as the Essenes had already done so at the beginning of the Common Era). Many of the above themes associated with the desert motivated and defined their spiritual quests. For one, their journeys to the desert were interpreted as a step in their detachment from the attractions and distractions of the world. By withdrawing to the desert, these ascetics would empty and void themselves of the comforts and pleasures of civilization. They welcomed the emptiness of the desert, an abyss or a void, as a partner in their search for a naked, unearthly wisdom. Away from the noise of city life, they might hear God in the silence of the desert wind as Elijah once did. For these hermits, the model of the spiritual life was the nakedness and stillness of the desert. And they sought to cultivate this desert life within the depths of their own souls.

In the Middle Ages, Christian monks would appeal to desert metaphors for similar purposes: to advocate a turning away from the emptiness of the world and to sing of the benefits of solitude. In interpreting the desert as an inner condition of the spirit, many medieval monks dreamed of nuptial union with God in the inner recesses of the human heart, not literally in the geography of the desert. The Cistercian monk, Isaac of Stella, invokes the prophet Hosea in speaking of the followers of Christ in the desert: "They seek the desert and the secret places where they can be open to God . . . where he himself will answer and speak to their heart, as the prophet says: 'I will lead you into solitude and there I will speak to your heart.'"[4]

In spite of the belief among many Eastern and Western monks that God may be encountered in the simplicity and emptiness of the desert, however, very few of them actually referred to God as desert. Bernard McGinn insists that none of the early monks used desert language to describe the nature of God. It was left to medieval Christian thinkers to create desert language about God. Why was this theological language so slow in coming? Is it because the desert was a dwelling place of demons, not God? Was the emptiness and void of the ancient Near Eastern desert too life-threatening to ascribe to God? For those monks with long-suffering experiences of the desert, was this region too hostile, too fierce to associate with the merciful God of scripture? And finally, why did this reluctance give way to a daring willingness to use desert language to describe God among some medievals?

In the west, it was Pseudo-Dionysius who first connected the Exodus story with the theory of divine incomprehensibility. For Dionysius, reference to the desert nature of God suggested the unfathomable and vast nature of God, a nature that no intellect could plumb or exhaust. In this manner, a disciple of Dionysius, John the Scot Eriugena, expounded on the transcendent nature of God: "A more profound interpretation understands it as the desert of the divine nature, an inexpressible height removed from all things. It is deserted by every creature, because it surpasses all intellect, although it does not desert any intellect."[5] This emphasis on the inaccessibility of the divine nature to human conception would find a more elaborate and sustained formulation among various German theologians. It was in the verdant forests of Germany, ironically, that desert language of the divine became more pervasive.

The work of the German Beguine mystic, Mechtild of Magdeberg, was a step in this direction. She provided a prescription for dwelling in the desert and for speaking of the Divine.

> You shall love nothingness,
> You shall flee existence,
> You shall stand alone,
> And you shall go to no-one. . . .
> You shall drink the water of suffering
> And light the fire of love with the wood of virtue,
> Then you will live in the true desert.[6]

Besides recalling the ascetical traditions of desert language, this remarkable passage indicates a connection between the desert of the inner soul and the divine nothingness of the godhead. In a manner reminiscent of Dionysius or Eriugena, Mechtild names the divine as a reality beyond being, as a nothingness or emptiness that exceeds the realm of human knowledge and existence. God is no-thing.

We see this position even more clearly with Meister Eckhart. He explicitly and consistently used the desert as a symbol of God. In one of his sermons, he discusses the nature of a noble or just person in this way:

> Who then is nobler than he who on one side is born of the highest and the best among created things, and on the other side from the inmost ground of the divine nature and its desert? "I" says the Lord through the prophet Hosea, "will lead the noble soul out into the desert, and there I will speak to her heart," one with One, one from One, one in One, one everlastingly. Amen.[7]

In this passage, Eckhart implies a union of indistinction in which the soul merges into God, or more precisely, into the unnameable desert of God, the God beyond our conception. In this empty place of divine oneness, where all human conceptions are empty, the soul is united with the solitary wilderness of the divine: "God's ground and the soul's ground are one ground."[8]

Another German text, the *Granum sinapis,* is similar in its theology. One passage describes the journey of the intellect first in climbing a mountain and then in fleeing to the desert.

> The mountain of this point, Ascend without activity, O intellect!
> The road leads you into a marvelous desert, So broad, so wide,
> It stretches out immeasurably. The desert has neither time nor place,
> Its mode of being is unique. . . . It is here, it is there, It is far, it is near,
> It is deep, it is high, It exists in such a way that it is neither this nor that.[9]

The vastness of the desert terrain is an icon of the grandeur and inexhaustible nature of God. Other mystics—and surely many ancient peoples—chose the symbol of the ocean to make this point. The immeasurable depths and darkness of the abyss of the sea was a parable of the unfathomable abyss of the divine. And the ocean symbol would have a further benefit: the analogy of a river flowing into the sea would resonate strongly with those mystics seeking union with the Divine Beloved. So, why is it that Eckhart and other German theologians turned to desert language in their God-talk?

As we have seen, part of that answer is due to the influence of Dionysius among many German intellectuals in the Middle Ages. Perhaps, however, as McGinn states, this is also explained by the fact that there are more forest deserts in Germany than anywhere else in Europe.[10] Or perhaps the immensity of the desert sky and the brilliance of the sun proved alluring to these forest-dwellers, to a people eager for the feeling of sunlight bathing one's body. Regardless what the exact answer is, it is questionable whether or not these theologians understood the life-threatening and hostile effects of desert terrain. Perhaps this is why the early desert-dwelling hermits, including the Egyptians, were unwilling to ascribe desert-language to God. Even if they believed, vis-à-vis scripture, that the soul's betrothal to God occurs in the simplicity of the desert, they were too well schooled in the dangers and suffering of desert living to see the desert as a parable of divine nature. The desert is indifferent, merciless, devoid of forgiveness, a place of demonic dominion, a place of death. If the desert is divine, then it is a god too ambiguous and uncaring to be revered. A desert god shows signs of cruelty. This kind of god is all too close to the gods of tragedy, to the protests of Shakespeare, for instance: "As flies to wanton boys, are we to the gods, they kill us for their sport."[11] Perhaps this is what the biblical figure Job most feared, that his God was not a friend at all, but an enemy. As Job's life is undone by the experiences of physical and spiritual affliction, he files a lawsuit against the Almighty. Is the Almighty responsible for, or at least indifferent to, the suffering of his people? Does God, after all, contrary to Eriugena's claim above, desert his people in the scorching heat of the desert?

Such daring questions naturally arise when one tries to make sense of the deaths occurring in the desert regions of our borders today. I, for one, cannot help but share the reluctance of early Christian theologians to name God as Desert. In light of the harsh and meaningless deaths of immigrants in the desert regions of the border today, I find myself uneasy with a devotion to the "Divine Desert."

Death in the Desert

If some mystics saw in the emptiness and nothingness of the desert a symbol of divine emptiness, they also believed that the latter was a greater reality than anything humans could imagine or experience. Simone Weil put it this way, "Contact with human creatures is given to us through a sense of presence. Contact with God is given to us through the sense of absence. Compared with this absence, presence becomes more absent than absence."[12] In confronting the absence of God, and the emptiness of much of our ideas and beliefs about God, Weil believed that we might clear space for the entrance of the true God. After voiding our lives of false attachments and comforting illusions and entering a desert experience of vacancy and desolation, we will hear God speak to us heart to heart. As Weil also knew, however, the experiences of the void or emptiness in history and society are real, destructive threats to the human body and spirit. The human spirit is not invulnerable to the blows of fate and the weight of suffering. Our modern age seems to sense more acutely the abyss of suffering or the threat of meaninglessness. In our time, a time out of joint, the threat of emptiness seems to fill the air that many great modern intellectuals breathe. Modern expressions of nothingness or emptiness, then, are far removed from the reverential postures of the classic Christian mystics, or of classical Buddhism for that matter. Our age appears to be far more troubled. Robert Frost's poem "Desert Places" represents this modern experience of the desert of life:

> They cannot scare me with their empty spaces,
> Between stars, where no human race is.
> I have it with me, so much closer to home
> To scare myself with my own desert places.

This experience of the terrifying countenance of emptiness is already signaled in early modern times by Blaise Pascal, who cried out in terror, "The eternal silence of these infinite spaces fills me with dread."[13] Modern science, witnesses Pascal, emptied the universe of God. For many in modern times, then, the desert becomes a symbol of absence and loss, a representation of the death of God. Needless to say, this brand of emptiness is far removed from the meaningful descriptions of emptiness in Christian mysticism or in Buddhism (*sunyata*).

When Pablo Neruda wrote of the desert terrain of the mining regions of northern Chile, for instance, he recalled a traditional biblical setting—the desert as prophetic space—but now with characteristics of this modern age. Neruda speaks as a prophet of the old and new, of ancient and modern times. Neruda's poetry evokes feelings of modern, existential anxieties: "I've come once again to lonely bedrooms, / to have a cold lunch in restaurants, and once again / I throw my pants and shirts on the floor, / there are no hangers in my room, or pictures of anyone on the walls"[14]

In addition to this poignant reading of the desert as a location of suffering and injustice, desert language in Neruda evokes the experience of exile. "I am a wandering son of that which I love," Neruda writes. "I am a wanderer, I live the anguish of being / far from the prisoner and the flower."[15] Even before Neruda was exiled from Chile, his works resounded with a sense of alienation. He speaks to us from the perspective of a stranger and alien of this earth. As the title of one of his great works, *Residence on Earth,* suggests, Neruda wrote poetry of temporary residents, of pilgrims in exile.[16] And his words reflect this tragic sensibility. His poems are filled with plaintive and black tones. Neruda's poetry is an elegy dedicated to all who feel the desolation of desert space and time.

GOD IN THE DESERT

In *Canto General,* Neruda's desert language, however, describes the particular anguish of the downtrodden and destitute. In a poem entitled *El desierto,* Neruda describes the nakedness of the terrain and the struggle for life in such landscapes: "The sun breaks its glass in the empty space, and the earth agonizes with a dry and drowning noise of crying salt." In this place "without plants, without claws, without dung, the land revealed to me its naked dimension."[17] This nakedness, this vulnerability is shared by Neruda, the exiled poet and by all refugees and wandering peoples.

As the ancient Israelites knew firsthand, survival in such stark terrain is a battle. In awaiting God, man fights with death in the desert. The great Spanish poet, Garcia Lorca, who describes Spanish culture as death-obsessed, pictures death lurking in the empty desert, in this case in a vast dune:

> The North near to death
> had switched off its stars.
> The skies were shipwrecked,
> slowly rising and falling.[18]

Here the traveler is lost in the immense dune, oppressed by the darkness of the sky, drowned in the vast sea of arid, scorched terrain. The North is no longer the beacon of freedom. Death has extinguished the light.

God and Death in the Desert

If some Christian mystics interpreted the desert as a location of a possible divine encounter or even as a parable of the incomprehensibility of the divine nature, others, including the ancient Israelites, read more ominous and dark signs in the symbol of the desert. The desert to these latter figures was a sinister realm where hunger and thirst, unforgiving heat and vast stretches of land become the occasion for death's visitation. In our own times, for too many immigrants from the south, the journey to the north is a battle with these demons. The North is distant and lonely, forever absent, forever unattainable. If it is not the heat and thirst, the cause of countless deaths is the sheer vastness of the desert and the number of miles they travel. Exhaustion comes quickly in this terrain and dizziness and confusion often accompanies the physical experience of the heat and insatiable thirst. In this condition, it is easy to lose one's way in the labyrinth of the desert. Lorca's description of being lost, of locating neither road nor sky is a precise expression of many immigrants' experiences. The light summoning them to the promised land of the north has been extinguished and the sky, dark and undecipherable, hides the way. These desert pilgrims are shipwrecked by the immensity and abyss of the desert landscape. It is not difficult to imagine them repeating the mournful and protesting words of the Israelites, "Was it for want of graves in Egypt that you brought us into the desert to die?" (Ex 14:11).

I opened these reflections by speaking of the surprising beauty of the Sonoran desert in southern Arizona and northern Mexico. If there is a good amount of rain in the winter months, this terrain blooms with an intensity of color and scent and shape. Wildflowers are resurrected during the spring in locations that seem inhospitable to plant life. In staring at this sight, so unexpected, so holy, I recall what the Egyptian monks describe as a "desert blooming with the flowers of Christ."[19] Perhaps for similar reasons, the To-hono O'odham people (the "Desert Dwellers") consider much of this land sacred (especially the mountain of Baboquivari where the god I'itoi dwells in a cave). It is not an exaggeration to see in this terrain the aesthetical attrac-tiveness of a garden.

I wonder, then, how to make sense of the garden-like beauty of the desert in light of the suffering and deaths of hundreds of immigrants. If the ecology of the Sonoran desert cannot exactly be described as a waste-land, does not the reality of death witnessed by this terrain justify such a title nevertheless? Perhaps it is a wasteland, simply for the spent lives ex-hausted here if not for geography and flora. Or are there the seeds of a gar-den experience even here in the midst of suffering?

Perhaps what I am asking is the same question posed by many of us: how does one reconcile the stunning, even at times ecstatic experiences of the beauty of nature with the horror of history, with the experiences of exile and poverty, violence and war? Surely, Dante, another great poet of the desert, explored this terrain.[20] In *Inferno,* the pilgrim is lost in the *gran deserto* until Virgil appears and guides him to the Garden of Eden. As many critics have suggested, the metaphor of desert in Dante represents the desert of Exodus and the experience of exile in Dante's own life and in human history. At the same time, Dante alludes to the hope (a hope sustained by the possibility of beauty and love) that a garden will reveal itself in the midst of the desolation and suffering of history. Recall that in *Paradiso,* the third part of the *Divine Comedy,* it is Dante's beloved Beatrice who takes over as the pilgrim's guide. It is now love that allures the pilgrim and that impels his will and causes his wings to sprout. It is Dante's experience of love that makes possible the ascent into paradise where he will be astounded and silenced by a vision of God (symbolized by the rose).[21]

It is not surprising that images of a garden appear in much poetry of the desert, including the Bible. In the Ancient Near East, a garden would have been a place of salvation in the context of the threatening desert. In the *Song of Songs,* for instance, the delights and intensity of love, the rapture of beauty, the sensual joy of both nature and the human body are celebrated in the context of a garden. This garden appears to be a refuge from the trials of history, a Garden of Eden in the context of exile on earth.

Perhaps in these contexts the garden is nothing else but a symbol of hope. As I look across the expanse of the Sonoran desert—its garden-like terrain and awesome immensity—I'm filled with ambivalence. I witness beauty everywhere and yet also hear the laments of immigrants burnt by the sun. It's a tragic beauty that I recognize, a beauty that attests to the contradictory and ambiguous face of the human experience. This ambiguity is felt not only in the experiences of beauty and exile, nature and history, love and suffering, but dwells with the experience of the Holy itself, as Rudolph Otto once suggested. For Otto, the Holy is a *mysterium tremendum et fascinans.*[22] This power and mystery is felt as an awesome, even terrifying mystery on the one hand and as an attractive, beautiful, trustworthy mystery on the other.

As holy space, the desert wears these different masks, not unlike the ancient god Janus, a god of doorways, thresholds, and borders. He stands on the border and looks in one direction and at the same time in the opposite direction. He stands nowhere, in-between two different positions and places, in liminal territory. Janus is a contradictory figure, situated in a location of contradiction. It seems to me that exiles and immigrants—if not us all—wear the masks of Janus, looking toward different cultural and religious horizons, with lives marked by contradiction, paradox and ambiguity. If this is true of the human condition itself, perhaps exiles and migrants understand these facts better than anyone else.

The tragedy of our contemporary border situation, however, remains the fact that the ambiguous and liminal space of the border has now become a gravesite for numerous pilgrims. While some North Americans blame the immigrants themselves for their own deaths, viewing their deaths as a kind of punishment for the sin of illegal trespassing, others see in these deaths a loud cry for a change in border policy. For this to happen, we need the prophetic voices of justice in biblical texts, in the poetry of a Neruda, Lorca, or Dante joined with the deep spirituality of the mystical traditions. In following the paths of these great prophets, we might be led to the mysterious regions of the human soul, crossing and transgressing the limiting borders that confine and prevent our spirits from exploring new terrain and from discovering new possibilities that would allow us to grow as individuals and as a human community. In following the trails of the border-crossers of history, past and present, we might be led to discover the faces of strangers within our very selves and thus to respond to the other with justice and compassion. Perhaps only when this happens will we be able to announce, with T. S. Eliot, that "fire and the rose are one."[23] Only then will the roses of the garden bloom in the scorched fire-zone of the desert, and we might begin to find credible the hope of biblical texts and mystics that we will be united with God in an ecstatic and consuming love.

NOTES

1. See Bernard McGinn, "Ocean and Desert as Symbols of Mystical Absorption in the Christian Tradition," *Journal of Religion* 74 (1994): 155–81.
2. Ibid., 156–57. See George H. Williams, *Wilderness and Paradise in Christian Thought: The Biblical Experience of the Desert in the History of Christianity* (New York: Harper and Row, 1962), 18.
3. Bernard McGinn, "The God Beyond God: Theology and Mysticism in the Thought of Meister Eckhart," *Journal of Religion* 61 (1981): 1–19.
4. Ibid., 165.
5. Ibid., 162.
6. Ibid., 166
7. *Meister Eckhart: The Essential Sermons, Commentaries, Treatises, and Defense,* trans. Edmund Colledge and Bernard McGinn (New York: Paulist Press, 1981), 247.
8. Ibid., 192.
9. McGinn, "Ocean and Desert," 171.

10. Ibid.

11. *King Lear,* Act 4, Scene 1.

12. See Simone Weil, *The Notebooks,* vol. 1 (London: Routledge, 1956), 239–40.

13. See Blaise Pascal, *Pensees* (New York: Penguin Classics, 1995), 102.

14. As quoted in Enrico Mario Santí, *Pablo Neruda: The Poetics of Prophecy* (Ithaca: Cornell University Press, 1982), 92.

15. Ibid., 193.

16. See Pablo Neruda, *Residence on Earth* (New York: New Directions Publishing Corporation, 2004).

17. Ibid., 195–96.

18. See Federico Garcia Lorca, *Suites,* in *Federico Garcia Lorca: Selected Verse,* ed. Christopher Maurer (New York: Farrar, Straus, Giroux, 1994), 121.

19. McGinn, "Ocean and Desert."

20. See Giuseppe Mazzotta, *Dante, Poet of the Desert* (Princeton: Princeton University Press, 1979).

21. Ibid.

22. See Rudolph Otto, *The Idea of the Holy* (Oxford: Oxford University Press, 1950).

23. T. S. Eliot, "Little Gidding."

CHAPTER FIVE

Poverty, Migration, and the Option for the Poor

GUSTAVO GUTIÉRREZ

The challenge of over 175 million migrants and refugees from around the world today brings to mind the well-known parable from the Gospel of Luke: "And lying at his door was a poor man named Lazarus, covered with sores, who would gladly have eaten his fill of the scraps that fell from the rich man's table" (Lk 16:20–21). As we seek to understand the meaning of this text in the face of our current reality, we recognize that poor nations are lying at the door of rich nations, and the latter are ignoring the former. Three considerations give rise to such a comparison. First, the poor today are not only lying at the door, but they are entering in search of a better, more dignified life. Poverty and unemployment are pushing them to leave their families, subjecting them to risk death, and putting them under the constant threat of deportation. Although poverty is not the only reason behind migration in its contemporary forms, it is the main one.

Second, some people in developed countries react to this fact by rejecting the poor and the migrant. This has resulted in political strategies that rely on anti-immigrant platforms to win elections across Europe.[1] In our hemisphere, reaction in the U.S. against immigrants—especially Latin Americans—should also be of concern. Samuel Huntington argues, for example, that Latino immigrants, especially Mexicans, represent the greatest threat to unity and identity in the U.S. According to his reasoning the same did not hold true for the great immigrant waves of the nineteenth and twentieth centuries that originated in Europe.[2]

Third, parables in the Gospels do not include the names of their characters but in this case the opposite holds true. Not only does this Gospel text include the name of the poor man, but the rich man remains anonymous. Yet, the situation today is the exact opposite: it is the poor who are nameless. They are born, live, and die without having left footprints, or traces of their existence, in our history.

Although the reversal of social situations is a constant occurrence in both testaments, the Gospel of Luke presents them quite frequently. Perhaps this is a lesson for our time: the poor and the migrant must not remain nameless if their condition is to change. Their personhood must be acknowledged and their human dignity must be recognized. For these reasons a major concern for the theology of migration must be to understand the current context in order to identify how there could be Good News for the poor and the migrant today. Even though the Gospel is already present in their daily experience of God, the Good News must be witnessed in deed and word so that it may be translated from scripture into daily life. This is a central issue in any Christian's life. Announcing and giving witness to the gospel message of the kingdom of God is also the goal and meaning of any theological consideration. Outside of such service, theology is meaningless.

With this in mind, I would like to present some reflections on the relationship between poverty and immigration from the perspective of the option for the poor in three steps: identifying the relationship between migration and poverty, understanding the preferential option for the poor, and articulating some implications for our contemporary context. These steps will serve to reflect on the relationship between poverty and migration itself, even though they do not exhaust this important issue that needs further exploration.

The Contemporary Challenge of Migration

Migration is as old as the history of humankind. Sometimes it was a result of compulsory displacements as in the ignoble case of black slaves forced into the U.S. and other countries throughout Latin America. Today, however, among the millions of migrants and refugees that leave their countries in search of a better life and survival, the professional elite of impoverished nations are also undertaking a another type of migration, which is resulting in the so-called "brain drain."[3] Although these professional migrants do not make up the majority of the global population movement, they need to be mentioned because they represent an important trait of the relationship between migration and poverty. They represent an investment by the poorest countries in the richest countries.[4] As for poverty itself, it is necessary to become aware of new perspectives on its characteristics. For a long time poverty was viewed as a natural fact or even fate. Some people were born poor and others were born rich. People often considered poverty an expression of God's will.

Theologically, being born poor was also interpreted as God's will. This old view was explicitly or implicitly reflected in official statements by Christian churches until a few decades ago. Unfortunately, today these views, or a variant of them, are still prevalent among some of the poor themselves. A shift has taken place in today's more secular world, though, and the poor are now considered responsible for their own poverty, as if they were its first and only cause. Borrowing some analytical concepts from the social sciences and socialist theories, we must become conscious that poverty is the result of human agency. Poverty is not a misfortune but an injustice, and it is not a destiny but a condition.[5]

Another characteristic of poverty is its complexity. As recently as five years ago, international agencies have begun using the term "multidimensionality of poverty" to describe this characteristic.[6] From the perspective of liberation theology, the complexity is quite evident. The poor are people who are not considered and respected as persons: they are nonpersons.[7] One may be a nonperson or be insignificant for economic, cultural, political, gender, and racial reasons. Hence, we must be careful to understand that the economic dimension is not the only one that must be taken into consideration when dealing with poverty. The same holds true for migrants. Consider, for example, that the economic dimension is not the only aspect of the migration phenomenon nor is it the only reason for the suffering of the migrants. This multifaceted perspective on migration also has biblical and socioeconomic foundations. The biblical category of "poor" does not include just the economic poor, but all despised and marginalized persons as well. Socioeconomic foundations have been well documented and studied, but conclusions must also be drawn utilizing noneconomic lenses. A case in point is a declaration made some years ago by the president of the Inter-American Development Bank, Enrique Iglesias: "The next century will be a fascinating and a cruel century." This phrase, like most paradoxical ones, is at once attractive and foreboding. But at a close reading we must realize that this century will be fascinating for a minority of those who can participate in the latest advancement of technological knowledge or take advantage of the new economy, or both. But it will be cruel for the majority. The immediate future does not look fascinating and cruel for the same persons. It is likely that pointing this out was not the author's intention.

It is true that in some way for most who do research in migration theology or pastoral care of migrants, this is a fascinating time. We are not insignificant people. We try to be committed to migrants in a globalized planet, but globalization is an ambiguous process that has brought about an ambiguous world. The idea behind the term is that of one world, and yet we are going to end up with two. Those excluded from the modern socioeconomic, cultural, and political order—including migrants—belong to one world. Those included within that same order belong to the second world. Globalization, however, has some positive aspects, and to be against globalization per se is like being against electricity. The reaction though, is due in part to the manner in which globalization is being adopted today: its dynamics are being placed in the service of creating more inequalities around the world instead of doing the opposite.

The Preferential Option for the Poor

The preferential option for the poor also sheds some light on the relationship between immigration and poverty. This option is three-fold and may be approached from a social-pastoral, theological, and spiritual perspective.[8] The social-pastoral perspective is perhaps the most obvious one because we understand immediately that to *make* the option for the poor means to *go out* to the poor. It entails working, living, playing, and being in solidarity with the materially poor. Perhaps at first glance this does not appear to be a very biblical understanding, but the option for the poor must necessarily start from a commitment to the materially poor. However, there are other ways of understanding poverty in both testaments. For example, spiritual poverty or spiritual childhood is a biblical notion that means putting one's life in God's hands. Nonetheless, spiritual poverty must not obscure the fact that the focus here must remain on serving those who are materially poor.

The option for the poor entails solidarity with them as well as a willingness to suffer poverty in protest against poverty. The poverty described up to this point, however, should not be confused with austerity. The type of material poverty being described here is an inhuman situation that is itself contradictory to the will of God. Yet solidarity with the poor in protest of poverty and poverty itself are two sides to the same coin. Even so, it is important to be clear that poverty, as an inhuman situation, is never good. Poverty is always an evil. Therefore true solidarity must include attempts to eliminate the reasons behind such a cruel state of affairs. Otherwise, an understanding of how to witness the good news to the poor may be beyond us.

Still continuing with the social-pastoral perspective, several texts in both testaments give priority to announcing the kingdom of God to the poor.[9] The good news is about proclaiming God's gratuitous love for any person, especially to the least among us, and the term "preference" points out this priority. The option for the poor as a priority also involves the universality of God's love so that no one is excluded. This does not soften the meaning of preferential option for the poor but rather indicates that it is the ultimate route to experience, witness, and share in God's gratuitous love.

Ultimately the option for the poor is really a "theo-centric" option because it is God's option as revealed in the first testament and by Jesus. In proclaiming the gospel we must, therefore, emphasize a theological aspect of evangelization that has long been excluded: the struggle for justice. It is necessary to understand that the promotion of humankind is an integral part of evangelization. Some believe this is an old idea, but this is not so. This notion of the relationship between faith and justice was still not fully articulated by Vatican II, but since then this understanding of the good news has been made explicit and affirmed time and again. Consider the statements of the bishops of Latin America,[10] *Evangelii Nuntiandi* of Pope Paul VI (1975), or several interventions by Pope John Paul II,[11] calling the commitment for social justice an essential part of evangelization. For many decades people have emphasized a particular understanding that viewed social justice as a pre-evangelization because it did not speak directly of God. While seeking social justice is not the whole of evangelization, it *is* an essential part. How do we proclaim the kingdom to the migrants without defending their human dignity in solidarity with them? How do we defend their personhood without fighting against their marginalization and exploitation? How do we commit ourselves to our migrant brothers and sisters so that, in Daniel Groody's words, "the border of death" is transformed into "a valley of life"?[12] But how do we begin? Announcing the gospel and addressing the causes of poverty must go hand in hand. The first perspective of the preferential option for the poor in its social-pastoral level, therefore, requires the concrete commitment to be with and to work for the poor.

Theology provides a second perspective within the preferential option. The option for the poor is not only a question of social and pastoral commitment, but also it is a way of doing theology. Poverty, in the final analysis, means death. Poverty means death—physical, early, and unjust death—due to the lack of the most basic necessities for life. Poverty also means oppression and ultimately cultural death for racial and gender-related reasons.[13] These descriptions attest to the death the migrants suffer. Migrants are coming in search of work carrying with them their cultures and customs. They are coming to live here with their particular understanding of the Gospel message. The option for the poor is truly a theocentric option because Christians are called to be witnesses of the resurrection, of Jesus Christ's victory over death. The resurrection in the Gospel is never called a miracle; it is much more than that. The resurrection *is* the meaning of our human existence and of our lives as Christians. Our shared call to witness the resurrection requires of us to enter more fully into that meaning. Making the preferential option for the poor includes a way of doing theology that incorporates two distinct moments: exegesis of the scriptural texts themselves and interpretation of the experience of the migrants themselves.

Migration is an important subject in the Bible, especially as it brings out the notion of stranger. The stranger or the foreigner composes together with the orphan and the widow the trilogy of the poor *par excellence* in the first testament.[14] Hospitality is another biblical subject that is present throughout the second testament, particularly in the Gospel of Luke, the letter to the Hebrews, and the first letter of Peter.[15] From the perspective of the option for the poor, theology is done not only about the migrants and their situation, but *from* their situation. We must learn to read the Christian message from the poor and in our case from the migrants, or as Virgil Elizondo teaches us, from Galilee.[16] This approach to doing theology is attentive to other approaches. Still, doing theology from the option for the poor is like swimming upstream in a river in which stronger theological currents abound. Theology as it is done today, by and large, does not begin its reflections from the perspective of the poor. The dominant theology in many Christian churches today attempts to rid the Christian message from the modern mentality. A similar attempt exists in more recent times with postmodern mentality. Some approaches to doing theology have engaged a historical reality such as democracy and freedom of religion, and with these in mind seek to announce the Christian message. Why not, then, engage reality from the perspective of the poor? Poverty is a whole human reality that challenges prevailing ways of announcing the gospel. Not being open to this reality runs the risk of failing to find the right words to announce the gospel to the poor, including the migrants.

The third perspective offered by the preferential option for the poor, the spiritual one, is the deepest one. The option for the poor is not only a question of going to and working with them in solidarity, but it is also not just a way of doing theology. Above all it is a specific ground or foundation of the manner in which we follow Jesus. The preferential option for the poor is an essential aspect of discipleship, or what is called in the tradition *Sequela Christi*.[17]

The spirituality of the option for the poor is mindful that the poor belong to a specific gender and culture. These and other aspects constitute the world of the poor. Consider the parable of the Good Samaritan (Lk 10: 25–37) even if naming the parable's character as such is due to our own deductions. In it, a scribe asks Jesus who is his neighbor. He asks this question within the context of the great commandment: "You shall love the Lord, your God, with all your heart, with all your being, with all your strength, and with all your mind; and your neighbor as yourself" (Lk 10:27), and Jesus answers with a parable. It begins with a "half-dead" man that is lying next to the road, a victim of robbers. A priest and a Levite walk by and see the man but do not acknowledge him. Instead they both walk across to the other side of the road. The decision to respond is left up to a Samaritan who sees the person in need and acts accordingly by caring for him. Jesus's answer focused on what it truly means to be "neighbor." The neighbor is not the one I find on my way. It is the one who helps the person in need. Hence, it is the act of approaching the wounded man that truly makes the Samaritan neighbor. Being a neighbor and being a neighborhood is the result of specific actions and deeds. The poor are not those who are nearest but rather those who are distant but who become neighbors through one's commitment to them. Strictly speaking one has no neighbors. Instead, through commitment one must make neighbors. The migrants for many reasons (such as their different culture) are likewise the distant ones. Although neighborhood is always a relationship, entering the world of the poor requires a commitment to become their neighbors. Going through such a process—especially in relationship to migrants—is a complicated affair precisely because theirs is a distant world.

Furthermore, it is important to consider that the matter of becoming one's neighbor arose out of a previous question: "Teacher, what must I do to inherit eternal life?" (Lk 10:25). Loving the neighbor is a collective term that implies loving those most distant to one's world, those foreign to it, in the same way as those closest to it. In biblical terms, being and loving as neighbor simply means to make friends. The beautiful words of Jesus come to mind: "I no longer call you slaves, because a slave does not know what his master is doing. I have called you friends because I have told you everything I have heard from my Father" (Jn 15:15). Friendship and love presuppose equality and trust between friends. It must be clear, then, that the spiritual level is the foundation of the social-pastoral and theological perspectives.

Some Implications

The understanding of the relationship between poverty and migration from the perspective of the preferential option for the poor carries at least two implications by way of conclusion. First, our commitment to the poor and the migrants is concerned with their human dignity, which includes holding their own destiny in their hands. Once again we encounter a process that requires that each person become the subject of his or her history. Being a voice for the voiceless is important and in some circumstances necessary. But our aim should be for the voiceless to have their own voice. This is perhaps far from reality as we know it today. However, just as love requires equality, dignity necessitates that the poor be subjects of their history. In the case of those who live their lives marginalized from our society this objective may seem unrealistic, but such a situation must not be a reason to forget their personhood.

A second consequence of the understanding we have reached is that theology is always a hermeneutic of hope. In the First Letter of Peter, faith is presented as the reason for our hope (3:15), and that is what doing theology means. The theology of migration must therefore understand itself from this perspective. This does not in any way mean that illusions should be created among the poor and the migrants. That is not hope. Hope is a gift of God that needs to be rooted in the daily life of each person. On the one hand, theology must remain committed to a critical position against unjust inequalities that exist in our day. Although this is but one aspect of theology, it is perhaps a difficult one because it is indeed conflictive. On the other hand though, theology must remain committed to hope by having the capacity, freedom, and commitment to pay attention to the smallest of things.

In a personal note, I do not like to speak only about the suffering of the poor because they have also experienced joy, and have projects and intentions. These may be nothing more than little hopes and short moments of joy. Perhaps these small things are too little for those who are not excluded, but no hope is too small to go unnoticed. Without hope there is no personhood and hope is present even if surrounded by suffering. True theology, it seems to me, must interpret the reasons for hope in whatever way possible. In the painful case of the migrants we must not forget this. We must struggle to overcome their suffering while we pay attention to life in its many expressions, however insignificant and small. The theology of migration must be a hermeneutic of hope.

NOTES

1. For a discussion of current international trends in migration and politics see Stephen Castles and Mark J. Miller, *The Age of Migration: International Population Movement in the Modern World,* 3rd ed. (New York: Guilford Press, 2003), 255–77.

2. Samuel P. Huntington, *Who Are We? The Challenges to America's National Identity* (New York: Simon and Schuster, 2004).

3. See Castles and Miller, *Age of Migration.*

4. Even highly skilled immigrants experience discrimination and exploitation in terms of pay and professional advancement. Some scholars in the U.S. have drawn parallels between the "braceros" or contracted farmworkers (referring particularly to the Bracero Program, 1942–1964), and "high-tech braceros" or "cerebreros," who are these highly skilled immigrants working as computer experts, engineers, etc. See Rafael Alarcón, "Skilled Immigrants and Cerebreros: Foreign-Born Engineers and Scientists in the High Technology Industry of Silicon Valley," in *Immigration Research for a New Century: Multidisciplinary Perspectives,* ed. Nancy Foner, Rubén G. Rumbaut, and Steven J. Gold, 301–21 (New York: Russell Sage Foundation, 2000).

5. See Xabier Gorostiaga, "La Mediación de las Ciencias Sociales y los Cambios Internacionales," in *Cambio Social y Pensamiento Cristiano en América Latina,* ed. José Comblin, José I. González Faus, and Jon Sobrino, 123–44 (Madrid: Editorial Trotta, 1993).

6. On this concept see Siddiqur Rahman Osmani, "Evolving Views on Poverty: Concept, Assessment, and Strategy," Poverty and Social Development Paper, no. 7, Asian Development Bank (available online at www.adb.org, last accessed April 2007).

7. Gustavo Gutiérrez, *The Power of the Poor in History* (Maryknoll: Orbis Books, 1983), 92.

8. Gustavo Gutiérrez, "The Situation and Tasks of Liberation Theology Today," in *Opting for the Margins: Postmodernity and Liberation in Christian Theology,* ed. Joerg Rieger (Oxford: Oxford University Press, 2003), 95–96.

9. For example Is 61:1–3; Dn 4:17; Mt 11:5; Lk 4:18, 14:13.

10. Especially the ecclesial conferences of Medellin (1968) and Puebla (1979).

11. See particularly John Paul II, *Sollicitudo Rei Socialis* (1987) and *Centesimus Annus* (1991). These documents are available online at the Vatican web site: www.vatican.va.

12. This is the title of the insightful book by Daniel G. Groody, *Border of Death, Valley of Life: An Immigrant Journey of Heart and Spirit* (Lanham, MD: Rowman and Littlefield, 2002).

13. Gustavo Gutiérrez, "Liberation Theology and the Future of the Poor," in *Liberating the Future: God, Mammon, and Theology,* ed. Joerg Rieger (Minneapolis: Fortress Press, 1998), 121.

14. See for instance Ex 22:21–23; Dt 14:28, 24:19–21, 26:13.

15. See for instance Lk 24:13–35; Heb 13:2; 1 Pt 4:9.

16. Virgilio Elizondo, *Galilean Journey: The Mexican-American Promise,* rev. ed. (Maryknoll: Orbis Books, 2000).

17. Gustavo Gutiérrez, *The Density of the Present: Selected Writings* (Maryknoll: Orbis Books, 1999), 157–68.

PART TWO

Mission, Ministry, and Migration

CHAPTER SIX

Mission *among* Migrants, Mission *of* Migrants

Mission of the Church

STEPHEN BEVANS

In his marvelous book describing a number of "excellent Catholic parishes," journalist Paul Wilkes begins his description of St. Pius X parish in El Paso, Texas, with these words:

> The sun slips behind the imposing bank of buildings and high-rise ho-
> tels that flank Interstate 10, busy now with the beginning of afternoon
> rush-hour traffic. The last of its blazing shards, streaming across a broad
> expanse of plaza just a few blocks away, strikes and sets ablaze a bronze
> statue of Jesus Christ. It depicts not one of the usual images of Christ,
> the triumphant savior or the bleeding crucified one, but the peasant
> Christ, with a rough-woven serape over his shoulders, a walking stick
> in one hand, a small bag in the other. It seems an anomaly here in this
> quiet sanctuary, yet so close to the world of commerce and the bustling
> Basset Center Mall.[1]

Wilkes goes on to introduce his readers to Fr. Arturo Bañuelas, the pastor of
the parish, whose pastoral genius has inspired the people of St. Pius for some

twenty years and whose artistic sensibility gave vision to the parish's amaz-ing church. It also has a beautiful plaza and statue of the "Border Christ," Jesus the migrant. As Bañuelas says reflectively about the statue:

> El Paso is a border town. . . . Hispanics are on the borders of the Anglo world; to be a Catholic is to stand at the edge of a secular society. Even today, the Church is still on the border between old ways and new ways, the traditional Church of Sunday devotion versus the Church that we carry into the world each day. So, it was appropriate that our "Border Christ" would be the symbol of our church—always on the move, not ever at home, willing to go where he is needed, wearing the simplest of clothes, carrying no more than he needed, but, because of his marginalized status, capable of entering all cultures and bridging all people as one.[2]

I would like to propose that this image of the "border" or "migrant" Jesus might be a way to envision the connection between the mission of the church and the many-faceted situation of the world's migrants, whether forced or unforced, documented or undocumented,[3] whether refugees, dis-placed persons, persons without a homeland, or immigrants.[4] This image of the "border Christ" points first of all to the fact that the church's mission is *among* migrants. In many respects, migrants represent the face of Christ, and in their suffering they represent a continuing *via crucis* (way of the cross) of God's people. Or, as Jesus says of himself in the Gospel of Matthew, "I was a stranger and you welcomed me" (Mt 25:35). Secondly, however, as is clear from so much of the literature on the theology of and pastoral work with people on the move, migrants are also the *subjects* of the church's mis-sion. Christian migrants themselves have precious gifts to give to the church itself—to form it more fully into the body of Christ in the world. As mem-bers of the church, Christian migrants also number among the "saints" who need to be "equipped" for ministry both within the church and within the world (see Eph 4:12).[5] To paraphrase the words of Arturo Bañuelas: like Christ, whose body is the church, the *church* is always on the move, not ever at home, willing to go where it is needed, wearing the simplest of clothes, carrying no more than it needs, but, because of its marginalized status, ca-pable of entering all cultures and bridging all people as one.[6] The church lives out its mission by being both a servant to migrants on the one hand and an agent of service by migrants on the other. In the words of Mark Griffin and Theron Walker, the church needs to be "an *inn* for weary travelers of the borderlands/frontiers, and an *outpost of hope* for exiles bound for the city of God."[7]

This paper will focus on each of these two dimensions of the church's mission in the context of migration, one of the greatest challenges for the church and indeed for humanity itself in our day. In a first, brief section I will try to summarize today's thinking on the nature of the church's mission. Second, I will reflect on several aspects of how the church carries out its ministry among migrants in the world today. My third and final section will reflect on how Christian migrants themselves participate in the church's mission, both in terms of helping the church become what it is—the body of Christ—and in terms of the church continuing Christ's mission in the world.

Mission Theology Today

There was a time, says Félix Barrena Sánchez, when mission was understood as an aggressive imposition of faith upon people with little respect for the richness of what they already believed and little regard for their cultural heritage. While we have to acknowledge, as Peter Phan once observed, that mission is not an innocent word, we also have to admit that such a concept of mission "responds to another mentality and another era in history."[8] Today, mission is understood quite differently. It is, in the words of Pope John Paul II, "a single, but complex reality, and it develops in a variety of ways."[9] In this section I'll try to outline briefly what some of those ways are.

In the first place, mission today is understood as first and foremost *the mission of God*. Mission is not *our* mission, it is God's mission, and by God's grace we Christians are called to participate in it. Ultimately, it is this life of service that is constitutive of our salvation; it is service that makes us fully human, fully alive, fully healed. Mission is rooted in the trinitarian life of God, in a community of mutual love that spills over into mission in creation and redemption. God's mystery is poured out in creation through the power of the Spirit, God "inside out," in the world at all times, in all places, and among all peoples. That powerful yet somehow indeterminate presence became incarnate in Jesus "in the fullness of time" (Gal 4:4). The depths of God's love was revealed in the way Jesus spoke, the way he healed and performed exorcisms of evil, and the way in which he included all and excluded none.

Second, mission as God's call to participate in the divine mission, incarnate in Jesus's life of ministry, is what constitutes the church. Mission, in other words, is *prior* to the church. In many respects, the church does not so much have a mission as the mission has a church. Mission, therefore, is not simply one activity among many in which the church engages; it is, rather, the church's very *raison d'etre*. Vatican II described the church as "missionary by its very nature," and it is true, says missiologist J. Andrew Kirk, that "if it ceases to be missionary, it has not just failed in one of its tasks, it has ceased being Church."[10]

Third, the mission that is God's and thus prior to the church is not primarily about the church but about the reign of God. Mission is not about the church's expansion; it is about continuing Jesus's mission. The church is a sacrament of God's reign; it is a foretaste, sign, and instrument. This does not mean that mission does not include an invitation to belong to the church, but it does mean that its concerns are much wider than that. Mission is for the creation, not the church.

Fourth, since the church as such is missionary, it follows that every Christian, by virtue of her or his baptism, is called in some way to missionary service. There are no passive Christians; ministry of some kind is part and parcel of Christian life, whether it is the informal ministry of Christian parenthood, responsible citizenship or bearing witness to Christian values in one's professional life, or the more formal activities of lay ecclesial ministry, religious life, or ordained pastoral leadership.

Fifth, mission is carried out by preaching, serving, or witnessing to the reign of God within the church (*ad intra*), so that the church might be a clearer sign of God's saving presence, and in the world (*ad extra*), as God's saving instrument.[11] On the one hand, as Paul VI insisted, the church itself must be evangelized before it dares to evangelize others.[12] Similarly, as the 1971 Synod of Bishops has rightly said, "everyone who ventures to speak to people about justice must first be just in their eyes."[13] On the other hand, the church exists for the world, never for itself. We are a sign to the world. In order to be an instrument, we must move beyond the church into every part of the world, into every culture, engaging in dialogue with every religious system, working against all injustices and oppression.

This fifth point leads naturally to a sixth—the church's mission is about crossing boundaries, whether boundaries of nations, of cultures, of generations, of religions, of injustice, of unbelief.[14] Christians always have to be careful of crossing these boundaries; they must go as guests and strangers and always in humility and openness.[15] Mission is always done in dialogue and with respect. Recent missiological thinking has suggested that rather than speaking of a mission *ad gentes* (to the nations), we should speak of mission *inter gentes*, that is, *among* the women and men of the world, first of all sharing their lives and learning from them.[16] But crossing is always part of mission. The church is called to all; no one is excluded. This is the dynamic of its catholicity.

But, seventh, a caution is in order. The boundaries I speak of are not necessarily across national borders or oceans. Mission takes place today on six continents; it is, in the words of Kirk, "quite simply, though profoundly, what the Christian community is sent to do, beginning right where it is located."[17] As a powerful, contemporary hymn called "The Church of Christ in Every Age" puts it: "Across the world, across the street / the victims of injustice lie / for shelter and for bread to eat / and never live before they die. // Then let the servant church arise / a caring church that longs to be / a partner in Christ's sacrifice and clothed in Christ's humanity." This aspect of the church's mission is of utmost importance to the question of migration, since no longer do we here in North America, or in many places of the world, need speak of "going overseas" to encounter peoples of different cultures and religions. In the persons of migrants, the whole world has come to us.

Finally, mission today is understood as having many aspects or elements. In our recent book, *Constants in Context*, Roger Schroeder and I have spoken about six elements of mission.[18] Mission is about witness and proclamation; it recognizes that liturgy and prayer are dynamic, missionary acts; it involves commitment to justice, peace, and the integrity of creation; it engages in interreligious dialogue; it works for inculturation of the gospel; and it announces and works for the possibility of reconciliation.

In contemporary missionary practice, therefore, mission is a far cry from simply trying to convert immigrants to Roman Catholicism or, when they are already Catholics, to guard them from any kind of threat from Evangelicals or Pentecostals. As Barrena Sánchez forcefully expresses it, any kind of proselytism or economic or social pressure on non-Christians or non-Catholics would be a real betrayal of mission.[19] Mission, rather, must be done, in the wonderful phrase of missiologist David Bosch, in bold humility and humble boldness; or as Roger Schroeder and I suggest, borrowing a phrase from our religious congregation, it must be done in "prophetic dialogue."[20] While deeply respecting migrants' human rights and religious freedom, mission needs to be done in a way that both serves their deepest spiritual and physical needs, and shares with them our most precious treasures of faith. It is with this understanding of mission that we reflect on how the church engages in mission among migrants, is itself evangelized by the gifts of the migrant community, and calls and equips migrants—formerly members of other local churches—to join the local church in its own witness to the world of God's saving love.

Mission among Migrants: Mission of the Church

The first aspect of the church's mission in the context of the migration of peoples is the church's mission among migrants. As the Vatican document "Starting Afresh from Christ: Towards a Renewed Pastoral Care for Migrants and Refugees" expresses it, "the Church cannot remain indifferent in the way of the present plight of migrants and refugees. She wants to share their joys and grief, be with them where they are, and be with them in their search for a better and safer life, worthy of being children of God."[21] The motive for this love and concern, of course, is that these women, men, and children are creatures of God, made in God's image, and so possessing the fullness of human dignity and human rights.[22] In addition, scripture is a rich source of motivation for the care of migrants and strangers. Israel is constantly encouraged to see itself in strangers and foreigners and to treat them as equals (e.g. Ex 22:21, 23:9; Lv 19:33–34; Dt 10:17–19, 24:17–18, 27:19).[23] But perhaps the most sublime motivation is found in scripture's insight that coming to the aid of the stranger and the migrant is somehow touching the person of God. We see this in Abraham's encounter with the three strangers at the oaks of Mamre (Gn 18:1–15), perhaps most memorably depicted in Rublev's famous icon of the Trinity. We see it again in Jesus's parable in Matthew 25, where Jesus identifies himself with the very least of humanity. Jesus comes to us in the immigrant and the refugee, which is also alluded to in the statue of the "Border Christ." Robert Lentz's well-known icon, Christ of Maryknoll, expresses the same biblical intuition, as does a cartoon drawn of an African priest pointing to Rwanda on the map and saying "This is my body," as does a poster I have seen recently announcing "National Migration Week" with the legend "face of migrants, the face of God." Edwina Gateley writes eloquently: "It is time for all of us who follow Christ to recognize him and to proclaim him. It is time to be prophetic about the Christ we know is present in the folks who are pushed aside, dismissed, left out, undermined, underfed, unhoused, or simply unseen and unheard."[24] And among these, migrants—particularly refugees and undocumented immigrants—are some of the most prominent.

How can the church carry out its mission in service of today's migrants, many of whom share the *via crucis*[25] and suffering of Jesus Christ? When it comes to concrete action in mission, what I wrote elsewhere is true as well here: "It depends on the context."[26] We can, however, focus on several particular activities in which the church might be engaged.

First and foremost, we may speak of the task of welcoming and hospitality. In all the literature I have read, it is this task that seems to be of utmost importance for the church in its missionary outreach to migrants.[27] It certainly is part of the witness of the local church to either members of other local churches who have come into it, or to women and men of other religious faith traditions. Whether it is hosting refugees or migrants in their homes, helping them settle in the community, or just acknowledging their presence in the community by giving them times for their own liturgical celebrations or integrating their own cultural practices into the local community's celebrations, a sense of welcome and hospitality is the first task of the church community in mission. Certainly the network of "Casas del Migrante" operated by the Scalabrinian congregation is a model of this aspect of the church's mission. Christine Pohl suggests that "in a world of deadly ethnic tensions and vast socioeconomic differences and injustices, acts of hospitality are what Philip Hallie calls 'little moves against destructiveness.' . . .

Hospitality is an important expression of recognition and respect for those who are despised or overlooked by the larger society. When we offer hospitality, when we eat and drink together, when we share in conversations with persons significantly different from ourselves, we make powerful statements to the world about who is interesting, valuable, and important for us."[28] Hospitality calls us to do mission *inter culturas* (among the cultures), allowing ourselves to be touched and transformed by those considered as "others" in our midst.[29]

Second, hospitality needs to be connected with a strong commitment to justice, specifically a commitment to "construct a society of solidarity, neither racist nor xenophobic."[30] Individual Christians, in their speech, their attitudes, and their voting, need to be against any kind of "nativist" movement that would discriminate against new arrivals. This is particularly true in the aftermath of the attacks of 9/11, when "Arab looking" or "Muslim looking" women and men have been especially targeted for hate crimes and harassment. The episcopal leadership of the church has to express in official statements and in action its opposition to racism and xenophobia. Parish communities need to model and be signs of inclusion, and be vigilant against any racist or xenophobic sentiment or legislation. The fine statements of the U.S. Bishops, the joint statement of the bishops of the U.S. and Mexico, and Cardinal George's pastoral letter on racism are examples of how the institutional church can take a firm stand in this regard.[31] The work of such advocacy groups like Network and Conference of Major Superiors of Men (CMSM)/Leadership Conference of Women Religious (LCWR) are examples of how Christians can work at the highest levels of government to counter prejudice and unjust legislation, like some of the provisions in the Patriot Act or California's infamous Proposition 187.

Third, there is the ministry of education. Education is no doubt the key to the future for migrants, especially for youth. The great resources of the church for education need to be at the disposal of migrants, for it is only through education that they will be able to overcome poverty. Education will be on many different levels: language, negotiating the new culture, employment skills, religious education, and, of course, other education at the primary, secondary, and tertiary levels. Barrena Sánchez remarks that in the same way education has been such a central focus in "mission lands," and such a key factor in people's development there, so it can play the same crucial role in many of the former "home countries" from where so many migrants have come.

A fourth missionary activity of the church in the context of migration is the conscious practice of interreligious dialogue—"Not an option, but an obligation inherent in the church's mission in migration."[32] Many of today's migrants are not Christian, and so the relation of Christians to them should be one of respect for their religious convictions and a willingness to learn from and be challenged by them. As John Paul II points out in *Redemptoris Missio,* "each member of the faithful and all Christian communities are called to practice dialogue, although not always to the same degree or in the same way."[33] Church documents point out several ways dialogue can take place, and among these the most "accessible" to ordinary members of the church are the "dialogue of life" and the "dialogue of common action." In the dialogue of life, we are close to hospitality; it is simply the practice of getting to know women and men of other religions as persons, sharing with them, learning from them, living "in an open and neighborly spirit, sharing their joys and sorrows, their human problems and preoccupations."[34] In the dialogue of common action, both Christians and non-Christians collaborate with each other in actions which promote justice—working together for more humane immigration laws, for example, or for greater inclusion of immigrants within the larger community.

Fifthly—and this for Christian migrants—there is the missionary, cross-cultural activity of sacramental pastoral care. The ministers of the local church that is hosting new arrivals need to provide sacramental care, especially the Eucharist. But if there is no Eucharist in the migrants' local language, no confessor available who can communicate with them, no one who understands their baptismal and wedding customs, no one who understands their popular devotions, there is great probability that faith will wither and die, or that migrants will be susceptible to overtures from other Christian groups. In this regard it may be wise for the local church to invite pastoral ministers from the migrants' home countries to work with them, or for the church of their origin to provide ministers to accompany them. The Fifth World Congress for the Pastoral Care of Migrants and Refugees also suggests that the church of origin should provide adequate preparation for those emigrating to other parts of the world.[35] In addition, women and men in ministerial training in the receiving country might insist that such training include language and culture learning as well. There is no question that in the context of migration an adequate celebration of liturgy and leadership of prayer is an authentic missionary act.

Sixth, the local church hosting the migrants needs to be an advocate for the liberation and development of the countries from which they come. It is not enough to be welcoming and working for the just integration of migrants into the new society. The church needs also to be involved in getting to the root of the problems that force women, men, and children to leave their homes. Most migrants would prefer to stay home if they could, but it is often economic necessity or violence that drives them to other lands. Christian communities need to make their members aware of the causes of migrations, and these same communities need to mobilize themselves in whatever way possible to work, for example, for fairer work practices in these lands, more just compensation for labor, abolition of the weapons trade, and more equitable trade relations between rich and poor nations. Connecting with groups like Bread for the World, Catholic Relief Services, Oxfam, and Pax Christi would be ways to live out this aspect of mission.

In his article on mission in the context of migration, Barrena Sánchez asks when it is appropriate to explicitly proclaim the gospel and the person of Jesus Christ—to Christians and non-Christians alike—in the context of migration. That this is part of the church's missionary commitment is "beyond the shadow of a doubt,"[36] but it is also to be done within the context of a deep respect for the religious liberty of each person: "the Church proposes, she imposes nothing," writes Pope John Paul II.[37] The moment for proclamation will arrive, says Barrena Sánchez, when there has been a clear commitment on the part of the local church in terms of hospitality, antiracism and xenophobia, education, dialogue, pastoral care, and global justice. While proclamation certainly is "the permanent priority of mission,"[38] it may very well be one of the last things we should do. First and foremost, the church lives *inter culturas* and *inter gentes.*[39]

In mission we minister to the *cristos migrantes*[40] (the migrant Christs) of the world, accompanying them on their *via crucis* in a foreign and often hostile land. Mission in the context of migration involves movement beyond our comfort zones to be *inter migrantes* (among the migrants), *inter culturas* (among cultures), *inter gentes* (among the peoples). But these *cristos migrantes* are not only the *objects* of the church's missionary outreach; they are also *subjects* of mission, and those who are Christian share and continue Jesus's mission as his body in the world. The church serves not only as an inn of refuge, but also as an outpost of hope.[41] This is what we turn to in the third and final section of this paper.

Mission of Migrants: Mission of the Church

The image of the "Border Christ" that stands outside the parish church of St. Pius X in El Paso is an image of the church of migrants as the body of Christ. The mission of the world's migrants is, on the one hand, to call the church to its full catholic reality as the pilgrim people of God, a people who follow the lead of the "God of the Tent"; on the other hand, the local church's mission is to incorporate its newest arrivals into its full mission of preaching, serving, and witnessing to the reign of God. We will focus here on each of these two aspects.

Calling the Church to Be Church

The document "Starting Afresh from Christ: Towards a Renewed Pastoral Care for Migrants and Refugees" insists that "no one, be they migrants, refugees or members of the local population should be looked upon as a 'stranger,' but rather as a 'gift,' in parishes and other ecclesial communities. This is an authentic expression of the 'catholicity' of the church."[42] A first mission of migrants to the receiving church, therefore, is to offer their gifted-ness to the community. As Cardinal Paul Poupard points out, migrants are not required to simply assimilate into their new culture, but to enter into a dialogue with it, calling it beyond itself toward a richer multicultural (or perhaps better, *intercultural*) reality.[43] This, at times, will be a real prophetic activity, since often a local church will not want to be shaken in its cultural complacency, and shares the racism and xenophobia of the population at large. The duty of the receiving church nonetheless is to be open to receive these gifts and so allow itself to be transformed. Poupard insists that rather than constantly turning in on itself, the vitality of a culture actually depends on it being open to other cultures. Furthermore, "in the church, cultural pluralism is not the mere juxtaposition of opposing worlds, but the complementarity of many kinds of riches."[44] The mission of migrants, then, is to call the church to its own catholicity and, indeed, to its own mission, so that the church can be what it is called to be: a sign to the world of God's own unity-in-diversity, an "outpost of hope" in which peoples and cultures can work in harmony together. Migrants, to use the apt phrase of Raúl Fornet-Betancourt, provide the church with a "school of interculturality."[45]

Second, migrants call the church to recognize its provisional, pilgrim nature. What this means is that the "on the move" nature of migrant peoples can show the church itself that it is a community of "exiles of the dispersion," that "this earthly city in which we dwell, as wonderful as it may be, is not the heavenly city (Heb 13:14)."[46] Building on Korean theologian Jung Young Lee, Peter Phan has pointed to the "in-beyond" nature of the migrant experience as one that can be a rich source of theologizing in the context of migration.[47] Such "in-beyond-ness" certainly is an image of the church, which is in the world, part of its joys and struggles, but ultimately not *of* it. As Griffin and Walker suggest that "from this insider-outsider location the church can best resist the corrosive pressures of the melting pot and the consumer culture that follows in its wake. The church's mission is to be carried out from this vantage point. It is a location that implies neither complete withdrawal from the 'world' of political power . . . nor a bid to be at the commanding heights of that world. The church's finest hours are always at the borderlands of nations and empires, not at their centers."[48] The body of Christ is the "Border Christ," always on the move, never at home in one place, willing to go where needed, wearing the simplest of clothes, carrying no more than needed—but because of this able to enter into every situation.[49]

Third, migrants in their state of risk, uncertainty, and hope call the church to recognize more deeply the nature of the God of Jesus Christ. The experience of migration, writes Archbishop Agostino Marchetto, invites Christians to "leave the arid land of our egoism and self-sufficiency"[50] for an encounter with the other—with God as such. This is an invitation that calls Christians constantly to open themselves to the mystery that reveals God as the one who is always greater than we can imagine, who is most clearly found on the margins—in the desert, at the periphery, at the frontier[51]—calling us beyond, calling us forward, outside our comfort zones to new and unexpected life. Gioacchino Campese has eloquently written of the fact that our God is the "God of the Tent," a God who is found most fully on the road, crossing borders, not confined to special, holy buildings.[52]

Mission of the Church

In many ways, the mission of migrants *to* the church, as I have described it in the last section, could be done by Christians and non-Christians alike, although, of course, with very different levels of consciousness. Even those who do not believe in Christ can provide for us a "school of interculturation," can remind us of our radical pilgrim nature as church, and can help us encounter the God who is always beyond our grasp. The aspect of mission in this section, however, applies only to Christian migrants who are members of the church. Women, men, and children who are baptized are called to be the body of Christ in the world, and therefore need to be involved in the church's mission. The task of the local church is, therefore, not only to respond to migrants' needs and to accompany them on their journey, but also to call and equip them for ministry, both within the church and within the world.[53]

First of all, then, the local church has to call and equip migrants for ministry within the church. This could be in the more general area of religious educators, music ministers, social justice workers, members of parish, or diocesan councils. Or it could be in the more formal area of lay ecclesial ministry: pastoral associates, directors of religious education, or directors of diocesan offices of ethnic ministries. In any case, the point I want to make here is that the mission of the receiving church includes the incorporation of newly arrived Christians into its ministerial life. As migrants grow in their integration into the local church, they should be given opportunities not only for ministry among people of their own culture but for cross-cultural ministry as well.[54] To be acknowledged is the work of many undocumented women and men who have worked for years as lay ecclesial ministers in parishes, hospitals, and activist organizations.

Second, the local church with its native and migrant ministers exercises its mission by calling and challenging all the members of the community to a life of authentic Christian witness and ministry in their daily lives. Once more, there are no passive Christians. All Christians are called to witness by the integrity of their lives, express and defend their faith, live lives of commitment to social justice and inclusion, and relate to women and men of other faiths with deep respect and openness. This means then that the local church needs to ensure through religious education, homilies, liturgies, and organizations that all the members of their congregations— especially the migrant population—understand the ministerial and missionary dimension of their faith.

The Border Christ and the Challenge of Mission

As is captured in that marvelous image of Christ in El Paso, the "Border Christ" is the object of the church's mission, as well as its subject. If the church is to be the church, it must attend to the face of Christ reflected in the poor and neglected of the world—and that face is reflected with particular clarity in the millions of women, men, and children who have been forced to leave their homes in search of a better life. But also, if the church is to be the church, it must ensure that all its members, including migrants, participate in its identity as Christ's bodily presence in our world. The church is missionary by its very nature;[55] it exists by mission as a fire exists by burning.[56] The migrants of this world deserve the church's very special attention and accompaniment, and they can in turn be valuable gifts to the church as well, as the church shares and continues the mission of its Lord.

NOTES

1. Paul Wilkes, *Excellent Catholic Parishes: The Guide to Best Places and Practices* (Mahwah, NJ: Paulist Press, 2001), 19–20.

2. Ibid., 20.

3. As is often pointed out, "undocumented" migrants does not mean "illegal" migrants. There are, as Michael A. Blume points out, no illegal immigrants. Immigration, the church teaches, is a human right. See Michael A. Blume, SVD, "Migration and the Social Doctrine of the Church," in *Migration, Religious Experience, and Globalization,* ed. Gioacchino Campese and Peter Ciallella, 62–75 (New York: Center for Migration Studies, 2003).

4. This distinction is made in various places in the literature. Here I am following Félix Barrena Sánchez, "La inmigración como desafío a la misión" (available

at http://www.sedos.org/spanish/barrena_sanchez.htm, last accessed April 2007). See also Jorge Castillo Guerra, "Hacia una teología de la migración: Perspectivas y propuestas," *Chakana* 2, no. 3 (2004): 29–32.

5. See, for example, Agostino Marchetto, "Retomar el camino desde Cristo: Visión eclesial acerca de los emigrantes y de los refugiados, del postconcilio hasta hoy," *People on the Move* 35 (December 2003): 115–24; Graziano Battistella, "The Human Rights of Migrants: A Pastoral Challenge," in Campese and Ciallella, *Migration,* 93–94; Castillo Guerra, "Hacia una teología de la migración," 35–37, and "A Renewed Church in Asia: A Mission of Love and Service," in *FABC Papers No. 93* (Hong Kong: FABC), 11–12; Paolo Suess, "Relato y red: Migracion, peregrinación y camino como desafíos de la misión en el mundo globalizado," *Spiritus* (Edición hispanoamericana), 42/2, no. 163 (2001): 145–63.

6. Paraphrase of Bañuelas in Wilkes, *Excellent Catholic Parishes,* 20.

7. Mark Griffin and Theron Walker, *Living on the Borders: What the Church Can Learn from Ethnic Immigrant Cultures* (Grand Rapids, MI: Brazos Press, 2004), 182.

8. Barrena Sánchez, "La inmigración," 1. The remark of Peter Phan was made in a conversation held at Catholic Theological Union in 2001. See also Peter C. Phan, "Proclamation of the Reign of God as Mission of the Church: What for, to Whom, by Whom, and How?" in his *In Our Own Tongues: Perspectives from Asia on Mission and Inculturation,* 32–44 (Maryknoll, NY: Orbis Books, 2003).

9. John Paul II, encyclical letter *Redemptoris Missio,* 41, in *Redemption and Dialogue: Reading Redemptoris Missio and Dialogue and Proclamation,* ed. William R. Burrows (Maryknoll, NY: Orbis Books, 1993), 27.

10. Vatican Council II, Decree on the Church's Missionary Activity (*Ad Gentes*), paragraph 2; J. Andrew Kirk, *What is Mission? Theological Explorations* (London: Darton, Longman and Todd, 1999), 30.

11. Vatican Council II, Dogmatic Constitution on the Church (*Lumen Gentium*), paragraph 1.

12. Pope Paul VI, *Evangelii Nuntiandi,* paragraph 15.

13. 1971 Synod of Bishops, "Justice in the World," in *Catholic Social Thought: The Documentary Heritage,* ed. David J. O'Brien and Thomas A. Shannon (Maryknoll, NY: Orbis Books, 1992), 295.

14. See Peter C. Phan, "Crossing the Borders: A Spirituality for Mission in Our Times," in his *In Our Own Tongues,* 130–50.

15. See Anthony J. Gittins, *Gifts and Strangers: Meeting the Challenge of Inculturation* (New York: Paulist Press, 1989).

16. See Jonathan Y. Tan, "*Missio inter Gentes*: Towards a New Paradigm in the Mission Theology of the Federation of Asian Bishops' Conferences (FABC)," *Mission Studies* 21, no. 1 (2004): 65–95; Theo Sundemeier, "Theology of Mission," in *Dictionary of Mission: Theology, History, Perspectives,* ed. Karl Müller, Theo Sundemeier, Stephen B. Bevans, and Richard H. Bliese, 429–51 (Maryknoll, NY: Orbis Books, 1997). See also Claude Marie Barbour, Kathleen Billman, Peggy DesJarlait, and

Eleanor Doidge, "Ministry on the Boundaries: Cooperation without Exploitation," in *Beyond Theological Tourism: Mentoring as a Grassroots Approach to Theological Education,* ed. Susan B. Thistlethwaite and George F. Cairns, 72–91 (Maryknoll, NY: Orbis Books, 1994).

17. Kirk, *What is Mission?* 24.

18. Stephen B. Bevans and Roger P. Schroeder, *Constants in Context: A Theology of Mission for Today* (Maryknoll, NY: Orbis Books, 2004).

19. Barrena Sánchez, "La inmigración," 1. However, Samuel Escobar does seem to be rather favorably disposed to a vigorous effort of Protestants to seek converts from Catholicism. See his "Migration: Avenue and Challenge to Mission," *Missiology: An International Review* 31, no. 1 (January 2003): 17–28.

20. David J. Bosch, *Transforming Mission: Paradigm Shifts in Theology of Mission* (Maryknoll, NY: Orbis Books, 1991), 489; Bevans and Schroeder, *Constants in Context,* 284–85, 348–49.

21. Final Document, Part I, 3, *People on the Move* 35 (December 2003): 360. The version I cite is slightly different from the English translation. I have translated the Italian "lì dove essi sono" (see ibid., 374) as "being with them where they are" rather than "there where they are." See also "Starting Afresh from Christ: Towards a Renewed Pastoral Care for Migrants and Refugees, no. 3 (available through the Vatican web site, http://www.vatican.va).

22. See Theodore E. McCarrick, "Pastoral Challenges in the World of Migrants and Refugees," *People on the Move* 35 (December 2003): 39.

23. For the scriptural background here, see Joseph A. Mindling, "Chosen People in Foreign Lands: Scriptural Reflections on Immigration and the Uprooted," *New Theology Review* 12, no. 1 (1999): 4–14.

24. Edwina Gateley, "Finding Christ in the Margins: Excerpts from a New Book," *America* 189, no. 14 (2003): 18.

25. Flor Maria Rigoni and Gioacchino Campese, "Hacer teología desde el migrante: Diario de un camino," in Campese and Ciallella, *Migration,* 184.

26. Stephen Bevans, *Models of Contextual Theology,* rev. ed. (Maryknoll, NY: Orbis Books, 2004), 140.

27. See for example Cecelia Fandel, "The Border and Immigration: An Invitation to *Posada,*" *New Theology Review* 12, no. 1 (1999): 32–42; U.S. Catholic Bishops, "Welcoming the Stranger among Us: Unity in Diversity" (available at http://www.usccb.org/mrs/welcome.shtml, last accessed April 2007); U.S. Catholic Bishops and Mexican Bishops, "Strangers No Longer: Together on the Journey of Hope; A Pastoral Letter Concerning Migration from the Catholic Bishops of Mexico and the United States" (available at www.usccb.org/mrs/stranger.shtml, last accessed April 2007); Robert Schreiter, "Theology's Contribution to (Im)migration," in Campese and Ciallella, *Migration,* 175–80; Rigoni and Campese, "Hacer teología desde el migrante," 196–198; Christine Pohl, "Biblical Issues in Mission and Migration," in *Missiology: An International Review* 31, no. 1 (2003): 3–15.

28. Pohl, "Biblical Issues," 10. The internal quotation is from Philip Hallie, *Lest Innocent Blood Be Shed* (New York: HarperPerennial, 1994), 85.

29. See Gioacchino Campese, " 'I Will Make You Live in Tents Again' (Hosea 12:9): The Church in an Age of Mobility," unpublished research paper for "Missionary Dynamics of the Church," Catholic Theological Union, Fall 2003, 19–20.

30. Barrena Sánchez, "La inmigración," 5.

31. The U.S. Bishops' document and the joint pastoral of the U.S. and Mexican Bishops are cited above in note 27. While Cardinal George's pastoral letter focuses mostly on racism in the context of White–African American relations, he does deal with a wider racism in the context of migration. See Francis Cardinal George, "Dwell in My Love: A Pastoral Letter on Racism," April 4, 2001 (Chicago: Archdiocese of Chicago, 2001), esp. 11.

32. Final Statement, Part II, Dialogues, 2, in *People on the Move* 35 (December 2003): 368.

33. *Redemptoris Missio,* 57, in Burrows, *Redemption and Dialogue,* 36.

34. Pontifical Council for Inter-Religious Dialogue and Congregation for the Evangelization of Peoples, *Dialogue and Proclamation,* 42, in Burrows, *Redemption and Dialogue,* 104.

35. Final Statement, Part II, recommendation 10, in *People on the Move* 35 (December 2003): 366; see also recommendations 11 and 12.

36. Barrena Sánchez, "La inmigración," 9.

37. *Redemptoris Missio,* 39, in Burrows, *Redemption and Dialogue,* 27.

38. *Redemptoris Missio,* 44, in Burrows, *Redemption and Dialogue,* 28.

39. Campese, "I Will Make You Live in Tents Again," 19–20. Campese cites Jonathan Y. Tan, "*Missio inter Gentes,*" 65–95.

40. Renato Ascencio León, "La Eucharistía, signo e instrumento de la unidad de la comunidad cristiana," *People on the Move* 35 (December, 2003): 296.

41. Griffin and Walker, *Living on the Borders,* 182.

42. Final Statement, Part II, Pastoral Care, 9, in *People on the Move* 35 (December 2003): 365.

43. Paul Poupard, "Ripartire da Cristo: La visione ecclesiale per una societá multiculturale e interculturale," in *People on the Move* 35 (December 2003): 131.

44. Ibid., 132; see also Final Statement, Part I, 7, in *People on the Move* 35 (December 2003): 361.

45. Raúl Fournet-Betancourt, "La inmigración en contexto de globalización como diálogo intercultural," in Campese and Ciallella, *Migration,* 39.

46. Griffin and Walker, *Living on the Borders,* 22.

47. Peter C. Phan, "The Experience of Migration in the United States as a Source of Intercultural Theology," in Campese and Ciallella, *Migration,* 149–51. See Jung Young Lee, *Marginality: The Key to Multicultural Theology* (Minneapolis: Fortress Press, 1995), 29–79.

48. Griffin and Walker, *Living on the Borders,* 22.

49. Wilkes, *Excellent Catholic Parishes,* 20, in a paraphrase of Arturo Bañuelas.

50. Marchetto, "Retomar el camino desde Cristo," 122.

51. Jon Sobrino, *Resurrección de la verdadera iglesia: Los pobres, lugar teológico de la eclesiología* (Santander: Sal Terrae, 1981), 335. Referred to in Campese, "I Will Make You Live in Tents Again," 25.

52. Campese, "I Will Make You Live in Tents Again," 13.

53. See Stephen Bevans, "Equipping the Saints: Pastoral Work and the Missionary Imagination," presentation given at the annual convention of the National Federation of Priests' Councils, Atlanta, GA, April 2004. Publication forthcoming.

54. See Final Statement, Part II, Pastoral Care, 14, in *People on the Move* 35 (December 2003): 366.

55. *Ad Gentes,* 2.

56. See Emil Brunner, *The Word in the World* (London: SCM Press, 1931), 11.

CHAPTER SEVEN

Migrants and the Ministry of Reconciliation

ROBERT SCHREITER

According to the United Nations' World Economic and Social Survey 2004, one of every thirty-five persons on earth is a migrant; in the rich countries, the number rises to one of every twelve. The World Bank has rightly called migration "one of the determining forces of the twenty-first century."[1]

As has long been clear, the fact of migration calls forth a host of pastoral challenges. In the case of forced migration (that of dislocated persons or refugees) or reluctant migration (when economic deprivation leaves persons with no other alternative), there is the likelihood of injury or even trauma to the mental and spiritual well-being of the migrant. When such things occur, a very specific set of pastoral needs arise that must be addressed. They include dealing with the memories created by leaving one's homeland, the risks and dangers faced in the transit from the homeland to a new country, and the consequences of arriving in a new place. Together these needs might be addressed under the heading of a ministry of reconciliation.[2] In this essay I would like to outline some of the issues and the responses possible for such a ministry in a coherent and reflective manner. The presentation will be in three parts. The first part sketches out the three stages in the migration process and some of the issues for healing and reconciliation that arise. The second part looks at the different groups or audiences that have to be addressed and involved in the reconciliation process. The third part attempts to describe aspects of the work of reconciliation among migrant populations, both in terms of the goals of such a ministry and what steps can be undertaken to achieve them. Needless to say, such a preliminary sketch as this cannot pretend to be exhaustive, either in the general kinds of situations and issues that must be faced, nor the myriad variations that arise from the specificity of different situations. Those migrants who flee from situations of conflict face different challenges than those who migrate voluntarily, but reluctantly, for economic reasons. And those who migrate voluntarily (for example, highly skilled workers who are seeking more favorable working conditions) may escape some of the negative experiences of migration, but may still face loneliness, discrimination, and other setbacks in their new homeland. This presentation should be viewed therefore as a first attempt to develop a framework for a ministry of reconciliation and healing among migrants.[3]

Stages of Migration to Be Addressed

In order to set up a framework and list of issues that may need to be addressed in a ministry of reconciliation among migrants, I would like to sketch out three stages in the migration process, along with some of the issues that are likely to arise and will need attention in the process of healing and reconciliation. The stages are: leaving one's home or homeland, the transit to a new situation, and the process of arrival and settling in the new situation.

The first stage is *leaving one's home or one's homeland*. In the former instance, people are forced from the place where they are living and relocate or are relocated in another place in the same country. Such persons or populations are defined as *displaced persons*. Depending upon the circumstances that forced them to leave where they had been living, they may or may not be able to return. In instances where they do return, they may find their homes and means of livelihood occupied by other persons, damaged, or even destroyed. If they have to flee the country entirely they are considered *refugees*. If leaving the country more or less voluntarily they are called *emigrants*.

A common feature that may occur in any or all of these situations is *trauma*. Trauma might be defined here as psychic or spiritual injury incurred by the shock of having to leave, especially when such departure is accompanied by fear of the loss of one's life and the real or possible loss of life of loved ones. Trauma can be a temporary experience of shock or loss, but in some instances the experience becomes ongoing and severe to the point of disabling the person in terms of normal functioning in society. In the latter case, it may be an instance of what is called medically *post-traumatic stress disorder* (PTSD). In the case of PTSD, the person may experience recurrent, intrusive flashbacks of memory of the event that cause irritability, nervousness, inability to sleep or relax and, in some instances, even death.[4] In severe cases of PTSD, psychological and medical intervention is required. The psychological intervention needs to be culturally sensitive to images and models of illness and recovery specific to the people involved. Thus, the "talking cure" favored by Western psychology may be inappropriate in cultures where one does not share inner experiences with strangers. Use of culturally sanctioned practices and rituals may be more in order here. The knowledge of the neurochemistry of PTSD (focusing upon the middle cortex of the brain, especially the hippocampus) is still at early stages, but promises to add important pharmacological resources to the treatment of this disorder.

The stress involved in leaving one's home, therefore, may range from the "culture shock" experienced upon entering a different place, to traumatic memories of departure and concern about those who have been left behind. Identifying the nature of the difficult experience is the first step in responding to it. More will be said about this below under the idea of "healing of memories."

An additional feature or challenge in these settings is the fact that the one suffering has to deal with the experience once removed or several times removed from where the experience happened. The sufferer may not be able to revisit the site of this experience and so lay anxieties and fears to rest. In addition, there may be no one in the new environment who can easily understand the context of the event or aspects of the experience itself. In such instances, the healing process is complicated by an inability to engage the experience more directly.

The second stage of migration—*transit to the new situation*—creates a second set of challenges for migrants. In the case of those who migrate voluntarily through established legal channels, the bureaucracy and complexity of the process may leave scars. For those who migrate involuntarily or illegally, physical danger is part of the picture. Migrants entering countries illegally face a host of dangers, either from the difficulty of the transit itself (as in the case of African migrants crossing the Mediterranean to reach Europe, or Latin Americans entering the United States and having to cross the Rio Grande River or the desert), or from dangers along the way (Vietnamese boat people attacked by pirates in the South China Sea), or from potential capture and deportation by border guards. In the case of persons in bondage who are being trafficked to a new country (especially women and children) for purposes of enforced employment as workers or in the sex industry, migrants are in danger at every moment along the way, even at the hands of those who are transporting them.

Along with the physical dangers faced in the transit situation, there are psychological ones as well. The disorientation of being in unknown places, of having to face an uncertain future, of not knowing the language used in the transit place, of having to rely on strangers for safety and sustenance—all of these factors can contribute to anxieties that do not disappear when the transit has been completed. They can figure into PTSD, or remain with the migrant in terms of flashbacks or nightmares.

The depreciation of migrants in transit adds an additional psychic burden to them. When they are treated as chattel or quantifiable units to be bought and sold, or charged fees as so many goods to be transported, migrants are stripped of the dense set of relationships that marked their former lives and are reduced to objects to be moved from one place to another.

Finally, in the third stage of migration, migrants must *settle into their new situation,* which is the stage that most of the attention in ministry to and among migrants has focused upon. Often there is no welcome to the new migrant nor hospitality to help them find their ways in the new setting. Likewise what have been called "asymmetries" occur: the breakdown of human reciprocity and mutuality in the violation of human rights, discrimination, racism, xenophobia, and other phenomena.[5] Along with out-and-out legal violations, there is in addition often a failure upon the part of the receiving culture to recognize the achievements of migrants. Stories abound of how teachers', physicians', and engineers' education and status are ignored, and how they are consigned to menial physical employment. This too strikes at the self-esteem of the migrant and the migrant's "face" within his or her own community.

Each of these three points in the migrating process could be expanded upon in greater detail, but this sketch should at least indicate something of the range of experiences migrants may need to address in a process of healing and reconciliation.

Who Is Involved in the Reconciliation Process?

In thinking about the healing and reconciliation process for migrants, it is important to reflect upon the different groups or audiences who may be involved. For the sake of this outline of such a ministry of reconciliation, six such perspectives can be listed. They are: the migrant, the migrant's community, the descendants of the migrant, the autochthonous population of the country, the minister(s) involved in reconciliation, and the potential contribution to the Church as a whole.

The most obvious subject of a ministry of healing and reconciliation are *migrants themselves.* Key for the migrant is the goal of overcoming the harmful effects of the experience of migration, and the integration—in different ways or dimensions—of the migrant into his or her environment. "Integration" is to be understood here not as an assimilation that discounts or negates the specific aspects of the migrant's biography or experience, but rather as the capacity to function in a healthy way in the variety of roles and communities in which the migrant now lives. Aspects of the ministry have to concentrate therefore on what will facilitate such a development in the life of the migrant.

The migrant is not an isolated individual—even in situations where no one else of the migrant's family or ethnic group is present in the new situation—and thus *the migrant's community* is a part of the reconciliation process. This is especially true when the migrant comes from a strongly sociocentric culture, where the individual can only be understood from the community from which he or she originated. One's place and one's status within that community are central to the identity and the well-being of the migrant. What this means is that the ministry cannot only be directed to the individual, but must take into account the social context of family and ethnicity. This is complicated, to be sure, in situations where the migrant is alone (as, for example, is sometimes the case for female domestic workers).

Ways to integrate new or difficult information into one's identity have to respect the sociocentric rules of a community regarding identity formation (e.g., how innovation or contradictory signals are integrated into a shared identity), as well as other indices that make up a picture of the culture.[6]

Attention also has to be paid especially to the *migrant's children and grandchildren,* and how the experience of migration affects them. It is not uncommon—when the experience of migration was traumatic—that parents will want to shield their children from the unpleasant experience or trauma incurred. In such instances, the older generation will remain silent or refuse to talk about the experience. However, it frequently is not possible to provide such absolute protection. Behavior of the migrant might disorient the children in some way, and cause them to inquire into what exactly did happen. As the children come of age, it is quite common that sheer curiosity will prompt them to seek out details of the migration experience. This persistent quest can become even more pronounced in the grandchildren's interest in what exactly did happen.

Among migrants themselves, it sometimes also becomes important to transmit the experience of the trauma of migration at the end of their lives, lest the experience be forgotten by subsequent generations. This can be the case even if prior to that time migrants had been reluctant to speak of the experience.

Finally, the migrant may transmit—consciously or unconsciously—what has been called "chosen trauma," that is, a particular version or response to the trauma that becomes imbedded in the identity of subsequent generations.[7] Such chosen traumas can affect those generations profoundly, and be all the more difficult to deal with because of the oblique acquisition of them from their parents or grandparents.

One of the most difficult audiences to deal with in the healing process is the *autochthonous community,* or the community into which the migrant comes. The autochthonous community's not having had the experience of migrating, or not being able to understand the context or circumstances that gave rise to the migration experience, can diminish their capacity to accept the migrant into their midst. If there are reactions of racism, discrimination, or xenophobia against migrants, this makes the task even more difficult. Dealing with the "otherness" of the migrant often takes specific and focused instruction for autochthonous communities to be able to understand the plight of the migrant, together with an enlargement of the vision of the community to include people different from themselves.

People who minister among migrant populations often have to face within themselves some of the same obstacles that beget problems for autochthonous communities. They too can suffer from feelings of discrimination, racism, and xenophobia toward migrants, however unconsciously. If working with traumatic experiences becomes part of the ministry, it becomes important that these ministers are aware of unacknowledged or unresolved traumas in their own history, since these personal traumas can impede ministers' capacity to deal with trauma in the lives of others. What is likely to happen is that dealing with the traumas of others becomes a way of dealing with one's own trauma. At best, this obfuscates the healing process; at worst, it creates new damage to the migrant.[8]

Finally, in engaging in a ministry of healing and reconciliation for and among migrants, it is important to be aware that migrants are not passive receivers of such ministry. Migrants themselves can and do contribute insight not only to their own experiences of migration but also to understanding the catholicity of the church, as well as expanding the visions of *local communities of the church*.[9] This more proper theological understanding of the church involves the meaning of its worldwide and multicultural character, perspectives on what it means to live as a *communio* (the theological understanding of the church much favored in papal and other Vatican documents), as well as the church's understanding of its role on earth as pilgrim. It is within these dimensions that one can develop especially both a theology and a spirituality of migration and of migrants—something needed to sustain both ministry in these settings and the spiritual well-being of migrants themselves.[10]

The Ministry of Healing and Reconciliation

Having spoken of some of the issues entailed in the experience of migrants, and the various groups or audiences that need to be taken into account in ministry among and to migrants, we can now turn to the ministry of healing and reconciliation itself. In order to set out some of the important dimensions of this ministry, I will proceed through four points: (1) a general understanding of the Christian meaning of reconciliation, (2) the matter of pursuing justice for migrants, (3) the process of the healing of memories, and (4) recovering agency as a migrant.

Again, in a presentation of this compass it is impossible to provide all the details necessary. Keeping in mind what was said at the outset, this is meant to provide a general framework rather than a handbook for the ministry of healing and reconciliation among migrants.

The Christian Understanding of Reconciliation

The term "reconciliation" has come to be used in many different ways among those who are involved in the restoration or reconstruction of individual lives and of societies. Some of the understandings that arise have much in common across different methods of conflict transformation or of therapeutic processes. My focus here is upon the specifically Christian contribution to a larger reconciliation process. This focus helps us see what sustains the minister and the migrant in coming to terms with the migration process, and what constitutes a satisfactory resolution of the dilemmas and challenges faced along the way. These should not be seen as in contradistinction to other approaches to the healing process, but rather as the specific Christian perspective on the process as a whole. There are five such distinctive elements.[11]

First of all, *God is the agent of reconciliation.* This means that it is God who leads and resolves the reconciliation process. Human beings—both the minister and the migrants themselves—play an active role. But giving to God the ultimate agency underscores the realization that the experiences of migration are so complex and so far-reaching that only God can completely comprehend them. It has the added dimension of making the healing process a spiritual quest that both receives divine guidance and refrains from depending too heavily on one set of techniques or solutions to issues.

Second, *healing begins with the victim.* Reconciliation processes usually focus on the repentance, apology, or restitutive action of the wrongdoer as the condition for reconciliation. This is all well and good when the wrongdoer does change. But often the wrongdoer refuses to change or (in the case of the migrant) is not even present to engage in any transformative activity. Thus divine action in the life of the victim allows for healing even when the wrongdoer does not change or is not present. To be sure, such healing would never be complete without some action on the part of the wrongdoer, but substantial healing can take place even without action by those who have done wrong.

Third, *the healing brought about in the reconciliation process takes the victim to a new place.* While healing is initially imagined as a return to the *status quo ante,* such is most often not possible and is unlikely to happen even if it were possible. In the case of a migrant, returning home may not be an option. Even if it were possible, the migrant has been changed by the experience, and the home of the migrant may have changed as well. Hence, the healing process should be envisioned as coming to a new place. In Christian language, one becomes a "new creation" (2 Cor 5:17), that is, God brings the victim into a new, transformed state that does not forget or negate the past, but rather puts that past into a new setting.

Fourth, *the migration story has to be reframed.* The concept of "reframing" has become widely used in psychology to explain the process of placing an experience in a new framework of interpretation or perspective on understanding. By so doing, hidden meanings in the experience may come to the fore, and a new explanatory narrative of the event can situate the event in the victim's biography in a new way. The suffering experienced in the migration experience (in any of the three stages of migration outlined above) has to be put in a framework that gives some meaning to what looks otherwise as cruel, meaningless, and wrongful suffering. Again, such reframing does not condone the wrongdoing that took place; rather, it attempts to portray what happened in such a way that the victim is not degraded or diminished, but rather upholds the dignity and worth of the victim.

Fifth and finally, *the healing process of reconciliation is never complete.* That the process is never complete arises out of two experiences. First of all, there can be dimensions of a trauma that do not come to the surface in explicit treatment. It may take other, subsequent events to make those dimensions come forward. The fact that such events can recreate the trauma is a common experience. Hearing about the 9/11 attack, for example, reactivated previous traumas for some victims. Reports of the torture of inmates in the Abu Ghraib prison in Baghdad in 2004 had a similar effect on survivors of torture. Second, since human lives are webs of relationships, the full range of repercussions from a traumatic event can reverberate far beyond what might initially be perceived. To see that full range may take a comprehensive view and vision that only God has. This fifth and final point brings us back to the beginning point of the Christian understanding of reconciliation, namely, that it is ultimately God who is the agent of reconciliation.

Following these five points of the Christian understanding of reconciliation does not preclude other points of view, either religious or non-religious. Rather they should be seen as the specific contribution of a Christian approach in the midst of other possible approaches. They form the backdrop of how a Christian would go about addressing the experience of migration—as a Christian minister, and especially if the migrant is Christian. A non-Christian migrant may or may not find such perspectives helpful.

The Pursuit of Justice

Because of the way that the discourse of reconciliation is sometimes used, the impression can be given that reconciliation is an alternative to the pursuit of justice: that when justice is not possible, a person or a group finds a way to become resigned to the injustice and to get on with life. In Latin America in the 1980s, certain right-wing movements tried to oppose reconciliation to the theology of liberation, on the grounds that liberation was inherently conflictive and opposed to Christian views of love of neighbor and of enemies embodied in reconciliation.

As Richard Falk has pointedly observed, part of the religious perspective that can be brought to the current conduct of international affairs is that both justice *and* reconciliation are possible.[12] Justice is not seen as an alternative to reconciliation, but rather as a condition for its fulfilment. Thus, the pursuit of justice is not only compatible with efforts at reconciliation; such pursuit is a necessary component of reconciliation itself.

At the same time, the justice achieved is often unsatisfactory. Sometimes it is impossible ever to bring about the desired result: justice, after all, cannot bring back the dead even though it can acknowledge and honor those who have suffered unjustly. What is important to realize here is that, even if the situation cannot be completely resolved, action is still possible. We are not placed in suspension or paralysis because complete justice has not been achieved. Justice often remains an asymptotic goal—approached but never entirely realized.

That having been said, just how does one pursue justice in the healing and reconciliation process for migrants? I would suggest that there are three dimensions to it: gaining an acknowledgement of wrongdoing (on the part of the wrongdoer) or of innocence (of the victim); the overcoming of the asymmetries that have arisen; and the regaining of agency on the part of the migrant.

Acknowledgement of the trauma that has occurred and the pain and suffering inflicted is an important aspect of the pursuit of justice. Indeed, such acknowledgement is foundational for any further acts of justice. It involves the issues of *silence* and of *truth*. Because of the risky character of so much migration that takes place, the story of what happened—from leaving one's home through the transit experience to the arrival—remains shrouded in silence. The humiliation that occurred in treatment along the way, the places where migrants may have been hidden or given sanctuary—all of this seems to call for silence. But being silent about experiences that touch the core of one's being can be an act of disregard or even degradation of the migrant. It is as if one were saying that the migrant is not important enough as a human being for these things to matter, or that they were not as suffering-laden as the migrant makes them out to be. The migrant may well have experienced the transit as being treated like chattel or an object, rather than a human being. To give voice to the experience is essential to the migrant's becoming once again a subject of his or her own history, rather than some object acted upon. Breaking the silence allows the agent to participate in the historical process once again.

Connected to breaking the silence is the act of establishing the truth. Especially in the case of illegal migration, the migrant who achieves transit from one country to another may be viewed by the autochthonous community as a criminal, someone who has broken the law. To be sure, laws about entry into a country may have been transgressed, but taking priority over that are the tenets of basic human rights. Migration may be a matter of sheer survival. The deeper truth about human dignity and equal regard may supersede positive law. That is why so many countries, after a time of totalitarian oppression or civil war, have set up Truth Commissions of various kinds to establish a platform of truth on which the society may be reconstructed. Such commissions work to set the record straight about what really did happen in the time of violence.

Such truth-telling and ending of the silence is important for the migrant. To tell the story of suffering and to speak the truth about what happened is to restore right relationships with the past and the events that occurred. Such right relationships constitute the very definition of justice. Any redress that the migrant might seek has to be built upon those right relationships.

Once trauma has been acknowledged, *asymmetries can be realigned*. Asymmetries refer here to all the skewed relationships that have occurred in the process of migration. The migrant may have been exploited by those who have agreed to help them cross the border illegally (e.g., the notorious *coyotes* working the U.S.-Mexico border, or the intermediaries who traffic Chinese illegally into other countries). Arrival into the new country is frequently fraught with a host of injustices regarding housing, employment, and forms of social welfare. As already has been noted, the arrival dimension has been the focus of much of migrant ministry. It also figures prominently into Vatican and national episcopal statements on migration and migrant ministry. The discrimination, racism, and xenophobia to be overcome constitute a heavy agenda for ministers. Issues of restitutive or distributive justice are of the foremost immediate concern here. Closely following behind them are the structural justice issues surrounding adequate and humane legislation regarding immigration and settlement in the new country, as well as proper allocation of resources to make such settlement possible.

The third and final dimension of the pursuit of justice in a ministry of reconciliation is the migrant's *regaining agency*, that is, the capacity to function as a full and free person in accord with the Christian understanding of human dignity and equal regard. Such issues as language acquisition, knowledge of the culture of the autochthonous community, intercultural communication, and getting respect for the migrant's own language and culture all figure into this. In some instances, additional formal education may aid in helping migrants take their own place and promote their own cause in the public forum. Reconciliation as understood by Christians has at its base the restoring of human dignity to victims who have been robbed of that sense of value and equal regard.

The work of justice for migrants is not a short-term project, after which it is possible to move on to other things. All too often it will continue over the migrants' lifetime and into the lifetime of the next generation. Nor is it achieved in full before any other healing can take place. Life presents itself as a series of much smaller victories, whereby some justice is achieved that in turn reestablishes some measure of right relationships along the way. Because the pursuit of justice is often the most public or measurable dimension of a ministry of reconciliation, it gets the most attention and calls for the greatest social effort. That is all well and important, and should not be underestimated.

The Healing of Memories

A central aspect of a ministry of reconciliation among migrants is the healing of the painful and traumatic memories that can mark any of the three stages of migration. Healing of memories does not mean the forgetting and suppressing of such memories. To engage in such activities would be tantamount to victimizing the victim yet another time; it would be saying to the victim that either the event was not as significant as the victim remembers, or that the victim is not important enough as a human being for anyone to be so concerned. Healing entails rather a detoxifying of the memories, so that the memory no longer holds the victim hostage. Healing memories means to learn to remember the past in a different way. This remembering differently—in a way that frees the victim from the bondage of the past and allows the victim to integrate the memory into a life story in a constructive manner—is the goal of a ministry of healing memories.

There are two important stages in the healing of memory: gaining access to the memories, and the retelling and reframing of the memories. Access to the memories is often difficult because of the trauma that the memories have created. This is especially the case where the migrant's life was at risk, or where the migrant may have witnessed the death of loved ones. In such instances, the sheer pain generated by the memory may lead the brain to suppress parts of the memory. What is allowed to come to the surface in remembering are only fragments of the memory, perhaps not even in the sequence in which they actually took place. This is especially the case in the traumatic memories of children. On the other hand, the memories may keep coming back as intrusive, unwanted flashbacks that interrupt sleep and also waking consciousness. The memories have a life of their own, as it were, and control the victim rather than the victim controlling them.

Gaining access to the memories requires setting up secure pathways for the victim, so that they do not overwhelm the victim and renew the traumatic experience. In the hands of professionals, some people can undergo hypnosis and other therapeutic approaches, but these are not available for most victims (nor are they always effective for those who do have access to them). More available are what are called "healing circles," that is, safe and welcoming spaces where the victim can examine the past in the company of sympathetic listeners.[13] These are small groups of people committed to accompanying victims and listening to their stories. The circles have to be both safe and welcoming. Safety means that what is said in the circle must remain in the circle, because victims are deeply vulnerable when they explore traumatic memories. The safety experienced in the healing circle engenders an experience of *trust,* that very basic human experience that has been sundered by the traumatic experience. Being able to trust others again is central to the healing of traumatic memories.

The safety must be matched with a sense of welcome, that is, that the victim is valued and treasured as a human being, and that the listeners will stay with the victim through the conclusion of the healing process. The experience of trust and welcome has its theological counterparts in the experience of *faith* and *grace.* Faith is the experience of reconnection with God, and grace is the experience of healing coming from God, the author of reconciliation. Creating safe and welcoming spaces, then, is the human counterpart of God's healing work in the life of the victim.

Within those safe and welcoming places, the memories have to be retold and reframed. Human identities are constituted in stories, and stories become the ritual reenactment of what took place. For a memory to be detoxified, it must be told—and retold—until a new set of relationships or connections are made. That new set of relationships reframes the story within the larger life story of the victim. To achieve this, the victim has to be able to tell and retell the story until it comes out differently. This is what constitutes a healing of memories—being able to remember the story in a different way.[14]

As was noted already above, the healing of memories is never an utterly complete project. New events can trigger aspects of memory not reframed and retold in the healing process. Even recalling the memory itself can evoke new dimensions of pain or new insights into the past. For the migrant, the sense of loss of one's homeland and the ongoing strangeness of the new place may continue to evoke painful memories. But finding a safe and welcoming space in which to explore those memories may be one of the most important things that a ministry of reconciliation can provide.

Recovering Agency as a Migrant

The importance of the migrant's recovery of a sense of agency has already been touched upon in the treatment of the pursuit of justice. As memories are healed, certain goals or tasks of this recovery of agency come into fuller relief.

The experience of healing in the Christian understanding of reconciliation does take people to a new place. It is not a return to where the victim was before the trauma happened: too much has happened in between that has to be taken into the life story of the migrant. In all of this we are indeed called to become a "new creation," as St. Paul puts it (2 Cor 5:17). That standing in a new place means not only having a different relationship to the events and personages of the past, but also acknowledging that one is in a new place. In cases of human rights abuses, such as torture, this move is placed in the language of moving from being a "victim" to becoming a "survivor." Being called a survivor indicates that one is no longer a victim, but also that the experience of having been a victim does not leave one without wounds and memories. Being a survivor often connotes an ongoing struggle not to slip back into being a victim once again.

With that change of status often comes a sense of call or vocation. Standing in a new place gives perspective not only on one's own experience but also on one's relation to others. Many survivors experience a call to help other victims out of the strength of what they have learned in the healing process, and out of the weakness and vulnerability that only a survivor can know. Stories of both victims and wrongdoers having been healed abound. In John 21, Peter is commissioned to look after Jesus's followers, after he had been forgiven by Jesus and healed of betraying Jesus. Paul, the erstwhile persecutor of the followers of Jesus, becomes their most ardent apostle. This assuming of a task or a vocation represents a fullness of agency for the erstwhile victim that the victim could never have generated alone. That it is experienced as a call or vocation confirms once again the role of the principal agent of reconciliation: God. And in this moment, the migrant can assume his or her highest sense of agency as a minister of reconciliation, by moving from victim to the healer of others.

This presentation has tried to sketch out some of the distinctive features of a ministry of reconciliation among migrants. Because of the complexity of the migrant situation, only the boldest of lines could be drawn here. But it is hoped that these give enough of an idea of what is entailed to promote a wider discussion of how to develop a fuller program that helps the migrant heal memories and regain full status and dignity as a son or daughter of God.

NOTES

1. The report may be found at www.un.org/esa/policy/wess (last accessed April 2007).

2. I suggested that such be done in Robert Schreiter, "Theology's Contribution to (Im)migration," in *Migration, Religious Experience, and Globalizaton,* ed. Gioacchino Campese and Pietro Ciallella (New York: Center for Migration Studies, 2003), 176–77. This is an attempt to work out some of the implications of such a ministry.

3. Aspects of what will be presented here rely in part on Jorge Castillo Guerra, "Naar een theologie van de migratie," *Tijdschrift voor Theologie* 44 (2004): 241–58.

4. The best introduction to PTSD remains Judith Herman, *Trauma and Recovery,* rev. ed. (New York: Basic Books, 1997).

5. Castillo Guerra, "Naar een theologie van de migratie." The term "asymmetry" owes its origin to Latin American reflection on the effects of globalization.

6. Useful here is the work of Geert Hofstede, who has drawn up a series of six indices that have now been applied to and studied in some seventy-five countries. See his *Culture's Consequences: Comparing Values, Behaviours, Institutions, and Organizations across Nations,* rev. ed. (Thousand Oaks, CA: Sage Publications, 2001).

7. The term is Vamik Volkan's. See his *Bloodlines: From Ethnic Pride to Ethnic Terrorism* (Boulder, CO: Westview Press, 1998). "Chosen trauma" is the version or aspect of a traumatic experience that is transmitted to others in such a way that the experience has a traumatic experience in the life of the recipient, even though the recipient did not have the direct experience. Transmission of the experience of the Holocaust by Jewish survivors of that event is an example. Carlos Alvarez has found that Cubans born in the United States can have a nostalgia for prerevolutionary Cuba transmitted by their parents, even without ever having visited Cuba.

See his *Ethnic Identity: Understanding Contemporary Perspectives* (Upper Saddle River, NJ: Prentice Hall/Pearson, 2001).

8. I have dealt with this in more detail in "Preparing Missionaries for Situations of Violence," in *Mission—Violence and Reconciliation,* ed. Timothy Yates, 46–59 (Sheffield: Cliff College Publishing, 2003).

9. This is a point made repeatedly in the Instruction of the Pontifical Council for the Pastoral Care of Migrants and Itinerant Peoples, *Erga Migrantes Caritas Christi,* released May 14, 2004. Cf. especially nos. 89 and 103. An English translation of the Instruction may be found in *Origins* 34 (August 12, 2004): 147, 149–68.

10. On a theology of migrants and migration, see Campese and Ciallella, *Migration, Religious Experience, and Globalizaton,* especially the essays of Bergant, Blume, Phan, and Rigoni and Campese.

11. I develop these in more detail in my *Reconciliation: Mission and Ministry in a Changing Social Order* (Maryknoll, NY: Orbis Books, 1992) and *The Ministry of Reconciliation: Spirituality and Strategies* (Maryknoll, NY: Orbis Books, 1998).

12. Richard Falk, *Religion and Human Global Governance* (New York: Palgrave, 2001), 31.

13. I have explored this in more detail in "Entering the Healing Circle," in *The Healing Circle: Essays Presented to Claude Marie Barbour,* ed. Stephen Bevans, Eleanor Doidge, and Robert Schreiter, 176–87 (Chicago: CCGM Publications, 2000).

14. The power of story within reconstructing of identity is explored in Schreiter, *Reconciliation.* Remembering a story in a reframed manner is exemplified in Jesus's encounter with the disciples on the road to Emmaus in Luke 24. For a treatment of this story and other stories, see Schreiter, *Ministry of Reconciliation.*

CHAPTER EIGHT

For the Love of Migrants

The Scalabrinian Tradition

GIOVANNI GRAZIANO TASSELLO

We Scalabrinians are constantly faced with a dilemma. On the one hand we share a secret desire: to eliminate forced migration as a way of life because it produces devastating effects upon the persons involved and their families. We join forces with men and women of good will who advocate a widespread international solidarity and cooperation, so that no one shall ever again be forced to seek the means of survival in another land. We envision a planet in which people will naturally move from place to place, if they so desire, as passports are not God's invention. On the other hand this aspiration encounters many difficulties. In the Gospel of Mark, Jesus rightly makes us aware that the poor will always be with us (Mk 14:7). Thus the retiring age of our religious order is still far away, as the number of migrants throughout the world is steadily increasing rather than diminishing. In fact

> migrations due to political, economic, and religious causes, be they of single persons or of entire communities, can no longer be considered marginal events requiring only emergency intervention. They are now a structural phenomenon involving all nations and effecting far-reaching changes in the social, cultural, religious, and economic life of the nations from where migrants leave and of those who welcome them.[1]

In the past, Scalabrinians often thought theirs was a unique charism within the church. But the transformation of an Italian congregation into an international religious community compelled its members to question the originality of their ministry and to seek new bonding values, no longer stemming from a single ethnic group, or even in the care of immigrants per se, as many within the church were paying closer attention to this social phenomenon and were investing personnel commitment and resources in the particular field. Human migrations in fact are a common responsibility for church and society:

> Faithful to its evangelizing mission, the Church, as well as the countries of departure and arrival, shares a common responsibility in promoting new ways for people from diverse origins to come together, while respecting fundamental human rights. This calls for the promotion of mutual acceptance and good will between migrants and local residents alike.[2]

Searching for a Tradition

Recognizing the broadening of their mission, Scalabrinians have reviewed their specific vocation and mission in the church and society because "what is generic and vague cannot be an authentic gift to others."[3] This work in progress is not meant for our religious congregation only. Scalabrinians want to share the results of this search with other persons who are involved with the phenomenon of migration and are striving to persuade people from diverse origins to live together in communion. In other words, we are looking for a spiritual "tradition." The term is used here in its original meaning: inspirational guidelines handed down to us; a gift we have received as a legacy, to which we adhere with creative fidelity.

Inspired by John Baptist Scalabrini's Life and Vision

The originator of this tradition is John Baptist Scalabrini (1839–1905), bishop of Piacenza (Italy). A sentence taken from one of his homilies on the role of the bishop will help us grasp his commitment to migrants and his pastoral vision of the phenomenon:

To make every sacrifice to extend the kingdom of Jesus Christ in the hearts of people, to risk his life if necessary for the welfare of his beloved flock, to get down on his knees before the world, as it were, and beg from it, as a favor, the permission to do it some good.[4]

Analyzing Bishop Scalabrini's writings and activities, we are met with an original outlook on migration that, in turn, generates an innovative pastoral approach. For Bishop Scalabrini migrants are not merely objects, beneficiaries of charitable deeds we carry out when an emergency situation arises. They are persons with an inner dignity and with rights, sharing the gift of a different culture. We cannot go out to them with the intention of colonizing and assimilating them. Rather we serve them because only when migrants experience acceptance and love will they become a resource.

During his ministry as a priest and bishop, Scalabrini often witnessed the departure of migrants, and was challenged by this reality: "Faced with this lamentable situation, I have often asked myself: how can it be remedied?"[5] His was not an emotional response, as may happen to those who fall victims of the media system, constantly looking for newer images with a greater emotional impact, to be immediately discarded when more dramatic scenes are portrayed. His approach to human migration was a combination of mind and heart, sentiment and rationality, the way any immigration problem should be tackled.

He was aware that expertise was necessary, and he surrounded himself with competent people. His conferences on migration were the result of study as well as an attentive observation of reality. A famous Italian journalist, not particularly fond of Catholics, defined him as the first European migration sociologist.[6] Scalabrini's was not the knowledge of an erudite. He saw the phenomenon, he analyzed causes and effects, and then acted. Scalabrini believed in

freedom of emigration, not freedom to coerce it, because, while emigration is good when free, it is bad when coerced. If spontaneous, it is good because it is one of the great laws of divine Providence ruling over the destinies of peoples and their economic and moral progress. It is good because it is a social safety valve. It opens up the flowery paths of hope and sometimes of riches to the poverty-stricken and civilizes people through contact with other laws and other customs. It brings the light of the Gospel and Christian civilization to barbarians and idolaters. It ennobles human destiny by broadening the concept of motherland beyond the physical and political boundaries, making the whole world man's motherland. If coerced, emigration is bad because it substitutes true need with the fever of instant gain or with an ill-conceived spirit of adventure. Instead of helping and relieving the situation, it becomes an evil and a danger because, by unnecessarily de-populating the motherland beyond measure, it creates more uprooted and disillusioned people. It is bad, finally, because it deviates emigration from its natural channels, which are the most effective and least harmful ones. Experience teaches, in fact, that this kind of emigration is the cause of great evils that can and must be prevented by a provident civil government.[7]

He advocated the natural right to emigrate, which would later become a component of the teachings of the Church.[8] It is partly because of his conversations with the migrants themselves during his frequent pastoral visitations of his diocese of Piacenza that Scalabrini reached this conclusion. He describes one of these dramatic encounters with one of the many people of his diocese who had decided to migrate:

One day a wonderful man, an exemplary Christian, from a little mountain village where I was making my pastoral visitation, came to see me and to ask for my blessing and a memento for himself and his family on the eve of their departure for America. When I demurred, he countered with this simple but distressing dilemma: "Either you steal or you emigrate. I am not allowed to steal nor do I want to, because God and the law forbid it. But in this place there is no way I can earn a living for me and my children. So what can I do? I have to emigrate: it is the only thing left. . . ." I did not know what to answer. With a full heart, I blessed him and entrusted him to the protection of God. But once more I became convinced that emigration is a necessity, a heroic and ultimate cure one has to accept, just as a sick person accepts painful surgery to avoid death.[9]

It is very clear that at the time of Scalabrini, migration was for many people a matter of life and death, much like it happens today for many migrants and refugees around the world. It represented the only way for these people to support their families and maintain intact their decency and dignity. Therefore, it is not a surprise to hear Scalabrini say that the right to migrate is "a sacred human right":

> Those who would like to put a stop or a limit to emigration for patriotic or economic reasons and those who, because of a mistaken idea of freedom, want emigration left to itself, without direction or guidance, are either not using their heads or, in my opinion, are reasoning egoistically and insensitively. In fact, by blocking emigration, we are violating a sacred human right; and by leaving it to itself, we are making emigration ineffectual.[10]

Faced by this situation Scalabrini decided that as a pastor he could not be silent and still. He had to understand and act in order to protect and lead his flock. So he observed the reality around him, gathered data and facts, discussed this issue with other people, and in this process he realized that there was much confusion about the phenomenon of migration not only among the people, but also among the so-called experts:

> A theoretical debate on whether emigration is good or bad is a waste of time at this point. For my purpose, the important thing is that emigration exists. But during the research I undertook to gather the statistical data and facts for this humble work of mine and also during my conversations with friends, I came to realize that there are a lot of fuzzy ideas in this field, not only among the middle class and among private citizens but also among journalists and public figures. So I came to the conclusion that my observations are not at all out of place.[11]

Scalabrini breathed the intellectual atmosphere of his time, full of political ideologies and social visions. Karl Marx in *Das Kapital* described the life of people who had moved into the English industrial towns, the exploitations of these immigrant workers, and their abysmal living conditions.[12] He envisaged a political system to overcome these injustices. Socialists and anarchists were quite active among immigrants, hoping to start a new social order by focusing their attention on this special category of people. The First Zionist Congress, held in Basel in 1897, called for the creation of a Jewish homeland in Palestine through the immigration of Jews from many parts of the world. Emma Lazarus's poem engraved on the pedestal for the Statue of Liberty offered a very idyllic view of migration. The Russian philosopher and theologian Vladimir Soloviev spoke at the time of the vocations of nations. It is in this context that we are confronted with the most original trait of Scalabrini's theory on migration, that is the providential outlook on this social phenomenon:

> Human beings migrate, sometimes in groups, sometimes alone, and, in so doing, are always the free instruments of divine Providence, which presides over human destiny, leading all people, even through great calamities, to their final goal, the perfection of man on earth and the glory of God in heaven.[13]

Because of this belief, in 1887 and 1895 Scalabrini initiated two religious congregations to care for migrants, respectively the Missionaries of St. Charles (priests and brothers), and the Missionary Sisters of St. Charles. In 1892 he had also founded the St. Raphael's Society for the Protection of Emigrants, a lay association.

Scalabrini's providential vision of migration did not make him oblivious of the real situation of migrants. He knew how the U.S. Roman Catholic hierarchy and the local Irish American clergy felt about the Italian immigrants. Some American ordinaries nourished strong suspicions about Italian, Polish, and Filipino clergy. They had reached the conclusion that quite a few priests were leaving their countries to escape the consequences of improper behavior there.

Working on behalf of Italian immigrants in North America at the end of the nineteenth century was not a very gratifying experience. A U.S. Catholic newspaper published in Jacksonville, Florida, summed up adequately the general perception of what was then known as "the Italian question":

> The Italians especially are non-assimilative, and some measures should be taken to check the flood of immigration from that country . . . This country should no longer be the receptacle for the most degraded and

vicious of the population of Europe. The American labour market is overstocked to a serious extent, mainly through the importation of cheap labourers from Europe. It is our duty as a nation to take some measures for self-protection and for the protection of our superior civilization from too serious contamination.[14]

Italian immigrants reaching the shores of the U.S. were mostly illiterate. People considered them superstitious because of their popular religiosity. Often they were "birds of passage," a fact that rendered ministry among them even more difficult. Yet Scalabrini was not afraid of investing hope, energy, and human power in people considered hopeless, as God does all the time! They were regarded solely as a cheap labor force. He strived to make them aware of their human and divine dignity. Because the migrants are God's children, he defended their cultural and religious rights. He demanded that their religious practices and their time of adjustment and growth within church and society be respected. By asserting that the Church has a duty to serve them, he was making migrants—let us not forget Scalabrini was a great expert in catechesis—aware of their special vocation within the Church.

After Napoleon Bonaparte's fall, a missionary spirit permeated many dioceses in Europe. The desire to spread the gospel and "convert the infidels" was felt everywhere. The rejection of faith by many intellectuals during the age of Enlightenment and by many workers during the industrial revolution pushed the church to search for new venues and invest in new territories. There were years in Europe in which a new religious congregation, or pious society, was born every week.

Scalabrini was concerned with a seemingly apparent contradiction. The church was investing heavily in the propagation of faith, even though the numbers of conversions to Roman Catholicism were quite limited. At the same time many millions of Catholic immigrants were left unattended and risked losing their faith. He called for a greater effort in order to preserve their religious heritage. Once he had received a message from a migrant from his diocese that reflected dramatically the spiritual needs of many Catholic migrants: "Tell our Bishop that we always remember his advice. Tell him to pray for us and to send us a priest because here we live and die like animals."[15] This is why he professed his faith and hope in a church that cannot abandon any of its children, especially those who had to leave their homelands because of poverty and lack of work:

> The Church of Jesus Christ, which has sent her Gospel workers among the most barbarous peoples and most inhospitable regions, has not forgotten and will never neglect the mission God entrusted to her, namely, to preach the Gospel to the children of poverty and labor. She will always look with anxious heart on so many poor souls who, in forcible isolation, are losing the faith of their forebears and, with the faith, every sentiment of Christian and civil upbringing. Yes, where people are working and suffering, there is the Church because the Church is the mother, friend, and defender of the people and will always have a word of comfort, a smile, a blessing for them.[16]

The "salvation of souls" was not a rhetorical platitude for a saintly person like Scalabrini, living at the end of the nineteenth century. When the Bishop of Piacenza founded his first congregation in 1887, St. Theresa of the Child Jesus was in Rome, begging Leo XIII to enter a Carmelite monastery at the age of 15 in order to "save souls." In his encyclical letter on the education of the clergy in Europe in 1902, Pope Leo XIII stated:

> To work the eternal salvation of souls will always be the great commandment of which it must never fall short, as to faithfully fulfill it, it must never cease to have recourse to those supernatural aids and those divine rules of thought and of action which Jesus Christ gave His Apostles when He sent them throughout the whole world to convert the nations to the Gospel.[17]

Even though Scalabrini used the typical language of the time, saving migrants for him meant showing great concern for their human and religious promotion. To propose a providential outlook on migration in fact does not mean inability or unwillingness on his part to examine reality in all its contradictory elements or remain silent vis-à-vis the injustices perpetrated against migrants. Scalabrini had the courage to tell the president of the U.S. of an incident he had witnessed at Ellis Island, in which a guard had beaten an Italian immigrant unjustly.[18] He sent missionaries to preserve and enhance the faith of migrants. But he also sent them to protect immigrants from the time they left Italy to the time they arrived and settled down in their country of destination. For him, loving migrants went hand in hand with sensitizing society and local churches to the plight of migrants, denouncing injustices, favoring better legislation, promoting social and religious harmony, and endorsing true Catholic conduct within the faith communities.

Scalabrini's First Followers in North America

Bishop Scalabrini died in 1905 at the age of 65. At the end of his life he envisioned a long-term strategy on the pastoral care of migrants.[19] Only after several decades did his dream become a reality when Paul VI created the Pontifical Commission for the Pastoral Care of Migrants and Itinerant People in 1970.

Migrants' urgent needs compelled Scalabrini to gather priests and brothers from many dioceses and congregations and send them to the American continent. He told his priests journeying to the Americas: "Go, the Angel of the United States is beckoning you and presenting you with 500,000 abandoned Italians. Go, the Angels of Paraná, Peru, Argentina, Colombia and other provinces are calling you to their 1,300,000 Italians thirsting for truth."[20] Certainly the first Scalabrinian missionaries were not as well equipped as the German priests accompanying their compatriots, or the Italian priests that the Bishop of Cremona (Italy), Geremia Bonomelli, chose for the care of Italian immigrants in Europe. The latter groups of priests were usually very open minded, splendidly prepared on the intellectual level, often sent abroad by the bishop to avoid the danger of being accused of modernism—they were adhering to the tenets of social Catholicism—which would be sternly and pitilessly fought by Pius X and his entourage.

The first Scalabrinians were not well accepted by the hierarchy, nor as well organized as the German clergy. Certainly they were not particularly liked by the dominant Irish clerical elements who considered Italian Catholics turncoats because of their unwillingness to defend the Papal States. They had to minister to Italian immigrants accused of not attending church regularly; but when they did, sometimes they found Irish policemen barring them from entering the main church, sending them to the basement instead. Italian immigrants were apparently unwilling or unable to contribute to the support of the priest and parish structures. Therefore Scalabrinians assisting these people were judged to be poor administrators, while a sound administration for U.S. bishops was a clear sign of divine benevolence. Scalabrinians were even considered spies of the Vatican: "Some American priests consider the Saint Charles Missionaries in New York as spies of the Holy See and as an active part of the Apostolic Delegation."[21] During that time the so-called spy system seemed a rather common practice in church circles. But these priests had met Bishop Scalabrini and had been inspired by his love for migrants. They possessed a true missionary zeal. Their capacity to adapt to the American way of life was quite remarkable. Hence, it happened that "while Bishop Scalabrini had begun with the vision of itinerant missionaries, he had come to accept that parishes provided his missionaries with a foundation that set them free to determine the type of pastoral care the Italians ought to receive,"[22] so much so that in the 1930s and 1940s some Scalabrinian pastors turned into strong competitors of their ancient Irish American rivals.

At a time when U.S. nativism and assimilation methods were espoused by many people within the church, the national parish system was considered a necessary instrument in order to balance the search for control and power over the faithful, typical of a certain North American Catholicism. Through the national parish, Italian immigrants would be able to discover and strengthen their identity in order to start a journey of communion with other ethnic groups within the local church. The result would be the construction of a veritable U.S. Catholicism on an equal basis.

If national parishes in the United States played a significant role in the development of U.S. Catholicism, this was not because of the great interest bishops and clergy showed in their regard. The persistence of an "immigrant Catholicism," as J. P. Dolan calls it,[23] was mainly due to priests caring for migrants, who withstood pressure for assimilation—considered too often the only plausible pastoral solution—and fought bravely against those pastors who regarded migrants simply as potential prey in what looked like a religious safari hunt.

Having been imbued with a providential outlook on migration, the first Scalabrinian missionaries invested in long-term pastoral care, while many

North American bishops and priests thought or hoped Italian migration would be something temporary. It took some time for the missionaries to settle down and establish themselves, as the religious institute was entrusted with Italian national parishes in the U.S. As all migrants, they had learned the art of survival.

However, the passage from solving emergency situations to normalcy constituted a real danger for the Scalabrinian charism. The process of settling down and caring for Italians, and descendants of Italian immigrants, often meant becoming and acting like all the other pastors, and entering the arena of competition. Normalization carried with it the danger of fostering a ghetto mentality. This was not the fault of the parochial system per se: it was a clear sign of a profound crisis of the congregation and it called for a refounding effort. The Scalabrinians had become unable to use the parish as a springboard for living in a creative way and for spreading their charism. The neglect of the founder's vision had turned them into "generic" priests and brothers. They were running the risk of becoming good ethnic museum curators and preservationists, and not seamen venturing into uncharted waters. They had not yet learned the art of balancing the urgency to reach the frontiers where they could meet and care for the suffering migrant humanity, and the need to run permanent dwellings where one could practice hospitality, begin a new life, cultivate the memory of the exodus in order to help other migrants, and experience fellowship.

What is really unique in this time, that is the 1930s, is the fact that the rebirth of the congregation was financially supported by Scalabrinian missionaries of the United States, and later it was mainly from North and Latin American seminarians that a new vision and role within the church, and a deeper understanding of the charism of the institute, came about. Some of the fundamental moments of this rebirth include: (1) The reintroduction of the religious, vows which took place in the Mother House of Piacenza in 1934, giving new missionary and spiritual vitality to the younger members of the congregation. (2) The "aggiornamento" of the Constitutions of the Scalabrinian Congregation, which began with the special General Chapter in 1969–1972 and was ratified with the official approval of the new Constitutions in 1981. These new Constitutions, inspired by the spirit of Vatican II, extended the missionary outreach of the congregation to all migrants, and not only to Italian migrants and their descendants, and affirmed "the preferential option for those migrants who are more acutely living the drama of migration."[24] (3) The opening in 1987 of Casa del Migrante in Tijuana, right at the border between Mexico and the U.S., which began a new way of doing ministry with the migrants for the Scalabrinians in North America, a dynamic and holistic ministry performed in close collaboration with the laity and the NGOs. Until then these missionaries had been working almost exclusively in national and territorial parishes. This pastoral presence at some of the most trafficked and controversial border lines in our planet (U.S.-Mexico and Mexico-Guatemala) confirms the option of the Scalabrinians for most vulnerable migrants in their journey toward the U.S.

A Tradition in the Pastoral Care of Migrants: A Work in Progress

What are the guidelines that the Scalabrinian community has developed over time and proposes to others Christian ministers so that immigrants may be loved and served as true brothers and sisters? We have not yet systematically and thoroughly analyzed our documents and accomplishments. Historical essays on Scalabrinian ministry vary considerably. Mary Brown's excellent analysis of Scalabrinians in North America is quite different from the research carried out by Brazilian historians on the same topic.[25] A difficulty may derive from the fact that many pastoral experts, upholding a technocratic approach to ministry, limit their investigation exclusively to the analysis of pastoral models, which may vary from church to church, and from one migrant group to another.

Scalabrinians' main concern is no longer directed at pastoral structures and techniques. Pluralism in this field is part of our ministry and constitutes our first experiment in diversity. We may tackle emergency situations, we may staff multilingual parishes, we may cater to a single migrant group, we may work in study centers or in the field of medias, or we may coordinate activities for migrants at a diocesan, national, or international level.

We believe that the church, "pilgrim" and "missionary by her very nature,"[26] cannot become fixed in its modes. The temptation of a monocultural approach is ever present. We are part of the pilgrim church and go among the men and women of today's multicultural societies, announcing to them the mystery of communion. The Trinitarian dialogue becomes for us the model for all relationships. Rather than recommending pastoral exterior arrangements that are tied to particular circumstances and to the equitable demands of migrants, we prefer searching for ecclesiological principles to be adopted by those who wish to take up the challenge of an original pastoral approach to immigration. Migration in fact questions the true nature of the church. That is why during the past decades Scalabrinians, besides venturing into new modes of serving migrants, have been trying to highlight some ecclesiological and biblical traits that are meaningful to our specific ministry. Besides furthering the economic, the political, and the sociological study of the phenomenon, we have urged theologians, church historians, experts in spirituality, and biblical scholars to shed light on the phenomenon of human mobility in order to enlighten our journey in hope.[27]

Scalabrini's vision, together with the newer biblical and theological insights that accompany our pastoral journey, have led us to consider the virtues of welcoming, of itinerancy, and of communion in diversity as basic to our ministry. When we welcome other people, we share in the Father's loving project. Welcoming means first of all spreading appreciation for migrants. Thus, we contribute to God's plan to make of the earth a place of fellowship and gratuitousness, anticipating the banquet of the Kingdom, where no one is excluded and all are called by name by our gracious God.

Ministering to migrants requires us to become itinerant in order to reveal in our lives Jesus's paschal mystery of death and resurrection. We emigrate from ourselves, from our own mentality, and from our self-interest, and go out to meet the other. Dying to ourselves brings about the resurrection of the other. Our pilgrimage from ourselves to the migrants entails breaking with them the bread of our lives as baptized and consecrated persons, humbly washing their feet, pouring precious nard on the unexpected guests, pausing to look after our fellow pilgrims wounded or hurt in their dignity, caring for them with the tenderness and commitment of Jesus, the good Samaritan.

Often feeling powerless when confronted with persons and institutions that seek to eliminate differences and impose uniformity, we turn to the creator Spirit of Pentecost. In spite of our temptation to give up, the Spirit of God invites us to move constantly from communion to diversity and from diversity to communion.

Elements of a Scalabrinian Missionary Spirituality

Our ministry and presence within the church has brought about some results on a theoretical as well as on a practical level. Our ministry is not parallel to but is an integral part of the local church's ministry. Within the local church, migrants have the same rights as everybody else because "in the Church no one is a stranger, and the Church is not foreign to anyone, anywhere."[28] From a religious as well as from a cultural point of view migrants are not biodegradable. One of the first fruits of the Scalabrinian tradition is in fact the appreciation of diversity through personal, ecclesial, and social relations. As individuals and as community, we invite those we meet to walk with us in that spirit of communion which overcomes all temptations to uniformity and has the power to transform the affirmation of one's own identity into a celebration of diversity perceived as a gift.

We are meant to be ministers of communion, building bridges between migrants and local churches. Inspired by Scalabrini, we work with migrants for the growth of a church that must express fully the notes of catholicity and communion, where differences are not left at the door nor forced into uniformity. Our ministry aims at educating fellow Christians to welcome and not to refuse or merely tolerate migrants. In spite of their dramatic existence, which is often the result of injustice and exclusion, migrants are the hidden and providential builders of universal brotherhood and sisterhood. Their presence becomes for the church prophecy and sacrament of catholicity, reminding it of its universal vocation. We are asked to be the sentries of a new dawn, waiting together with migrants for new heavens and a new earth (Rv 21:1).

Quite a few church people do not consider migration as a problem any longer, but as a providential opportunity for both church and society. They emphasize that ministry to migrants is an essential part of the church's pastoral care and not a response to an emergency, or a passing whim. Religious ministry to migrants does not simply mean offering them linguistic assistance for their liturgical celebrations. It requires a long educational process in which migrants are taught to interpret their history through the eyes of faith and accept the responsibility of their new mission in life. In the past we were speaking of a mission of the church to migrants. Today we insist on the mission of migrants within the church.

A theological vision of the care of migrants is much more relevant than a technical service. Migrants are not numbers to be used for power games but a revelation of the good news. What in the beginning was solely a control issue has now become a theological concern. The effort to assimilate migrants has given way to an intercultural approach, which demands that the care of migrants, in order to be a true ministry, be specific, specialized, exemplary, and catholic in its outcome.

While the political issue is ever present (the fear of a "de-Americanization" of the U.S. through the influx of newer immigrants is apparent even today[29]), the church has become aware of its "new" image, from a theological as well as from a sociological point of view. In the past she worked for migrants, or with them; today she defines herself as a "pilgrim," a "migrant" church.

The history of the Scalabrinian congregation is a history of loss and recovery, of death and resurrection, of diversity and communion: a typical migrant history. We consider the discrepancy between the ideals handed to us and the daily reality we face as a laboratory in which it is possible to grow together. Every step toward communion, motivated by trust in the Father's promise, becomes prophecy and anticipation of the kingdom.

God's behavior has taught us to be patient with ourselves, with migrants, and with local Catholic communities. During our pilgrimage we have felt the necessity to seek companions, people who share our vision and our hopes. With them and by the grace of God we can journey toward the future:

> Some day . . . all nations will have in this land numerous rich, happy, moral, and God-fearing descendants who, while retaining the characteristics of their respective nationalities, will be closely united. This land of blessings will give rise to inspirations, develop principles, unfurl new mysterious forces that will regenerate and revitalize the Old World, teaching it the true economy of liberty, brotherhood, and equality, showing it that, though politically and religiously united, people of different

origins can very well keep their own language and nationality, without the barriers that divide people and make them envious, without armed forces to dominate and destroy one another. . . . Yes, this is my hope! For while the world is dazzled by its progress, while man exults in his conquests over matter and lords it over nature, disemboweling the earth, yoking the lightning, cutting isthmuses to mingle the waters of the oceans, eliminating distances; while nations fall and rise and renew themselves; while races mingle, spread, and fuse; above the roar of our machines, above all this feverish activity, over and beyond all these gigantic achievements and not without them, a much vaster, nobler, and more sublime work is developing: the union in God through Jesus Christ of all people of good will.[30]

This was Scalabrini's dream. This is also our dream. Our task is not yet finished. We are not people of the past, but together with many other persons working with migrants we are the forerunners of the future. And this is a great challenge and a great responsibility.

NOTES

1. *Traditio Scalabriniana,* no. 1, available at http://www.scalabrini.org/Traditio_Scalabriniana/traditio_inglese.htm (last accessed April 2007).

2. Ibid.

3. Ibid.

4. Bishop John Baptist Scalabrini, *A Living Voice: Excerpts from His Writing,* trans. Gino Dalpiaz (Oak Park, IL: Missionaries of St. Charles-Scalabrinians, 1987), 157.

5. Ibid., 377.

6. Furio Colombo, "Un vescovo tra gli immigrati: Un precursore della moderna sociologia," *La Repubblica,* October 14, 1997.

7. Scalabrini, *A Living Voice,* 382–83.

8. Pope John XXIII, *Pacem In Terris,* no. 25, available at the Vatican web site, http://www.vatican.va.

9. Scalabrini, *A Living Voice,* 379–80.

10. Ibid., 380.

11. Ibid., 380–81.

12. Karl Marx, *Das Kapital,* is available at http://www.marxists.org/archive/marx/works/cw/index.htm (last accessed April 2007).

13. Scalabrini, *A Living Voice,* 390.

14. Quoted in Mario Francesconi, *Giovanni Battista Scalabrini Vescovo di Piacenza e degli Emigrati* (Roma: Città Nuova Editrice, 1985), 971n18.

15. Scalabrini, *A Living Voice,* 377.

16. Ibid., 394–95.

17. Pope Leo XIII, *Fin dal Principio,* no. 3, available at the Vatican website, http://www.vatican.va.

18. This incident is reported in Francesconi, *Giovanni Battista Scalabrini,* 1161.

19. See especially the "Memorial of Bishop G. B. Scalabrini on a Commission for Catholic Migrants" written in Piacenza on May 4, 1905. This document is found in Silvano M. Tomasi, ed., *For the Love of Immigrants: Migration Writings and Letters of Bishop John Baptist Scalabrini, 1839–1905* (New York: Center For Migration Studies, 2000), 218–30.

20. Scalabrini, *A Living Voice,* 456.

21. Mary Elizabeth Brown, *The Scalabrinians in North America, 1887–1934* (New York: Center for Migration Studies, 1996), 82.

22. Ibid., 49–50.

23. Jay P. Dolan, *The American Catholic Experience: A History from Colonial Times to the Present* (Notre Dame, IN: University of Notre Dame Press, 1992).

24. Congregation of the Missionaries of St. Charles (Scalabrinians), *Rules of Life* (Rome, 1999) n. 5.

25. Brown, *Scalabrinians.*

26. *Ad Gentes,* no. 2, available at the Vatican web site, http://www.vatican.va.

27. For an analysis of the theological and philosophical essays on migration published recently see C. Lubos and G. G. Tassello, "Scienze teologiche e mobilità umana: Excursus bibliografico (1980–1997)," *Studi Emigrazione* 34, no. 128 (1997): 578–734; G. G. Tassello, L. Deponti, and C. Lubos, "Filosofia e teologia in contesto migratorio: Un aggiornamento bibliografico," *Studi Emigrazione* 38, no. 143 (2001): 655–739.

28. John Paul II, "Message for World Migration Day, 1995–1996," no. 5, available at the Vatican web site, http://www.vatican.va.

29. This view has been recently championed in Samuel P. Huntington, *Who Are We? The Challenges to America's National Identity* (New York: Simon and Schuster, 2004).

30. Scalabrini, *A Living Voice,* 391–92.

CHAPTER NINE

The Ninety-Nine Sheep and the Mission of the Church

The Pastoral Care of Hispanic Immigrants

PATRICK MURPHY

For the last couple of years I have been working in the heartland of the United States as the animator of Hispanic Ministry for the Archdiocese of Kansas City in Kansas. Consequently, I have had many opportunities to reflect and plan new and challenging ways of trying to help the archdiocese provide adequate pastoral care for the increasing number of Latinos who continue to arrive in our region on a daily basis. In fact, this ministry has challenged me to reflect more creatively and concretely on how our church can provide a more complete and cohesive plan for the pastoral care of Hispanic migrants. Out of this context of ministerial experience and thoughtful reflection, I would like to share some suggestions regarding the pastoral care of Hispanic migrants.

My reflections on this theme can be divided into three sections. First, I would like to prepare the way with a few introductory comments on this topic, which I believe will demonstrate the urgency for concrete and specific action. Secondly, I will outline a few key challenges that confront us as a church in providing more comprehensive pastoral care for Hispanic migrants. Thirdly, I will offer some final thoughts on a model of ministry that I am currently implementing in an effort to reach out to Spanish-speaking migrants of Kansas City. Through these reflections, I hope to provide some food for thought in what must certainly be seen as a critical ongoing conversation that involves the very future of our church in the United States.

The Re-emergence of the Immigrant Church

A familiar parable from the Gospel of Luke (15:1–7) provides us with an excellent place to begin our reflection. The story of the good shepherd, in particular, demonstrates God's sense of duty and care for every single sheep, by leaving behind in the wilderness the ninety-nine, so that he may go in search of the lost one until he finds it. Indeed it is a very noble and loving gesture that points towards God's absolute care for all his lost sheep. However, it seems to me that when it comes to the lost sheep of the Hispanic community here in the United States, we might think of the pastoral challenge of reflecting on this parable in reverse. As a church, when it comes to the Catholic Hispanic migrants in the United States, we often seem so content to have *one sheep* in the fold that we often fail to notice the *ninety-nine* that have escaped our pastoral care. Consequently, the critical question remains for us: "are we willing to make the pastoral effort and missionary commitment to leave behind the one sheep and go in search of the ninety-nine who have escaped our care?" It seems clear to me that our window of opportunity is closing quickly, and that as a church we need to make a concerted effort to provide for a more intense pastoral care for all the lost sheep of the Catholic Hispanic community.

There is no doubt that every immigrant group that has ever landed on the shores of our country has presented to the church a unique set of challenges and opportunities. *Extension Magazine* (July 2005) in an article entitled "Hispanic Catholics in the U.S.: Surprises, Challenges and Blessings," summarized this very issue with the following words: "The struggle of U.S. dioceses today to serve the burgeoning Hispanic population repeats the story of America as a land of opportunity. How that story plays out depends largely on whether the Church can marshal sufficient personnel and resources to serve them adequately—and whether their fellow Catholics fully embrace their presence as equal members of the Body of Christ."

I contend that the current reemergence of the immigrant church in the presence of new immigrants offers us a unique set of challenges for the Catholic Church in the United States:

1. The vast majority of new immigrants that are arriving are Hispanic, Catholic, and young.
2. The Catholic Hispanic immigrant of today, unlike many immigrant groups of yesterday, is by and large not bringing their own clergy to care for their pastoral needs. Although some Hispanic clergy are arriving, their numbers are insufficient to offer adequate pastoral care.
3. The majority of Hispanic immigrants coming to our shores are not separated by an immense ocean, and so the ties and even the dreams to go back home remain quite strong.
4. The large number of undocumented Hispanic immigrants, as well as the number of families living in a situation of a mixed status (some members legal and some illegal within the same household), has never been seen before, and the numbers continue to rise on a daily basis.
5. The lingering challenge of living in a post-9/11 era, which makes all immigrants suspected of terrorist activities, cannot be underestimated when it comes to creating welcoming churches.
6. The youthfulness of the Hispanic community presents the church with abundant hope, as well as a call to provide a creative outreach.
7. Finally the large numbers of Hispanic Catholics who arrive in our neighborhoods on a daily basis offer us the possibility to revitalize and transform our churches almost overnight.

I remain more convinced than ever before that we are not living in a post-immigration church, but rather that on a daily basis we are once again becoming more and more an immigrant church.[1] Consequently, depending on how we handle the pastoral care of Hispanic migrants, our churches will be either overflowing with joyful noise or they will fast become empty echo chambers. In a real sense the pastoral care of Hispanic migrants is a life or death issue for our church, which calls for immediate attention and drastic action. The number of Hispanics that have recently arrived and continue to arrive every day, in spite of the best efforts to control the borders, challenges our church to cross other borders and be more creative in our pastoral care of migrants.

At the same time, we cannot afford to talk ourselves into a false sense of security and simply think that the new Hispanic immigrants have the same needs or concerns of the Mexican Americans who have been here awhile. Their names may be similar and their chili spicy hot but the pastoral reality of the new Hispanic immigrants is an entirely different story that calls for a unique response from the church. The Hispanics who are arriving here have been deeply marked by their immigration experience, clearly suggesting they will need specific and intentional pastoral care. Obviously the journey of any immigrant can be long and lonely, but the migrants of today so often arrive beaten and broken physically, emotionally, and spiritually that they present us with an unprecedented pastoral challenge. The special ministry of accompaniment is something that only a church community can provide when it says *Bienvenido* (welcome) in words, actions, and spirit. In essence the church must provide a place where the Hispanic immigrant can feel safe at home in his or her new country, convinced that someone cares for them and is willing to accompany them as they continue their pilgrim journey in their new environment. This happens best when a parish community makes a deliberate decision and option to open wide the doors of their churches as well as the doors of their hearts.

In addressing the importance of this issue, the bishops of the United States have set the tone and have offered us much to reflect on in terms of the pastoral care of immigrants.[2] In the document "Encuentro and Mission," the U.S. bishops have provided us with a treasure chest of theologically sound reflections on the pastoral care of Hispanic migrants.[3] However, this theological treasure is too often buried by those called to put this pastoral plan into action. While we have many wonderfully written documents, the biggest challenge remains how to implement them in the daily life of our multicultural church. In one sense we have come a long way, but in another sense we cannot be content with having in our possession some wonderfully written documents. We cannot afford to pretend that the journey is over with the publication of a series of good intentions, but rather we need to push forward for the implementation of this body of church teaching on the local level in all of our parishes.

All the signs seem to indicate that we are presently entering a critical phase in terms of providing pastoral care for Hispanic migrants. The challenge is this: the number of newly arrived Spanish-speaking migrants is indeed startling and increasing as never before.[4] The most conservative statistics seem to indicate that at least 39 percent of all United States Catholics are Hispanic. To put it bluntly, the future of the church is Hispanic. This is true not only in the big cities but throughout the country. Hispanics continue to arrive in large numbers and settle in places they never dreamed of going before. This trend is likely to continue into the foreseeable future.[5] Consequently, pastoral care for the Hispanic community is urgent. It also provides us with a unique opportunity to show concern for the lost sheep of our Catholic Church and to create pastoral planning that corresponds with this great need.

At the very heart of this process, pastoral planning has an intrinsic missionary dimension. First and foremost, we are being called to evaluate our previous pastoral responses and approaches, so that we may provide some new alternatives for the care of Hispanic migrants. In this process, we might let go of some of the traditional ways of doing things and seek more creative alternatives to effectively reach out to the lost sheep that continue to migrate towards our local churches on a daily basis. Oscar Andrés Cardinal Rodríguez from Tegucigalpa, Honduras, summed up the current challenge with these words: "when our people migrate to the United States, they migrate with their faith, and unfortunately at times they keep migrating to other churches."[6]

A greater percentage of Hispanic Catholics are leaving the church than ever before. Andrew Greeley notes that in the 1970s, 77 percent of Hispanics were Catholic.[7] However by the mid-1980s, that number dropped to 71 percent, and by the middle of the 1990s the number dropped to 67 percent.[8] Greeley estimates that one-fifth of those who were raised Catholics have left the church.[9] Allan Deck also observes that, even though many Hispanics have cultural roots that lie deep at the heart of Catholicism, they are migrating elsewhere.[10]

The landscape that is being painted by a serious reflection on these numbers clearly indicates that Hispanic ministry must have a very distinctive tone. We simply cannot continue to do things the way we are accustomed to doing them or else we will lose the unique evangelization opportunity being presented to us. At the core of all this must be the subtle but significant idea that our ministry is not just *to the Hispanic immigrant* but must also be *with the Hispanic immigrant*. It must be about accompanying these people of

God on their immigrant journey and meeting them where they are, rather than where we wish them to be. The ultimate goal of being in ministry with the immigrant is that eventually they will be strengthened in the process and able to assume the pastoral accompaniment of their brothers and sisters on the migration journey.

Consequently those involved in Hispanic ministry must always be actively encouraging Hispanic immigrants to take ownership of their faith lives and in a sense give them official permission to be who they are called to be as disciples of the Lord. At the same time we can never underestimate the lingering effects of culture shock, which often happens on many levels (language, food, customs, religious traditions), and so we need to always remember that the Church can play a very significant role in providing immigrants with a safe space and place to be themselves and to grow in their faith. The distinctiveness of the ministry of accompanying the migrant as he or she continues the journey in the new land plays itself out in several areas of pastoral concern that are worth delineating.

Language: Providing basic services, sacraments, and liturgies in the Spanish language is indispensably foundational to the ministry. A Catholic community should not have to fight a battle to have a Mass celebrated in Spanish!

Religious Education: The challenge of both immigrant children and teens caught between two cultures must never be overlooked. If the faith is to be caught and not simply taught, we must be willing to stretch ourselves and our pastoral systems to fit the newcomers. Consequently when in doubt we should pass on the faith in the language of love, which is the language spoken to one from the moment of birth.

Adult Faith Formation: We are being called to adapt our ways of sharing the faith with adults and meeting the migrant where he or she is. We must make every effort to tailor specific faith formation programs to the reality of the immigrants we serve, or we will risk not having a sufficient number of people to do the ministry of accompaniment.

Religious Traditions: For a great many of the Hispanic immigrants arriving in our country the Catholic faith has been maintained and nourished by key religious traditions and customs passed on from generation to generation by their ancestors. Those in active ministry with the community need to reverence the sacredness of these traditions and seek to create ways for them to be shared and passed on to the next generation.

Youth and Young Adults: This ministry is a challenge at all times but even more so for immigrant youth who feel they belong neither here nor there. The large number of Hispanic youth residing in the U.S. urgently call us to practice radical hospitality in terms of welcoming them in our churches.

Being Catholic and Hispanic: The sense and way of being Catholic is very unique for the Hispanic immigrant. Many come from places where there has traditionally been a lack of clergy, and so the idea of going to Sunday mass was not always a possibility. Likewise the concepts of registering in a parish and using the Sunday envelopes remain totally unfamiliar concepts. However, the vast majority arriving feel that they are Catholic to the bone, and so we need a great deal of pastoral sensitivity in order not to rip the spiritual heart out of the Hispanic community simply in order to be liturgically or pastorally correct.

Forming a New People of God: The challenge inherent in what Fr. Virgilio Elizondo often refers to as *mestisaje* is the beautiful intermingling of cultures that calls all those involved in ministry to Hispanics to enter into a process of transformation. This pilgrimage will enable the movement from an attitude of them versus us to the formation of a completely new us. This creative process of *mestisaje* is always ongoing and developing and cannot be boxed in or limited, and at its best it is about the creation of a new people of God. The new Hispanic pilgrim is changed by the journey of immigration, as are those who accompany the immigrant on the journey. In this scenario the concept of being companions on a journey is much more than a song to be sung because it has the unlimited potential to form us into a new people of God.

Active Advocacy for Immigrants: The huge number of undocumented immigrants attending our parishes calls us as a church to be a voice for those who have no voice. We cannot allow advocacy on behalf of immigrants to become the hobby of a precious few, but rather it must be a constituent part of the gospel we preach and teach. To advocate on behalf of defenseless and voiceless immigrants is, in a real sense, to be pro-life because it is about protecting the life of a very vulnerable group of people. Obviously this pastoral position will create some pastoral tensions in our communities, but it was Jesus himself who advocated for immigrants so clearly when he said, "I was a stranger and you welcomed me" (Mt 25:35). The undocumented Hispanic immigrant presents the Catholic community with a unique challenge that demands creative pastoral approaches.

Five Key Challenges for the Pastoral Care of Hispanic Migrants

In light of these concerns let us reflect on five of the key challenges confronting us as we seek to provide for the pastoral care of Hispanic migrants.

The Challenge to Provide Hospitality that Is Both Real and Welcoming to Our Migrant Brothers and Sisters

In the year 2000 as we gathered to celebrate the jubilee, we often heard the very beautiful call *to open wide the doors.* This refrain was subject to a variety of interpretations on many different and important levels, but part of the implication of this jubilee deals with the pastoral care of migrants. More than simply a catchy jubilee motto, the theme of "opening wide the doors" has many implications for the Hispanic community. Yet opening these doors is a decision for mission, not only to benefit the migrants but the entire church.[11]

At the very minimum an open church is a church without borders. In my experience over the years it has become increasingly clear to me that the biggest borders that need to be crossed are not the borders of countries but the borders of our own hearts. In this context, the hospitality we must embody needs to go beyond mere lip service and become as real and as welcoming as possible. By breaking down the barriers and opening all the doors of our local churches, newcomers can make our church into something new. The pastoral care of migrants means providing spaces and places for people to feel welcome and to practice their Catholic faith. While Hispanics need a worship space for the celebration of the Mass and sacraments in their language, this pastoral gesture is only the tip of the hospitality iceberg. Opening wide the doors of our churches means going beneath the surface and providing spaces and places for migrants to pray and meet, to play and eat, and basically find a new home for the practice of their Catholic faith. Practicing true Catholic hospitality means making a real effort to accept the other as other without sacrificing their traditions and customs.

Opening wide the doors opens up the possibility of meeting Christ in the migrant, and hopefully in the process these same migrants will reveal a new face of Christ to others. In the end, true hospitality is accepting and welcoming the migrant and even allowing ourselves to be changed in the process.[12] The challenge of creating authentic hospitality must involve the pastoral practice of both physically opening wide the doors of our local churches, as well as prying open the gates of our individual hearts.

The Challenge to Provide a Missionary Outreach in the Pastoral Care of Migrants

In thinking about the parable of the Good Shepherd in reverse, it seems to me that we have a lot of pastoral work to do if we are to take seriously the missionary call to actively search for the ninety-nine lost sheep. Some say the second biggest religious denomination in the United States, after Roman Catholics, is the so-called "unchurched." Many of these are nonpracticing Roman Catholics, and many of these nonpracticing Catholics are Hispanics. While some complain and lament about those who have left the Catholic Church to attend other denominations, at least they are going somewhere to practice their faith. However, many Hispanic Catholics are not practicing any faith because no one has invited them to come back home. The pastoral implications of this challenge are enormous.

This challenge calls us to be more creative in our pastoral approaches and not be content with the hope that the Hispanic community will automatically feel at home just because they have a *Misa en Español* (Mass in Spanish) on Sunday afternoons at 2:00. In a real sense the increasing presence of the Hispanic community in the United States constantly calls us as a Church to literally move from the pews to the shoes. In particular, I would suggest we are being called to move and work in two rather distinct pastoral dimensions.

First, we are urgently called to actively evangelize in the Hispanic community. At this moment in our history, the Church must make a missionary option for the Hispanic migrant. This means viewing the Hispanic community with missionary eyes and ears and doing pastoral planning with this focus in mind. The U.S. Bishops' document "Encuentro and Mission" is an excellent beginning, but what is most needed now is a way to put this document into action in all the local churches. There is an urgent need to re-implement the document on evangelization "Go and Make Disciples" and see how this can be applied to a more active process of evangelization in the Hispanic community.[13]

In concrete terms I think our evangelization efforts among Hispanics should have a dual focus: Spanish radio and personal outreach. One of the key places the Church can reach Hispanics is through the radio. Spanish radio ministry is one of the easiest and most convenient ways to reach thousands of Spanish-speaking Catholics and to let them know that their church is alive and ready to welcome them into the local parishes. However, with few exceptions, the radio has been a greatly underused ministry in the Catholic Church, and other religious traditions have done a better job utilizing it as a tool for mission and outreach.

A second means to focus our evangelization efforts is what I would call the ministry of door-to-door visitation. This is an essential missionary option in our pastoral approach to the Hispanic community. An active door-to-door evangelization ministry is a concrete way of moving from the pews to the shoes. Over one hundred years ago Blessed John Baptist Scalabrini in a similar vein exhorted his priests to "leave their sacristies and care for the immigrants."[14] I believe Bishop Scalabrini's advice is still valid for us today when it comes to the pastoral care of Hispanic migrants. We must be willing to take the good news to the streets and go beyond the self-imposed boundaries of our sacristies and church offices. This means not simply waiting for immigrants to come to the church but calling the church to go out to the immigrants.

The second pastoral dimension of providing outreach to migration is the call for a more serious training and formation of pastoral agents.[15] As a church we are at a point where we must prepare people seriously to minister to the Hispanic community. We can no longer afford for this ministry to be treated like a hobby for a few dedicated priests, religious, and lay people. The missionary option for the Hispanic community needs to be treated seriously and everyone needs to take an active part of that mission. I would suggest that there are three concrete steps that are critical to the future of this missionary option.

First, every diocese in the United States is directly touched by the presence of the Hispanic community. To meet the ever growing needs of these Hispanics, more priests are needed, but priests alone are only one part of this mission. Active cultivation of lay vocations is also urgently needed so that Hispanics are not only passive recipients of the missionary activity of the Church but active participants in it.

Second, for those who are ordained, I would also suggest that priests who are the most fluent in Spanish be freed from all administrative duties associated with being a pastor so that they are free to do pastoral ministry among the many migrants who speak only Spanish. At this juncture I do not think we can afford to wait for more Spanish-speaking priests to arrive from elsewhere to offer pastoral care for the people who are part of our local diocesan communities. Each local church needs to assume responsibility for the pastoral care of its own people and act accordingly to make sure their faith needs are being met.

Third, I think we need to actively invest money and resources in the serious formation of lay people for ministry. Let us be humble and honest enough to admit that we will never have enough priests and religious prepared to keep up with the pastoral needs of the Hispanic community. Consequently it is quite obvious that we are being challenged to prepare lay people for this important ministry of preserving the faith of the Hispanic community.

The Challenge to Be More Aware of the Hispanic
Reality that Surrounds Us

One of the great challenges for many communities is simply understanding the reality of the Hispanic presence. Many Catholics, including many good intentioned pastors, do not realize how many Hispanics are living in their parish boundaries. Becoming aware of the increasing presence of the Hispanic community can make the transition to a multicultural world easier, although such transition is inevitably messy and difficult at times. However, denying this reality will make matters even more frustrating in the long run and create many new and unresolved tensions. In practical terms, a pro-active stance towards the pastoral care of Hispanic migrants should include two important attitudes.

Becoming aware of our surroundings is the first crucial step, and one we cannot take for granted. I have heard many times: "Of course we do not have any Hispanics in our parish because I never see them in Church." Hispanics are everywhere, including all the Marts (that is the Wal-Marts and the K Marts, etc.) and all you have to do is see who is shopping there, but this implies leaving our comfort zones and ordinary places of activity to recognize the newcomers in our community. They are also present in great numbers in the local public schools and obviously provide opportunities for new students in our Catholic schools. In other words the presence of these Hispanics is a sign of the times, but it is also an invitation to a greater pastoral commitment.[16]

The concrete presence of the new migrants in local neighborhoods represents the second step: the opportunity for the receiving community to truly practice hospitality. This immigrant presence, however, will already make some people quite nervous about the changing neighborhood and even more upset about the possibility of offering even a minimal pastoral response. The arrival of newcomers to the neighborhood and the possibility of opening wide the doors of the churches could be viewed as a major threat. Actively working to prepare people for the arrival of newcomers into the local church community, however, is a part of the process. While there is no perfect moment to begin this preparation nor a perfect process, such preparation is vital.

In my experience, one very nonthreatening approach is what I call the ministry of food and piñatas, which is a way of gathering people together into community. Through such activities, adults and children can begin to break down the barriers of language and culture in a nonthreatening manner. Another activity to help prepare people for this kind of pastoral transition is to gather a few leaders for informal roundtable discussions that would focus on sharing what they have in common in view of building a future together, rather than accentuating the differences. Common activities such as these, or a common cause, can do wonders to unite the community in spite of its many cultural differences, but this is a task that must be worked in an intentional sort of way.

The Challenge to Develop More Realistic Pastoral Responses for Migrants

The world of reality TV claims to bring us into the depths of the real world of real people in an effort to show us how they tick under the stresses of their real lives. No one can argue that reality TV presents reality in its totality, but hopefully this basic concept of searching for reality could serve as an inspiration for all of us as we reflect on providing pastoral care for migrants. For the church, getting in touch with this reality means a commitment to getting in touch with the Hispanic presence. The church is being challenged as never before to offer a more comprehensive pastoral response to the Hispanic reality of our time. What seems clear about reality is this: Hispanics are here to stay. We need to believe in the reality that has been promulgated to us by our bishops time and time again, namely, that *the Hispanic community is a blessing for our Church*.[17] We can no longer romantically fantasize that Hispanics are the Church of yesterday or tomorrow because the clear reality is they are the Church of today.

While many feel threatened by this emerging Hispanic presence, my own experience has proven over and over again that the presence of new immigrants renews the life of our parishes and brings new hope to our neighborhoods. However, this only becomes a reality when we are open to accepting the newcomer and work at creatively providing them with adequate pastoral care. In the end we can only develop more realistic pastoral responses if we are in tune with the reality of the Hispanic migrant in our local communities.

The Challenge of the Youth in the Hispanic Community

The biggest and most serious challenge of the Hispanic community depends on how the church responds to its younger members. Hispanic youth, by virtue of their numbers, demand immediate and serious pastoral attention. In a research study published in 2003 entitled *Welcoming Hispanic Youth/Jóvenes in Catholic Parishes and Dioceses,* Ken Johnson-Mondragón notes that Hispanics account for more than 45 percent of all Catholics under the age of 30.[18] Accordingly, Hispanic youth are no longer an option but rather an urgent and absolute priority. Reaching out to them requires resources, personnel, and formation opportunities, as well as a sense of hospitality that truly welcomes them to be an active part of their Church. The great work being done by the Institute of Faith and Life in their efforts to provide pastoral care for the youth is one important model, but there are other possibilities as well. Regardless of the model, what is most needed are the pastoral tools, as well as the professional expertise, to help all of us confront the great challenge of Hispanic youth in our church.[19]

A Test Case for Pastoral Care of Migrants:
St. Mary/St. Anthony Church, Kansas City

I wish to conclude by sharing some of the initial results of a test case of the type of pastoral ministry that we have tried to implement in the Archdiocese of Kansas City. But first I need to start with a story that has become a metaphor for what ministry to Hispanic immigrants is all about.

The story of Fr. Matt, the pastor of St. Mary/St. Anthony Church in Kansas City, Kansas, gives me great hope that in the future we can continue to provide better pastoral care for migrants, when as a church we make the commitment to cross the borders of our hearts and authentically reach out to the other. Fr. Matt, who has been instrumental in opening the doors of St. Mary/St. Anthony, is in his mid-70s and recently took us all by surprise when he announced that he wanted to study Spanish. Of course we all agreed that was indeed a wonderful symbolic gesture on his part. However, this gesture became a source of inspiration for all of us when we heard that during the course of his classes he has mentioned at least three times why he wanted to study Spanish: "I have to learn the Spanish language because 80 percent of my parishioners are now from the Hispanic community." Of course whether he learns the language or not is totally immaterial because what counts most is that Fr. Matt has crossed over the border of his heart in a spirit of welcoming hospitality. Now if a priest in his mid-70s can cross over such borders when it comes to working with the Hispanic community, then I believe this should be a source of encouragement for all of us. This is the good news that needs to be shared as a moment of inspiring hope that should move our Church to continue to work at offering better pastoral care for Hispanic migrants

The welcoming attitude of Fr. Matt is what encouraged us in January 2004 to begin to make plans to start a Spanish Mass in the parish of St. Mary/St. Anthony, a downtown parish. The parish constituency was primarily made up of an elderly population of second- and third-generation German and Irish immigrants. In working with this close-knit group of people, it became obvious that they had a deep love for their parish, but at the same time they also acknowledged the reality that the neighborhood was changing and becoming more and more Hispanic. In a sense the time was ripe for a missionary outreach and to open wide the doors of the parish.

It was with this in mind that, together with the archdiocesan vicar general, I met with the pastor and the parish council and presented to them the possibility of starting up a weekly Sunday Spanish Mass as a way of reaching out to their neighbors and giving new life to the parish family. The atmosphere of the parish council meeting was somewhat cordial but at the same time a bit tense as they presented me with a long list of questions. In this process we soon found out that one of the most important foundations for this type of work was creating an atmosphere of hospitality where all felt at ease and truly welcomed.

We started a Sunday Mass in Spanish on the first Sunday of Lent 2004 at 11:00 am, which took the place of one of the English Masses. There were some initial negative reactions from a few people, but by and large there was acceptance of this new missionary outreach as it was seen as a sure way of continuing to give life to the parish. At the first Mass there were about 250 people in attendance, but within ten months a weekly crowd of over 400 people gathered to worship, and after fifteen months more than 600 people attended the Sunday liturgy.

At the core of our pastoral plan has been a commitment to the implementation of the *Pastoral de Conjunto,* which we have come to call "Shared Leadership." We currently have in place a mission team of twelve people who have worked closely in developing our pastoral plan and missionary outreach. I have offered them ongoing formation, supervision, and support, as well as encouraging them to take advantage of any other formation opportunities offered in our area. They have responded with enthusiastic zeal and a deep sense of missionary commitment. It has been great to see them come alive and share both their gifts and their faith with this newly formed community. One of the positive signs that we have witnessed is that in the course of this missionary outreach new leaders have come to the surface and are making use of their talents to serve the community. Our ongoing effort to be a parish that practices authentic hospitality and is committed to promoting a sense of shared leadership has led to the rapid development of this faith community. There is no doubt that this immigrant community in a very short time has felt at home in this new safe place where they live out their Catholic faith as members of St. Mary/St. Anthony parish.

Consequently, in collaboration with a missionary team of volunteers, and with no budget to speak of, during the course of the first year at our new parish we have been able to implement the following ministries: lectors, eucharistic ministers, altar servers, a choir, a program of family catechesis, confirmation classes, monthly baptism preparation, a door-to-door evangelization team, the Disciples In Mission Lenten Program, a faith formation program, a social committee, and Youth and Young Adult Communities (the latter based on the small community model proposed by Institute of Faith and Life). In addition we have been able to secure a valuable meeting place, as well as some significant office space. We have regular office hours where the needs of the community can be addressed three evenings each week. I would say that the parish has gone out of its way to provide us with a sincere and genuine welcome, and so the people have responded with a deep sense of feeling at home in their new parish. Of course what makes all this so unique is that none of these pastoral structures existed before the Hispanic community arrived. In a sense the parish was a bit stagnant. These newly arrived immigrants have been active agents in this effort at missionary outreach, and that in turn has given the parish a new lease on life.

A key moment in this transition process came at the annual St. Mary/ St. Anthony June Fest in 2004. This is a traditional and important fundraising event in the life of the parish. On the occasion of this celebration a great effort was made to invite the Hispanic community to attend and work at the June Fest. The people came out in great numbers and not only participated, but also donated food, prizes, and entertainment, and became involved in both the set-up and clean-up for this big parish event. It was a very simple but profound moment in the faith life of these two cultural communities coming together and working as one parish family. In fact I would dare to say that at the parish June Fest of 2004 a lot of old barriers were torn down and new bridges were built that will go a long way towards the continued growth and development of this faith community.

The experience at St. Mary/St. Anthony has been a good one because a conscious effort was made to work at offering a pastoral response to the five key challenges presented by the Hispanic community to the local church. That is to say we have provided authentic hospitality to newcomers, we have organized a specific missionary outreach, we have tried to be aware of the Hispanic reality around us, we have strived to develop realistic pastoral approaches, and we have made ministry to youth a pastoral priority.

I would say we have made an intentional effort to do things differently in providing pastoral care for the newcomers, and so far the initial results have been fantastic. Perhaps it is a bit too early in the process to draw any final conclusions, but at this point I feel very optimistic about the future of this faith community. In fact I would venture to say that what we are learning from our experience at St. Mary/St. Anthony could very easily become a model for doing a missionary outreach that provides an authentic pastoral care for Hispanic migrants in many other areas of the Archdiocese.

In summary I would simply suggest that any authentic ministry to Hispanic immigrants will have three key moments:

1. *Acceptance:* The actual giving to Hispanic immigrants a space and place to be at home is a key moment in their pilgrimage and obviously the most logical place for this to happen is at the local parish.
2. *Accompaniment:* The act of walking with immigrants on their journey towards a new homeland where they will seek out a new Christian identity can be a reassuring way of helping them to keep the faith.
3. *Assertiveness:* In the course of the journey we need to begin to encourage the immigrants to be fully alive in their faith so that they can transition from being passive sheep to active shepherds in the community.

In conclusion I really believe that the future of the Church in our country depends on how we welcome and activate the potential of Hispanic immigrants. Time is of the essence, and in a sense we are running against the clock to take advantage of this window of pastoral opportunity. Consequently, I suggest that we need to be preparing Hispanic immigrants on several levels to be active participants in this missionary activity.

1. We need to prepare people to minister to themselves so they can become active agents of their own evangelization in their new country.
2. We need to prepare people to minister to fellow Hispanic immigrants who might be reluctant to commit themselves to be active members of their faith community.
3. We need to be preparing Hispanic immigrants to minister to the Church at large. We cannot be content in allowing this new people of God to stay in their barrios, but rather we should encourage them to keep on migrating and using their gifts, talents, and unique faith expressions to transform the world and activate the kingdom of God in new and wonderful ways.

NOTES

1. The "post-immigrant" and "newly immigrant" church typology has been proposed by J. Bryan Hehir, "With No Vision, People Perish," in *All Come Bearing Gifts,* Proceedings of the National Migration Conference 2003 (Washington, DC: United States Conference of Catholic Bishops, 2003), 21.

2. See for example "Welcoming the Stranger Among Us: Unity in Diversity" (2000) and "Strangers No Longer: Together on the Journey of Hope" (2003), the latter a joint document on migration issued together with the Mexican Conference of Catholic Bishops. Both documents can be downloaded at www.usccb .org/mrs/pastoralstatements.shtml (last accessed April 2007).

3. This document, both in English and Spanish, can be downloaded at www .usccb.org/hispanicaffairs/encuentromission.shtml (last accessed April 2007).

4. The statistics of the 2000 census showed that Hispanics represent already the largest minority in the U.S. (more than 35 million). The major source of the rapid growth of the Latino population in the U.S. is, without any doubt, sustained migration. See Alejandro Portes, "The New Latin Nation: Immigration and the Hispanic Population of the United States," (working paper 04-02, The Center for Migration and Development, Princeton University, February 2004 available at http://cmd.princeton.edu/papers/wp0402.pdf, last accessed April 2007).

5. Immigration scholars have been pointing out for some years now the movement of Mexican immigrants away from traditional destinations, like Texas and California, toward nontraditional destinations like Georgia and North Carolina. See Douglas S. Massey, Jorge Durand, and Nolan J. Malone, *Beyond Smoke and Mirrors: Mexican Immigration in an Era of Economic Integration* (New York: Russell Sage Foundation, 2002), 126–28.

6. This quote comes from Cardinal Rodríguez's concluding remarks at the "Migration and Theology" conference at the University of Notre Dame, September 22, 2004.

7. Andrew M. Greeley, "A Defection Among Hispanics," *America,* July 30, 1988, 61.

8. Andrew M. Greeley, "A Defection Among Hispanics," (updated) in *America,* September 27, 1997, 12–13.

9. Ibid., 13.

10. Andrew M. Greeley, "A Defection Among Hispanics," (1988), 61–62; J. Juan Diaz Vilar, "The Success of the Sects among the Hispanics in the United States," *America,* February 25, 1989, 174–75, 181; Allan Figueroa Deck, "Proselytism and Hispanic Catholics: How Long Can We Cry Wolf?" *America,* December 10, 1988, 485–90; Allan Figueroa Deck, "A Latino Practical Theology: Mapping the Road Ahead," *Theological Studies* 65, no. 2 (2004): 291–92.

11. Recently theologians have become more attentive to hospitality as an integral element of our Christian tradition. See for instance Christine D. Pohl, *Making Room: Recovering Hospitality as a Christian Tradition* (Grand Rapids, MI: W. B. Eerdmans, 1999).

12. Henri J. M. Nouwen, *Reaching Out: The Three Movements of the Spiritual Life* (New York: Doubleday, 1975), 71. Nouwen points out that, "Hospitality is not to change people, but to offer them a space where change can take place."

13. This document was originally published in 1992. A special tenth anniversary edition has been issued in 2002. It can be downloaded at www.usccb.org/evangelization/goandmake/eng.shtml

14. John Baptist Scalabrini (1839–1905) was bishop of Piacenza (Italy). He has been a pioneer in the ministry among immigrants within the Roman Catholic Church. For this purpose he founded in 1887 a religious congregation, the Missionaries of St. Charles Borromeo (Scalabrinians); in 1892 a lay association, the St. Raphael's Society for the Protection of the Emigrants; and in 1895 a second religious congregation, the Missionary Sisters of St. Charles. His writings on migration have been edited and translated into English in Silvano Tomasi, ed., *For the Love of Immigrants: Migration Writings and Letters of Bishop John Baptist Scalabrini, 1839–1905* (New York: Center for Migration Studies, 2000). For further information on Scalabrini and the Scalabrinians, see Giovanni Graziano Tasello, "For the Love of Migrants: The Scalabrinian Tradition," this volume.

15. Some of these issues are touched on in the bishops' "Welcoming the Stranger Among Us."

16. Vatican II's document *Gaudium et Spes,* 4, affirms it clearly: "At all times the Church carries the responsibility of reading the signs of the time and of interpreting them in the light of the Gospel, if it is to carry out its task."

17. "Encuentro and Mission," 6.

18. For more information see the website of the Institute for Faith & Life, www.feyvida.org (last accessed April 2007).

19. For a challenging and insightful reflection on the issue of Hispanic youth, see Gary-Riebe Estrella, "A Youthful Community: Theological and Ministerial Challenges," *Theological Studies* 65, no. 2 (2004): 298–316.

CHAPTER TEN

The Story of Humane Borders

ROBIN HOOVER

Since 1993, when new U.S. border policies were enacted, thousands of immigrants have died in the deserts of the Southwestern United States. This is a profound social, economic, and political problem that has many theological ramifications. Humane Borders was created as a faith-based response to this problem of migrant deaths. It is appropriate to examine Humane Borders in light of structural injustices that have contributed to these deaths, and in consideration of current border strategy's function and dysfunction along the U.S.-Mexico border. Simply stated, the goal of Humane Borders is to take death out of the immigration equation. Immigration reform presents daunting challenges and complex factors that make it difficult to create a more humane border control strategy. The contribution of and controversy over our efforts gives us much room to reflect on the sociopolitical contours of our work.

The Current U.S. Border Strategy and Immigration Policies

United States Border Patrol officials devised a strategy to deter economic migrants from crossing the U.S.-Mexico border in 1993. Beginning in El Paso, Texas, and later replicated in areas like San Diego, Nogales, Laredo, and other urban areas along the border, Congress began implementing this strategy by doubling the number of Border Patrol agents stationed along the southwest border. In doing so, political leaders wanted to push migrants away from major urban areas and out into the desert where Border Patrol agents could more easily apprehend them.

By design, a "prevention through deterrence" strategy was meant to dissuade migrants from coming across the U.S.-Mexico border, and help federal agents gain better control of the borders.[1] While such was the intention, this strategy has failed miserably. Instead of controlling the flow of undocumented immigrants, it has merely redirected them into more dangerous territory.[2] The rise in the number of desert deaths has been most notable in southern Arizona, where migrants have to walk as many as fifty miles in temperatures that can reach 120 degrees in the summer time.

Since 1993, on average more than one migrant a day has died crossing the U.S.-Mexico border. Many deaths go unaccounted for, and some estimate that the actual number of deaths in any one year may be as high as five hundred to six hundred. Using a conservative daily death rate of 1.25 persons, more than five thousand migrants have died since these policies began. Though only an estimate, this number is not an exaggeration. These conclusions are not inflated figures of border activists or those of a few scholars pointing to unsubstantiated data. The U.S. General Accounting Office has studied the pattern of militarization of the border for more than a decade and has reached the same conclusions.[3] Even when the precise figures differ, border activists and government officials all agree the number of people dying is significant. As a result, the large, expensive deployment of personnel, technologies, and ill-conceived strategies have not controlled the border and have succeeded only in escalating the number of migrant deaths.[4]

The human costs of this border policy require a more adequate analysis than can be generated by mere political expediency and economic efficiency. Beneath the rhetoric are serious structural flaws in a system that dehumanizes and degrades, and results in the death of thousands. Regardless of the good intentions behind these strategies and the values they are meant to protect, border policies and border law enforcement efforts that lead to migrant dehydration in the deserts, freezing in the mountains, or confinement in train-box cars must be changed. Humane border policies, in the end, should be evaluated not only in terms of economic, social, and political costs, but above all in terms of human costs.

The Birth and Development of Humane Borders

The Humane Borders organization was founded June 11, 2000, when a very clear mission statement was written.

> Humane Borders, motivated by faith, will work to create a just and humane border environment. Members will respond with humanitarian assistance to those who are risking their lives and safety crossing the United States border with Mexico. We encourage the creation of public policies toward a humane, non-militarized border with legalized work opportunities for migrants in the U.S. and legitimate economic opportunities in migrants' countries of origin. We welcome all persons of good faith.

Based in Tucson, Arizona, it is a compassionate response to the intense human suffering and deaths that migrants experience along the U.S.-Mexican border. In addition to providing humanitarian aid, Humane Borders challenges unjust and inhumane U.S. border policies that contribute to these deaths. A humane and moral strategy counters an inhumane border policy.

Hundreds of volunteers carrying out the mission of Humane Borders save lives by the simple action of placing water in the desert for migrants who would otherwise die without it. The administration of Humane Borders, however, is complex. The mission is carried out by a network of organizations and volunteers who deploy and maintain water stations in remote, strategic desert areas on both sides of the border where most migrants travel and where, unfortunately, most migrants die. While there are many different aspects of Humane Borders, looking at the core strategy, core philosophy, and our core membership captures the essence of the organization.

The Core Strategy of Humane Borders. The concept of Humane Borders began in the spring of 2000 when the Border Patrol reported forty-four deaths in the Tucson sector. During the spring of that year, an eighteen-year-old mother named Yolanda Gonzales Garcia died in the desert after giving her last drop of water to her infant child, who survived. In response to the tragedy of unnecessary human deaths, a group of pastors and activists gathered at the Pima Friends House in Tucson, Arizona, to formulate a concerted response. At this meeting were Rev. Robin Hoover, Ph.D.; Rev. Phil Anderson, a Lutheran pastor/activist from Washington, DC; Rick Chase of BorderLinks; the Rev. John Fife of Southside Presbyterian Church; David Perkins of Pima Friends Meeting; Amy Schubitz and Marianna Neil of the Center for Prevention and Resolution of Violence; Sister Elizabeth Ohmann; and others. On Pentecost Sunday, June 11, 2000, the group of approximately eighty-five people focused upon two questions: (1) how can we respond with compassion to the migrants who are risking their lives crossing the deserts along the U.S.-Mexico border? and (2) how can we work to change the U.S. immigration policies that place these persons at risk in the desert?

During the discussion, the group formulated eight points which became the core of the Humane Borders platform:

(1) Place water in the desert to prevent dehydration deaths.
(2) Challenge the current border policy.
(3) Assemble a faith-based organization.
(4) Structurally become an organization of organizations interested in the mission.
(5) Work binationally and as cooperatively as possible.
(6) Develop a logo, which became the big dipper and the North Star.[5]
(7) Create a steering committee.
(8) Utilize the media to tell the story of the plight of the migrant.

Writing the mission statement, the early organization of the corporation, and the coordination of volunteers were all focused on reducing the number of deaths at the border and changing the U.S. policies that were designed to force migrants into dangerous desert environments.

Our Core Philosophy. Although organized as faith-based, Humane Borders does not require nor expect volunteers to represent any particular faith or religion, and all are welcomed. The biblical phrase "what you do to the least of our brothers and sisters" guides many participants in their volunteer efforts. From a social point of view, concern for the most vulnerable of our society motivates action. From the political perspective creating a more just community becomes a driving force. And in ethical terms, valuing and fostering life dictates conservation of human lives. Regardless of people's starting point, as an organization Humane Borders examines not only what kind of world we live in but what kind of world we want it to become.

With this philosophy in mind, volunteers carry out the mission in deeds. Growing from the deployment of the first two water stations in March 2001, to eighty-seven in 2005, Humane Borders has dispensed water on both sides of the border. In five years volunteers have dispensed more than 100,000 gallons of water, driven more than 225,000 miles and have made more than 2,600 trips to the desert, including some trips which are more than 300 miles in length. The contribution of approximately 40,000 hours of volunteer time per year carries out the mission to save lives with a simple drink of water.

Our Core Membership. More than 10,000 volunteers have made trips to the desert to service water stations while donating thousands of hours delivering water and even more hours building and preparing equipment, plus staffing educational and fundraising events. This effort requires substantial coordination and significant resources in terms of equipment, trucks, insurance, fuel, tanks, stands, and other essential support. Our volunteers receive special training. Vehicles carry supplies for water stations and are stocked with food packs, first aid, satellite telephones, Global Positioning System (GPS) devices, maps, tools, and other resources for the volunteer crews and for the migrants. People from around the state, country, and world join us in this mission, and five interns have each given a year of work to Humane Borders.

Efforts to reduce migrant deaths have drawn the attention of all interested persons, groups, authorities, and jurisdictions to engage in conversations designed to change the politics of migration. The story of Humane Borders has been exceptionally magnetic and effective at engaging local, regional, national, and international media in telling the story of the plight of the migrant to people in places away from the border. Over 1,500 print articles and over 150 video news articles concerning the water station efforts have been archived in the Humane Borders office. As a result of publicity, engagement in various kinds of advocacy followed, including conversations with national politicians in immigration reform and legislative proposals.

The Sociopolitical Contours of Humane Borders

Although the work of Humane Borders is faith-based, it has political consequences. The contribution and the controversy of this life-saving mission gives room to reflect on its sociopolitical contours. In observing volunteers' activities over time, a theoretical model for social change emerges in the interactions between Humane Borders' volunteers, various migration stakeholders, public administrators, and elected officials. While efforts appear as a simple mission, it is helpful to distinguish some of the social, theological, political, and media dimensions of our work in order to understand better this relationship of migration to theology.

Social Dimensions. While Humane Borders begins its mission statement with the words, "Motivated by faith," the primary interest is not doctrinal but behavioral. The focus is upon the migrant, not theology. Theology is the source of motivation for many, but theologies traditionally divide organizations. Humane Borders unites people around a common mission. Nonetheless, it can be recognized that theology has the potential to shape and influence public policy and help create a more just and humane community.[6]

The social theory is geared more towards collaboration than division. Even when volunteers have held up their arms in protest, pointed to death in the desert, and declared that what is happening in the desert is immoral, no one has been excluded from the discourse. Hearing has been given to legitimate arguments, including those of the Border Patrol, federal land managers, health care providers, elected officials, and others. Humane Borders has chosen to speak with all interested parties in a nonadversarial way.

As might be expected, saving lives of migrants brings conflict with other people who do not share similar views, and who voice hostility to our actions or create obstacles to the mission. To cite but one example, sometimes permission has been denied to put water stations on public lands because some see acts of humanitarian aid as obstructing the law or aiding those who break it.

Theological Dimensions. Humane Borders draws deeply upon traditional, biblical models for organizing its work. Theology shapes much of what people do and how they live. Even in media interactions, spokespersons are forthright in stating that actions stem from moral judgments based upon religious convictions. Those actions are demonstrated when moments of silence are offered to remember migrants who have died or when memorial worship services include crosses that bear the names of the dead. In the Annual Memorial and March for Migrants each September, crosses with deceased migrant names parade through Tucson's public streets in protest of inhumane border policies.

Part of our organization is inspired by the priestly, kingly, and prophetic traditions of biblical Christian and Jewish faiths. While there are many scriptural passages that have direct bearing on the mission, one of the key narratives is that of the Good Samaritan parable in Luke's Gospel (Lk 10:25–37). This story highlights the prophetic ideal in challenging all people to see the common, human ties each person shares with his or her neighbor. It highlights the kingly ideal in calling all people to be ruled by love and compassion, which manifests itself in caring for the injured person found on the side of the road. It highlights the priestly function of inviting all people to engage in actions that build community, which includes binding up the wounds of the injured. For us, this priestly, kingly, and prophetic ministry manifests itself not only in individual acts of charity but in a collective effort of outreach aimed at assisting those who are most vulnerable in our society, which means assisting migrants in the desert.

Although Humane Borders has worked hard to establish its own theological coordinates, social theology and social theory have also greatly influenced the work. While many other faith-based groups have been active in migrant outreach programs, one of the unusual aspects of Humane Borders is that it provides a unique nexus between the secular organizations and the religious communities along the border, as well as between the social activists and government representatives.[7]

Political Dimensions. Migration is a complex issue with a wide variety of political perspectives. Amidst an often fiery debate both for and against immigration, Humane Borders situates itself in the middle of the U.S. immigration reform discourse.[8] Praise, endorsement, and support has been received from multiple sources: (1) many major newspaper editorial boards from Los Angeles to Boston, (2) individual donors in 37 states plus Canada, England, and Mexico, (3) churches in several denominations, (4) elected officials on both sides of the aisle in Congress, and (5) governmental agencies including the Department of the Interior, Pima County Health Department, and City of Tucson Water. While the support far exceeds the criticism, the list of detractors looks very similar to the support list and includes: (1) a few print media editorial boards, (2) individuals with opposing viewpoints expressing them through media interviews and letters or email to the Humane Borders office, (3) some religious extremists, and (4) a few elected officials on both sides of the aisle. The Border Patrol has both praised us publicly for saving the lives of thirty-three migrants who were rescued alive because they took water from a Humane Borders water station, and criticized us publicly because a drug mule could carry more marijuana and less water by knowing how to walk from water station to water station.

While the primary concern focuses upon the well-being of migrants, there are also questions of ecology and justice. While complexity is acknowledged in the immigration debate, including multi-faceted economic interests, theological viewpoints add an important and often neglected dimension to the analysis and response to migration today.

By focusing upon the deaths of the migrants, Humane Borders has concentrated its efforts on direct aid for migrants and policy changes. In bringing the problem of migrant death to the forefront of the immigration debate, Humane Borders has tried to identify the deeper, underlying problems that cause these deaths. More than simply treating the symptoms of a broken border policy, it is imperative to identify, analyze, and ultimately change unjust and inhumane social structures.

Media Dimensions. Humane Borders has received national and international attention. More than 1,500 articles have been published referencing or portraying the work of Humane Borders. Between the founding of the organization in 2000 and the end of 2005, news articles were printed or reproduced in multiple languages around the world, including Russian, Mandarin Chinese, French, Italian, Japanese, and more. Stories have been done on Humane Borders in Pakistan, Pacific Rim countries, European countries, and in the Spanish-speaking world. Humane Borders has archived more than 150 video clips ranging from a few seconds of local news to hour-long network features, some of which have been shown internationally. Several documentary film makers have included the work of Humane Borders in their stories. In January 2006, *Crossing Arizona,* a documentary by Joseph Matthew and Daniel DeVivio, featuring a Humane Borders volunteer, was one of the top entries in the Sundance Film Festival in Park City, Utah.

Each year, journalists, activists, administrators, and academics produce an enormous body of raw data, analysis, and commentary about migration through the border lands. The work of Humane Borders and the need for it precipitated by US border policy using the desert as a form of deterrence, causing migrants to have to march down death trails in the desert where some pay the price of an illegal border crossing with their lives, is an issue that generates great passion among these journalists, broadcasters, and others. Through contact with the press, we tell the story of the border in places away from the border, engender public discourse, and thereby convey information that shapes the way people think about the issue, and ultimately influence legislation.

The Challenge of Immigration Reform

The complex and polemical debate over immigration raises many challenging questions, and most everyone agrees that serious immigration reform is necessary. How this reform is to be accomplished, and which direction it will take, is still a matter of serious controversy. There are many interwoven policies that, when combined, have deleterious effects on people and lands, and comprise border issues. These include policies for immigration, trade, law enforcement, labor, environment, drugs, health care, education, and national security. Considering all the challenges of reform, creating solutions that are possible, logical, and practical has been overwhelming. Space does not permit examination of the multiple complexities that need to be studied here. Two often overlooked challenges are the stresses imposed upon the fragile desert environment and the local infrastructure of many communities.

The Environmental Challenges. The U.S.-Mexico border spans a stretch of approximately two thousand miles from the shores of San Diego, California, to the shores of Brownsville, Texas. Within Arizona where the highest migrant traffic occurs, the US federal government owns approximately 85 percent of all of the land. The rest of Arizona's land is urban, Arizona state trust lands, designated Indian Nations, or private rural. The trust lands produce income for state public education, predominantly from livestock grazing leases. Because of Arizona's land surface management distribution, when migrants cross the border into Arizona, they are usually crossing public land for part of their journey.

Approximately seventy-five miles of the border between Arizona and Sonora, Mexico, is shared by the Tohono O'odham Indian Reservation, a dependent, sovereign nation roughly the size of Connecticut. It is unique in that part of their tribal land is located in Mexico and part in the United States. This raises many challenging issues in regard to national sovereignty, civil law, and humanitarian assistance.

Undocumented immigration has taken a huge toll on the Tohono O'odham Nation. Because the area is sparsely populated and has very few roads to assist Border Patrol or tribal law enforcement officials, many migrants journey through this land on their way into the United States. During peak migration time, as many as 1500 to 1800 migrants are crossing the border daily into the Tohono O'odham property.

The problems associated with the flow of migration impact Tohono O'odham residents and ranchers, as well as all land owners and managers along the border and as far as one hundred miles north of the border into the state. Some become outraged at the environmental impact of migrant traffic: fences are cut, water systems drained or disturbed, and migrant trash litters huge, expansive areas. The trash includes every conceivable kind of garbage one would find at a picnic site, every article of clothing that can be imagined, as well as Bibles, hymnals, family photos, love letters, employment records, educational documents, medicines, bicycles, cell phones, and more. The remnants of migration in the desert affect not only the natural environment but also endanger livestock. In addition to the millions of dollars being spent by various agencies to clean up the trash, Humane Borders' volunteers contribute many hours to removing trash from the desert every month. Several environmental groups active in southern Arizona are working with Humane Borders and share the vision of immigration reform as the avenue to saving the desert and the desert's vegetation and wildlife.

The Local Infrastructure Challenges. The movement of hundreds of thousands of undocumented migrants through the borderlands each year poses great challenges to the infrastructures of local communities, particularly in areas of health and education. County governments in Southern Arizona spend tens of millions of dollars to help migrants rehydrate, dialyze, and rehabilitate from their dangerous trek across the desert. These funds are not reimbursed by the federal government. Any kind of comprehensive border reform would have to include some systematic reimbursements for such services. To the many educational and health care delivery needs, exceedingly high demands are placed upon services that respond to emergencies, including ambulance companies, rural tax-based fire departments, law enforcement, and others. The abundance of nonreimbursed, federally mandated expenditures threatens the viability of many of these organizations.

Law enforcement jurisdictions in southern Arizona report they are ill-prepared to deal with the demands of increased migrant traffic. They report insufficient training, equipment, and personnel in responding to the desperate, complex needs that migrants pose to them. In 2005, some Arizona legislators proposed legislation preventing undocumented immigrants from receiving any state services. While this response might have some pragmatic benefits, it raises much more serious ethical issues. Much of the social teaching of Christian churches would assert that the moral viability of any community is intimately tied to how it treats its most vulnerable members.

Because of budget constraints, elected officials face complex dilemmas in responding to the influx of migrants. Humane Borders builds bridges with local civic agencies. Pima County Government ratified contracts with Humane Borders to erect and maintain water stations in the county. County leaders provided financial resources as a cost-effective measure to keep dehydrating persons out of the hospitals and morgues. When each medical examiner's report costs the county $1500, and over two hundred dehydrated migrant bodies must be handled in a year's time, it makes fiscal sense to provide a drink of water.

The tensions along the border are exacerbated by various groups who seek to take the problems of border control into their own hands. Notable examples in southern Arizona include Ranch Rescue, Civil Homeland Defense, the American Border Patrol, and Minutemen. Though well-intended, they create problems not only for the migrants but also the law enforcement officials. They frequently set off motion detectors belonging to the Border Patrol, which compounds the efforts at organized enforcement.

Amidst the environmental and infrastructure challenges, there are many questions about human rights and sovereign rights, civil law and divine law, charity and justice. Humane Borders poses questions on the border of Mexico and the United States and equally important questions on the edge of human suffering, human responsibility, and civic order. In every discussion of border issues, the value of human life must be brought to the forefront and not relegated to the background.

Towards a More Humane Border

In light of the complex challenges, many proposals for immigration reform have been put forward by legislators, advocacy groups, and executive branch personnel, including the president of the United States. Generally, the proposals focus on economic interests or upon human and labor rights questions. Earlier worker programs, most notably the Bracero program, were abusive. All parties agree that abuses of the previous systems will have to be avoided in comprehensive reform proposals before Congress.

Humane Borders holds several proposals for immigration reform. As a matter of justice, the first priority is to extend legal status to those who are living in the United States of America without basic legal recognition or protection. While the particulars may vary, reform must include certain nonnegotiable rights: (1) to travel back and forth across borders using public transportation, (2) to organize and be organized, and (3) to have family protection. Otherwise, undocumented migrants in the United States are reduced to slaves who are constantly living in the shadows of American society.

The second proposal is to provide legal work opportunities for those who wish to work in the U.S. The organized work opportunities for up to 750,000 persons a year should be made available to foreign nationals who are not participating in other programs. Visas should go directly to the migrants to seek employment in the U.S. economy at will. This would allow for migrants to organize, have their families follow them, and be able to move from employer to employer at will, avoiding exploitative working conditions. With this framework, migrants have the right to enjoy Labor Department protections and judicial relief, and generally have the pleasure and benefit of living among the citizenry without prejudice.

Finally, cooperative work between nations engenders economic development in the migrants' countries of origin. In point of fact, most migrants leave their home countries not because they want to, but because they have to. And the reasons they leave are intimately tied to the socioeconomic forces of globalization, which greatly impact many of the communities from which these migrants come. Unless the causes of immigration are addressed, migrants will continue to seek opportunities where there are employers hiring workers. Simply putting more law enforcement officials on a border will not, in the end, curtail the human drive migrants have to look for more dignified lives outside their impoverished economies.

While there are many more complexities and dimensions woven into migration issues that merit further examination, Humane Borders responds to the problem with a clear mission to lower the number of deaths in the desert by giving a drink of water, and working toward immigration reform by telling the story of the border. As the mission continues it involves engagement of public leaders, activists, and various stakeholders in the immigration policy discourse.

As with the very first gathering on June 11, 2000, all persons of good faith are invited to join the life-saving work. For information visit www .humaneborders.org.

NOTES

1. Doris Meissner, *Border Patrol Strategic Plan 1994 and Beyond* (United States Department of Justice: United States Border Patrol, 1994).

2. Border control is a relatively recent phenomenon in this area. In Arizona, indigenous populations, Spaniards, Mestizos, Texians, and early U.S. citizen populations have crossed the area with almost no restriction for centuries, and the U.S. Border Patrol is a relative newcomer to this area, as it was not formed until 1924. Now it is part of the Department of Homeland Security, and it is known as the Bureau of Customs and Border Protection (CBP).

3. United States General Accounting Office, *Illegal Immigration: Southwest Border Strategy Results Inconclusive; More Evaluation Needed* (Report to the Committee on the Judiciary, U.S. Senate and the Committee on the Judiciary, House of Representatives, 1997), GAO/GGD-98-21. *Illegal Immigration: Status of Southwest Border Strategy Implementation* (Report to Congressional Committees, 1999), GAO/GGD-99-44. *INS Southwest Border Strategy: Resource and Impact Issues Remain after Seven Years* (Report to Congressional Committees, 2001), GAO-01-842.

4. Karl Eschbach, Jaqueline Hagan, and Nestor Rodriquez, *Causes and Trends in Migrant Deaths Along the U.S.-Mexico Border, 1985–1998* (Houston, TX: University of Houston, Center for Immigration Research, 2001).

4>4>4>4>4>4>4>4>4>4>4>4>

5. The "drinking gourd," reminiscent of the U.S. antislavery movement of the 1800s, shows water being poured.

6. Robert Lane Hoover, "Social Theology and Religiously Affiliated Nonprofits in Migration Policy" (PhD dissertation, Texas Tech University, 1998).

7. Hoover, *Social Theology*.

8. Humane Borders utilizes some of the communicative democratic theory of Jurgen Habermas as adapted by Fox and Miller; see Charles J. Fox and Hugh T. Miller, *Postmodern Public Administration: Toward Discourse,* rev. ed. (Thousand Oaks, CA: Sharpe Reference, 2006). One must learn the arguments in a policy area, fully prepare for the public conversations, allow for discursive redemption, and push for substantive policy decision making. Until the literature and dynamics of the public policy area of interest to a group is mastered along with an understanding of public administration (the world of the influential players), the new organization should expect limited results.

PART THREE

The Politics of Sovereign Rights, Cultural Rights, and Human Rights

CHAPTER ELEVEN

Migration and Human Dignity

From Policies of Exclusion to Policies Based on Human Rights

GRAZIANO BATTISTELLA

Usually migration is handled from the perspective of interest: more from the interest of states, employers, recruiters and travel agents, banks and money changers, real estate brokers, and the receiving community, and less from the perspective of the interest of migrants. If migration is approached only from the interest perspective, it will be difficult to manage it properly because of competing interests. A more common ground must be sought, and that is found in the human rights approach.

The human rights approach is necessary also to overcome the inadequacies of the politicoeconomic approach. Inevitably, in the politicoeconomic approach, migrants are reduced to labor providers. Other than their role as workers in the labor market, migrants are otherwise viewed as a burden for the welfare system, as strangers and potential criminals in the local community, and lately as possible terrorists. This framework has to be countered with one that begins from the human dimension, which establishes a common responsibility toward others regardless of their ethnicity or nationality. Such responsibility is grounded on the notion of common belonging to the human family—from which originates responsibility for the common good—and on the sacredness of human dignity, from which human rights derive. However, even the human rights discourse presents weaknesses, which do not simply derive from the inadequate recognition and application of human rights instruments, but also from unresolved flaws. A more solid ethical basis should be established for migration policies.

In this paper I will first highlight the exclusionary dimension inherent in migration policies responding to a pure politicoeconomic agenda. I will then present the contribution that a human rights–based platform can make to migration policies and explore also some of its weaknesses. Finally, I will discuss the ethical basis for migration policies, especially an ethics based on Christian principles which leads to inclusionary migration policies.

Policies of Exclusion

Migration policies, a set of measures that states adopt to manage the inflow—but in some major countries of origin also the outflow—of migrants, are not the shiniest examples of successful public policies. These policies often are not crafted to properly manage a very complex issue such as migration but to gain political mileage in response to political pressure. They tend to respond to short-term aspects of the problem and are limited in addressing the long-term impact. Concerned mostly with the control of migrant flows, they do not sufficiently deal with integration. Finally, although migration is an inherently multilateral issue, migration policies are established exclusively by each national state. With such shortcomings, it is no wonder that migration policies reveal in general an exclusionary approach to migration. This notion is somehow paradoxical, as policies are crafted precisely to admit migrants, and therefore to include them in the country of destination. However, the result is often civic stratification, in other words, apportioning different rights to different categories of migrants.[1]

Economic exclusion. Apart from those few countries that consider themselves as countries of settlement and do not place restrictions on the economic activities of immigrants, most labor-receiving countries have admission policies restricting the insertion of migrants in the labor market. Often the result is a segmented labor market, with migrants constantly confined to economic activities rejected by nationals. Furthermore, the tendency to escape economic seclusion produces normally a growth of the informal economy and unregulated involvement in different jobs. Irregularities in the migration system are also dependent on migration and labor policies. To avoid the possibility for migrants to grow in their job, acquire skills, and improve their economic insertion, receiving countries often limit the duration of contracts. Exclusion also takes the form of violation of labor rights toward hired migrants. For instance, it is estimated that fifty percent of Indonesian domestic workers in Hong Kong are only paid half of the stipulated HK$3,270 minimum wage.[2] Reports about migrants not being paid their wages are common, such as the case of the four hundred construction workers who were not paid for five months in Singapore.[3]

Social exclusion. Migrants have been suspected of entering another country simply to exploit its better welfare system. For this reason, various countries, such as the U.S., have passed legislation to limit access of migrants to social benefits.[4] The issue has received further attention in the U.S. after an analysis of the high concentration of migrants in just a few states was correlated to the social benefits provisions of those states.[5] In countries with a labor migration system, social exclusion is even more pronounced as migrants often lack health insurance, and lodging is provided in substandard housing. Temporary contracts are designed to avoid the accumulation of social security and pension benefits.

Cultural exclusion. After a season in which assimilation was displaced and various nations formally or informally adopted a multicultural program (Australia, Canada, Sweden, the Netherlands), scholars are noticing a return to assimilation in various countries, and multiculturalism seems now to be on the retreat.[6] Although globalization facilitates the simultaneous belongings of migrants to various cultural communities, in fact the negotiation of culture and identity remains an ongoing struggle. Increased communication possibilities might even damage the potentials for intercultural dialogue, as migrants could settle for the ghetto of virtual space.

Political exclusion. By definition migrants do not belong to the political community of the receiving country. Often they cannot exercise their political rights, since many countries of origin do not provide for absentee voting. They contribute to the economy and society of the country in which they work as well as of the countries of origin, where their remittances constitute a sizeable portion of the gross national product (GNP), but they cannot have a say on how such societies should evolve. Some countries are increasingly recognizing these anomalies and extending migrants the right to participate in administrative elections. A movement is spreading to facilitate the incorporation of more migrants, and concepts such as "residence" citizenship are gaining ground. But in other contexts the opposition remains strong.

Policies of exclusion, based on maximizing the interest of all except the migrants, tend to get as much as possible out of migrants while giving them the barest minimum. Such policies reveal shortsightedness and are bound to fail. Keeping the developmental divide among nations at the present level and even increasing it is a sure recipe for intensifying migration pressures. If pressure is handled only through control, migration will be irrepressible. Economists have foreseen a great economic benefit out of freer circulation of workers across boundaries, but politicians are not convinced. Contrary to public belief, migrants contribute more than what they get out of the welfare system. Nevertheless, better access to such a system will certainly improve social cohesion and reduce migrants' marginal status. Discouraging intercultural dialogue only creates tension and leads to extreme positions, generating suspicion and stress where there was none before. Potential terrorist cells in receiving countries are also the result of lack of opportunities for cultural dialogue. Finally, lack of participation in the political arena is increasing the divide between institutions and people, and among persons living, working, studying side by side, but not participating in shaping their common reality. In sum, it is hard to find examples of successful management of migration, and the reason is the exclusionary approach behind the current practices.

The Role of Human Rights in the Management of Migration

Adopting a human rights approach modifies the management of migration in at least three directions:

1. It sets the priority on respecting the dignity of migrants. Recognizing such priority requires examining labor standards, living and working conditions, safety, and insurance to eliminate any possible abuse. The state inevitably becomes an interested party in the relation between migrants and employers or migrants and citizens, to balance the otherwise unequal distribution of power.

2. It recognizes that migrants' identity goes beyond their migration condition. Migrants, even temporary workers with only a limited working contract, cannot simply suspend, for whatever period of time, their spiritual and cultural dimension. Obstacles to such dimensions cannot be maintained in a rights-based policy.

3. It limits the power of the state itself. The temptation of sovereignty is to feel free from obligations toward foreigners, who have no claims on the state. But a human rights approach brings the state to recognize that even foreigners, even irregular migrants, have rights that the state must respect. The recent ruling of the Italian Supreme Court on the non-constitutionality of a migration law (a provision that allows the state to proceed with repatriation without counsel assistance to migrants) indicates how things can be different when human rights are considered.[7]

In general, the admission of migrants as persons with rights, rights that can be claimed in the receiving state, changes their "natural" condition from excluded to included. Although perhaps in a minimal and unsatisfactory way, recognizing the rights of migrants is recognizing that they belong. Recognition because of exclusion is substituted by recognition because of entitlements. This is a minimal but real basis for incorporation.

When assessing the role of human rights in terms of the three key aspects of migration policies—admission, selection, and integration—the result is a mixture of successes and failures. In the admission process, human rights do not have much impact, as all instruments constantly repeat that nothing contained in various conventions impinges on the sovereign right of the state to decide on the criteria governing the admission of migrants.[8] The duty to admit asylum seekers is considered to be of a different nature, although migrants have sometimes utilized it to gain access to a foreign country. The admission of migrants' family members is at best a recommendation to governments, not a recognized right of migrants, except perhaps in the case of children.[9]

In addition to the number of migrants to be admitted, the selection of such migrants also remains an exclusive privilege of the receiving country, and human rights cannot much influence this selection process. In fact, in the past, the admission policies of some countries had outright racist objectives, excluding migrants coming from specific races or nationalities.[10] Today it is recognized that states should not discriminate, but nondiscrimination is limited to a few aspects.

Human rights have greater relevance in incorporation policies, precisely because such policies consist of rights that governments grant to migrants in their territory. The state maintains a vast latitude on additional rights that may be extended to migrants, and this normally occurs when incorporation is possible: the longer and more stable the incorporation, the richer the package of rights granted to migrants. Obviously, incorporation and admission policies go hand in hand. A country admits and selects those migrants to whom it is willing to extend certain rights, and the rights that are given determine which migrants are admitted.

In the discourse on social cohesion, particular attention must be given to cultural rights. In fact, the latest chapter in the human rights battle is for cultural rights and migration. Immigrants protest because they feel constrained in their right to maintain and express in public their cultural traditions.[11] Natives protest because they feel that immigrants are threatening their cultural identity. In the background are some misconceptions. One is that persons should have only one identity, as if identity is a zero-sum game, that acquiring one means losing another. The other misconception is that multiple identities imply divided loyalties.[12] In the interrelation between immigrants and the receiving society, intercultural dialogue must be established, based on the assumption that cultures are not static entities but always in flux, and that opening the nation's borders requires breaking down confines within the nation. A static concept of culture would create barriers, while intercultural dialogue allows for the trespassing of such confines, which leads to the sharing of common purposes. A confine is simultaneously a limit but also a determination of commonality of purposes.[13] Intercultural dialogue should go beyond the traditional approaches to social cohesion (differentialism, assimilation, and multiculturalism); but intercultural dialogue is not possible without addressing cultural, socioeconomic, and civic exclusion. A human rights–based policy, which implies also specific attention to cultural rights, extends its influence not only on policies toward migrants but also on policies that manage identity within a territory.

If, however limited, the human rights approach can make a difference in the treatment of migrants, particularly by influencing migration policies, why is the problem of abuse of migrants' rights still so widespread? The reason lies behind inherent weaknesses in the human rights approach, as well as inadequate implementation and inadequate recognition of human rights.

Weaknesses in the Human Rights Approach

The effectiveness of human rights in ensuring protection to migrants seems very limited first of all for reasons of a general nature, such as the difficulty to provide real protection for social, economic and cultural rights; the pre-occupation for the protection of individual rights without challenging the systems that originate abuse; the ideological use of human rights to maintain advantages in trading and commerce relations; and the recurrent impression that the human rights system protects those who are already protected, rather than the real victims. Other reasons are more specific to the condition of migrants, in particular the difficulty for victims to accede to the human rights protection system.[14]

Furthermore, there are many problems concerning the inadequate implementation of human rights standards, which are well documented by countless reports, particularly of Non-Government Organizations (NGOs). The simple fact that so many NGOs and migrant associations have emerged in recent years is an indication of the vastness and seriousness of abuses against migrants, which do not simply occur in countries that have not ratified international conventions, but also in those that have. Actually, abuse is found also in countries of origin, at the beginning of the migration process and during the recruiting phase. The difference between countries with and without adherence to international instruments is the availability of mechanisms for redress, provided that international principles are properly implemented in national legislation. However, between international principles and performance at home there is a "yawning gap."[15]

To speak of inadequate recognition of the rights of migrants apparently seems a wrong statement. In fact, because their status touches on various dimensions, migrants can appeal to principles of international law protecting foreigners; they can appeal to international labor conventions and to regional conventions drafted specifically to protect them; and they can appeal to humanitarian law, insofar as it applies to all without exclusions based on nationality.

Nevertheless, migrants' protection is still inadequate because some categories of migrants are not sufficiently protected in the law. The most cited case is always that of domestic workers, for whom there is no legislation in many countries. But the most difficult issue concerns the protection of unauthorized migrants, whose undocumented status should not be considered as fully deprived of rights, but whose protection makes states uneasy even to mention, as they do not want to be taken as encouraging unauthorized migration.[16]

Most of all, migrants' protection is inadequate because standards are not universally accepted or recognized. The small number of ratifications of the International Labour Organization (ILO) or other conventions for the protection of migrants speaks volumes about this. The most recent case in point is that of the United Nations *International Convention on the Protection of the Rights of All Migrant Workers and Members of Their Families*. It was entered into force in 2003 and has been ratified by 37 countries.[17] As the convention protects migrants within member countries, it has been calculated that those that will be able to invoke the principles of the convention will only be approximately four million, about 5 percent of the estimated eighty-six million migrant workers in the world. Why are the other countries not ratifying the convention? Is it because it is a badly drafted and ultimately unacceptable instrument, or is it something else?

Actually, various shortcomings have been pointed out in the text of the United Nations convention, among them: not addressing gender-based vulnerability; ignoring trainees, who are often employed as migrant workers; lacking specific concerns for the second generation of migrants; and envisioning a supervisory mechanism that does not have true effectiveness in forcing governments to comply with the measures in the convention. Nevertheless, these weaknesses do not detract from the merits of the convention, the most complete international instrument for the protection of migrants. In addition, the text is the result of negotiations among governments. In fact, the major effort in drafting the text was undertaken by some European countries. If such text was acceptable to them in 1990, when the convention was adopted (the UK, Belgium, and Germany were among the major countries in Europe that either did not participate in the drafting or expressed serious reservations on the text), it should still be acceptable now. Furthermore, some studies have confirmed that ratification of the convention would not require excessive changes in the domestic law.[18] This could lead to the counter argument on the actual benefit of ratifying a convention that does not change much of what the national system already provides. But the answer is that ratifying an international instrument places an additional obligation on the government to respect those standards and most of all to respect the human rights–based approach to migration. On the other hand, unwillingness to ratify confirms that governments intend to maintain migration mostly as a political-economic issue, to be managed according to the fluctuations of domestic economic and political climates.

But there is also another reason for the weakness of human rights and that is their dependence for actual implementation on the recognition by the state. When the issue is exclusion, such dependence becomes crucial. The symbol of exclusion is the refugee or, in a different way, the unauthorized migrant. Agamben has resurrected from the old Roman law the figure of *homo sacer*—the person that could be eliminated without penalty but not according to sacrificial rites—and applied it to the refugee.[19] Like the *homo sacer,* who have nothing but their lives, naked lives, and over whom the sovereign nation has the power of exclusion, so do the refugees; excluded from the nation, they only have their lives and cannot count on the protection of the nation. Similarly, unauthorized migrants, affirming a right to belong in a nation to which they do not belong, finds themselves excluded, with only human rights to count on. However, human rights only find protection in the same state that is the source of exclusion. While human rights are founded on the naked life, on the idea that first comes membership in the human family, their exercise depends on being a subject of a state, members of a nation, a legal resident in its territory.[20] The crisis of the nation state in the transnational world, to which migrants belong, is also the result of the progressive affirmation of human rights, which are inherently transnational. But while eroding the power of the state, human rights also erode their own basis for implementation.

The Ethical Basis for Migration Policies

The whole reflection on the relation between human rights and migration policies inevitably leads to the issue of the ethical basis for migration policies.

The issue has been thoroughly debated but keeps coming back. The divide is well-defined between liberal egalitarians and political realists. The first, beginning with the equal moral worth of all people, which cannot be diminished by such accidents as the place of birth or the nationality of parents, conclude that justice requires an open border migration policy. Nevertheless, this principle should be applied with prudence, as some restrictions could be necessary in extreme cases, such as an invasion of migrants or the subversion of a national culture. On the other side of the spectrum, the political realists or communitarians would start from the fact that, in the current world, divided into nation states, migration is not a basic human right, and the first duty of the state is toward its citizens. Migrants can be admitted but purely on a cost-benefit analysis basis, in which priority is not given to the welfare of migrants but to the welfare of citizens.[21]

Needless to say, it is the realist perspective that rules, only mitigated by the recognition that humanitarian principles must be applied specifically in the duty to admit people in danger, such as asylum seekers. Moreover, as mentioned before, there is substantial agreement, at least in principle if not in practice, that the basic human rights of migrants admitted in the territory of the state must be respected. However, the introduction of the humanitarian principle pushes the ethical reflection beyond the realist approach, questioning the current divide among states and economies as unjust and expanding the state's and people's responsibilities beyond the confines of the national community, also because such a gap is not simply in the nature of things or the result of bad management but because of unfair relations among nations.

It is not difficult to see the fundamentally different points of the two camps: realists begin with how things are, egalitarians begin with how things ought to be. The problem with realistic and idealistic positions, however, is that both have shortcomings. As well illustrated by Carens,[22] the realist position tends to justify and leave unjust situations unchanged, whereas the idealist position tends to require more radical changes, such as a new world order,[23] without explaining how to do it and therefore becoming of little use in current situations.

A human rights perspective on migration policies might be considered an idealistic position, as if the rights of migrants distort the benefits of migration, and a migration system without human rights would yield better results for all parties involved. This is the position of consequentialists, such as Ruhs and Chang. In a recent article on the ethics of labor immigration policy, where policies are evaluated on the basis of rights granted to immigrants and the types of consequences they generate, they conclude that many of the existing labor immigration policies are based on "relatively low moral standing for noncitizens and relatively high weights assigned to economic efficiency, distribution and national identity (rather than citizens' rights) as policy outcome parameters."[24] This is well illustrated by the low number of ratifications of international conventions on the rights of migrants. Operating on the assumption that "the promotion of migrant workers' rights and economic betterment may be negatively correlated," they conclude that policies should be based on a framework "characterized by moderate degrees of consequentialism and moderate degrees of moral standing for noncitizens."[25] Therefore, policies that severely restrict the rights of migrant workers should be rejected and so should policies that grant too many rights to migrants.

Although apparently reasonable, such a position has several problems, inherent with consequentialist ethics. If an action is to be judged solely on consequences, from where are the criteria for such judgment derived? On what ground do parties agree on what constitutes severe restriction of rights? Moreover, we find it hard to accept that economic development for migrants would necessarily require lowering the protection of rights. It is true, as Weiner put it, that "incorporating morality in public policy often entails making difficult choices among divergent values."[26] But in our view, human rights cannot be included in a cost-benefit analysis. They constitute a prerequisite for life to remain human. Therefore, the human rights approach is a prerequisite to migration policies, and all governments should agree on standards that are nonnegotiable. If current policies give insufficient regard to human rights principles, those policies need to be reformed rather than lowering human rights standards.

What Is the Church's Position? Toward an Ethics of Inclusion

The church position on migration, which spans a variety of aspects but does not enter into details of migration policies that supersedes the Church's competence, is that policies should be examined against four basic principles.

The human dignity of the person. John XXIII made the human dignity of the person the foundation for his presentation of the rights of the human person. Likewise, *Gaudium et Spes* (12–22) finds in that dignity the foundation of its understanding of the human person. As a consequence of his or her dignity, the person's "rights and duties are universal and inviolable. Therefore, there must be made available to all persons everything necessary for leading a life truly human" (*Gaudium et Spes,* 26). Migration is the search for dignity when this dignity is not available in one's own country. It is the right of the person to do so and to deny it is to deny dignity to human beings.

The common good. A central tenet in the church's social teaching, the common good is defined in *Mater et Magistra* as "the sum total of conditions of social living, whereby persons are enabled more fully and readily to achieve their own perfection" (65), which also affirms that it is the duty of the state to realize the common good in the temporary order (20). The concept is further elaborated in *Pacem in Terris* (54). Although much discussed in the postmodern perspective, which finds hardly anything in common in the current time marked by fragmentation, the principle upholding the need to respect the good of the community remains valid. Therefore, the state has the right to regulate migration. However, the church also constantly adds that the principle of the common good must be properly understood, as it could lead to oppressive consequences for the person.

The universal common good. The duty of the state towards migrants, and therefore the limitations of the state in its migration policies, derives from the larger community to which all belong, the human family. According to *Pacem in Terris,* "the fact that he [the migrant] is a citizen of a particular state does not deprive him of membership in the human family, nor of citizenship in that universal society, the common, world-wide fellowship of men" (25). The common good of the state "cannot be divorced from the common good of the entire human family" (98). Logically, there should be a public authority to supervise issues, such as migration, that concern the whole human family, and John Paul II referred to the need for international norms "to prevent unilateral decisions that are harmful to the weakest" ("Message for World Migration Day," 2001).

Solidarity. The Church's moral teaching, although recommending the respect of human rights, is not ultimately founded on human rights but on the gospel. Solidarity as a principle that should guide public action was elaborated in particular by John Paul II, who, after observing the interdependence of nations in our world, concluded that "interdependence must be transformed into solidarity, based upon the principle that the goods of creation are meant for all." Therefore, "the stronger and richer nations must have a sense of moral responsibility for the other nations" (*Sollicitudo Rei Socialis,* 39). Consequently, the "other," the migrant, must be seen as "our 'neighbor,' a 'helper' (cf. Gn 2:18–20), to be made a sharer, on a par with ourselves, in the banquet of life to which all are equally invited by God" ("Message for World Migration Day," 2001).

The church, while not denying the state the right to regulate migration, provides a rather different approach to the issue, one which is not exclusive, but inclusive; which requires examining responsibilities beyond the confines of the national community; and which gives priority to the underprivileged by establishing that solidarity is not an option, but a duty. In addition to the church, other organizations share similar thinking. In fact, the United Nations *Millennium Declaration,* adopted by 189 countries stated: "We recognize that, in addition to our separate responsibilities to our individual societies, we have a collective responsibility to uphold the principles of human dignity, equality, and equity at the global level. As leaders we have a duty therefore to all the world's people, especially the most vulnerable and, in particular, the children of the world, to whom the future belongs."[27] What is still missing is coherent and adequate action to apply those principles. As the 2003 *Human Development Report* stated, what is needed is policy, not charity.[28]

A good ethical foundation is essential for the elaboration of policies that are inclusive, and such policies begin with the recognition of the human rights of migrants. However, principles alone do not change reality. Policies of inclusion, which cannot be examined in detail in this presentation, imply addressing some major issues: the political participation of diverse cultural groups, religious practices, legal pluralism, the use of multiple languages, and redressing socioeconomic exclusion."[29]

Policies based on human rights require responsibility for the other as simply the other. As emphasized in Bruno Forte's book *L'uno per l'altro,* it is possible to have an ethics without explicitly recognizing and adoring God, but it is not possible to have an ethics without the "other," and therefore without transcendence, that is, without going out of oneself toward the other and without a movement of the other toward oneself.[30] Ultimately, an ethics of inclusion leads toward overcoming the individualism on which the human rights approach is founded. If in Western culture the self comes before anything else, in the Christian worldview the relationship to others comes first.

NOTES

1. Lydia Morris, *Managing Migration: Civic Stratification and Migrants Rights* (New York: Routledge, 2002).

2. These statistics and others are available through the biweekly Internet digest Asian Migration News (AMN). See http://www.smc.org.ph/amnews/amnews.htm (last accessed April 2007).

3. Ibid., June 30, 2004.

4. See the *Personal Responsibility, Work Opportunity and Medicaid Restructuring Act of 1996,* which is part of the law of the 104th U.S. Congress, referenced as H. R. 3734 of July 23, 1996. This has led to a sudden increase in naturalizations.

5. George Borjas, *Heaven's Door: Immigration Policy and the American Economy* (Princeton, NJ: Princeton University Press, 1999).

6. Christian Joppke and Ewa Morawska, "Integrating Immigrants in Liberal Nation-States: Policies and Practices," in *Toward Assimilation and Citizenship: Immigrants in Liberal Nation-States,* eds. Christian Joppke and Ewa Morawska (New York: Palgrave Macmillan, 2003).

7. Corte Costituzionale della Repubblica Italiana, Sentenza 222, 8 luglio 2004. The text of the court's rulings are available online: http://www.giurcost.org/decisioni/index.html.

8. See for instance the United Nations *International Convention for the Protection of the Rights of All Migrant Workers and Members of their Families,* n. 79, available online through the Office of the High Commissioner for Human Rights web site (http://www.ohchr.org, last accessed April 2007).

9. See *United Nations Convention on the Rights of the Child,* n. 10, available online through the Office of the High Commissioner for Human Rights web site (http://www.ohchr.org, last accessed April 2007).

10. See for instance the exclusion of the Chinese from the U.S. and Canada, and the White Australia policy in general.

11. The most renowned case refers to the prohibition in France for minor students to wear ostensible religious symbols in school.

12. United Nations Development Program (UNDP), *Human Development Report 2004* (New York: Oxford University Press, 2004).

13. Renato Martino, "La Chiesa e la globalizzazione," in *The Governance of Globalisation,* ed. E. Malinvaud and L. Sabourin (Vatican City: The Pontifical Academy of Social Sciences, 2004).

14. This is particularly true of unauthorized migrants, who are always afraid of prosecution and punishment (Bosniak 1991).

15. Bimal Ghosh, *Elusive Protection, Uncertain Lands: Migrants' Access to Human Rights* (Geneva: IOM, 2003).

16. Antoine Pécoud and Paul de Guchteneire, "Migration, Human Rights and the United Nations: An Investigation of the Obstacles to the UN Convention on Migrant Workers' Rights," in *Global Migration Perspectives,* no. 3 (Paris: UNESCO, 2004), 1–28.

17. As of June 2007.

18. For the case of Italy, see R. Baratta, "La Convenzione sui diritti dei migranti e la normativa italiana sull'immigrazione," *Studi Emigrazione* 153 (March 2004).

19. Giorgio Agamben, *Homo sacer: Il potere sovrano e la nuda vita* (Torino: Einaudi, 1995).

20. Zygmunt Bauman, *Amore liquido* (Bari: Editori Laterza, 2004), 205.

21. A discussion of the various arguments can be found in Brain Barry and Robert E. Goodin, eds., *Free Movement* (Hemel Hempstead: Harvester Wheatsheaf, 1992).

22. Joseph H. Carens, "Realistic and Idealistic Approaches to the Ethics of Migration," *International Migration Review* 30 (1996): 156–70.

23. The call for a new world order resounds often in the international arena and it is repeated also by the church. The recent instruction *Erga Migrantes Caritas Christi* (8), stated: "At the same time, however, migration raises a truly ethical question: the search for a new international economic order for a more equitable distribution of the goods of the earth."

24. Martin Ruhs and Ha-Joon Chang. "The Ethics of Labor Immigration Policy," *International Organization* 58 (2004): 92.

25. Ibid., 94.

26. Myron Weiner. "Ethics, National Sovereignty and the Control of Immigration," *International Migration Review* 30 (1996): 13.

27. United Nations *Millennium Declaration,* no. 2, available online through the Office of the High Commissioner for Human Rights web site (http://www.ohchr.org, accessed April 2007).

28. United Nations Development Program (UNDP), *Human Development Report 2003* (New York: Oxford University Press, 2003), 145.

29. UNDP, *Human Development Report 2004* (New York: Oxford University Press, 2004).

30. Bruno Forte, *L'uno per l'altro: Per un'etica della trascendenza* (Brescia: Morcelliana, 2003).

CHAPTER TWELVE

The Natural Rights of Migrants and Newcomers

A Challenge to U.S. Law and Policy

DONALD KERWIN

United States law and policy does not fully reflect the natural (human) rights of migrants and newcomers. This should come as no surprise. Any nation would find difficulty in protecting or giving content to all the natural rights of its residents. Legal norms will invariably fall short of rights rooted in human dignity.[1] In addition, newcomers and, in particular, migrants have more tenuous ties and arguably less claim than citizens to state-based protections. To recognize these complexities is not to argue that domestic (or international) standards should have no reference to natural rights. To the contrary, the "inalienable" rights protected by the U.S. Constitution and enunciated by the Universal Declaration of Human Rights serve as an essential measure of the legitimacy of legal standards and practices.

This paper will explore the disparity between U.S. law and practice and the natural rights attributed to migrants and newcomers in the Catholic tradition. It will analyze U.S. policies as they impact undocumented immigrants and their families, low-wage laborers, persons fleeing persecution, and those deemed security risks. It will end with a discussion of how these policies might be brought into greater harmony with the Catholic natural rights tradition.

Natural Rights

Catholic teaching recognizes a full contingent of natural rights. Since these rights derive from human dignity, they include "all that is necessary for living a genuinely human life: for example, food, clothing, housing, the right freely to choose their state of life and set up a family, the right to education, work, to their good name, to respect, to proper knowledge, the right to act according to the dictates of conscience and to safeguard their privacy, and rightful freedom, including freedom of religion."[2]

Persons fleeing persecution occupy a privileged position in the Catholic tradition. Present-day refugees follow the path of the holy family who, in their flight to Egypt, represent "the archetype of every refugee family" and are "the models and protectors of every migrant, alien and refugee of whatever kind who, whether compelled by fear of persecution or by want, is forced to leave his native land, his beloved parents and relatives, his close friends, and to seek a foreign soil."[3]

The Catholic Church supports the international regime of refugee protection and has urged all nations to adopt its relevant instruments.[4] The church would also protect those who experience refugee-like hardship but who do not meet the narrow refugee definition.[5] These include the internally displaced, and those who flee natural disaster, generalized violence, and other rights deprivations.[6] The Catholic tradition also recognizes a right to economic migration: "[W]here a State which suffers from poverty combined with great population cannot supply such use of goods to its inhabitants, or where the State places conditions which offend human dignity, people possess a right to emigrate, to select a new home in foreign lands, and to seek conditions of life worthy of man."[7] The right to self-preservation has been recognized in Christian jurisprudence and philosophy since the Middle Ages.[8] Although originally considered in the context of condemned prisoners, this right has obvious application to migrants fleeing persecution or privation. Furthermore, it was conceived as both a power and a duty, making it an "inalienable" right. The notion of rights and corresponding responsibilities remains a defining characteristic of the Catholic tradition.

Newcomers also enjoy natural "political" rights, including the right to full membership in the civic life of their adopted countries: "Now among the rights of a human person there must be included that by which a man may enter a political community where he hopes he can more fittingly provide a future for himself and his dependents. Wherefore, as far as the common good rightly understood permits, it is the duty of that State to accept such immigrants and to help them into itself as new members."[9] Natural rights also extend to the workplace, encompassing just pay, fair treatment, and the right to join labor unions.[10]

These teachings might be dismissed as trite or even dangerous in light of the catastrophic terrorist attacks suffered (and the ongoing risk faced) by the United States. The Mexican and U.S. bishops considered migration in the post-9/11 world in their joint pastoral statement *Strangers No Longer: Together on the Journey of Hope.*[11] In it, they sought to reconcile a (relative) right and duty of a sovereign state—to control its borders in furtherance of the common good—with the natural rights of migrants. They did not qualify church teaching on the "absolute," "inalienable," and God-given rights of migrants, nor did they perceive a conflict between migrant rights and border control. Instead, they viewed the rights as consistent based on an understanding of the "common good." They concluded:

> The Church recognizes the rights of a sovereign state to control its borders in furtherance of the common good. It also recognizes the right of human persons to migrate so that they can realize their God-given rights. These teachings complement each other. While the sovereign state may impose reasonable limits on immigration, the common good is not served when the basic human rights of the individual are violated.[12]

The "common good"—defined as the "sum total of social conditions which allow people, either as groups or as individuals, to reach their fulfillment"[13]—requires states to protect the rights of migrants and newcomers. *Strangers No Longer* affirmed that in the Catholic tradition civil authority exists to promote the common good and, by extension, natural rights.[14]

An objection might be raised that, in practice, this interpretation would eviscerate a nation's ability to control its borders. To the contrary, a nation could still enforce orderly immigration procedures for those exercising their natural rights and could exclude migrants who sought entry for less worthy or for harmful reasons, or whose entry otherwise would not further the common good. However, in a world of rampant poverty and persecution, the bishops established a "presumption" that persons "must migrate in order to support and protect themselves and that nations who are able to receive them should do so whenever possible."[15] "The common good will not be attained by excluding people," said Archbishop Romero in a different context. "We can't enrich the common good of our country by driving out those we don't care for."[16]

Legal Norms

One need not dispute the United States' generosity towards immigrants—past and present—to recognize the ways in which its current laws and policies fail to honor their natural rights. These shortcomings can be found in the treatment of immigrant families, laborers, border crossers, persons seeking protection, and those deemed security risks. As always, the poor suffer the most from unjust policies.

Immigrant Families

The U.S. immigration system attempts to facilitate family reunification. Nearly 70 percent of foreign-born persons who obtain lawful permanent residence in the United States—492,297 of 705,827 in 2003—do so through a close family relationship to a petitioning U.S. citizen or a lawful permanent resident.[17] Immigrants also maintain strong ties to family members in their countries of birth. Annual remittances to Latin America and the Caribbean have reached $30 billion, with 23 percent of all Central Americans and 18 percent of Mexicans receiving money from abroad.[18] Remittances can be seen as a form of foreign aid that results from labor that directly benefits the U.S. economy.

Unfortunately, U.S. policy also undermines immigrant families. To begin with, it ties family reunification to income. Under the Illegal Immigration Reform and Immigrant Responsibility Act of 1996 ("the 1996 Immigration Act"),[19] a petitioning U.S. citizen or lawful permanent resident must demonstrate an income at least 125 percent of the federal poverty line and the ability to maintain the family member (beneficiary) at the same level.[20] The petitioner bears this responsibility until the family member naturalizes or works for 40 "qualifying quarters," normally ten years.[21] Co-sponsors can be used to satisfy this requirement. Nonetheless, 20 percent of petitioners who seek the services of charitable immigration programs to immigrate family members cannot meet this standard and, thus, do not apply.[22] Forty-two percent must rely on joint sponsors to meet these requirements.[23] Others must immigrate family members on a staggered basis.[24] These families face either long-term separation or lengthy periods of uncertainty and vulnerability (to deportation) in the United States.

The immediate family members of adult U.S. citizens—their minor children, spouses, and parents—can be admitted without numerical limitation. However, family members with other "qualifying relationships" face caps by both type of relationship ("preference category") and by nationality. As a result, millions who qualify for family-based visas are mired in multiyear backlogs. The spouses and unmarried sons and daughters of lawful permanent residents from Mexico, for example, face a seven-year backlog. In other categories, backlogs extend more than two decades. In 1997, the U.S. Department of State stopped providing statistics on the number of persons approved for family-based visas who had not yet received them. At that point, 3.5 million languished in backlogs.[25] Persons in this group who opt to live with their family members in the United States represent a significant percentage of U.S. undocumented residents.

Once a family-based visa becomes available, the beneficiary must apply for lawful permanent residence. At this point, he or she faces a wide range of bars to permanent residence based on undocumented presence in the United States, past deportations, and other violations of U.S. immigration law. The beneficiary also faces further "processing" delays. Between 2000 and 2003, the total number of pending immigration applications grew from 3.9 to 6.2 million.[26] The number of pending "adjustment of status" applications (for permanent residence) has reached 1,188,482, with average processing times of 24 months.[27] Before the yearly adjustment cap of 10,000 was removed, thereby improving the situation, roughly 160,000 persons granted political asylum faced 13- to 14-year waits for permanent residence.[28] Since it typically requires five years in lawful permanent resident status to naturalize, these delays significantly postpone naturalization. Once eligible to naturalize, applicants face further processing delays that average 14 months.[29]

Although legally present, lawful permanent residents can still be deported based on relatively minor crimes—like shoplifting—that they committed years in the past. Ten percent of all families in the United States include at least one noncitizen parent and one U.S. citizen child.[30] The deportation of a parent and spouse can be emotionally and financially devastating for the members of these so-called "mixed status" families. Most of those in removal proceedings for criminal offenses face mandatory detention in the troubled Department of Homeland Security (DHS) prison system.[31] By 2003, the DHS detained an average of 21,133 persons per night, nearly triple the number detained at the time that the 1996 Immigration Act passed.[32]

Between 1993 and 2003, Border Patrol funding more than quadrupled (from $361 million to $1.5 billion). During the same period, the undocumented population tripled from 3.4 million to nearly 10 million persons.[33] Since 2003, this anomaly has become even more pronounced. While increased border control efforts have failed in their primary purpose, they have succeeded in pushing migrants to more perilous crossing routes, in causing more crossing deaths due to dehydration and exposure, and in fostering the emergence of ruthless smuggling syndicates.[34] On average, more than one migrant per day perishes along the U.S.-Mexico border, and countless others fall victim in Mexico.[35]

The success of immigrant families (relative to natives) has historically turned on their length of time in the United States. This trend persists. However, due to these laws, many families with undocumented members may be more fixed in their poverty and lack of status than past immigrant families. Exacerbating matters, the United States has an "immigration" policy that determines who can enter and stay, but it lacks a coherent "immigrant" policy to address the integration, educational, and myriad social needs of the nation's 35 million foreign-born persons. This deficiency harms not only individual newcomers but also U.S. civic life.

Immigrant Laborers

United States labor realities also contribute to the poverty of newcomers. The foreign-born represent 11 percent of the population, but 15 percent of U.S. workers.[36] The undocumented alone represent 5 percent of the U.S. workforce, and have become a structural reality in the U.S. economy.[37]

In the 1990s, the foreign-born filled 47 percent of the new jobs created.[38] Between 2000 and the first four months of 2004, they constituted 60 percent of the growth in the U.S. workforce.[39] The U.S. economy needs immigrants; it is projected to create 21.3 million jobs between 2002 and 2012, with much of the fastest growth in "service," "construction," and other jobs that immigrants dominate.[40] Immigrants also represent one answer to the demographic problems caused by an aging work force; 44 percent of foreign-born workers (compared to 27 percent of the native-born) are between the prime working ages of 25 and 44.

The new federal minimum wage of $5.85 an hour, effective July 24, 2007—which is the first increase since 1997—does not represent a "living wage," and immigrants in many industries fail to earn even sub-minimum wages.[41] As a result, poverty among the foreign-born has reached scandalous levels. In 1980, the poverty rate of the foreign-born narrowly exceeded that of the native-born.[42] By 2003, 21.7 percent of noncitizens and 17.2 percent of all foreign-born persons (including naturalized citizens) lived in poverty, compared to 11.8 percent of natives.[43] By 2002, 51.4 percent of the children of immigrants lived in families that earned less than 200 percent of the federal poverty line, compared to 33.1 percent of children in native-born households.[44] Immigrants also work at high rates in jobs that do not provide health and other benefits. Nationally, 45 million U.S. residents lack health care, including 13 percent of the native-born, 34.5 percent of the foreign-born, and 45.3 percent of noncitizens.[45] Eighteen percent of immigrant children lack health care, compared to 7.5 percent of children with native parents.[46]

States and localities offer tax and financial incentives to lure meat packing, poultry processing, and other industries to rural, low-cost areas. The companies recruit immigrant laborers but do not provide them with sufficient wages or benefits.[47] In effect, they realize the profits created by these workers, but leave it to the local communities to meet their health, educational, and social service needs. High numbers of immigrants also endure perilous working conditions. Mexican nationals, for example, are 80 percent more likely to suffer fatal injuries on the job than the native-born.[48]

Newcomers have entered the job market during a period of historic weakness for the U.S. labor movement. Between 1954 and 2003, membership in unions fell from 39 percent of the U.S. workforce[49] to 12.9 percent.[50] Only 8 percent of private sector employees belong to unions, even though the earnings of union members significantly exceed those of unrepresented workers.[51]

Overall, U.S. labor and workplace protections do not cover large numbers of immigrant laborers, do not carry penalties that deter misconduct, and are not adequately enforced. The National Labor Relations Act (NLRA),[52] for example, prohibits employers from engaging in antiunion activities. However, millions of workers in immigrant-prominent industries fall outside its protections, including an estimated three million agricultural laborers, one million domestic employees, and seven million independent contractors.[53] Not surprisingly, agricultural laborers and domestic workers endure some of the worst conditions in the U.S. labor force.[54] The National Labor Relations Board (NLRB) can order an employer to reinstate an employee, pay back wages and benefits, and undo the illegal steps taken.[55] However, illegally fired undocumented workers cannot receive back pay and benefits.[56] These penalties do not deter antiorganizing tactics.[57] Unscrupulous employers use the threat of deportation to suppress organizing activities.[58] Finally, while unfair labor practice cases have tripled since 1950, NLRB staff has recently fallen back to 2,000 people, just above 1950 levels.[59]

Refugees and Asylum-Seekers

Refugees, asylum-seekers, and others fleeing violence and terror have a natural right to protection, but face security-related concerns and longstanding gaps in the U.S. and international protection regimes.[60] Refugee determinations take place outside the United States, while asylum cases are decided within the country, but the standards are identical.

An estimated twelve million persons worldwide qualify as refugees.[61] The refugee definition does not cover, however, twenty-three million persons who are displaced within their own countries.[62] Nor does it apply to the millions who flee civil war, generalized violence, natural disaster, or poverty. The United States provides temporary protection to nationals from designated countries that are experiencing armed conflict, environmental disaster, or other extraordinary conditions.[63] Although sorely needed, a complementary international protection regime for these near refugees does not exist.

In fiscal year 2001, the United States resettled nearly 70,000 refugees from abroad.[64] After the 9/11 attacks, it temporarily suspended and (appropriately) initiated a security review of this program. In 2002 and 2003, it admitted a total of 55,000 refugees.[65] These diminished numbers—the fewest admitted in 25 years—came at a time of long-term refugee populations with no "durable solution" but resettlement. Refugee admissions increased to 52,868 in 2004, but still remain well below historical averages.[66]

Other migrants fleeing persecution have also found it difficult to reach the United States since 9/11. The number of persons who request asylum at U.S. ports-of-entry plummeted between 2002 and 2003.[67] This may be due, in part, to preinspection programs that do not allow persons with improper documents to board planes to the United States. It may also be due to U.S.-supported migrant interception programs. Even prior to 9/11 Mexico intercepted thousands of migrants each year as part of a trinational effort to create a "North American security zone."[68] This program did not include adequate refugee protections and as a result almost certainly returned persons fleeing persecution to perilous situations. Advocates have not been able to obtain reliable information on the scope of U.S.-supported interception programs since 9/11.

Similarly, the United States continues to interdict, return, and detain Haitian boat people. However, in a novel twist, it now defends these policies on national security grounds, claiming that they deter large-scale migrations that would divert the Coast Guard from its other security responsibilities.[69] This attenuated application of the "national security" paradigm effectively punishes Haitians when they most need protection. One could scarcely imagine a more desperate situation than present-day Haiti in the wake of natural disaster and the reemergence of military and paramilitary human rights abusers.[70]

The right of nonrefoulement precludes a refugee's return to where his "life or freedom would be threatened" on an enumerated ground. The U.N. Refugee Convention also provides a "bill of rights" for refugees—the right to property, to free association, to work, to courts, to housing, to education, to public benefits—that are more observed in the breach.[71] Essentially, refugees cannot be warehoused under international law. However, of twelve million refugees worldwide, more than seven million have been in camps or segregated settlements for ten years or more.[72]

Asylum-seekers who flee their countries with false or no documents must request asylum or express a fear of persecution to U.S. immigration officials on arrival or face immediate removal. The United States has recently extended the "expedited removal" program to cover all non-Mexican migrants caught within 100 miles of the southwest border who have been in the United States for less than 14 days.[73] This raises particular concerns in light of findings by the United Nations High Commissioner for Refugees[74] and the U.S. Commission on International Religious Freedom that many migrants who express a fear of return at ports-of-entry are not referred to pursue asylum claims.[75]

In Miami and elsewhere, U.S. Attorneys have also effectively criminalized the asylum process by selectively prosecuting certain arriving asylum-seekers for document fraud.[76] In these cases, asylees—those ultimately granted asylum—begin life in the United States with a criminal record, with all the negative social and immigration consequences that this entails.

Other asylum-seekers have also been targeted. The United States and Canada, for example, have agreed to require migrants to seek political asylum in whichever country that they first reach.[77] The asylum-seeker from Colombia who visits Miami on his way to Toronto is now to be returned by Canadian officials to the United States. Since its implementation in late December 2004, this agreement has led to significant decreases in Canadian refugee claims.[78] Under the 1996 Immigration Act, migrants must also seek asylum within a year of their entry into the United States, with narrow exceptions.[79]

Under the U.N. Convention against Torture, no state can expel, return, or extradite a person to a country "where there are substantial grounds for believing that he would be subject to torture."[80] Unlike the refugee convention, the torture convention does not include exceptions for criminals or security risks, and does not require that the torture be directed at the applicant for a particular reason. However, claims for relief under the torture convention have been approved at extraordinarily low rates, three percent in 2003.[81]

More troubling, the United States employs a procedure known as "extraordinary rendition" to turn over suspected terrorists to foreign governments known to torture prisoners.[82] In one case, U.S. officials arrested a Canadian citizen, Maher Arar, passing through John F. Kennedy International Airport in New York, and sent him through Jordan to Syria where he suffered months of interrogation and torture.[83]

Persons Deemed Threats to National Security

In a comprehensive report on the 9/11 attacks, the National Commission on Terrorist Attacks upon the United States emphasized the need for a balanced and coordinated approach to terrorism that involves "all elements of national power," including military, "diplomacy, intelligence, covert action, law enforcement, economic policy, foreign aid, public diplomacy, and homeland defense."[84] The report highlighted the crucial role played by intelligence in the counter-terror fight. Improved intelligence collection, mining, and sharing represent key counter-terror priorities. Assuming that intelligence can be accessed by the appropriate officials, the U.S. immigration process can prevent a noncitizen terrorist from securing a visa or entering the country. The system should also be able to track an immigrant who has already entered.

While there has been support for many post-9/11 immigration-related initiatives, there has also been widespread concern over the targeting of certain groups of immigrants. As has been observed, terrorism is a tactic, not an enemy. This enemy needs to be defined and countered with tactics that respect civil liberties, promote national unity, and prevent further attacks.

After 9/11, the United States arrested and detained hundreds of Middle Eastern and South Asian noncitizens. It placed nearly eight hundred in closed deportation proceedings.[85] Many were held without charge for weeks under a new regulation that extended the charging period to forty-eight hours or, in an emergency or other extraordinary circumstance, a "reasonable period."[86] The regulation did not specify how an emergency or extraordinary circumstance would be determined or when a detainee would be notified of the charge. A report by the Department of Justice's Office of Inspector General studied a sample of the 762 noncitizens who were detained at the Metropolitan Detention Center in Brooklyn, New York, and the Passaic County Jail in Paterson, New Jersey.[87] The report highlights the investigation's underlying assumption that the "enemy" would be in violation of U.S. immigration laws. Yet al Qaeda does not typically recruit people with immigration difficulties or who otherwise meet U.S. terrorist profiles.[88]

As the report documents, the investigation led to the arrest and detention of hundreds of persons with no connection to terrorism.[89] The Federal Bureau of Investigation (FBI) often classified detainees to be of "high interest" based "on little or no concrete information."[90] Prison officials held these detainees in the most restrictive, maximum security conditions. For weeks, they could receive no calls, visits, mail, or otherwise communicate with anybody outside the prison.[91] They suffered mental and physical abuse and, even after the communications blackout ended, faced strict limits on access to counsel and visitors.[92] The FBI took an average of 80 days to clear innocent detainees; in more than a quarter of the cases, it took more than three months.[93] These delays occurred even after it "became clear that many of the September 11 detainees had no immediately apparent nexus to terrorism."[94]

Another controversial program required the registration of men from 25 countries who entered the United States on temporary visas before September 30, 2002. Of the 83,519 people who came forward, 13,799 were placed in removal proceedings.[95] This program led to the flight of thousands of visa "over-stayers" (mostly Pakistanis) to Canada. According to counter-terror experts, by punishing those who voluntarily came forward and driving countless others underground, and still others out of the country, the program may well have undermined U.S. security.

Since 9/11, the Department of Justice (DOJ) has also targeted undocumented employees at "critical infrastructure" work sites, like airports, water supplies, and nuclear facilities, as well as those working at events of national significance like the Super Bowl.[96] Few would dispute that employees in sensitive jobs need to undergo security screening. However, screening should not be limited to the undocumented. In fact, al Qaeda tries to recruit "clean" operatives who do not raise security, criminal, or immigration concerns.[97]

In the same period, there has also been a significant push to enlist the police in immigration enforcement. However, as many police forces and associations have recognized, this will make immigrants less likely to report crimes, to cooperate in investigations, and to assist in community policing activities. Law enforcement measures that target the undocumented erode immigrants' trust in institutions created for the common good—like schools and hospitals—that depend on their participation.

Harmonizing Natural Rights and Legal Norms

The U.S. immigration system falls short of the natural right ideal in significant ways. In outline, U.S. law values family reunification. However, it conditions family unity on income. It also divides families whose members have committed immigration violations, including those convicted of minor criminal activity. Multiyear backlogs and processing delays also separate and undermine families. These laws frustrate the natural right to live with one's family. They also create and perpetuate a population of second-class residents, a situation inimical to the exercise of political and economic rights. Immigration reform, combining legalization of the undocumented and greater legal avenues for future migrants to enter, would address these shortcomings. It would also alleviate the tragedy of migrant crossing deaths. The United States also needs to develop a national "immigrant" policy to respond to the integration, educational, social service, and other needs of newcomers.

Immigrants possess a natural right to earn enough to support themselves and their families. To achieve this goal, the U.S. minimum wage, even in light of the 2007 adjustment, should be increased to a living wage. Health coverage must be extended to the forty-five million U.S. residents—a disproportionate number of them immigrants—who do not have it. Businesses should be awarded tax breaks and financial incentives only if they provide a living wage and basic benefits. U.S. labor and worker protection laws should be extended, strengthened, and enforced.

The U.S. and international regime of refugee protection honors natural rights. Nonetheless, millions of refugees stagnate in camps without prospects. The refugee definition also excludes the internally displaced, those fleeing generalized violence, natural disaster and hardship, and economic migrants. A complementary protection regime should be created for these migrants. In addition, migrant interdiction and expedited removal programs need to provide adequate protections against nonrefoulement. Bona fide asylum-seekers should not be detained. Migrants should never be returned to nations where they might be tortured.

National security, at its core, implicates the right to self-preservation. The Catholic natural rights tradition, however, cautions against turning security into an "idol" or an absolute good. Archbishop Romero reminded us that a "society's or political community's reason for being is not the security of the state but the human person."[98] The Catholic tradition does not see a conflict between security and the protection and defense of rights. In the post-9/11 world, this insight must not be lost.

NOTES

1. Natural or human rights can be defined as the "rights that people have, not by virtue of any particular role or status they have in society, but by virtue of

their very humanity." Brian Tierney, *The Idea of Natural Rights* (Grand Rapids, MI: Eerdmans Publishing, 2001), 2n4.

2. Vatican II, *Gaudium et Spes,* 66. Works issuing from the Vatican and papal texts can be accessed throught the Vatican website, http://www.vatican.va.

3. Pius XX, Apostolic Constitution, *Exsul Familia,* Introduction.

4. Pontifical Council "Cor Unum" and Pontifical Council for the Pastoral Care of Migrants and Itinerant People, "Refugees: A Challenge to Solidarity" (1992), § 13.

5. Under international and domestic law, a refugee is a person outside his or her country who is unable to return due to a "well-founded fear of persecution on account of race, religion, nationality, membership in a particular social group or political opinion." *Immigration and Nationality Act,* §101(a)(42)(A).

6. Pontifical Council, "A Challenge to Solidarity," §§ 4–5, 67.

7. Sacred Congregation for Bishops, "Instruction on the Pastoral Care of People Who Migrate" (August 22, 1969), § 7.

8. Tierney, *The Idea of Natural Rights,* 79.

9. John XXIII, *Pacem in Terris,* 106.

10. Leo XIII, *Rerum Novarum,* 32, 51, 59, 63, 72, 76.

11. Mexican Catholic Bishops' Conference and United States Conference of Catholic Bishops, *Strangers No Longer: Together on the Journey of Hope* (Washington, DC: United States Conference of Catholic Bishops, 2003).

12. Ibid., 39.

13. Vatican II, *Gaudium et Spes,* 26.

14. John XXIII, *Pacem in Terris,* 54.

15. *Strangers No Longer,* 39.

16. Oscar Romero, *The Violence of Love* (Maryknoll, NY: Orbis Books, 2004), 3.

17. U.S. Department of Homeland Security, Office of Immigration Statistics, "2003 Yearbook of Immigration Statistics" (September 2004), 7. The reader is advised to consult relevant governmental websites for items in these notes that do not have further publication information.

18. Pew Hispanic Center and the Multilateral Investment Fund of the Inter-American Development Bank, "Remittance Senders and Receivers: Tracking the Transnational Channels" (Washington, DC: Pew Hispanic Center, Nov. 24, 2003), 3–4.

19. The Illegal Immigration Reform and Immigrant Responsibility Act of 1996, Pub. L. No. 104-208, 110 Stat. 3009 (Sept. 30, 1996).

20. Immigration and Nationality Act, §§ 213A(f)(1)(E) and 213A(a)(1)(A).

21. Ibid., § 213A(a)(2)–(3).

22. Catholic Legal Immigration Network, Inc., "The Affidavit of Support and Its Effect on Low-Income Families" (Washington, DC: August 2000), 7.

23. Ibid., 8.

24. Ibid.

25. U.S. Department of State, Bureau of Consular Affairs, *Immigrant Visa Waiting List in the Family-Sponsored and Employment-Based Preferences as of January 1997* (March 1997).

26. U.S. General Accounting Office, "Immigration Application Fees: Current Fees Are Not Sufficient to Fund U.S. Citizenship and Immigration Services' Operations," GAO-04-309R (Jan. 5, 2004), 36, 40.

27. U.S. Department of Homeland Security, "I-485, Application for Adjustment of Status: Fiscal Year 2004 Year to Date" (July 31, 2004); U.S. Department of Homeland Security, "I-485 Projected Processing Time" (July 31, 2004).

28. U.S. Citizenship and Immigration Services, "Adjustment of Status for Asylees," http://uscis.gov/graphics/fieldoffices/nebraska/asyleeadj.htm (accessed Oct. 6, 2004).

29. U.S. Department of Homeland Security, "N-400, Application for Naturalization: Fiscal Year 2004 Year to Date" (July 31, 2004); U.S. Department of Homeland Security, "N-400 Projected Processing Time" (July 31, 2004).

30. Michael Fix and Wendy Zimmerman, "All Under One Roof: Mixed Status Families in an Era of Reform" (The Urban Institute, 1999), 2.

31. Mark Dow, *American Gulag: Inside U.S. Immigration Prisons* (Berkeley: University of California Press, 2004).

32. U.S. Department of Homeland Security, "2003 Yearbook of Immigration Statistics," 148.

33. Jeffrey Passel, R. Capps, and Michael Fix, "Undocumented Immigrants: Facts and Figures" (Urban Institute, Immigration Studies Program, Jan. 12, 2004); U.S. Immigration and Naturalization Service, "1993 Statistical Yearbook" (Sept. 1994), 183.

34. Karl Eschbach, Jacqueline Hagan, and Nestor Rodriguez, "Causes and Trends in Migrant Deaths Along the U.S. Mexico Border, 1985–1998" (University of Houston: Center for Immigration Research, Mar. 2001), 41; Catholic Legal Immigration Network, Inc., "Chaos on the U.S.-Mexico Border: A Report on Migrant Crossing Deaths, Immigrant Families and Subsistence-Level Laborers" (Nov. 2001), 8–15, 20–21.

35. Wayne Cornelius, "Controlling Unwanted Immigration: Lessons from the United States, 1993–2004," Working Paper 92 (San Diego, CA: University of California, The Center for Comparative Immigration Studies, Dec. 2004; available at http://www.ccis-ucsd.org/publications/wrkg92.pdf, last accessed April 2007).

36. Sum, Fogg, Khatiwada, and Palma, "Foreign Immigration and the Labor Force of the U.S.: The Contributions of New Foreign Immigration to the Growth of the Nation's Labor Force and its Employed Population, 2000 to 2004" (Boston: Center for Labor Market Studies, Northeastern University, July 2004), 7.

37. Jeffrey Passel, "Estimates of the Size and Characteristics of the Undocumented Population" (Washington, DC: Pew Hispanic Center, Mar. 21, 2005), 1, 4.

38. Sum, Fogg, Khatiwada, and Palma, "Foreign Immigration," 2.

39. Ibid., 12.

40. D. Hecker, "Occupational Employment Projections to 2012," *Bureau of Labor Statistics, Monthly Labor Review* (Feb. 2004): 80–81, 87, and 91.

41. Catholic Legal Immigration Network, Inc., "Work without Justice: Low-Wage Immigrant Laborers" (Washington, DC: Catholic Legal Immigration Network, Inc., 2000).

42. Michael Fix and Wendy Zimmerman, "The Integration of Immigrant Families in the United States," (The Urban Institute, June 2000), v.

43. U.S. Census Bureau, "Income, Poverty, and Health Insurance Coverage in the United States: 2003," *Current Population Reports, P60-226* (U.S. Government Printing Office, 2004), 11.

44. Urban Institute, "Children of Immigrants Show Slight Reductions in Poverty, Hardship," in *Snapshots of America's Families III Series* (Nov. 7, 2003).

45. U.S. Census Bureau, "Income, Poverty, and Health Insurance Coverage," 17.

46. Urban Institute, "Children of Immigrants."

47. Catholic Legal Immigration Network, Inc., "Work Without Justice," 22–26.

48. J. Pritchard, "Mexican Worker Deaths Rise Sharply," *Associated Press,* Mar. 12, 2004.

49. Human Rights Watch, "Unfair Advantage: Workers' Freedom of Association in the United States Under International Human Rights Standards" (Aug. 2000), 7n11.

50. U.S. Department of Labor, Bureau of Labor Statistics, "Union Members in 2003," USDL 04-53 (Jan. 21, 2004).

51. Ibid.

52. *National Labor Relations Act, U.S. Code* 29), §§ 151–169.

53. Human Rights Watch, "Unfair Advantage," 189.

54. J. Bowe, "Nobodies: Does Slavery Exist in America," *The New Yorker,* Apr. 21 and 28, 2003; D. France, "Slavery's New Face," *Newsweek,* Dec.18, 2000; Catholic Legal Immigration Network, Inc., "Work Without Justice," 7–8, 16–21; Human Rights Watch, "Unfair Advantage," 176–78.

55. *U.S. Code* 29, §160(c).

56. *Hoffman Plastics Compound, Inc. v. NLRB,* 122 S. Ct. 1275 (2002).

57. Human Rights Watch, "Unfair Advantage," 18.

58. R.H. Taylor, "Undocumented Hotel Workers Who Formed Union Are Released," *Star Tribune,* Oct. 20, 1999; Steven Greenhouse, "Immigrants in the Middle of Union Push at Bakery," *New York Times,* Oct. 9, 2000; Nancy Cleeland, "Unionizing Is Catch-22 for Illegal Immigrants," *Los Angeles Times,* Jan. 16, 2000.

59. Human Rights Watch, "Unfair Advantage," 26.

60. In 1968, the United States acceded to the 1967 UN Protocol Relating to the Status of Refugees which, in turn, adopted Articles 2 to 34 of the 1951 UN Convention Relating to the Status of Refugees.

61. U.S. Committee for Refugees, *World Refugee Survey 2004* (Immigration and Refugee Services of America, 2004), 1.

62. Ibid.

63. *Immigration and Nationality Act,* §244 (b).

64. U.S. Department of Homeland Security, "2003 Yearbook of Immigration Statistics," 53.

65. The Refugee Council USA, *U.S. Refugee Admissions Program for Fiscal Year 2004* (May 2003), 4.

66. U.S. Citizenship and Immigration Services, Office of Refugee, Asylum, and International Operations, *2004 Year in Review* (2005), 4–5.

67. U.S. Department of Homeland Security, "2002 Yearbook of Immigration Statistics" (Oct. 2003), 57; "2003 Yearbook of Immigration Statistics," 48.

68. Catholic Legal Immigration Network, Inc., "Chaos on the U.S.-Mexico Border," 35–37; M. Flynn, "Dónde Está La Frontera?" *Bulletin of the Atomic Scientists* (2002); M. Flynn, "U.S. Anti-Migration Efforts Move South," *Americas Program* (Interhemispheric Resource Center, July 8, 2002).

69. 67 Fed. Reg. 68924 (Nov. 13, 2002); "A surge in illegal migration by sea threatens national security by diverting valuable United States Coast Guard and other resources from counter-terrorism." *In re D-J-,* 23 I&N Dec. 572 (A.G. 2003); "there is a substantial prospect that the release of such aliens into the United States would . . . encourage future surges in illegal migration by sea . . . diverting valuable Coast Guard and DOJ resources from counterterrorism and homeland security responsibilities."

70. Deborah Sontag and Lydia Polgreen, "Storm-Battered Haiti's Endless Crises Deepen," *New York Times,* Oct. 16, 2004.

71. U.S. Committee for Refugees, "World Refugee Survey," 38.

72. Ibid.

73. U.S. Department of Homeland Security, "DHS Expands Expedited Removal Authority Along Southwest Border" (Sept. 14, 2005).

74. Rachel Swarns, "U. N. Report Cites Harassment at American Airports of Asylum Seekers," *New York Times,* Aug. 13, 2004.

75. Commission investigators observed that asylum referrals did not occur in one-sixth of the cases in which migrants expressed a fear of return. United States Commission on International Religious Freedom, "Report on Asylum Seekers in Expedited Removal, Volume II: Expert Reports" (Feb. 2005), 20.

76. Associated Press, "Prosecution of Asylum Seekers Challenged," Aug. 12, 2003.

77. "U.S.-Canada Safe Third Country Agreement" (available at www.cic.gc.ca/english/policy/safe-third.html, last accessed April 2007).

78. Canadian Council for Refugees, "Closing the Front Door on Refugees: Report on Safe Third Country Agreement 6 Months after Implementation" (Aug. 2005), 10–13.

79. Immigration and Nationality Act, § 208(a)(2).

80. United Nations' Convention against Torture, opened for signature Feb. 4, 1985, 1465 U. N. T. S. 85.

81. Donald Kerwin, "Charitable Legal Programs for Immigrants: What They Do, Why They Matter, and How They Can Be Expanded," *Immigration Briefings,* no. 04-06 (June 2004): 11–12.

82. D. Brown and D. Priest, "Deported Terror Suspect Details Torture in Syria: Canadian's Case Called Typical of CIA," *Washington Post,* November 5, 2003.

83. Ibid.

84. National Commission on Terrorist Attacks Upon the United States, *The 9/11 Commission Report* (New York: W. W. Norton and Company, 2004), 363–64.

85. Associated Press, "Supreme Court Rejects Dispute Over Closed Deportation Hearings," May 27, 2003. According to the Solicitor General, 766 noncitizens have been deemed of "special interest" and subjected to closed hearings; of these, 505 have been deported.

86. 66 Fed. Reg. 48334 (Sept. 20, 2001).

87. U.S. Department of Justice, Office of the Inspector General, "The September 11 Detainees: A Review of the Treatment of Aliens Held on Immigration Charges in Connection with the Investigation of the September 11 Attacks," April 2003.

88. Center for Migration Studies, Special Report, "Immigration Policy, Law Enforcement and National Security," (2003), 13.

89. U.S. Department of Justice, "The September 11 Detainees," 16, 41–42.

90. Ibid., 18.

91. Ibid., 19, 112–14.

92. Ibid., 112.

93. Ibid., 51.

94. Ibid., 47.

95. U.S. Department of Homeland Security, "Fact Sheet: Changes to National Security Entry/Exit Registration System (NSEERS)," Dec. 1, 2003.

96. For more on Immigration and Customs Enforcement directives to the Department of Homeland Security targeting "critical infrastructure" work sites, see http://www.ice.gov/pi/news/factsheets/immigration_enforcement_initiatives.htm and http://www.ice.gov/partners/employers/worksite/index.htm (last accessed July 2007).

97. National Commission on Terrorist Attacks Upon the United States, *The 9/11 Commission Report,* 234; Migration Policy Institute, "America's Challenge: Domestic Security, Civil Liberties, and National Unity After September 11" (2003), 9–11.

98. Romero, *The Violence of Love,* 29.

CHAPTER THIRTEEN

Hermeneutics and Politics of Strangers

*A Philosophical Contribution on the Challenge
of* Convivencia *in Multicultural Societies*

RAÚL FORNET-BETANCOURT

The word *convivencia* is a Spanish term that is difficult to translate into English. Its roots are derived from the Latin verb *convivire,* which literally means "to live with or together." Its connotations however are far richer. *Convivencia* does not just mean to physically live together. Rather it is used in the sense of sharing in such a way that there is celebration and a mutuality of enrichment.

The purpose of this essay is to reflect on what is foreign or strange, but only in its cultural sense, that is, the foreign and strange as they appear to us in another language, culture, or religion. Therefore, we will not deal here with "the other" that emerges from social differences, conflicts of interpretation, or biographical breaks within one culture or one person, and which, as a consequence, in spite of how foreign it may appear to us, could be perceived and understood *intraculturally* or *intrasubjectively* as the foreign within one's own context. Therefore, since we are going to deal only with what is culturally strange to us, our topic will be introduced by means of the following question: Is a stranger, as a member of a "strange" culture, the one whose presence causes the members of another culture to have a feeling of "strangeness"?

By asking this question, I do not mean to bring to mind the thesis, which is in itself evident, that what is strange provokes strangeness. That is to say, we are not interested in problematizing *how* what is strange presents itself to us nor *how* we feel or experience what is strange. Rather, with this question we postulate as a starting point the idea that the necessary condition to experience what is strange does not consist only in the existence of what is strange in general, but above all in the fact that what is strange *makes itself present* to us as some particular "strange entity" that presents itself in this or that form and, that through its presence visible in space, can affect us with a definite and specific form of strangeness.

We will also anticipate that when we speak here of what is culturally foreign to us, we refer to an otherness that is always contextualized. It is equally important to underline the contextuality of the stranger that, in our opinion, always implies a double dimension inasmuch as we encounter what is foreign in the concrete figure of a cultural difference constituted historically—a difference that comes from another place and that has its home in another place, but that at the same time irrupts into the context of what we call our own space to transform itself in what is strange, which "interferes" in our order precisely because we can see, listen to, and smell it. We are not just talking about the stranger seen from the distance of its original foreign contextuality, but also of the stranger that presents himself or herself near us, that is to say, a stranger in our own field of action. For this reason, the question about the treatment or relationship with respect to what is strange becomes—also in its strictly hermeneutic dimension—an eminently political question.

The purpose of these introductory remarks is to clarify that I am not interested here in problematizing the abstract experience of what is strange, but rather the experience marked by the particular contexts of the contextualized "strange entity." I am convinced that what is strange presents itself in the context of the world of our life, and that it does so neither as an abstract cultural tradition nor as an isolated individual apparition, since it presents itself from and with its original context. In the encounter with the stranger in a particular context it is not only human beings who meet, but also their respective worlds. For this reason we want to concretize and mark in a more precise way in which sense I am speaking here of the stranger or of what is strange. This will be the first point of this essay. The second and third points—as is indicated by the title—deal respectively with the hermeneutics and the politics of strangers. It must be noted that in my opinion these two aspects correspond to one another, since between the hermeneutics and the politics of strangers—as will be shown later—exists an internal practical-theoretical link.

What Are We Talking about in this Text When We Speak of What Is Strange?

It is obvious that we speak of what is strange. But, what is strange? Who is the stranger of whom we want to speak? Let us say, first, that "the stranger" is not an ontological category nor a homogeneous cultural-philosophical construction, but an anthropological-historical reality that approaches us or becomes present to us in the diversity of linguistic worlds, worlds of life, religions, traditions, cultures, and horizons of understanding. What is strange exists because plurality exists. Plurality manifests itself in phenomena that represent originals, which cannot be reduced to variations of a single identity, even if it is widely defined. For this reason, when one speaks of what is strange one must speak in the plural. That is the reason why I will no longer speak here of *what is* strange or *the* stranger, but of the *strangers.*

Second, the strangers of whom we will speak are concretely those human beings who we call foreigners or strangers, or better, those who are foreign or strange to us. But the human beings that are foreign to us are not simply those whom we call "the others." The others are those human beings from whom, through the demarcation of our personal identity, we want to differentiate ourselves in order to express the difference of our identity, as the old use of the German term *ander* in the sense of "the second" shows. But, inasmuch as those human beings who as a result of this differentiation, or better, "duplication," represent "the second half," the others are always also those whom we can experience as "our fellow human beings,"[1] that is to say, those who belong to our surroundings, because, in spite of their differences, they are part of our order.

On the other hand, culturally strange human beings or foreigners are those with whom, when we encounter them, we miss that immediate experience of belonging to "our" group that could perhaps be explained by the participation in a tradition that we claim as our own. For this reason we are not familiarized with who they are. It is true that they are in "our" world, that is to say, in our world of origin, but they are not native to that world, so we cannot understand them from the horizon of our world. Thus we develop a very special relationship with those human beings, above all when, as it happens with many of the migrants workers, "they arrive today and tomorrow they remain here,"[2] because that relationship is marked by "the distance that exists in the relationship."[3] Strangers are *for us* those human beings for whom our history, our language, and culture do not represent, by themselves, any reference or protection but on the contrary represent a labyrinth[4] in which they feel alienated and they do not know how to move. For this reason their "accessibility" is *for us* above all, as Husserl affirms, "accessibility in our own inaccessibility, in the form of incomprehensibility."[5] To speak today about such a stranger in the Federal Republic of Germany means to speak of those whom some German regional ideologists demand to assimilate to the "leader [dominant] German culture" so that they can live, perhaps not as God in France, but at least as true Germans in Germany.[6]

Thus I speak of strangers who live, for whatever reason, in a foreign land, that is, in our native world, and of those who, precisely because they are not at home in our country, are expected to assimilate to the social and cultural world order of the place that welcomes them. My reflections on the hermeneutics and politics of strangers will try to do justice to this contextual situation from which we start. But before going further with my argument, it is important to round up this point summarizing briefly the perspective from which I speak.

The title of the essay, insofar as it indicates that it deals with a philosophical contribution, obviously informs us on the perspective that we must follow. And we could believe that, with that statement, enough has been said on our point of departure, since it is evident that philosophical contributions must have something to do with philosophy! In effect, this essay deals with philosophy. But, what is philosophy? Every answer to this question is and always will be problematic, and every effort to try to solve it in a definitive form seems to be pure vanity and arrogance. Therefore, I will refrain from trying to answer that question in a definitive way. Nevertheless, as an orientation to better situate my argument, I want at least to outline briefly the concept of philosophy from which I start.

Philosophy is much more than the discipline that carries that name. Even more, there is no "philosophy" by the mere fact that philosophy exists as an academic discipline; on the contrary, the discipline called philosophy exists because "philosophy" exists, which in the exteriority of its institutionalized structure and also outside the margins of its own history as a discipline, tries to be philosophy in and for the world, that is to say, a contextual reflection. It is the philosophy that, as Hegel[7] demanded—to the surprise of many of today's Hegelians—does not build any world of its own but confronts its time and tries to understand each contextual moment and situation, precisely because its vocation consists in contributing to the contextual understanding of the problems of its time, as well as to the transformation of the historical world of humanity

The philosophy that makes of history its *locus philosophicus* is a philosophy for which the *logos* and the *ethos* form part of one and the same reality. For this reason, the exercise of its theoretical function is, by definition, fundamentally linked to the acceptance of responsibility in regards to the real course of humanity's practical world.

This concept of philosophy explains why I am not interested here in the question whether what is strange is a topic of philosophy or how it becomes so, that is to say, the question about how philosophy conceptualizes what is strange as a philosophical question. I am much more interested in problematizing the reality of the strangers, their situation, history, and culture, as a reality that challenges our way of thinking and acting. How can philosophy contribute contextually to overcome this challenge? What can philosophy offer us so that we may understand about strangers and behave ethically with them? This is the question in which we are really interested here.

For a Hermeneutics of Strangers

Hermeneutics, to the development of which theology and jurisprudence made contributions of fundamental importance, is considered today in fact as a distinct discipline. It is the theory, or better, the scientific method for the interpretation and explanation of texts, but also of the conditions for understanding what is human. Moreover, in this sense hermeneutics is inscribed "in the scientific tradition of Modernity. The corresponding utilization of hermeneutics begins precisely in that time, that is to say, with the emergence of the modern concept of method and science."[8] But, on the other hand, it is precisely that particular development of hermeneutics within the horizon of the European scientific tradition that turns it today into a problematic tradition for intercultural research. Let us put this question aside, since we do not want to use the term hermeneutics in the sense that is generally given to this discipline that belongs to the history of the differentiation of European philosophy. We will rather use the term hermeneutics in its wider etymological meaning.

As it is well known, the word "hermeneutics" comes from the Greek and—among other things—it means "to interpret," "to translate," "to announce." In Greek mythology this etymological meaning is expressed by the figure of Hermes. Hermes was the messenger of the gods, the "spokesperson" whose function was to transmit the messages of the *strange* world of the gods to that of human beings, which meant to translate and announce it to humans in a language that would be understood by them. It is interesting to remember here, however briefly, that Hermes' role as announcer and spokesperson explains why the inhabitants of Listra used the name "Hermes" when speaking of Paul.[9] In continuity with this insight, the starting point of a hermeneutics of strangers should be the fundamental idea that *to translate* is a necessary condition to understand the strangers. Whoever wants to understand the stranger must, then, deal with them by *translating.* But in that process the only thing that is clear is what needs to be translated, that is, what is strange in the strangers. The messenger Hermes is not anymore among us, and we have to ask ourselves who is actually the subject or the carrier of that *interpretation,* that is, who transmits the world of the strangers to our world. It seems obvious that we ourselves are the ones who are now in charge of that task. Our working hypothesis goes also in that direction, but only partially. In fact, we must assume the work of Hermes, not as the unique subject that demotes the strangers to an object of interpretation, but as a subject that perceives the strangers as subjects in their own right. They question us as interpreters of their own world and self-interpreters of their own condition, and for this reason do not consider themselves as beings that are merely at the disposition of the interpreter as a silent object of soliloquy, but that on the contrary understand themselves as speakers having the same rights as the one who is interpreting them.

The translation of the strangeness of the strangers has to be posed as a *collective* task, understanding by this the patient and challenging cooperation of a *community of translators* that—like the famous translators' school of Toledo in the still partially Muslim Spain of the eleventh and twelfth centuries—is the expression of a community of *convivencia* with the stranger and for that reason it also allows the stranger to serve as co-translator. Thus the translation of the strangeness of strangers is a task that needs to be carried out by an intersubjectivity that is interculturally qualified. To express it in a clearer way: fundamentally the strangeness of strangers can only be translated by human beings who are aware that one cannot understand the strangers without their cooperation as subjects and that, consequently, to really understand them, one must learn to understand *together with* them. Besides, we have to become aware that the participation in the collective task of translation of the strangeness of strangers—precisely because, insofar as it is an exercise of understanding achieved through the accompaniment of strangers, it represents also a process of learning about our own reality—is a work that implies important consequences as much for our own self-interpretation as for the positioning of our own culture in relation to that of the stranger.

Nevertheless, this idea of an intersubjectivity that is interculturally qualified presupposes that one works intersubjectively at the level of our way of thinking and intraculturally at the level of our own culture. This is the second essential characteristic of the hermeneutics of strangers I propose here. I am speaking of the work that we have to carry out *in our very selves,* that is to say, to be willing for the experience of being with what is strange to become the starting point to achieve a process of collective learning. In this area we would distinguish two complementary moments. Firstly, I would mention the historicization of our way of thinking. Our way of thinking is not innate, but has been developing through history, and, in fact, under conditions marked by social conflicts. Our way of thinking, could be said, has a familiar history. It is precisely for this reason that we have to ask ourselves, particularly in our encounter with the strangers, the following question: why do we think or understand exactly in the way that we do, and not in another way? The importance of this question increases in the encounter with strangers, since the form of our thinking is, at the same time, an expression of ourselves. Our way or form of understanding says much about ourselves, and through it, therefore, we make ourselves understood by others.[10] In relation to this question we also have to think deeply and critically about the concepts that shape our way of thinking. For example, it would be necessary to question if the concepts from whose horizons we encounter the strangers are suitable instruments to approach them or if these are the result of "prejudgements" that we continue to cultivate, since what basically interests us is not knowledge of the strangers but controlled and interested dealings with them.

Secondly, I would mention the critique of the hegemonic way of knowing in European culture that conceptualizes knowledge on the basis of the division between subject and object, with which it is precisely assumed as evident that, supposedly, the subject "appropriates" the object, that is to say, "takes possession" of it. In this case, knowledge does not lead to *recognition* but to *assimilation*. The well-known German master of hermeneutics writes in this respect the following: "Recognizing what is our own in what is strange, getting comfortable in it, that is the fundamental movement of the spirit, whose being is only to return to himself from that otherness."[11] In this quotation a way of knowing becomes evident, ideal of which is the dissolution of what is strange, and it could be expressed by comparing it with the processes of eating and digesting.[12] Nevertheless, its aggressive character and its real threats for the strangers make themselves evident when we consider that the modern way of this form of knowing is intimately linked with the history of European colonialism. Further, seen in a more precise way, this form of knowing represents in reality a chapter of the history of the colonial relationships with respect to the strangers.

Therefore, the hermeneutics of strangers that follows the principle according to which strangers can only be understood with their help as self-interpreters of their condition would have to be then, and this is its third characteristic, a hermeneutics that is both liberated from the habits of colonial thinking and allows itself to be influenced by the strangers. Strangers, then, would not represent only that which our hermeneutics has to take possession of—by means of an assimilating knowledge—to incorporate them into what is our own, but they would better represent the exteriority that widens the frontiers of our horizon of understanding. Thus, the praxis of hermeneutics of strangers implies a commitment with a horizon of understanding transformed by the strangers, and in which we ourselves are transformed, since by means of this experience we discover a new world and—above all—because we become aware that with the strangers "we are reborn."

In summary, I would conclude with the following: a hermeneutics of strangers has to orient itself following the principle that advocates the participation of the strangers in the process of self-understanding. It is only the cooperation of the strangers in such a process that can prevent us both from raising what is our own as the rule or norm, and that we consider, from the beginning, that to understand the strangers and our *own* experience of them is one and the same thing.[13]

Toward an Intercultural Politics of Strangers

In the last part of this essay, I will concentrate on the question of the challenges that the *convivencia* with strangers poses to our political action. While I mentioned this word in the title of the essay, I also used the term "multicultural society." In order to avoid possible misunderstandings, I must clarify that. I use the concept "multicultural society" for contextual reasons, that is, because this concept has become a common term in Germany. Nevertheless, at the same time in Germany this concept is the object of a strong public debate, as revealed in the actual debate on the politics of immigration. Let me give an example. For the politicians of the Green group, like Daniel Cohn-Bendit,[14] the term "multicultural society" is used as part of a political program that responds to the demands of a reality which de facto already exists. For the politicians of the conservative German party, the Christian Democratic Union, like Jörg Schönbohm,[15] however, this term symbolizes the flag of a political struggle with which the German left outlines its ultimate utopia. Because a common definition for multiculturalism does not exist, it is resolutely put aside as a possible model for the future.

As I have pointed out, the use of the concept "multicultural society" here is due to these contextual reasons, but that should not be interpreted as an indication that we are to identify with the position of those who consider "multicultural society" as the only future alternative and, consequently, propose it as the *only* model for the organization of the *convivencia* of human beings who come from different cultures. Yet, I also do not share the criticism of the right to the "multicultural society" in Germany, which tries to seek salvation in a self-affirmation of a German culture, understood as a national homogeneous culture. Rather, I identify more closely with the proposal of a leftist critique of the "multicultural society," taking as a guiding light the vision of an *intercultural* community of worlds that are different and yet in solidarity with each other, that is to say, of worlds that are reshaped by means of the interaction of their members in their daily life, and that in this way are understood as processes in which the borders between what is our own and what is "other" are conceived as places of encounter and "negotiation." Here, the organizing principle is not the self-preservation of diversity or the adaptation of the strangers to a unifying leader [dominant] culture (*Leitkultur*),[16] but the leading and normative idea of "mutuality."

On the other hand, I want also to point out, that when I speak of politics, I are not talking only of party politics, namely, the politics of professional politicians. The meaning of this term includes also the social action of human beings in relation to the *res publica,* that is, the things that concern each human being as a citizen. Politics, understood as the space for political action, deals with things that human beings can change. In other words, politics—as Hannah Arendt showed—draws life from the idea that human beings can change the historical world in which they live.[17] In light of this insight I will now try to posit a first moment of an intercultural politics of relationships with and among strangers, a moment which, in reality, indicates something evident. In connection with Hannah Arendt's thought which I have just cited, I would say that we are talking about the following: a politics of strangers must be, above all, a reflection of the evidence that the way to deal with strangers is one of the things that we can actively change with our behavior and that is, therefore, a practice the real quality for which we are responsible. Thus, the politics of strangers must be a daily, concrete politics for the betterment of the quality of our relationships with strangers. But, for it to be such, it must also be critical of the actual contextual conditions in which we live with strangers, and with this we are already anticipating the second aspect of our proposal of an intercultural politics of strangers.

Here, I am referring to the need of a critique of the reigning asymmetric conditions that we can notice, for example, in the limited possibilities for the participation of strangers in the organization of our society. Nevertheless, in this context the politics of strangers should not be a politics of *integration* but a politics of elimination of borders that delimit the present order.

Therefore, it must not point to the reestablishment of a supposed unity, which was supposedly disturbed by the strangers. Its goal should rather be to work with the strangeness of the stranger in order to achieve an ecumenical reconstruction of the social order in which the strangers *are not deprived of their rights* but that, on the contrary, *are authorized* and *recognized* in their difference in such a way that the guarantee of their physical and vital *integrity* does not depend on their social or cultural *integration*.

From this follows the third aspect: a politics of strangers should be not only a politics of recognition but a politics of *public* recognition. Whoever speaks of recognition speaks also of identity.[18] This means that a politics of recognition of the strangers has to be a politics of differences, a politics that recognizes the strangers not only as *equal*, that is, as subjects to whom, as citizens, are given the same rights of political integration to the order of the majority's culture, but also and precisely as *strangers*, that is, as those before whom the established political community commits itself to create a new ecumenical order in which—as the Zapatistas of Mexico claim—all the worlds have a place and belong. In other words, a politics of recognition of the strangers has to go beyond the mere acknowledgement of their human dignity as the source of equality for the civil rights of all. It needs to go beyond the acknowledgement of what belongs to each one on the basis of equality in order to recognize also the difference of their respective worlds.[19] Human dignity is not an abstract universality, but a reality always incarnated in cultural identities. Thus, the acknowledgement of dignity implies the acknowledgement of the cultural differences in which the human dignity is concretely realized. Therefore, a politics of recognition of the strangers must be a politics of acknowledgement of the strangers as subjects who have the right to difference, or better, the right to live their culture.

The recognition of strangers as *bearers* of culture and difference does not imply, nevertheless, that the cultures of strangers be reduced to mere monuments placed under protection. Respect towards difference should not lead to consider the members of foreign cultures as "traditionalists," that is, as mere "upholders of the monuments," of the traditions of their place of origin. Cultures represent historical processes that not only facilitate what is known, but also can serve to investigate what is new and unknown, since they are always moving within the tension between tradition and innovation.[20] The recognition of foreign cultures implies certainly the public *authorization* (*Berechtigung*) of its members so that they may live their cultural difference. But this implies, at the same time, a commitment to dialogue and interchange. In this sense, the recognition, understood as authorization, is the condition necessary to achieve relationships of equality among all, but it is also the condition for the cultures to begin a process of *correction* (*Berichtigung*) according to the spirit of "mutuality."

For this reason—and this is our fourth point—a politics of strangers must go beyond the horizon of the model of a multicultural liberal society, which is based on a cultural pluralism that brings out the ethnic origin and for that reason tends[21] to consider cultures as ghettos, in order to foster a praxis of "overflowing" of borders that put limits to differences, starting with daily experiences in which in fact we share our worlds and continually cross borders. By means of this praxis of "overflowing" of borders, the fact of multiculturality must begin to acquire a new quality: the quality of intercultural *convivencia*. What we aspire to, therefore, with this new political practice is the transformation of a multicultural society into an intercultural community in which human beings do not change their culture of origin into barricades for the defense of a self-affirmation of the difference, which in reality yearns for hegemonic power. According to the politics proposed here, the cultures of origin must, on the contrary, represent the starting point from which concrete human beings enter into contact with a daily world marked by multiculturalism, deal with what is their own or foreign, and develop a new relationship, not only in regard to the others but also in relation to themselves. And perhaps in this way they will also learn to situate and define identity beginning with the relationship and practical dealings with differences, and not only from the centrality of one culture.

On the other hand, it is clear that a politics of strangers inspired by interculturality has to reject the program that is debated today in Germany under the slogan of "leader [dominant] German culture" (*Deutsche Leitkultur*). On one hand, the expression "leader culture" (*Leitkultur*)—I consciously consider this term as an "expression" because for me "leader culture" is not a concept—is a contradiction because it changes the cultural heritage of a community into a static order of culture, culturally untransformable, although the cultural heritage of a people has been developed historically and is, therefore, something variable and continues also subjected to the historical changes proper of the daily world of the human beings who live in it.[22] And we must still say that this contradiction has to deal with the fact that this expression, in truth, does not distinguish between culture and values, which by consensus can be recognized as *basic values* for the members of a given culture.

On the other hand, the expression "leader German culture" may be perhaps only another variant of "collective narcissism"[23] on the part of those who have to use tradition for compensatory ends because in reality their central interest is the control of society, and not cultural development. But what is decisive for the topic treated here is the following: for a politics of strangers, which really aims at the realization of interculturality in our world of today, the idea of *one* leader [dominant] culture, understood as the organizing principle for living together with human beings coming from strange cultures, represents a project of assimilation of these cultures to the dominant culture of the majority. To this project one must oppose a politics of strangers interculturally inspired that, as we have tried to outline here, does not advocate assimilation to the predominant culture, but the intercultural transformation of the cultures and their members.

Nevertheless, we must acknowledge that we still find ourselves very far from this intercultural politics of strangers. But we are aware of it, and for this reason I will end with the following observation: as long as a politics of intercultural *convivencia* does not characterize the reality of our daily living, and xenophobia is tolerated, as if it were something normal, we should at least make some efforts to assume the practice of civil courage that, according to a German translation of the Hebrew term for the established stranger (*gēr*), welcomes our strangers as "citizens who must be protected"[24] (*Schutzbürger*).

NOTES

This paper was translated from Spanish by Sister Rosa María Icaza, C.C.V.I.

1. See Edmund Husserl, *Zur Phänomenologie der Intersubjektivität,* ed. W. Biemel, *Husserliana,* Bd. XV (Den Haag: Martinus Nijhoff, 1973), 38. With respect to the distinction between the other and the stranger see Bernhard Waldenfels, *Der Stachel des Fremden* (Frankfurt: Suhrkamp, 1990) and his book *Topographie des Fremden* (Frankfurt: Suhrkamp, 1997). In relation to the question on the other within Western philosophy, cf. Pedro Laín Entralgo, *Teoría y realidad del otro* (Madrid: Revista de Occidente, 1961) and Paul Ricœur, *Soi-même comme un autre* (Paris: Seuil, 1990).

2. George Simmel, "Exkurs über den Fremden," in *Soziologie* (Berlin: de Gruyter, 1968), 509.

3. Ibid.

4. Cf. Alfred Schütz, "Der Fremde," in *Gesammelte Schriften II* (Den Haag: Martinus Nijhoff, 1972), 68.

5. Husserl, *Zur Phänomenologie der Intersubjektivität, 631.*

6. The reader must keep in mind that this article takes as concrete experience the context of the most intense moment of the debate on the "leader [dominant] culture" (*Deutsche Leitkultur*) in Germany.

7. Cf. G. W. F. Hegel, *Grundlinien der Philosophie des Rechts,* in *Theorie-Werkausgabe,* vol. 7 (Frankfurt: Suhrkamp, 1970), 26.

8. H. G. Gadamer, "Hermeneutik," in *Historisches Wörterbuch der Philosophie,* ed. Joachim Ritter, vol. 3 (Basel: Schwab, 1974), 1062.

9. Acts 14:12.

10. Cf. Anette C. Hammerschmidt, *Fremdverstehen: Interkulturelle Hermeneutik zwischen Eigenem und Fremdem* (München: Iudicium, 1997), 241.

11. H. G. Gadamer, *Wahrheit und Methode* (Tübingen: J. C. B. Mohr, 1975), 11.

12. Cf. Jean-Paul Sartre, "Une idée fondamentale de la phénomémologie de Husserl: L'intentionnalité," in *Situations I* (Paris: Gallimard, 1974), 29.

13. Cf. Hammerschmidt, *Fremdverstehen,* 12.

14. Cf. Daniel Cohn-Bendit and Thomas Schmid, *Heimat Babylon* (Hamburg: Junius, 1993), and Daniel Cohn-Bendit, "Ganz einfache Sachen," in *Multi Kulti: Spielregeln für die Vielvölkerrepublik,* ed. Claus Leggewie, 61–68 (Berlin: Rotbuch, 1993).

15. Cf. Jörg Schönbohm, "Die letzte Utopie der Linken wird auch scheitern," *Berliner Zeitung,* June 22, 1998.

16. This term literally means "leader culture."

17. Hannah Arendt, *Wahrheit und Politik* (München: Fink, 1967).

18. Cf. Charles Taylor, *Multikulturalismus und die Politik der Anerkennung* (Frankfurt: Fischer, 1997), 13.

19. Ibid., 28.

20. Cf. Raúl Fornet-Betancourt, ed., *Kulturen zwischen Tradition und Innovation: Sind wir am Ende der traditionellen Kulturen?* (Frankfurt: IKO-Verlag, 2001).

21. Cf. Karl-Otto Apel, "El problema de la justicia en una sociedad multicultural," in *Filosofía para la convivencia,* ed. Raúl Fornet-Betancourt and Juan A. Senent, 195–216 (Sevilla: MAD, Editorial Universitaria, 2004), and his study "Das Problem des Multikulturalismus aus der Sicht der Diskursethik," in *Gemeinschaft und Gerechtigkeit,* ed. Micha Brumlik and Hanke Brunhorst, 149–172 (Frankfurt: Suhrkamp, 1993); D. Cohn-Bendit and Th. Schmid, *Heimat Babylon* (Hamburg: Hoffman und Campe, 1992); Jürgen Habermas, *Faktizität und Geltung* (Frankfurt: Suhrkamp, 1992), and his study "Anerkennungskämpfe im demokratischen Rechtsstaat," in Taylor, *Multikulturalismus,* 147–96; W. Kymlicka, *Liberalism, Community, and Culture* (Oxford:

Oxford University Press, 1989); and above all, Diana de Vallescar Palanca, *Cultura, Multiculturalismo e interculturalidad* (Madrid: Editorial PS, 2000).

22. Cf. Christian Geyer, "Spiel nicht mit der Leitkultur," *Frankfurter Allgemeine Zeitung-FAZ,* November 1, 2000, N5.

23. Th. W. Adorno, "Theorie der Halbbildung," in *Eine Auswahl,* ed. Rolf Tiedemann (Stuttgart: Deutscher Bücherbund, 1971), 314.

24. Cf. Artikel "gēr" in Wilhelm Gesenius, *Hebräisches und aramäisches Handwörterbuch über das Alte Testament* (Leipzig: Mayer, 1910), 145; and the German edition of *Jerusalemer Bibel* (Freiburg: Herder, 1979), 2 Sam 1:13 and 2 Sam 4:3, among others. This information I owe to I. Homey of the University of Bonn.

CHAPTER FOURTEEN

The Gender of Risk

Sexual Violence against Undocumented Women

OLIVIA RUIZ MARRUJO

If risk plays a role in most international undocumented migration, it underlies especially the experiences of undocumented women migrants from Central America, the focus of this essay. To be sure, like men who migrate, women face the possibility of robbery, assault, extortion, and mistreatment at the hands of authorities. Likewise, in search of the most economical ways to travel, women risk falling from freight trains or tumbling off the backs of trucks.[1] Among the dangers Central American migrant women face, however, sexual violence, due to the frequency of its occurrence and the degree of suffering it necessarily inflicts, occupies a singular and terrifying place.[2] Indeed, it is hardly an exaggeration to state that the possibility of falling victim to this aggression sits foremost in the minds of women who leave their countries without documents. According to one director of Beta Sur, the Mexican police force established to protect the rights of migrants on the Mexico-Guatemala border, sexual assault of migrant women forms part of the modus operandi of robbers who daily attack migrants in the region. On Mexico's northern border, the Attorney General of Human Rights and Citizen Protection (*Procuraduría de Derechos Humanos y Protección Ciudadana de Baja California*) states that, among undocumented migrants, both in California and Baja, California, women are especially vulnerable to mistreatment by authorities and frequent victims not only of robbery and threats but of sexual aggression.[3] Furthermore, we can expect more cases of this type of violence in years to come, judging from the growing numbers of women leaving their homes without documents. Estimates for the northern border show that women now make up 20 percent of the migratory flows across that border, while data from the southern border reveal even higher rates.

Yet, despite the reality of sexual violence against undocumented women migrants, Central Americans in this case, it is a poorly documented risk, if and when it is registered at all. Notwithstanding the familiar cautionary tales of sexual abuse and rape, stories told by migrants (both male and female) to warn women and their companions of the dangers ahead, relatively little attention has been paid to the subject. As such, any effort to bring to light the facts of this injury, to understand why and to whom it occurs along the migratory route, presents a difficult challenge. Indeed, not until the 1990s, when "the physical, sexual, and emotional violence . . . that many women experience because of their gender" was added to the long list of officially recognized human rights violations did attention begin to turn to the specific situation of the sexual abuse of female migrants.[4]

What follows are some initial observations on sexual violence in the context of undocumented migration on Mexico's southern border with Guatemala, specifically in the long sliver of western coastal land known as the Soconusco in the state of Chiapas. The essay draws on testimonies of migrant women and men from Guatemala, Honduras, El Salvador, and Nicaragua, participant observation especially in two missions in Chiapas and Guatemala, as well as interviews with individuals, groups, and organizations dedicated to helping undocumented migrants in the region.[5] In this essay I hope to contribute to an understanding of sexual violence against women migrants by examining why this type of violence occurs and why it does so with such frequency along Mexico's southern border. I also propose ways to address this urgent issue.

Defining Sexual Violence

What is sexual violence? While many of us have an intuitive understanding of the term, its meanings vary in place and time, a point I will return to at the end of the essay. To emphasize, the literature on migration makes almost no mention of sexual violence against women migrants. Sexual violence, however, occupies an important place in the literature on women and gender studies. Due to its emphasis on sexuality and on the role men play in the subordination of women, radical feminism, in particular, has placed the issue at the center of its analysis.[6] Kate Millet, for example, suggests that sexual violence is intrinsic to patriarchy, which "relies on a form of violence particularly sexual in character and realized most completely in the act of rape."[7] Later studies, widening the scope of analysis, focus on the political character of sexual violence and its diverse and complex origins.[8] They underline the need to situate its occurrence in historical, sociocultural, political, and economic perspectives, on the one hand, and the configurations of class, race, and ethnicity, on the other. These studies emphasize how different contexts, from the individual to the institutional, give rise to patriarchal ideology and, by implication, to sexual violence.[9] In the words of Brickman, such acts are "social statements [which] embody central themes and tensions of the civilization" in which they take place.[10]

To be sure, sexual violence against undocumented women migrants repeats many of the patterns that characterize this aggression against women in general. Consequently, the definition I offer here reflects ideas critical to the issue in the population at large. As defined here it refers to an act that is physical or psychological-emotional in nature—a sexual assault as well as a threat of sexual assault—aimed at the sexuality of the woman migrant, at attacking her physical, emotional, spiritual, and psychic integrity. More specifically it has the following characteristics.

First, to repeat, "sexual violence" refers to a physical and verbal affront that *a migrant woman identifies* as an offense to her sexuality and, by implication, her physical, psychological, spiritual, and emotional constitution as a woman. When classifying acts as expressions of sexual violence we must always keep in mind these women's points of view.

Second, it refers to abuses aimed at the bodies of women migrants. It is an aggression directed at those parts of the body which physiologically distinguish her as a woman—her breasts and genitals—and lie at the heart of her identity as a woman.[11] As such, sexual violence includes physical attacks to her sexuality as well as verbal assaults, for example, a threat of rape.

Third, these attacks are aggressions that transgress norms (whether set down in law or daily practice), themselves socially and culturally configured, that shape behavior, especially sexual behavior, towards the feminine body. In the life of a woman, these standards determine which man or men can (or cannot) approach her body; they also govern how, if, when, and where he or they may do so. In other words, cultures develop and establish an array of precepts to treat women's bodies, and conventions of respect as well as rules governing the transgression of female bodies. Sexual violence involves a violation of one or more of them.

It is important to note that a migrant woman's interpretation of a specific act or event as sexually violent will reflect how the cultures and societies in which she first became conscious of her sexuality—the behaviors and norms that shape and give meaning to sexuality—define transgressive and nontrangressive sexual behavior. Consequently, the place (or places) where a woman has lived and the sociocultural landscape where she has developed as a woman necessarily influence her interpretation of an act or event as sexually violent or not. An undocumented Central American woman for whom sexual relations have been rarely, if ever, consensual, may consider a *coyote's* demand for sex, in exchange for assuring her "safe" passage, a repulsive kind of hounding but not necessarily deviant behavior. Indeed, she may even consider it "expected" or "usual" adult male conduct, "what one can expect from a man if you are a woman."[12] In other words, a woman will or will not associate an experience with sexual violence depending, to a certain extent, on whether her culture of origin has equipped her to identify that experience as such.

In that process of identification, the degree to which a woman understands her personal, civil, and human rights plays a critical role. Preparing for the worst, a possible sexual assault on the journey north, and seeking to avoid the additional hardship of a forced pregnancy, a woman migrant may take birth control pills. She may not name this scenario (facing the possibility of assault, acquiring birth control pills, and taking them) "sexual violence," but from the standpoint of human rights it is difficult not to see it as such. In the end whether or not she recognizes this psychological terror and the horrible choice it imposes as sexual violence will depend to a large extent upon the degree to which her society of origin has encouraged the education and socialization of human rights, especially her civil and gender rights as a woman. It is important to take into account both the perceptions of migrant women who undergo such violence and an analysis based on fundamental principles of human rights.

The Whys of Sexual Violence

The literature on sexual violence offers a number of explanations for this abuse. One approach suggests that sexually abusive behavior has clearly defined motives and occurs in specific and recurrent situations. The rape of women during a robbery is one such case. Assailants rape women, according to this explanation, to "reward" themselves for a successful robbery or as a "gratification" after the assault. Some forms of male-bonding or rites to establish loyalties and hierarchies in a group of boys or men include, may even require, the sexual abuse of women.[13] The initiation rituals of some gangs involve the collective rape of a woman.

Coyotes, or migrant traffickers, insofar as they have almost exclusive control over the people who have paid them to go north, often gain access to the bodies of women migrants. *Coyotes* may refuse to take a woman north, threaten to turn her over to unknown men, or abandon her midway if she refuses his advances. A woman, aware of the possibility of such a demand, and seeking to avoid a confrontation and possibly greater violence, may "agree" from the beginning of her negotiations with a *coyote* to have sex with him in exchange for his "help" or "protection."

There also exists a trafficking of women, a buying and selling of their bodies, most often for sex work. While the people who buy and sell women may or may not abuse the women themselves, they force their hostages into a cycle of abuse, the sale of their bodies for the sexual gratification of customers.

Yet the question remains: why are women migrants in the border between Mexico and Guatemala so vulnerable to this form of aggression? Parting from the premise that the number of men who sexually abuse women varies from society to society, we need to ask what, if anything, in the sociocultural configuration of societies where this aggression occurs frequently produces sexual aggressors or permits men, with a predisposition towards this kind of aggression, to act on it. Is there, in the specific case of the Soconusco, anything in the social and cultural makeup of the region that permits some men to commit acts of sexual violence against women migrants?

I suggest we can begin to answer this question by examining what makes this kind of violence not only permissible but gratifying, or even rewarding, in a society and culture—in the Soconusco, for example. Specifically, and following the advice of much of the literature on sexual violence, we should look at the interrelationship of four factors: the uses and abuses of power, the role of violence in society, the normative and legal construction of gender, and the culture of gender.[14] In the case of women migrants, especially in a border context, we need to look, in addition, at local erotic culture and the culture and structure of interethnic and interracial relations.

The Uses and Abuses of Power

Sexual violence reflects and shapes inequalities of power in a society. In incidences of sexual violence the uses and abuses of power manifest themselves; they become concrete. Above all such acts reflect inequalities of power in sex and gender relations. As such, they mirror the inequalities that subordinate a woman, or group of women, to a man or group of men in a particular society.[15] MacKinnon states that in incidences of sexual violence "a man takes possession of the sexuality of a woman, as it is mediated by her body" and, by way of this act, proclaims that her sexuality "belongs to him, is subordinated to him."[16]

Sexual violence, to be sure, may also reflect inequalities of power among men, revealing attempts of one group to dominate another. History documents time and again how groups of men have strategically employed sexual violence to humiliate and demoralize the "other." Since women—exclusive access to them as well as the treatment and control of their bodies—are symbols of honor and shame in many societies, sexual violence against them, especially when carried out collectively, may have origins and aims rooted in broader societal aggressions, such as ethnic cleansing or war.[17] The collective rape of women migrants degrades and humiliates its victims; if carried out in front of husbands, boyfriends, brothers, or sons, it will humiliate and defeat them as well.

The Role of Violence

In this light, we need to look at the role that violence plays in a society. Indeed, studies show that its generalized use to solve social conflicts corresponds to a high incidence of sexual abuse.[18] In other words, we need to examine sexual abuse in the context of societal violence, since the frequent use of violence, in any form, reflects a predisposition towards aggression in a society and belies a high incidence of abuse of women. In the case of the southern border, we need to determine if, and to what extent, violence constitutes a culturally appropriate, accessible, and permissible response to conflicts and disagreements. Regarding its practice in the Soconusco, for example, we should ask whether people in the region employ it frequently. Also, is it tolerated or punished? Is it used in a wide range of situations or limited to specific circumstances? In other words, we should ask if and to what extent, in the words of Bandura, there exists a "social learning of aggression," that is, a reinforcement and reproduction of aggressive behavior in the repertoire of acceptable responses to conflict. We also need to examine whether there exists a "social learning" that represses violence, that is, a social and self-condemnation of it.[19]

The Normative-Judicial Rights of Women

The degree to which a society accepts or condemns sexual violence also depends upon how its judicial system defines and defends the rights of women. As such, we need to ask to what extent the system supports a woman who says she has been sexually mistreated and facilitates or hampers the judicial process—the apprehension and punishment of those who abused her.[20] In addition, in the case of Central American women migrants, we need to know to what extent the judicial process can accommodate migrants, particularly when they have crossed international boundaries without documents. Women migrants on the southern border, for example, will most likely avoid public institutions and places, and remain in transit unless money is lacking, work is available, or physical incapacity (an accident, disease) makes traveling north impossible. Today, in light of the dynamics of migration and the judicial system's limitations, it should not surprise us that so few cases of sexual violence against women migrants appear in official records in the Soconusco. A case of rape on the Guatemalan side of the border takes three months to be expedited; the process on the Mexican side requires comparable lengths of time.

The Culture of Gender

Acts of sexual violence also have roots in the cultures of gender, which order and give meaning to relations between men and women in societies. In the words of Scully, sexual violence occurs more frequently in societies where women are portrayed as property and extreme distrust or hostility marks relations between the sexes.[21] At bottom lies a recurrent absence often associated with a propensity for violence in general: the incapacity to identify with the "other," to feel empathy for her or him.[22] In other words, in societies where images of women as property dominate, where an acute and generalized distrust of women prevails, and hostility marks relations between the sexes, men are, in general, less likely to identify with women as equals—as people who feel and suffer as they do—and more likely to feel less empathy for them when they do suffer.[23] In this light, I suggest we need to explore to what extent, if at all, these elements form part of the culture of gender on the southern border.

Any effort to determine the presence or absence of these characteristics in the culture of gender alerts us to the need to develop ways of naming and measuring their identifying signs. While that analysis lies beyond the scope of this essay, I suggest that we might start by determining the degree of control men have over women, especially over their bodies and sexuality. What do women reveal about gender relations in the Soconusco, for example, when in daily conversation they refer to sexual relations with their partners as "cuando hace uso de mi"—"when he makes use of me"? Likewise, emergency rooms of local hospitals attend daily to women who arrive unconscious after suffering "fainting spells," the result, almost always, of disagreements or conflicts with a spouse or partner. By implication, what reception and treatment can Central American migrant women expect in a society that has built a culture of gender around the appropriation of women's bodies and sexualities by the men closest to them or where women "faint" when faced with an angry mate or husband?

Erotic Culture

In reflecting on the way the culture of gender influences the treatment of Central American migrant women, we also need to look at local erotic culture, that is, the way women and men in the region imagine, construct, and live sexual desire. This is important in understanding sexual violence in the Soconusco, I suggest, for erotic culture plays a role not only in the daily life of relations between men and women but in the acceptance or rejection of the abuse of women. Following Tong's advice, we should look for the balance between sexual impulse and *thanatos,* or death instinct, in the local practice of erotic relations, between a sexuality characterized by the full participation of two people and one shaped by subordination and domination.[24] In this respect, even a cursory observation of the public practice of erotic life in the Soconusco reveals worrisome signs.

Bars, for example, predominately masculine domains, except for the waitresses and dancers (who often double as sex workers), are the principal places of male recreation in the region. Men go there, most often in groups of friends and acquaintances, to talk, drink, play pool, watch sports, and amuse themselves with the table dancers, almost exclusively from Honduras, El Salvador, Guatemala, and to a lesser extent Nicaragua. Indeed, men go to bars expecting Central American table dancers to entertain them. In a similar vein, young men in the Soconusco will often seek out Central Americans for their first sexual experiences, due to the ease and impersonality of the encounters. In short, Central American women play a singular and important role in male erotic life in the region, in the unfolding and life experiences of their sexual desire. These women occupy a central place in the growth of personal sexual behavior and norms of conduct—in their development into a sexuality of subordination or full participation—that shape men's erotic relations with women.

The Context of Ethnic-Racial Relations

Addressing the issue described above also entails examining the place Central Americans, especially Central American women, occupy in the social structure and day to day life of the Soconusco, as well as in this Mexican border region's historical relationship with communities and nations south of the border. The configuration of society and daily life in the Soconusco and the region's historical ties to the south rest, in turn, on what may be referred to, borrowing from Omi and Winnant, as an *ethno-racial and national project.* Shaped by and adapted to local circumstances, such a project is "an interpretation, representation or explanation of the racial [and I would include, as well, ethnic and national] dynamics" between peoples, communities and societies—those of the Soconusco and the distinct peoples of Central America in this case. It emerges out of a struggle to fix a hegemonic notion of community, people, and nation. As such it relies inherently on a *racial, ethnic, and national classification and stratification* of the distinct peoples who make up a society, region, or nation.[25] By implication, the place minority social groups—Central Americans, for example—occupy in the local classification and stratification of social groups—that of the Soconusco—influences how local residents will perceive and treat them.

Since the late nineteenth century, large numbers of rural laborers as well as domestic workers, many from Guatemala, have crossed the border to look for work in the Soconusco. As such, many residents identify Guatemalans, especially when poor and indigenous, with rural and domestic labor; they are, by definition of their employment in Chiapas, a subordinated and exploited social group. By extension, anyone from Central America who works in agriculture or domestic service is profiled in a similar way. Also, to repeat, most sex workers in the region come from Central America; today the association between Central America and sex work remains well established in the region. I suggest that these images set the stage for abuse; any explanation of sexual violence against women migrants needs to look at the role played by these popular images and representations of Central American migrants as low-wage, if not impoverished, expendable, agricultural laborers, domestic workers, and prostitutes.

What We Can Do

What can we do and how do we proceed in light of the profound consequences and ramifications of this abuse, both in the immediate present, in the day to day of women's migrations, and in the future, as these women begin to settle and participate in society, possibly in another country? What is to be done in the worst cases of sexual violence, such as rape, which can alter a woman's sense of self to such a degree she may feel stigmatized and marked for life?[26] To be sure, the findings of recent research on the consequences of sexual abuse of minors, young victims of rape, for example, are especially alarming, since they indicate that severe mistreatment may provoke irreversible neurobiological damage.[27] The growing numbers of women migrants along the southern border, a scenario repeated in Mexico's northern border and reflected worldwide, where female migrants make up almost 50 percent of the planet's migratory flows, renders sexual violence against women an urgent issue in the arena of migration policy.[28]

I make the following proposals taking into account the seriousness of the injury, the lack of information, and the need to respond to the situation with the aid of people knowledgeable about the abuse, especially in the context of migration. To begin, in specific cases of abuse we need to learn more about what occurred. We need to know what happened, when and where it happened, and who was responsible. Women should be able to give this information and talk about the abuse in an environment where they feel safe. This involves preparing people who are knowledgeable, helpful, and nonjudgmental. It also requires respecting a woman's desire and need for confidentiality, at least until she wants to speak about what occurred.

In general terms, individuals, groups, and organizations in the Soconusco dedicated to helping women victims need more information about this type of violence. Again, they should listen to the victims, to know what women migrants identify as sexually violent behavior. Over what parts of their bodies do these women believe they should have or want to have control? Those interested in helping victims of violence also need to know what other victims of similar types of abuse have done to lessen the possibility of future aggressions and to minimize the effects of the abuse, which may surface in the future.

Programs need to be set up in the region to prepare people to attend to women migrants who have been mistreated. These programs should provide guidelines indicating what legal and medical measures to take and how to address the psychological, emotional, and spiritual needs of women migrants. This requires adapting procedures, designed to address the needs of local victims of sexual abuse, to the special requirements of undocumented women migrants who are probably unfamiliar with local Mexican culture and only temporarily in the area, that is, en route to somewhere else.

In addition, help should be available for male victims of abuse, who may have suffered some form of sexual violence themselves or had to witness the abuse of wives, mothers, sisters, daughters, girlfriends, friends, or companions. The availability of this care should be well publicized and accessible in centers dedicated to providing medical, legal, psychological, and spiritual attention to migrants.

At the same time, taking into account the social and cultural roots of sexual violence, an effort should be made to disseminate in society at large knowledge about this form of abuse against women. Residents of the Soconusco should know about the existence of this violence. Those most knowledgeable about the local reality of sexual violence can educate and sensitize the local population to the causes and consequences of this abuse. This effort could begin with local authorities. To emphasize, sexual violence is not only an individual act, but a social and cultural expression of a deteriorated image and an abusive treatment of women in general and, in this case, of Central American women in particular.

Since most of the women affected entered the country without documents and with few resources (money or family, for example), which precludes them from staying for any length of time in the area (they may also fear being apprehended if they remain in one place for too long), those women who want to take legal action against their abuser should be able to do so with the least amount of difficulty and time. This requires making the legal process more agile. Legal action should not take months to process and resolve. This is especially urgent in border areas where a case may entail working with two legal systems. Such incidences may require the exchange of information across international lines between authorities responsible for managing, attending to, or prosecuting the case in their respective countries. This occurs frequently when the event took place on one side of the border and the victim seeks legal action on another.

The Matter of Healing

If, as Daniel Groody suggests, the United States is the Mexican migrant's Golgotha, then Mexico, beginning at the border with Guatemala, has become the Central American's way of the cross.[29] This is especially so for Central American women, whose suffering, the violence they endure in search of a more promising life, embodies the essentials of human despair and hope. In reminding us of the universal experience of suffering, these women become metaphors for the breadth of our human potential in its disfiguring and more noble forms. They bring into our line of sight human violence, injustice, cruelty, and fear as well as our compassion, solidarity, love, resilience, and strength. Perhaps above all, they embody faith, for while their suffering contains enormous grief, it also potentially contains the gift of healing. As a young Salvadoran woman explained to me after escaping the two men who kidnapped and gang-raped her for three days until she managed to flee, faith, the bedrock of her spirituality, kept her alive during her harrowing captivity. In the days we met she spoke often of her faith in an effort to recapture her sense of self, so necessary for her survival. In short, if suffering threatened to tear apart her identity as woman, her spirituality, her sustenance in the aftermath of the assault, was helping to rejoin the fragments and restore the unity shattered by violence.

Yet, in what became abundantly clear to me the more I listened to women migrants, victims of sexual violence, healing and the spirituality that enables it are not individual experiences. Rather they emanate from communities of souls, from the sharing of stories of journeys and the trials of those journeys. They lie in the awakening fellowship with one's neighbors, or *prójimos,* in a renewed trust of one's neighbor which allows the bruised and sometimes shattered pieces of the self to rebuild bridges to the world. This is the relational nature of the self, in Brison's words, the ability to find something of one's self, lost and damaged, in another. This ability—to see oneself and one's place in the world through fellowship with another—lies at the heart of these women's healing, which in turn, I suggest, rests at the heart of a migrant woman's spirituality.

NOTES

1. On Mexico's southern border, migrants frequently ride in the backs of trucks already loaded with bags of coffee beans, regularly piled seven to eight meters high.

2. Although men are victims of sexual violence, of rape, for example, the number of male victims is significantly lower. As such, this type of abuse may be considered gender specific, that is, overwhelmingly a threat to women. M. Azu, "Violence Against Migrant Women" in *Migrant Women's Human Rights in G-7 Countries: Organizing Strategies,* ed. Mallika Dutt, Leni Marin, and Helen Zia (San Francisco: Family Violence Prevention Fund, and New Brunswick: Center for Women's Global Leadership, 1997). Amnesty International, *Israel: Human Rights Abuses of Women Trafficked from Countries of the Former Soviet Union into Israel's Sex Industry* (AI Index: MDE 15/17/00; 2000). "Niñas traficadas detenidas como si ellas fueran

criminales," *Adital* (Agencia de Informacao, Frei Tito para a América Latina), November 19, 2002.

3. "Mujeres, sureños e indígenas, víctimas usuales," *La Opinión,* April 16, 1997. "Reportan abusos en la frontera," *La Opinión,* May 2, 1997. "Reporta ONG denuncias en frontera Tijuana," *Reforma,* July 23, 1997.

4. E. Maier, "Deconstruyendo las violencias de género," in Equipo Editorial, *Los Rostros de la Violencia* (Tijuana: El Colegio de la Frontera Norte, 2001), 122.

5. The missions are the Casa del Migrante of Tapachula, Chiapas, Mexico, and Tecun Uman, San Marcos, Guatemala, established and run by the congregation of the Fathers of St. Charles Borromeo, otherwise known as Scalabrinians.

6. R. Tong, *Feminist Thought: A Comprehensive Introduction* (Boulder, CO: Westview Press, 1989), 9–123.

7. Kate Millett, *Sexual Politics* (Garden City, NY: Doubleday, 1977), 44.

8. Ana Bergareche, *Tiempos de ambivalencia: Violencia sexual, religión e identidad en las trabajadoras de la maquiladora* (unpublished manuscript, 2002).

9. Ibid.

10. J. Brickman, "Female Lives, Feminist Deaths: The Relationship of the Montreal Massacre to Dissociation, Incest, and Violence against Women" in *States of Rage: Emotional Eruption, Violence, and Social Change,* ed. Reneé R Curry and Terry L. Allison, eds. (New York: New York University Press, 1996), 16.

11. C. Schafer and M. Frye, "Rape and Respect" in *Women and Values,* ed. Marilyn Pearsall (Belmont, CA: Wadsworth, 1986), 195.

12. This is not meant to imply that she is unaware or insensitive to the hostility in the behavior. Rather the aggression is understood as a common expression of a type of normal behavior, sex, which, in turn, is considered intrinsic to relations between men and women in general.

13. L. Segal, *Slow Motion: Changing Masculinities, Changing Men* (New Brunswick, NJ: Rutgers University Press, 1990), and 246.

14. D. Scully, *Understanding Sexual Violence: A Study of Convicted Rapists* (Boston: Wellington, Unwin Hyman, 1990), and Segal, *Slow Motion.*

15. They may also reflect and reproduce other inequalities, such as those of class, ethnicity, and race.

16. C. MacKinnon, "Feminism, Marxism, Method, and the State: An Agenda for Theory," *Signs: Journal of Women and Culture in Society* 7, no. 3 (1982): 532–34.

17. Amy Friedman, "Rape and Domestic Violence: The Experience of Refugee Women," in *Refugee Women and Their Mental Health,* ed. Ellen Cole, Oliva M. Espin, and Esther D. Rothblum (New York: Harrington Park Press, 1992), 67.

18. J. Lorber, *Paradoxes of Gender* (New Haven: Yale University Press, 1994), 76–77. Segal, *Slow Motion,* 238.

19. A. Bandura, "Análisis del aprendizaje social de la agresión," in *Modificación de conducta: Análisis de la agresión y la delincuencia,* ed. Emilio Ribes Iñesta and Albert Bandura (México: Editorial Trillas, 1975). I. Dobles, "Psicología de la Tortura," in

Aportes Críticos a la Psicología en Latinoamérica, ed. Bernardo Jiménez–Domínguez (México: Universidad de Guadalajara, 1990).

20. Scully, *Understanding Sexual Violence,* 163.

21. Ibid.

22. F. Butterfield, *All God's Children: The Boskett Family and the American Tradition of Violence* (New York: Avon Books, 1996), 103.

23. It should be noted that women in such a society are also less likely to see men as their equals or to see themselves as men's equals; by implication, they may not identify with men's suffering.

24. Tong, *Feminist Thought,* 113.

25. M. Omi and Howard Winnant, *Racial Formation in the United States, from the 1960s to the 1990s* (New York: Routledge, 1994), 56.

26. S. Brison, *Violence and the Remaking of a Self* (Princeton, NJ: Princeton University Press, 2002), 49.

27. M. Teicher, "Scars That Won't Heal: The Neurobiology of Child Abuse," *Scientific American,* March 2002.

28. "Migration on Rise Worldwide, especially among Women, IOM Says," *cnn.com, US News,* November 11, 2000. "Creció el número de mujeres migrantes desde 1997," *La Jornada,* September 17, 2000.

29. Daniel G. Groody, *Border of Death, Valley of Life: An Immigrant Journey of Heart and Spirit* (Lanham, MD: Rowman and Littlefield, 2002), 33.

PART FOUR

Constructive Theologies
of Immigration

CHAPTER FIFTEEN

A Theology of Migration

Toward an Intercultural Methodology

JORGE E. CASTILLO GUERRA

A theology of migration is not the answer to a theological fashion, and even less to the purpose of covering a demand for exotic themes. Theology of migration does not want to be a fashion, but a critical and faith-filled answer to the demands that come from individuals, groups, and processes linked to the phenomenon of human mobility.[1] Very far from being a fashion, the centrality that the theme of migration is given in theological reflection comes from an organic development, where a Christian attitude and spirit have been accompanied by practices that are prophetic, communal, hope-filled, and based on *convivencia* and solidarity.[2] The theology of migration already exists, therefore, in daily practices and in convictions of Christian communities of migrants. The scientific and academic theology of migration, about which we are talking here, springs from the experiences, claims, and testimonies of migrants and of groups in solidarity with their cause. It springs from the discernment that migrants represent a major sign of the presence of God within our contemporary history.

The theology of migration is polycentric and intertopical. It has been developing in various *topoi*—locations—because in today's world migration is a world answer to neoliberal expansionism; to religious, political, and cultural radicalization; and to gender oppression, which accompanies glob-alization. The theology of migration springs up in order to reflect and make known a peculiar dimension of God's journey through our history, in a positive and a negative way. In a positive way, that is to say, as a testimony, the theology of migration pays attention to those places where elemental rights of the migrants are defended and respected and where the possibility of human *convivencia* is becoming credible among groups of persons from different places of origin, cultural orientations, and religious convictions. In a negative way, as a prophetic discourse, the theology of migration is affected by and tries to transform realities of suffering, where the dignity and life of migrants is stepped on. The lethal walls; the migrants who perish in the waters of the Indian Ocean, the Mediterranean Sea, the English Channel, or along the "filtering" borders in the U.S. Southwest; the xenophobic reaction in the societies where they arrive; the tensions between diverse groups or generations of migrants—these are all extreme ways of impeding the journey of God through our world, and give all of us something new to think about faith, hope, and love.

In other words, to speak of a theology of migration is to accept a challenge, so that theology may deal scientifically with the foundations of faith that are (re)discovered in the realities linked with migration, in the daily living of those who, having a great faith, go as pilgrims to secure a decent life. Those realities are an opportunity for theology to constitute itself as a sensitized reason and wisdom that makes known, first, how the migrants and the groups in solidarity with them make credible the discourse about God today, and, second under which signs God gives meaning to and fosters the construction of societies of human *convivencia*.

I want to make it clear that up to this moment, what I call theology of migration does not count on well-defined conceptual frameworks, and its epistemology—its theory for knowing reality—its hermeneutic mediations, and even less its relationship with the different theological trends or fields, have not been outlined. As a scientific reflection, the theology of migration finds itself at a germinal stage, and its methodology will be something that will be found along the journey, following the intercultural logic of a dialogue-encounter that articulates and respects differences and mutualities.

In recent years different authors have published works that place the migration theme in the field of reflection of some theological disciplines.

The great majority of these works approach migration as a pastoral, ethical, or missiological challenge.[3] Few have posited the need to elaborate a contextual and intercultural theology from the faith, life, and journey of migrant communities,[4] and methodological-dialogical paths of reflections have yet to be proposed. In general, the publications that can be gathered under the theology of migration are dispersed in different continents. Until now, three international congresses have been celebrated on this topic, and there is only an interdisciplinary network, founded in 2003 and coordinated by Raúl Fornet-Betancourt in Aachen, Germany.[5]

The methodological proposals that I will share with you must be placed in the context of the germinal stage of the theology of migration. My proposals are an essay, an indication; they are a desire to put something in movement. My intention is to channel part of what has been reflected upon separately until now: migration and theology have to begin to be considered as "theology of migration." For this reason these methodological reflections are an invitation to elaborate together—*en conjunto,* as the U.S. Latino/a theologians are trying to do—theological and intercultural methodologies about migration that, consequently, will deal with the different realities and faces of migration.

In the present essay, I propose some suggestions in order to lead, methodologically, the way for a reflection on several themes of a theology of migration. With this, we take a step forward in the elaboration of a theology of migration, since we do not pay attention only to *what* its contents are, but also on *how* to reflect on them. Precisely here, I want to make clear that this reflection must be understood as an open suggestion conscious of its contextual and cultural limitations. With that openness for dialogue, I want to remain alert and aware of the danger that our suggestion may get caught between the mono-logical, mono-cultural, and universalistic margins of those who identify wisdom, and the cognitive or reflective ability, exclusively with the model of Western civilization. Therefore, our reflection must be understood as a part of the challenge of intercultural transformation[6] where different realities, memories, wisdoms, reflections, and traditions weave a polycentric theology.

This article begins with an explanation of the terminology—migrations and migrant—from my point of view, followed by the identification of the theology of migration as a specific liberation theology with its own identity, rationality, and methodology. Later I will characterize theology of migration as an intercultural theology from the point of view of the migrants. Finally, after the preliminary clarifications, I will deal with the central theme of my contribution: an essay about an intercultural methodology for the theology of migration, where I will suggest the systematization of a method for a theology of migration.

Migration and Migrants

As a phenomenon of human mobility, of transference from one specific reality to another, migration is accompanied by a series of tensions between the human groups that inhabit the new territory, of political, restrictive, and exclusive reactions which aim at closing the borders to impede the crossing of undesirable people, and the so-called industry of human traffic, where the life of migrants is extorted and played with. Both human mobility and tensions in the territories of immigration, accompanied by the creation of new iron curtains, become each time more important on a world scale. As a phenomenon, migration contains a great variety of themes in several areas: sociopolitical, cultural, juridical, religious, anthropological. I propose, then, a phenomenological outline as the first approach to our theme: migration and migrants.

What Is Migration?

The International Organization for Migration (IOM) calculates that at the beginning of the twenty-first century there were 175 million migrants. Among them, about 10.4 million are refugees,[7] that is, 1 of every 35 persons is involved in this type of human mobility. The greatest amount of migration movement does not go from the south to the north, but occurs within the area of the countries in the south, that is to say, migration from the south to the south. Of the 175 million migrants about 65 million live in industrialized countries or in those where oil is the basis of economy, while the rest remain in the south.[8]

   As I understand it, the term "migration" means human mobility in relation to a territory, and it can happen inside as well as outside the country of origin. As a movement in the interior of a country it is called *displacement*;[9] as a movement out of a country, it is called *emigration;* and as introduction into a new territory it is called *immigration*. But the migratory process does not end with the arrival into a new territory, which represents only the first phase. Once they arrive in this new territory, the second stage begins, which we can call an *inter* space, which is the space of struggle between the native culture and the resident culture. This space could be cultural, sociopolitical, economic, or religious, all of which contribute to the process of forming a new identity. The third phase deals with building a new life and new identity in a new and often different land.

Many studies have been written on the situations that cause today's massive flows of migrants.[10] There are two chief causes for leaving one's habitat: forced emigration and voluntary emigration. In forced emigration, the flight is an answer to situations that place life in danger. Leaving behind one's own country is in this case a radical answer to political, religious, ethnic, sexist, or sexual orientation conflicts, or extreme poverty. The above-mentioned conflicts also play a role in voluntary emigration, but with less intensity. There are also other causes for voluntary emigration: lack of fulfilment of expectations, unemployment, marriages between mixed nationalities, ecological catastrophes, overpopulation, and the symbolic-magnetic force that first-world countries have.

With respect to the duration of the migration, two categories can be distinguished: permanent and semipermanent migration.[11] Permanent migration—or, at least long-term—is strongly linked to the continuation of the situations that were the cause for leaving (whether by obligation or by choice) the place of origin, to the development of the migrating process (social participation, working conditions, and so forth), and to the legal possibilities of remaining in the new country (undocumented migrants obliged to abandon the country: refugees who are forced to reemigrate or to return to their country). Semipermanent migration is a limited-time stay, and in many cases it is agreed upon, by contract, before the border is crossed. This group is formed first of all by temporary workers or privilege persons, such as impresarios, students, or persons known as *expats,* those that "constantly crossing the border every day . . . become more invisible"[12] Second, this group is formed by undocumented migrants, a situation that makes them extremely vulnerable (working and sexual abuses, economic blackmail), and forces them to live in constant fear of being caught and sent back. Finally, this semipermanent category includes what is called circular migration, generally practiced by undocumented workers. They move through different regions of one country, following, for example, the cycles of seeding and harvesting, and alternating these with other short employment opportunities in industrial production.

Who Are the Migrants?

The above approach to the phenomenon of migration helps us to understand who is a migrant. This understanding is guided above all by an ethical, human, and Christian option for and with the migrants—victims of realities that oblige them to leave and of realities that they find in the society where they arrive. The migrant is the person that after initiating his or her history of migration, in a forced or voluntary way, has assumed different identities (emigrant, immigrant) and now in a new territory must build his or her identity as migrant. This identity is built within two processes, each one with its unique dynamics. The first process includes the possibility or impossibility of developing roots in the new land, a dynamic that varies between interaction and exclusion. The second process includes the relation with the territory or country of origin, a dynamic that varies between nostalgic romanticism and complete break with or denial of origin (the logic of assimilation).

A result of the process of transformation of identity—as we will describe later—is what is called double belonging, the experience of being *in-between* and *in-both,* or in other cases double denial, belonging neither to the territory of origin nor to the territory of destination. In other words, migrants are above all persons who have left their homeland, the place or country of origin in search of a new home, a refuge, work, or family unity.[13] Migrants, and in a special way refugees, are those who flee and leave their territory to save their own life and that of the family or community they leave behind. They leave because they are seeking freedom, well-being, and dignity. Finally, migrants are those who, starting with what is most basic— love for life—are unveiling one of the major facts of our time when they uncover the asymmetric and exclusive regulations that govern our world, and when they begin to judge the validity and objectivity of the values that guide the societies where they arrive: freedom, equality, and fraternity. In terms of the human condition, the migrant offers a hermeneutic key to get to know how the world is, where it is going, and to what type of world we must aspire.

Methodological Contributions from a Theology of the Specific Liberations

My point of departure is the search of contributions and insights that could guide the process of elaboration of a methodology for the emerging theology of migration. Some important insights are found in liberation theology because of its interest for the specific contexts where theology is done and due to its sensitivity towards the victims of oppression.

The Legacy of Liberation Theology

Toward the end of the 1980s, Enrique Dussel affirmed in his *Ética comunitaria* that liberation theology has been a fundamental theology, as it opted for the poor, trying to discover them and to understand and transform their situation. In the decade of the '90s, Dussel affirmed that the next development of the theology of liberation is linked to its transformation, as a process of diversification will change it into a theology of specific liberations.[14] During the '90s we witnessed the rise of theological interest for new historical subjects. There will be no more reductionism or homogenization of all victims to the socioeconomic category of the poor, just as it had been criticized by groups with specific asymmetries, above all women.[15] Now there will be feminist theologies, indigenous theologies, and Afro-American theologies, just to mention a few. The question of the subjects, culture, race, sex, and reorientation of liberation beginning with specific liberations is going to determine the development of liberation theology.[16] This development creates a space of theological sensitivity vis-à-vis the reality of migration.

A theology of migration is not simply an update or a reelaboration of the theology of liberation. A theology of migration is inspired by the liberating and martyr legacy, and wants to contribute to the liberation of all creation from its specific subjects, the migrants. In the first place, a theology of migration makes use of the fundamental bases of the theology of liberation:

A theology of migration values the so-called Medellín heritage, which calls for the option for the poor and interprets it as the option for and with the migrants, and for the formation of societies of *convivencia*.

A theology of migration pays attention to migrants because it sees in them an actual irruption of victims with specific oppressions (racism, assimilation, patriarchy, exclusion, xenophobia, or the constant nearness of death during the migrant exodus).[17] From their human condition, from tragedy and hope, from their situation of grace and disgrace, the migrants make known the passing of God through our history and are considered by the theology of migration as a "major fact," as "signs of the times" according to the expression of Vatican II.[18]

A theology of migration draws from the contents that Jon Sobrino has gathered in the principles of mercy, liberation, and reality, where the attitude of the theologian, the context of his reflections, and the sociopolitical and religious relevance of it are reflected. Through them, the theology of migration is equipped with the analytical means to support human intercultural encounters, which help reality to give "more of itself," as Ignacio Ellacuría affirms, and liberates theology of its complicity with systems of oppression, as Juan Luis Segundo has shown.[19]

A theology of migration values the understanding of God systematized by the theology of liberation: God of the poor, God of life, God of the victims,[20] and puts them again in context as the pilgrim God, who does not remain on the other side of the border. Likewise, it captures the meaning of Christ the liberator as the migrant Christ, and the Holy Spirit as the strength that inspires a welcome in solidarity, unity, and mutual understanding, and the plan of salvation of the reign of God as a hope that gives courage to struggle for intercultural *convivencia*.

Finally, a theology of migration lets itself be inspired by ecclesiological models of the ecclesiology of liberation: the ecclesiogenesis, the church of the poor, the resurrection of the true Church, and the Church of mercy. With the help of those models, the theology of migration will find specific ways to discover Catholicity as "globalized universality,"[21] and to articulate the great sociopolitical, ethnic, and cultural variety of the people of God.[22]

Methodological Contribution of the Theology of
Liberation to the Theology of Migration

I want to point out the methodological contribution of the theology of
liberation to a theology of migration. The theology of liberation histori-
cized the "theology as anthropology" program of Karl Rahner,[23] and the
return to the world called for by the conciliar *aggiornamento* as liberation
and return to the poor. Today, from the diverse contexts of migration, theology turns to the migrants and springs up again from them, from their *sensus pauperum* and *sensus migratorum*. For this reason it is a theology that tries
to be an expression of the human situation of the migrants; it tries to be a
Christian science from the cultural diversities and affinities that the migrants
and the native groups are forming in the countries of destination.

Just as Peter C. Phan emphasized in his conference during the congress
Migration, Religious Experience, and Globalization (Tijuana 2002), the
method of the theology of liberation is important in the theological elaboration of the situation of migrants and in the transformation of unjust realities. Just as Phan did, I find in Clodovis Boff a valuable contribution—
the socioanalytical mediation—to approach the situation and the subjects
of migration to elevate it to a theological category, and to motivate communities of the faithful to continue their praxis of approaching the Reign
of God.[24] Nevertheless, together with the socioanalytic mediation we must
consider the value of philosophical mediation in the method of theology
of liberation, just as it has been suggested by Juan Carlos Scannone, Ignacio
Ellacuría, and, in a more practical way, Jon Sobrino. According to Scannone, the approach to the material object, to what is historical-social, presupposes a previous approach where the meaning is captured and wisdom
is gained, that is to say, a *sapiential knowledge*. For Scannone "that sapiential
moment can only be reflected theoretically . . . by sciences that are not regional, but belong to the human totality, that is to say, by philosophy and—
in its *theologal* aspects—by theology. For this reason they are needed, even
though they are not sufficient, for a human and Christian *seeing* and *analyzing*
of society."[25] According to Ellacuría, philosophy, whether as philosophy of
history or as intraworldly metaphysics, is interested in historical new approaches where in a dialectical way superior or inferior forms of reality

appear. Thus he proposed the concept of "historical reality" to help the process in which already within reality one advances towards more, that is to say, towards a moment that increases the superior forms of reality.[26] Sobrino, in turn, uses the socioanalytical mediation to study reality and the philosophy of history—Ellacuría's concept of historical reality—in order to interpret how the events bring reality "to give more of itself." Now, without using a detailed analysis of the contributions of the authors mentioned, it is enough to say that we find here the fundamental arguments for the use of a philosophical mediation, in our case an intercultural one, as we will see later.

Another methodological contribution by Ellacuría has been reworked by Sobrino as a "compassionate reason." Its value is rooted in its capacity to save the dislocations that in the name of objectivism have occurred between the object of reflection and the subject who is reflecting. Therefore, it is not about a methodology of management, function, or legitimization of the socioanalytical mediation. It is about the perceptive capacity of the subject before those situations that call for justice. Thus, for Sobrino the reality of the poor sensitizes the theologian: her theological task and understanding of faith (the logic, presuppositions, and relevance of theology). From it a sensitized theology for the reality of the victims springs up. Let us see now the steps that lead towards a compassionate theology:[27]

(1) "Realizing the weight of things" [*hacerse cargo de las cosas*] as a moment of the *location* that allows direct access to reality. The knowledge of the truth of reality comes from the *location* or the incarnation.

(2) "Shouldering the reality of things" [*cargar con la realidad de las cosas*], that is, the *commitment* that follows because of the implications of the moment of shouldering reality. Knowledge is liberated from its sinfulness, of its contribution to the cover-up of reality.

(3) "Taking charge of things" [*encargarse de las cosas*] where the *practices* for the transformation of reality are revealed.

(4) Discernment of the reality of God today: theological and liberating intelligence establishes its preliminary point in those realities that are presented to us today as the word of God and in the answers to that word.

(5) "Reality carries the one who shoulders it": reality is not anymore only a place that mediates the presence of God in our history, but it is also a fertile soil for the conversion of the reflection on God, a fertile soil for God's grace to act in the theological task.

The compassionate theologian, reason, and theology are the result of processes where a human, methodological, and practical development takes place. Finally, the method introduced by Ellacuría and completed by Sobrino presents two demands to theology. First, it must be articulated methodologically and cognitively so that it may be able to apprehend reality. Secondly, it may allow itself to be fertilized by reality, when the theologian allows reality to outline both the method and the content of theology. A theology of migration receives the philosophical and socioanalytic mediation of the theology of liberation. Without ignoring the second mediation, it emphasizes the philosophical mediation, because it wants to start from the faith, experience, and sapiential knowledge of the migrants. It is from this starting point that the difficult process of building itself as a compassionate theology begins.

Theological Identity of the Theology of Migration

Our remarks on the theology of liberation could raise suspicions about the identity of a theology of migration. With the following, I want to dissipate those doubts by clarifying what is proper to a theology of migration. Starting from the reality of migration and of the migrant, of the cultural encounters and clashes, a theology of migration proposes for theological reflection a specific content, one therefore different from the context that up to now has been central for liberation theology. Liberation theology, as I pointed out, offers analytical and methodological instruments to capture the sociopolitical situation of the victims, to value the liberating practice and the faith present there, and to contribute to the transformation of reality. In the face of the phenomenon of migration those instruments are not sufficient because we are before a new context that presents new problems. This context is worthy in turn of new theoretical approaches, for example, to cultural identity: the ways of expressing faith and of communicating, strategies to insure life, or the type of leadership to organize a social or religious community. And one must not forget the problems created by the reaction—often violent—of the native population against the migrants: racism, exclusion, or oppression. The theology of liberation has made clear the importance of a sensitized openness to the context. Therefore, a theology of migration that allows itself to be affected by and filled with the hopes of the migrants proposes a reflection beginning from the type of specific oppression and small liberations of its primordial interlocutors. As it is fed by and filled with hope among the migrants, it assumes its double belonging, or double loyalty, a situation also known as "in-between" or "in-both,"[28] and that causes the migrants the feeling of simultaneous reference to both contexts: the one of origin and the one of destination. In other words, the theology of migration accepts the challenge of bicultural or multiple identities. For this reason a theology of migration must get rid of the logic of application in its relation with the theology of liberation. If it does not do that it would be using a decontextualized terminology, without the capacity of reflecting on the different historical realities of migration. Its fruit would not be other than to favor the groups of migrants who isolate themselves from the other groups that constitute the new society to which they have immigrated. The same happens when it deals with the question of migration only from the perspective of theologies that come from the contexts of the origin of the migrants, even if the country to which they arrive belongs to the same geographic region as the country of origin. The theology of the context of origin does not respond to the new questions or to the new identity of the migrant: How can we live together with other human groups in a Christian way? How must they resolve the dilemma of fidelity to the traditions of origin and to the temptations of sociocultural assimilation? And how do they keep the faith in situations of xenophobia, cultural oppression, or secularization? In the same way, it is not proper to include the theme of migration only from the perspective of theologies that have been articulated for the contexts of destination. As it is expected, the society in the place of arrival has particular situations and the theological reflections that spring from there, in general, do not know the meaning of migration for theology.[29]

A theology of migration emerges as a theology that wants to deal, in a Christian way, with the "in-between" situation of the migrants, situated between the reality of origin and the reality of the society where they arrive. At the same time a theology of migration pays attention to the places of "in-both" that mediate social, cultural, political, and religious realities of communion. This space of in-both and in-between is the intercultural space. A theology of migration assumes that space through an intercultural perspective and pays attention to the otherness or affinity between persons or communities with the same context. With the help of the intercultural perspective it focuses, especially, on the *inter* spaces which mediate the encounters. It is there where true and communitarian fellowship encounters take place, there where truths are shared, there where due to daily practices borders begin to fade among different ways of being and living in the world. In the context of a theology of migration the intercultural perspective means a call to its constant decentralizing and openness to conceive criteria with the purpose of understanding the truths of faith from diverse traditions, experiences of faith, and realities, both in the country of origin of its interlocutors and the new place where the migrants struggle to build a new home.

Allow me to illustrate the impact of the intercultural perspective at a social level. In a multicultural logic, diversities are recognized, and cultural and religious behaviors and orientations are studied among what are called multicultural mosaics. Such learning has a limited reach since it is not interested in relationships, in that which promotes or avoids mutual interaction among different members of a multicultural society. A theology of migration is interested because of the dialogue-communion in the contexts where migration is generating societies of cultural, religious, or ethnic diversity or plurality. Its goal is to facilitate the dialogue-communion through the acknowledgement of the otherness and affinities in a relational way. It deals, then, with a transforming dialogue-communion, where identities are not changed or exchanged but reciprocally sensitized through the practices of proximity. It is from there that the process for intercultural transformation begins in society and the church.

A theology of migration is an intercultural theology from the migrants. It assumes the following criterion basic to intercultural theology: "Intercultural theology starts from the insight that all theologies—including the biblical ones—are contextually conditioned. There is no pure gospel. The gospel appears to us *per definitionem* in an incarnate form."[30] A theology of migration understands itself as an intercultural theology. It wants to offer from the migrants a concrete universal in order to achieve "the more" of reality—in Ellacuría's sense to which we referred previously—when it transmits the Christian message from and among different cultural places. And this is why it is a polycentric and intertopical theology; it promotes the praxis of transformation of multicultural contexts incited in contexts of intercultural *convivencia*.

Essay on an Intercultural Methodology for the Theology of Migration

As an intercultural theology, the theology of migration cannot renounce the contributions of other sciences dedicated to the study or possibility of *convivencia* among human beings with different cultural orientations. We are talking about the intercultural sciences that assume a dynamic interpretation of cultures. Instead of making them perennial, it understands them as cultural orientations, in a constant pendulum movement between tradition and innovation. Besides, intercultural sciences study the differences and commonalities in order to facilitate dialogue and *convivencia*. Among the intercultural sciences, a theology of migration finds in intercultural philosophy[31] resources for criteria to have access to the wisdom—as sapiential knowledge according to Scannone—that is a primary moment where one can see, analyze, and understand that which makes us more human, better neighbors, and better Christians. We are referring, therefore, to the philosophical-intercultural mediation as a moment of elemental truth and belief that contributes to capturing the sense of things, to link us to the *inter* space, and to begin and maintain a process of subjective conversion from an interculturally situated perspective. Having an intercultural sense or sensitivity, a theology of migration is able to judge the data coming from the sciences that deal with the human or social context, the socioanalytic mediation.

An Intercultural Rationality

My central suggestion is that intercultural mediation holds a primary role in the method of a theology of migration, both for its basic epistemology and for the very rationality of its theological reflection. With the help of the intercultural perspective or mediation we hope to have access to the new rationality needed for a discourse dedicated to grasp the limits, tensions, encounters, and clashes among diverse human groups, particularly between migrants and natives. As part of the new rationality there are the fields of interculturation and intercontextualization.[32] By interculturation we understand the process where the mutual acknowledgement and a reciprocal interchange of cultural orientations, values, traditions, or behaviors takes place. And by intercontextualization we understand the process that goes together with interculturation, and that points to a mutual openness not only in the narrative or formal scope, but also in the practical and material scope. Inter-contextualization is the exercise to save fragmentations and to share contextual realities, when the openness of what is one's own opens the way to a contextual relocation. Therefore, a new otherness is born and the *other* begins to be also acknowledged as what I call the *affin*.[33] From the intercontextualization exercise, each person or group proposes from its own context some ideas for the construction of situations of *convivencia*. Therefore, from the processes of interculturation and intercontextualization the new intercultural rationality is being built up as a project of deconstruction of three projects of the dominant rationalities: monocultural, ethnocentric, and monological projects.[34] When it chooses the task to reconstruct rationality through intercultural perspective, a theology of migration joins a project that above all is being proposed in the context of the "philosophy of relation."[35] We can understand how far the intercultural project reaches with the words of Raúl Fornet-Betancourt, a pioneer of intercultural philosophy: "Interculturality does not point, then, to the incorporation of the other in one's own, whether it is in the religious, moral, or aesthetic sense. It rather looks for the transfiguration of one's own and of the other in order to interact and search for the creation of a common shared space determined by *convivencia*."[36] For Fornet-Betancourt such a project obeys

the imperative that commits us to recognize the interdependence [*respectividad*] of our own cultural identity, that is to say, that elemental time to understand and appreciate the other, in order to perceive him/her as subject that interprets from his/her order or relation with history, world, and truth; and thus to be able to take charge of his/her interpellation in the sense of an invitation to enter into the process of intercultural communication.[37]

Now, the goal of contributing to a society of *convivencia* and to establish dialogical relations is full of tensions, since it is about establishing bridges between individuals and communities removed from one another by socio-political, cultural, and religious asymmetries. Within the experience of intercultural theology there is proof that struggle often accompanies intercultural encounters.[38] When I spoke about the contributions of liberation theology to a theology of migration I already pointed out the importance of the approach that transforms thought and the thinking subject. Now I only have to remember another criterion of the theology of liberation to react before the asymmetries. This is "honesty toward reality"[39] as a spiritual attitude opposed to the dishonesty of those who hide situations of sin and imprison truth by means of injustice (Rom 1:18). For Sobrino, honesty toward reality is an attitude of Christological honesty: to be aware of the present evil and to do justice. Therefore, we find ourselves confronting the challenge of how to be aware and how to meet the truths of faith in situations of *convivencia* and confrontation. We try to respond to this challenge from three points of view proper to the intercultural perspective, the criticism of the asymmetries created by cultures, and the proposal of a new rationality and of a new hermeneutics.

First, according to Fornet-Betancourt, there is, within the intercultural perspective, the concern for *the transformation of unjust situations.* This concern is presented in a double criticism of the way power is used and asymmetries are created.[40] On one side, there are the asymmetries *between* the cultures; on the other side, there are the asymmetries *in* the cultures. The asymmetry between cultures is more evident each time through the neoliberal globalization, as a world order that is built by oppressing cultures. This type of asymmetry also takes place in multicultural societies when the dominant cultural group alone decides the path to be followed by the whole society.[41] The asymmetries in the cultures occur through processes of organization, gender issues, and group or personal dynamics. For this reason, intercultural philosophy has a clear political dimension.[42]

Second, in the project of intercultural philosophy the suggestion is to build *a new representative rationality* of consensus, dialoguing and less exposed to be manipulated by ethnocentric cultures. Josef Estermann has formulated criteria for building this intercultural rationality based on the European reality.[43] From his valuable list we glean the formal and material criteria. According to the formal criteria, an intercultural rationality has its base in a discourse that will be anticentric, antitotalizing, free of domination, and theoretical-practical. And according to the material criteria, it tries to formalize another paradigm of rationality based in the *logos* of the dialogue and understanding "interculturality" above all as a fact of life, not beyond culture or transcultural, but as a concrete experience.

Third, the proposals for a new intercultural rationality go together with a new *intertopical hermeneutics* that relates the different contexts. According to Raimon Panikkar, an intercultural hermeneutics is not the one that dedicates itself to the interpretation of texts, nor the one that dedicates itself to the interpretation of contexts. For Panikkar, intercultural hermeneutics is *diatopical:* it is a way of relating contexts, "*topoi* or cultural locations," and of understanding them knowing that the texts come from plural cultural and contextual orientations. To do this, it is necessary to recognize different ways of intelligibility, of using symbols or concepts. This is a need that deserves access to the meaning of a different way of thinking, not in order to search for an equivalent of that which we know—for example, the concepts of Greek philosophy—but an equivalent of "functional sense." This is what Panikkar calls "homeomorphic equivalents." Intercultural hermeneutics is not, therefore, a translation or comparison of concepts—in the sense of philosophy or certain comparative theologies. Still less does it work as a superior instance that judges or rejects a type of intelligibility in the measure that would reproduce theoretical patterns of a dominant (colonialist) reason. Intercultural hermeneutics is the search for a *via media* between colonial mentality, which believes that the totality of human experience can be expressed with the ideas of only one culture, and the opposite extreme, which believes that there is no possible communication between diverse cultures that should then condemn themselves to a cultural apartheid to preserve their identity.[44]

The contributions of Fornet-Betancourt, Estermann, and Panikkar help us to think of a new rationality critical and honest toward reality. We are thus safe from possible risks that suppose the abandonment of the liberation paradigm or the tendency to cover up the relations of oppression with a purely sociocultural analysis at the margin of the relations of power. Finally, they propose that the intercultural reflection-discourse begins from everyday life—*lo cotidiano*—and one's own intelligibility of cultures and their contexts, avoiding the risk of the universalizations of one context only and one rationality only, for example, the Greco-Roman.[45] Today, those dialogical and analytical traps are called supra-cultural, trans-cultural or the *tertium mediationis,*[46] and are no more than an attempt to identify a common place without taste or color, where nobody feels represented and that can exist only in theory.[47]

Methodological Systematization

In this last part I want to conclude with the methodological systematization of the perspectives that I have been introducing throughout this essay.

First step: The starting point of a theology of migration is the reality of migration
On one side the theologian of migration discovers the migrants' faith, hope, and love, the mysticism of migration, and the practical-sapiential theology of migration. On the other side, she discovers the idolatry, hopelessness, and hate—xenophobia, racism, ethnocentrism, intolerance, and exclusion—that place the migrants in a situation of suffering and marginality. In this theologal moment,[48] a theology of migration begins to emerge as daily wisdom from the professionals of the experience of migration, from those about whom many speak and few invite to dialogue. With the help of the hermeneutical instruments of intercultural philosophy, the sapiential contribution of the migrants and their communities is valued here to sketch a fundamental epistemology. This epistemology will be the critical background that will give meaning to the next analytical steps.

Second step: Sociopolitical and intercultural approach
The sociopolitical analysis is indispensable to have access to the dynamics that generate poverty and marginality, and to study and value the praxis that reclaims justice or full citizenship so that they can be promoted. A sociocultural analysis also becomes absolutely necessary to study in a critical way the asymmetries that are generated between and in cultures. In particular, there will be special interest in cultural interaction: problems will be analyzed, doubts will be clarified and solutions will be suggested to the problems that spring up, among others, about polarizations of cultural identities or about the absence of *inter* spaces to achieve social and cultural communion. Besides, the intercultural analysis offers instruments to discover the *convivencia* that already exists through daily intercultural encounters[49] in the barrios, schools, parishes, and health centers. The two types of privileged analysis in this second step for a theology of migration make use of different scientific branches: philosophy, political and social science, anthropology, history, and communication. Such sciences contribute empirical data that the theology of migration values from its fundamental intercultural epistemology.

In this way it is empowered to do a scientific and critical reading of the contextual reality of the migrants.

Third step: Theological systematization

This step cannot be taken without the previous ones, because the three of them belong to the same journey. As a theology, the theology of migration has begun its journey in the situation and wisdom of migration; as a theology it has established an interdisciplinary dialogue to understand better the mechanisms that intervene in the context of the migrants; and now as a theology from this background it questions itself and its theological sources, and establishes contacts with other theological trends. Therefore, in the theological systematization the challenges, impulses, or expressions that come from the faith of the migrant communities or peoples, from the reality of migration, from multicultural societies, from the need of interreligious dialogue, and the project of a society of *convivencia* are theologically reworked. The theology of migration will use here different historical, contextual, and intercultural hermeneutical models. Besides, insofar as it enters into a critical dialogue with other theological trends it will receive contents or theological hermeneutics elaborated in the contexts of the migrants' origins and in the contexts where they struggle to build a new home.[50] In order to give light to the contents of the faith that it finds among the migrants, a theology of migration establishes links with "the other sides" in its theological systematization:

- theological sources: Bible, tradition, and the Magisterium;
- theological traditions of the places of origin and of the societies where migrants arrive;
- theologies, popular traditions, and experiences of other migrant communities.

These three steps will give birth to christologies, ecclesiologies, missiologies, spiritualities, exegeses, mariologies, and liturgies of migration. The theology that emerges here finds its identity when it thinks of itself as a theoretical and theological systematization of the situation, life, and expressions of faith of the migrants. Systematizing elements for a Christian intercultural theory, a theology of migration becomes, paraphrasing the philosophical definition of Fornet-Betancourt, a "theology of relationship," and prepares itself to take the next step, where it directs and fosters intercultural practices. In this step, its theoretical systematizations are verified according to its ability for practical workability.

Fourth step: The generation of a society of convivencia
The theology of migration has now theoretical and "praxical"[51] arguments to capture and give continuity to God's message and to God's saving plan, and to value the great human and Christian contributions that the migrants offer today. On the basis of new hermeneutical and intercultural criteria it will be able to sensitize other theological activities in favor of a society of *convivencia*. It will be able to contribute to the transformation of ethnocentric rationalities and to support initiatives directed to propose the intercultural transformation of the societies: migrant communities and groups in solidarity, and projects for interreligious dialogue from the asymmetries of the migrants, NGOs, world forums, churches, and others. It is precisely here where a theology of migration is made relevant to the situations from which it has taken its intercultural option. But the same theology of migration will be transforming—interculturating—itself insofar as it reflects on and fosters the *inter* spaces of intercontextual, intercultural, interreligious and interdisciplinary dialogue.

Tasks of a Theology of Migration

A theology that springs up as the expression of migrant persons is directed first of all to them and to the situation of migration. A theology of migration aims to be the result of experiences, convictions, and practices of intercultural and interreligious dialogue directed towards the realization of migration projects. To this end they seek to empower economic, social, cultural, political, and religious rootedness. Such commitment has to be accompanied by the task of humanization of the societies of destination, so that they are hospitable societies, facilitating full citizenship for the migrants. Let us see some urgent tasks, according to my point of view, for the theology of migration:[52]

(1) To support the struggle for justice and dignity of migrant persons by backing its project of migration, humanizing the society of destina-

tion, defending the rights of migrants, and raising awareness about the human condition of the migrants.

(2) To give a theological response to the feminization of migration by means of denouncing the different types of exploitation to which women are submitted (home, work, domestic environment, and trafficking of women); supporting their struggle against patriarchal oppression; valuing their humanizing and Christian potential; and valuing their quality as bearers of the memory of first rootedness in the land of origin.

(3) Cultivating intercultural dialogue from the asymmetries experienced by migrants with the purpose of fostering human encounters and alternatives to new forms of instrumentalization or exclusion by the dominant groups through the systematized support of pastoral or systematic reflections (theology would be a good companion in the field within the process—many times painful—of appropriating new elements of identity); through valuing intercultural dialogue as a theological expression of diversities and cultural, ethnic, religious, and spiritual affinities; and through the proposal of new interdisciplinary mediations (intercultural hermeneutics, intercultural philosophy, intercultural communication) in order to find theoretical, practical, and strategic criteria to affirm the values that emerge from intercultural encounters.

(4) Favoring interreligious dialogue through an interreligious option for migrants by means of reaching out to the human condition of the migrants, to their life, expectations and religious perception, and pursuing a collaborative work for the most humble and needy migrants (avoiding a pietistic charity and paternalism). From there a common ground could be agreed upon, a common house for encounters among Christians, Muslims, Buddhists, or Hindus—a theological accompaniment in order to capture the double experience of God of many migrants, who profess a creed where two religions (African Americans, Amerindians) coexist.

The themes briefly outlined here constitute, in my opinion, the central axis for the discourse of a theology of migration. They are themes that, just as they have been already worked by some theologians, will be reflected upon from different fields (exegesis, spirituality, missiology, and others) and will form the torrent of the theology of migration. Through these themes, the theology of migration will contribute a meaningful discourse, that is to say, it will answer doubts, expectations, expressions, and practices of the migrant communities and of their new society.

In this essay I have asserted that the theology of migration is not an improvised theology, but the fruit of a long process of pastoral maturation beginning with faith, hope, and love of migrant communities. A theology of migration springs up as an expression of the daily life of migrants, of their agonies and celebrations, to take charge of the asymmetries linked to the phenomenon of migration, while at the same time discerning those signs of God's word in our times, which are offered to us today by migrants. I have also made reference to the theology of migration as one that identifies itself as a theology of liberation from specific oppressions, and as an intercultural theology situated in the agonizing and hopeful world of migrants. With the help of these theological perspectives, the theology of migration has a great task to accomplish: to assume different themes that shape the reality of the migrant—feminization of migration, intercultural dialogue, defense of the rights of migrants, and others. Assuming these realities, the theology of migration encounters two problems. First, it cannot be just a theology that looks at the situation of migrants; it must deal with the challenge of finding a rationality able to understand the plurality of human and religious convictions or diverse cultural traditions or orientations. And when the first problem is resolved, the question remains open about how to systematically channel and interpret the contributions of a reason interculturally sensitized and how the journey will be interculturally transformed.

It is my opinion that the theology of migration will be able to remove these doubts by means of an interdisciplinary dialogue with other sciences mentioned in the process of interculturation. Particularly, I mentioned intercultural philosophy, because it offers critical and hermeneutical resources to accept the theoretical and practical challenges of migration. With the help of these criteria, I proposed an intercultural method for a theology of migration. My method is not the definitive methodological model, but it is one that can start a methodological debate within the newborn theology of migration, so that it may be able to represent the diversities and affinities of the migrants. To the degree that it assumes and reflects the reality of migration, the divine and human dimensions of the project, of a society of an intercultural *convivencia,* it will give theoretical and practical instruments that will make it relevant when it can promote practices in favor of a society of *convivencia,* because it sees in it a specific form of witnessing to its faith and of bringing closer the reign of God.

NOTES

1. The following reflections come from a European context, particularly from the Netherlands, but I want to contribute to the theology of migration expressed from different cultural, social, and political realities and from a plurality of nationalities, spiritualities, and perceptions of what is human and divine, all of them present in the world of the migrants.

2. The term *convivencia* refers to the creation of common and harmonic spaces that make true encounter between human beings possible.

3. See for instance R. Krockauer, "'Was willst du, Fremder?' Eine Pfarrgemeinde und das Asylantenproblem," in *Die Fremden,* ed. O. Fuchs, 74–88 (Düsseldorf: Patmos, 1988); K.-H. Kleber, ed., *Migration und Menschenwürde* (Passau: Passavia Universitätsverlag, 1988); M. Delgado, "Lebendige Katholizität gestalten: Auf dem Weg zu einem Miteinander von einheimischen und zugewanderten Katholiken," *Stimmen der Zeit* 125 (2000): 595–608; P. Suess, "Migração, peregrinação e caminhada como desafios da missão no mundo globalizado," *Revista Eclesiástica Brasileira* 38 (2002): 294–311; S. Escobar, "Migration: Avenue and Challenge to Mission," *Missiology* 31 (2003): 29–34; D. Rodríguez, "No Longer Foreigners and Aliens: Toward a Missiological Christology for Hispanics in the United States," *Missiology* 31 (2003): 51–68; the journal *Chakana* 2, no. 3 (2004) is dedicated to the theme of religious identity and migration. I also point out the work of the magisterium on the dignity, ministry, and theological aspects of migration: the encyclical *Mater et Magistra* by John XXIII; the constitution *Gaudium et spes* in the Second Vatican Council documents; the document by Paul VI *Pastoralis Migratorum Cura* (August 15, 1969); the Pope's yearly messages for Migrants' World Day; the documents of the Pontifical Council for the Pastoral Care of Migrants and Itinerant People, which also publishes the journal *People on the Move;* and the recent instruction *Erga migrantes caritas Christi* (May 1, 2004).

4. See Peter C. Phan, "The Experience of Migration in the United States as Source of Intercultural Theology," in *Migration, Religious Experience, and Globalization,* ed. Gioacchino Campese and P. Ciallella, 143–69 (New York: Center for Migration Studies, 2003); Jorge Castillo Guerra, "Hacia una teología de la migración: Perspectivas y propuestas," *Chakana* 2, no. 3 (2004): 27–51.

5. In chronological order: Migration, Religious Experience, and Globalization Congress, (Tijuana, Mexico, 2002), see Campese and Ciallella, *Migration, Religious Experience, and Globalization;* Migration and Interculturality: Theological and Philosophical challenges conference (Aachen, Germany, 2003), where the

interdisciplinary network for the study of migration is founded, see Raúl Fornet-Betancourt, ed., *Migration and Interculturality: Theological and Philosophical Challenges* (Aachen: Agustinus, 2004); Migration and Theology Conference (University of Notre Dame, 2004). A series of events that I want to point out are the international seminars on ministry and pastoral counseling that have been organized since 1986 (Kaiserswerth, Germany) and that have opened the way to the Interkulturelles Forum. See H. Weiss, "Die Entdeckung interkultureller Seelsorge: Entwicklung interkultureller Kompetenz in Seelsorge und Beratung durch internationale Begegnungen," in *Handbuch Interkulturelle Seelsorge,* ed. H. Weiss et al., 17–37 (Neukirchen-Vluyn: Neukirchener, 2002); Ch. F. W. Schneider-Harpprecht, *Interkulturelle Seelsorge* (Göttingen: Vandenhoeck and Ruprecht, 2001).

6. Raúl Fornet-Betancourt, *Transformación intercultural de la filosofía: Ejercicios teóricos y prácticos de filosofía intercultural desde Latinoamérica en el contexto de la globalización* (Bilbao: Desclée, 2001).

7. International Organization for Migration, Migration in a Globalized World conference, 86th session, October 10, 2003.

8. Th. Faist, *The Volume and Dynamics of International Migration and Transnational Social Spaces* (Oxford: Oxford University Press, 2000), 7.

9. According to the committee of the United Nations for Refugees (ACNUR in Spanish) the number of displaced persons is between 20 and 25 million worldwide.

10. H. Moussa, P. A. Taran, and M. Robra, eds., *Ha llegado el momento de optar por la solidaridad con las personas desarraigadas: Documento de Referencia* (Geneva: World Council of Churches, 1996); P. Taran and E. Geronimi, *Globalización y migraciones laborales: Importancia de la protección* (Geneva: OIT, 2003).

11. S. Sassen, *Guests and Aliens* (New York: New Press, 1999); Faist, *Volume and Dynamics.*

12. ACNUR, "La evolución de la dinámica del desplazamiento," in *La situación de los refugiados en el mundo 2000: Cincuenta años de acción humanitaria,* available at http://www.acnur.org/publicaciones/SRM/cap111.htm (last accessed May 2007).

13. Moussa, Taran, and Robra, *Ha llegado el momento*; MaP. Aquino, "La Humanidad peregrina viviente: migración y experiencia religiosa," *Chakana* 1 (2003): 85–120.

14. E. Dussel, *Ética comunitaria* (Madrid: Paulinas, 1986), 244–47; "Teología de la liberación: Transformaciones de los supuestos epistemológicos," *Theologica Xaveriana* 47 (1997): 203–14.

15. I. Gebara, "Presencia de lo femenino en el pensamiento latinoamericano," in *Cambio social y pensamiento cristiano en América latina,* ed. J. Comblin et al., 199–213 (Madrid: Trotta, 1993).

16. P. Richard, "El futuro de la Iglesia de los pobres: Identidad y resistencia en el sistema de globalización neo-liberal," *Pasos* 65 (1996): 9–10; J. J. Tamayo, "Las teologías de Abya-Yala: Valoración desde la teología sistemática," *Pasos* 109 (2003).

17. Gustavo Gutiérrez, *The Power of the Poor in History* (Maryknoll, NY: Orbis Books, 1983).

18. *Gaudium et Spes*, no. 4, 11. Available at www.vatican.va.

19. Jon Sobrino, "Teología en el mundo sufriente: La teología de la liberación como '*intellectus amoris,*'" *Revista Latinoamericana de Teología* 5 (1988): 243–66; "La teología y el 'principio liberación,'" *Revista Latinoamericana de Teología* 12 (1995): 115–40; "Ignacio Ellacuría: El hombre y el cristiano; Bajar de la cruz al pueblo crucificado," *Revista Latinoamericana de Teología* 11 (1994): 131–61, 215–24; J. L. Segundo, *Liberación de la teología* (Buenos Aires: Lohlé, 1975).

20. V. Araya, *El Dios de los pobres: El misterio de Dios en la teología de la liberación* (San José, Costa Rica: DEI, 1983); Gustavo Gutiérrez, *El Dios de la vida* (Lima: Instituto Bartolomé de las Casas–Rimac, 1989).

21. N. García Canclini, *La globalización imaginada* (Buenos Aires: Paidós, 1999).

22. Jorge Castillo Guerra, "Interculturele kerkopbouw: Kerkvorming met migranten," in *Kerk aan de stadsrand,* ed. C. Sterkens and J. van der Meer, 191–214 (Damon: Budel, 2004).

23. Karl Rahner, "Theologische Anthropologie," in *Lexikon für Theologie und Kirche,* ed. Josef Höfer and Karl Rahner (Freiburg: Herder, 1957–65), 1:618–27.

24. See Peter Phan, "Experience of Migration"; Clodovis Boff, *Teologia de lo político: Sus mediaciones* (Salamanca: Cristiandad, 1980), and "Epistemología y método de la teología de la liberación," in *Mysterium Liberationis,* ed. Jon Sobrino and Ignacio Ellacuría, 1:79–114 (Madrid: Trotta, 1990); X. Gorostiaga, "La mediación de las ciencas sociales y los cambios internacionales," in Comblin et al., *Cambio social,* 123–44.

25. Juan C. Scannone, "Reflexiones epistemológicas acerca de las tres dimensiones (histórica, teórica y práctica) de la doctrina social de la iglesia," in *América Latina y la doctrina social de la iglesia; diálogo latinoamericano-alemán,* ed. P. Hünermann and J. C. Scannone (Buenos Aires: Paulinas, 1991), 71; the term "theologal" refers to the presence of God in history, and in this case, to the divine aspects of wisdom, previous to all theological systematization. See also his *Evangelización y cultura* (Buenos Aires: Paulinas, 1990), and *Teología de la liberación y doctrina social de la iglesia* (Buenos Aires: Paulinas, 1987), 21–133.

26. Ignacio Ellacuría, *Filosofía de la realidad histórica* (San Salvador: UCA, 1990), 41.

27. In the following steps I synthesized the methodological reflections of Sobrino and Ellacuría. See Jorge Castillo Guerra, *Iglesia: Identidad, misión y testimonio; Un análisis contextual de la eclesiología de la liberación de Jon Sobrino* (forthcoming); Jon Sobrino, "Lo fundamental de la teología de la liberación." *Proyección* 32 (1985): 171–80, and "La teología y el 'principio liberación.'"

28. Virgilio P. Elizondo, "Transformation of Borders: Border Separation or New Identity," in *Theology: Expanding The Borders,* ed. Ma.P. Aquino and R. S. Goizueta, 22–39 (Mystic: Twenty-Third Publications, 1998); J. Y. Lee, *Marginality:*

The Key To Multicultural Theology (Minneapolis: Fortress Press, 1995). See also the studies on transcultural identity such as V. Mazzucato, "De dubbele economische gerichtheid van Ghanese migranten: Een transnationaal perspectief op integratie en ontwikkelingsbeleid," *Migrantenstudies* 4 (2004): 177–95; R. Gowricharn, "De duurzaamheid van het transnationalisme: De tweede generatie Hindoestanen in Nederland," *Migrantenstudies* 4 (2004): 252–68.

29. In the case of the Netherlands, many migrants are not able to understand that here, within the process of secularization and postmodernity, people are suggesting nonpersonal and, in other words, abstract images of God. See H. M. Kuitert, *Over religie: Aan de liefhebbers onder haar beoefenaars* (Baarn: Ten Have, 2000). Greek, Italian, Filipino, Polish or Latin American migrants, for example, in their iconography conceive the divine as a nearby and personal reality that can be symbolized and is even tangible.

30. W. Hollenweger, "Intercultural Theology: Some Remarks On The Term," in *Towards an Intercultural Theology: Essays in Honor of J.A.B. Jongeneel,* ed. M. Frederiks et al. (Zoetermeer: Boekencentrum, 2003), 90. It is the missiologists Walter Hollenweger, Hans-Jochen Margull and Richard Friedeli who introduced the trend of "studies in the intercultural history of Christianity," which later would be known as "intercultural theology" through the publications by Hollenweger. See W. Hollenweger, *Interkulturelle Theologie* (München: Kaiser, 1979).

31. I refer here to a number of intercultural congresses initiated in México in 1995 whose proceedings have been edited by Raúl Fornet-Betancourt: *Kulturen der Philosophie: Dokumentation des I. Kongresses für interkulturelle Philosophie* (Aachen: Concordia Monogrraphien, 1996); *Unterwegs zur interkulturellen Philosophie: Dokumentation des II. Internationales Kongresses für interkulturelle Philosophie* (Frankfurt: IKO, 1998); *Kulturen zwischen Tradition und Innovation: Stehen wir am Ende der traditionellen Kulturen? Dokumentation des III. Internationales Kongresses für interkulturelle Philosophie* (Frankfurt: IKO, 2001); *Culturas y poder: Interacción y asimetrías entre las culturas en el contexto de la globalización; Documentos del IV Congreso Internacional de Filosofía Intercultural* (Bilbao: Desclée, 2003). Among the intercultural philosophers participating in these congresses, I single out Raúl Fornet-Betancourt, Franz Wimmer, Ram A. Mall, Raimón Pannikar, and Josef Estermann.

32. F. X. D'Sa, "Inkulturation und Interkulturation: Versuch einer Begriffserklärung," in *Inkulturation als Herausforderung und Chance,* ed. M. Heberling, G. Rott, and H. Sing, 32–54 (Aachen: Riese Springer, 2001).

33. The *affin*—from affinity—is a category I am introducing to save the unilaterality of the "other" that places the emphasis on distance and difference. An example of the exercise of intercontextualization is the intercultural encounter within the Christian communities of mixed origins, when the interest for the other gives way to the reciprocal valuing of the contextual backgrounds of life and faith. We find in some parishes in the Netherlands that were formed by migrants and natives, situations of true encounters in which the distant and unknown

"other" is treated as the *affin* who is close and appreciated. The discovery of common references will also give way to a contextual relocation, to a rediscovery of what is one's own with the help of the other. An example of rediscovery can be found in H. Wagenaar, A. van der Meiden, and Y. Schaaf, *Een eigen theologie? Friese en Saksische antwoorden op Afrikaanse vragen* (Kampen: Kok, 2000). Missionaries in Africa discovered that the Christian message is more accessible in the local language than in the national one, and later, in Europe, they rediscovered the value of their own languages and contexts for the elaboration of a theology from the native minorities. Another example is the work of H. de Wit et al., eds., *Through the Eyes of Another: Intercultural Reading of the Bible* (Elkhart, IN: Institute of Mennonite Studies, 2004) where strong intercultural and intercontextual bridges are established among the Christian communities dispersed in various continents, by means of the interchange of their own biblical interpretations (intercultural hermeneutics).

34. Jorge Castillo Guerra, "Hacia una teología de la migración," in Fornet-Betancourt, *Migration and Interculturality,* 170.

35. Raúl Fornet-Betancourt, *Interculturalidad y filosofía en América Latina* (Aachen: Concordia, 2003), 87.

36. Ibid., 47 (translation my own).

37. Ibid., 52 (translation my own).

38. H. Rücker, "Zur symbolischen Sprache des Fremden," in *Mit dem Fremden Leben,* ed. D. Becker and A. Feldtkeller (Erlangen: Erlanger Verlag für Mission und Ökumene, 2000), 176.

39. See Jon Sobrino, "Espiritualidad de Jesús y espiritualidad de la liberación," *Christus* 44 (1979–80): 529–30, 559–63; "La honradez con lo real," *Sal Terrae* 80, no. 5 (1992): 375–88; *La fe en Jesucristo: Ensayo desde las víctimas* (Madrid: Trotta, 1999), 272–76.

40. Raúl Fornet-Betancourt, "Interacción y asimetrías entre las culturas en el contexto de la globalización: Una introducción," in *Culturas y poder: Interacción y asimetría entre las culturas en el contexto de la globalización,* ed. R. Fornet-Betancourt (Bilbao: Desclée, 2003), 20–22.

41. S. P. Huntington, *Who Are We: The Challenges to America's National Identity* (New York: Simon and Schuster, 2004).

42. Raúl Fornet-Betancourt, "Interacción y asimetrías," 27, states: "the cultural interaction has to be looked at as essentially joined to an alternative political project; a project that critically shows that the dialogue on the supposed need for integration in the world market of the hegemonic system is an ideological dialogue and that it must foster contextual models as a plural basis of *convivencia* in solidarity in the midst of diversity."

43. J. Estermann, "Hacia una filosofía del escuchar: Perspectivas de desarrollo para el pensamiento intercultural desde la tradición europea," in Fornet-Betancourt, *Kulturen der Philosophie,* 119–49.

44. R. Panikkar, "Filosofía y cultura: Una relación problemática," in Fornet-Betancourt, *Kulturen der Philosophie,* 19.

45. To the criteria for a new intercultural rationality we could add the philosophy of Pierre Bourdieu and his critique of ethnocentrism, which he also calls "intellectual ethnocentrism." See P. Bourdieu, "Het denken van granzen," *Crisis* 42 (1991): 5–15.

46. J. Estermann, "Anatopismo como alienación cultural: Culturas dominantes y dominadas en el ámbito andino d América Latina," in Fornet-Betancourt, *Culturas y poder,* 177–202.

47. R. Edmondson, "Interreligiöses Verstehen: Kultursoziologische Probleme und Paradoxien," in *Verstehen an der Grenze; Beiträge zur Hermeneutik interkultureller und interreligiöser Kommunikation,* ed. M. Bongardt et al. (Münster: Aschendorff, 2003), 45–79.

48. Rahner, "Theologische Anthropologie."

49. See W. A. Shadid, *Grondslagen van interculturele communicatie: Studieveld en werkterrein* (Houten: Bohn Stafleu Van Loghum, 1988); N. Vink, *Dealing With Differences* (Amsterdam: KIT Publishers, 2005).

50. A fruit of this use could be the process of *mestizaje* and *mulatez* of European or U.S. theologies. In this way, those theologies will be sensitized to other images of God, other cultural expressions of Christian faith, and other local ways of having ecumenical, interreligious, or intercultural encounters.

51. Using Ellacuría's criteria, the term "praxical" means the qualification of practices to discern those that stimulate reality to give "more of itself."

52. In what follows, I present, in a summary way, some of the themes of my own proposals for a theology of migration. See Jorge Castillo Guerra, "Hacia una teología."

CHAPTER SIXTEEN

¿Cuantos Más?

The Crucified Peoples at the U.S.-Mexico Border

GIOACCHINO CAMPESE

One of the most heartbreaking aspects of my seven-year experience at Casa del Migrante en Tijuana[1] has been without any doubt to confront the tragic reality of thousands of migrant men, women, and children dying in the process of crossing the U.S.-Mexico border. During that experience it became very clear to me that migration is for many people a dangerous and often deadly journey. In many informal conversations migrants described to me in vivid terms the ordeal of crossing the border through the mountains, the desert, or water channels.[2] I remember one of the survivors of a high-speed chase by the Border Patrol on a California highway speaking with profound sadness about the loss of his brother in the accident in which at least ten more migrants died trapped in a van. I think about the group of fourteen migrants from Veracruz, Mexico, who died in the Arizona desert in 2001. I have seen the graphic pictures of the bloated and almost mummified corpses of migrants who have died crossing the same desert.[3] I am reminded of the nineteen migrants who died of asphyxia in a truck in Victoria County, Texas, in the spring of 2003.

When is this slaughter going to end? How many more migrants have to die to convince the U.S government and society that something is terribly wrong with the current border policy? *Cuantos más?* How many more? This has been the rallying cry of many protest marches and religious celebrations—like *El Día de los Muertos* (All Souls' Day), *Posada sin Fronteras* (Posada Without Borders), *Via Crucis del Migrante* (Way of the Cross of the Migrant)—that human rights and religious activists groups have organized and staged at the border to denounce the senseless death of so many migrants whose sole "crime" is the dream of a new and better life. During these events we have planted hundreds of crosses with the names and ages of migrants who died crossing the border. Many of these crosses had no names because a significant number of these migrants have not yet been identified. In this way we have tried to remind ourselves, the churches, and society at large that these migrants are first and foremost human beings. This has been part of our effort to carve some space in our society for the "cry of the undocumented,"[4] a cry that is most often ignored, when it is not completely silenced.

U.S. mass media have definitely chosen not to tell the stories of the unbelievable faith and resilience of the human spirit found among the migrants. On the contrary, they have carved the image of a border that is out of control and needs to be protected against the invasion of "illegal aliens."[5] Especially after 9/11, mass media prefer to discuss "broken borders,"[6] and how easy it is for "illegal aliens" to "sneak into" the U.S. The message is that the situation at the U.S.-Mexico border represents an extremely serious threat for the security of this country, and some drastic decisions have to be taken by the U.S. government on this matter.[7] Not much is said about the causes and dynamics of undocumented immigration, and even less about the human dimension of this phenomenon. Few people have the courage and honesty to ask the hard questions: If it is so easy to "sneak in," why do thousands of people die crossing the border? And why do these deaths not burden the conscience of a country that loves to define itself as a "Christian" nation?[8]

This essay is an attempt to answer some of the hard questions that spring up from the reality of the U.S.-Mexico border. It is a reflection urged by the conviction that Christian theology has to confront this reality honestly and squarely from the perspective of the marginalized victims of history—in this case, undocumented migrants—in order to transform it. At the same time it is a reflection stirred by the belief that this reality is not only made up of suffering and death, and undocumented migrants are not just victims.

Used with permission of David Fitzsimmons.

In the midst of pain and sin we can discover God's abundant grace in un-expected and amazing ways. Two main resources have inspired this essay. First of all, the concept of the "crucified peoples" coined by Ignacio El-lacuría and further developed by Jon Sobrino. Second, a cartoon by David Fitzsimmons published in the *Arizona Daily Star* in 2001 which vividly sets the "crucified peoples" in the context of the U. S southern border region: a migrant is crucified under the scorching heat of the Arizona desert by the "U.S. Border Policy." The headline of the cartoon is the famous Matthean passage: "I was thirsty and ye gave me no drink; I was a stranger and ye took me not in" (Mt 25:42). Fitzsimmons's drawing represents, to my mind, a challenging and insightful expression of a sinful and, literally, mortal human and political reality interpreted in the light of some of the main tenets of the Christian faith: the crucifixion and the belief that Jesus is present in the least of our sisters and brothers.

This article consists of four main sections. First, I will describe the situ-ation at the U.S.-Mexico border, especially in terms of official U.S. border policy and its lethal consequences. Second, I will offer a critical assessment of this policy following the insights of social scientists and human rights activists. Third, I will introduce the metaphor of the "crucified peoples" as it has been developed by Ellacuría and Sobrino. And finally I will use this concept as a key to interpret theologically the current immigration and border predicament and explore its significance for theology today in the U.S.

Death at the U.S.-Mexico Border

Except for the Bracero Program that began in 1942 and Operation Wetback in the 1950s, prior to the 1960s the U.S.-Mexico border did not receive any significant national attention. In the late 1960s the perception that the national boundary was being overrun started gaining momentum, and in the 1970s this sentiment was heightened by the rise of a neorestrictionist movement that started clamoring about the growing undocumented migration from Mexico. Federal officials, politicians, and the mass media helped construct the public perception of a "border crisis," and began fostering public fear of a "border out of control," of "an invasion" in the making by "illegal aliens" from Mexico, and the image of this country as a "time bomb."[9] These perceptions were further encouraged in 1978 by former CIA director William Colby, who described Mexican immigration as the single greatest security threat facing the United States, greater even than the Soviet threat. He was quoted as saying that by the end of the twentieth century there would be more than 120 million Mexicans and that the Border Patrol would not have enough bullets to stop them from entering the U.S.[10] In 1984 Ronald Reagan gave a presidential slant to this discourse when he warned: "The simple truth is that we've lost control of our borders and no nation can do that and survive."[11] It was Reagan again who, in the context of the Cold War hysteria, made the connection between border control and international terrorism in a 1986 televised speech.[12] In the 1990s this process reached its peak when the effort to control and stop undocumented immigrants was "elevated from one of the most neglected areas of federal law enforcement to one of the most politically popular."[13] The tragic events of 9/11, and the ideology of the "war on terror" that was declared in the aftermath, have further strengthened the arguments of those who see the U.S.-Mexico border as the main strategic site of the country's national security.

While national security has become the buzzword after 9/11, it is just one dimension of the whole security issue in the U.S. In fact, for people who are concerned about the erosion of U.S. cultural and national identity caused especially by immigration, what is at stake is not only national security, but also, and more importantly, "societal security." Harvard scholar Samuel Huntington makes this point very clearly in his most recent, and perhaps most controversial, book *Who Are We?*: "[W]hile national security is concerned, above all, with sovereignty, societal security is concerned above all with identity, the ability of a people to maintain their culture, institutions, and way of life."[14] One of Huntington's main objectives is precisely to protect "true" U.S. culture and ideals—which are represented by the Anglo-Saxon culture—from the invasion of Third World immigrants (particularly Spanish-speaking immigrants) who, according to him, are not learning English and are definitely not assimilating to the "American way of life." In this scheme the border becomes an extremely critical site since it is primarily there that the "illegal alien" threat to national and societal security has to be eliminated. And the beginning of this whole process is the construction of a U.S.-Mexico border in crisis and "out of control."

Néstor Rodríguez has observed that the manufacturing and representation of the border crisis as a threat to the "American way of life" has been constructed at three main levels: first, at the level of federal officials and presidential political candidates who have visited the border to show their patriotism and concern for the security of the nation; second, at the local level where officials in border states have depicted "illegal aliens" as a fiscal burden and have used this issue to boost their political campaigns (in this case the example of California Governor Pete Wilson and his campaign for Proposition 187 in 1994 comes readily to mind[15]); third, at the level of institutions and think tanks that have contributed to this restrictionist agenda by organizing conferences and supplying "academic" papers to provide "scientific" and credible arguments to support the image of a border "out of control."[16] To these three levels we must add the impact of U.S. mass media, which continues to feed, as I noted above, public opinion with negative images of the border and immigrants.[17]

Together with the construction of the border crisis comes also the construction of the "illegal alien."[18] Hugh Megan explains this image in the following way:

The illegal alien designation invokes a representation of people who are outside of society. The illegal alien designation invokes images of foreign, repulsive, threatening, even extra-terrestrial beings . . . people from outside our world, who are invading and threatening our lives, "the quality of our lives."[19]

Now it is crucial to realize that the "illegal alien," this foreign and threatening being, is not just any immigrant. Today this extremely negative image is used to refer to Third World immigrants, and not, for instance, to European immigrants. The former are, according to this discourse, lacking the positive characteristics that the earlier European immigrants had, just as later Southern European immigrants were considered inferior to the earlier Northern European immigrants in the U.S. So it happens that while European immigrants in general are celebrated as pioneers and heroes at Ellis Island, commemoration of Mexican immigrants who entered through the southern border is absent. In fact, Mexican and other "new" immigrants are considered "aliens" while their European counterparts are portrayed as "immigrants."[20] In other words, we are witnessing the process of "alienization," and concomitant "criminalization," of Third World immigrants in the U.S., which is based on powerful racial motives and a totally misleading narrative of the dynamics and history of immigration in this country.

The border policy that was implemented by the U.S. during the 1990s has to be seen as a response to this widespread perception of a border "out of control" and of an "invasion" of "illegal aliens," which was unabashedly used by scores of local and federal officials and politicians to boost their campaigns. Something had to be done to stop "illegal" immigration right at the border, and so placate the public opinion. This is when INS[21] bureaucrats took the opportunity to expand their federal prestige and increase their resources by coming up with a border strategy whose rationale is "prevention through deterrence." This strategy was activated by pouring thousands of Border Patrol agents and sophisticated surveillance devices into the rural areas, and building metal and concrete fences in the urban areas of the border region, which had become the normal corridors through which undocumented immigrants crossed the U.S.-Mexico boundary. Once these critical border sites were sealed, the "illegal flows" would be forcibly channeled toward the most inhospitable and indeed dangerous terrain in the border region, like mountains, desert, rivers, and water channels. Faced by these rugged terrains, and by extreme meteorological conditions the immigrants would be discouraged from entering the U.S. The first experiment in the application of "prevention through deterrence" took place in the El Paso/Ciudad Juarez area with Operation Hold the Line in 1993. Because of the "success" of this experiment in terms of an increasing number of apprehensions of undocumented immigrants, and a consequent decrease of "illegal traffic" in that area, the strategy was officially approved and expanded to the whole border. Thus, Operation Gatekeeper followed in California in 1994, and Operations Safeguard and Rio Grande a few years later respectively in the Arizona and Texas border region. As a result apprehensions skyrocketed and the "illegal aliens" were no longer that visible. INS pundits took this as a proof that undocumented immigration was finally declining and that federal authorities were regaining control of the border. Yet, there was another consequence of this border strategy that was not receiving the same attention as those previously mentioned but was quickly noticed by human rights and religious activists at the U.S.-Mexico border: the number of undocumented immigrants dying while crossing the border was dramatically increasing.

Despite many objections, this strategy has been maintained by George W. Bush's administration, especially in the aftermath of 9/11 and in view of the 2004 presidential campaign, and so the number of dead immigrants has continued to climb, reaching more than 3,000 casualties since 1994, many of them still unidentified. The causes are mainly related to the border's extreme geographical and meteorological environment, which leads to dehydration, hypothermia, drowning, and so on. A smaller number of immigrants have died in high-speed chases and shootings, or have asphyxiated in small truck, van, or train compartments. These are somehow the official statistics, which do not account for the many bodies that according to the witness of immigrants and Border Patrol agents are still to be found in the deserts, natural and artificial rivers, and mountains of the border region.[22]

After all the controversies and debates that the U.S.-Mexico border generates, we are left with the reality of a fortified border that has been created to supposedly prevent illegal substances (drugs) and "illegal" beings from entering the U.S.,[23] but that in the end "has been more than 10 times deadlier to migrants from Mexico during the past nine years than the Berlin Wall was to East Germans throughout its 28-year existence."[24]

A Critical Assessment of U.S. Border Policy

After more than ten years since the implementation of the new border strategy, the results have been mostly negative: the federal government has spent billions of dollars in taxpayers' money; because of border enforcement the smugglers' industry has boomed to the point of becoming basically indispensable; the violation of the human rights of immigrants continues unabated; there is no real proof that this strategy has substantially reduced "illegal" immigration in the USA; the border build-up, rather than deterring undocumented immigrants from entering the USA, discourages them from returning home; and, most tragically, the number of immigrants dying at the border has simply skyrocketed.[25] To deal with this latter problem the Border Patrol launched in 1998—five years after the El Paso experiment—search-and-rescue operations to help immigrants stranded in the deserts and mountains of the border region. But despite these efforts the number of deaths continues to rise because it is the strategy itself—the rerouting of the immigrants toward the most dangerous terrains—that is causing these deaths. The U.S. government refuses to take any responsibility for all these casualties, which are considered one of the "unintended" consequences of the nation's effort to protect its sovereignty.

Therefore, even after the considerable shortcomings that we have just mentioned, the U.S. continues to stand by this policy. The question is: why? Among the many factors that need to be considered, I will just mention a number of critical ones that can help us to understand the real, and often hidden, reasons and objectives of this border strategy. First of all, the whole border issue has to be looked at within the framework of the immigration "problem" in the U.S. I use the term "problem" on purpose because of the basic ambivalence with which immigration, and particularly undocumented immigration, is seen in the U.S. On one side we find the rhetoric of the poem by Emma Lazarus engraved on the pedestal of the Statue of Liberty, which depicts a generous nation that has welcomed the "poor, tired, and huddled masses yearning to be free," a "nation of immigrants"; on the other side, there is the true story of these masses who had to struggle against racism and nativism in order to show that they really belonged. On one side there is the anti-immigrant rhetoric of a country that is being invaded by "illegal aliens" and other "foreign menaces," an invasion that is causing the demise of the Western—White and Anglo-Saxon—civilization;[26] on the other side there is the reality of a nation that with its aggressive and neocolonial foreign policy, its economic policies, and structural dependence on and "insatiable appetite" for cheap immigrant labor is practically inviting immigrants into its territory.[27] This is the game of "they are responsible not us," which covers up the true story of immigration in the U.S. In this regard sociologist Yen Le Espiritu observes that the anti-immigrant rhetoric

> by portraying immigration to the United States as a matter of desperate individuals seeking opportunities, . . . completely disregards the aggressive role that U.S. government and U.S. corporations have played— through colonialism, imperialist wars and occupations, capital investment and material extraction in Third World countries and through active recruitment of racialized and gendered immigrant labor—in generating out-migration from key sending countries.[28]

Renowned immigration scholars such as Massey, Durand, and Malone explain this situation in terms of hypocrisy and the refusal to accept the humanity of immigrants:

> If there is one constant in U.S. border policy, it is hypocrisy. Throughout the twentieth century the United States has arranged to import Mexican workers while pretending not to. With the sole exception of the 1930s, when the Great Depression effectively extinguished U.S. labor demand, politicians and public officials have persistently sought ways of accepting Mexicans as workers while limiting their claims as human beings.[29]

Secondly, there exists a clear contradiction between the current U.S. border strategy, the objective of which is to fortify the border, and the "borderless world" that supporters of the free market economy, like the U.S., preach. Here we have the North American Free Trade Agreement (NAFTA) as a testimonial of the economic integration among Canada, the U.S., and Mexico. But at the same time we have also a border that has to be protected against "illegal" substances and human beings, and, especially after 9/11, against terrorists. Peter Andreas has observed that at the U.S.-Mexico border "the imperatives of security and those of economic integration appear to be on a collision course" and threaten the project of North American economic integration.[30]

Thirdly, in answer to those who wonder why this border strategy is still in place, despite being a policy failure, Andreas explains that this is an example of a "politically successful policy failure," which has succeeded in terms of its symbolic and image effects while largely failing in terms of its deterrent effects.[31] As such, this is more a political game than a successful strategy: "Border policing, in other words, is very much a spectator sport, but in this particular case the objective is to pacify rather than inflame the passion of the spectators."[32] Andreas continues:

> Indeed, even when some of the shortcomings of the strategy are recognized and acknowledged, the solution is assumed to be escalation rather than any fundamental reevaluation. Such policy persistence and escalation points to an underappreciated fact: failing and flawed policies can nevertheless be successful from a political and psychological perspective. The border *appears* more orderly at those crossing points that are most visible to the public and the media's eye.[33]

The theme of escalation of the current policy as a solution to the "border problem" has been at the forefront of the most recent debate on immigration in the U.S. Some politicians and pundits, galvanized by the ideology of the "war on terror" and by anti-immigrant movements such as the Minuteman Project,[34] are actually saying that the existing U.S. border policy is failing because it does not stop all "illegal aliens" from entering the country. The solution is to implement tougher measures such as sealing the whole Southern border—to build a border security fence from the Pacific Ocean to the Gulf of Mexico—an initiative that will stop the flow of "aliens" and protect the homeland from terrorist attacks.[35] On December 17, 2005, the House of Representatives passed the "Border Protection, Antiterrorism, and Illegal Immigration Control Act of 2005," which among the other things will authorize 2.2 billion dollars to build double-layer fences in some border areas of California and Arizona, and makes it a crime to assist any immigrant who enters the U.S. without authorization.[36] This escalation rhetoric is, after all, part and parcel of the main objective of this "spectator sport," that is, to give the public what they want: the *impression* of a border under control, even if immigrants are still entering the country in large numbers. This brings us to the notion of the hidden agendas of migration policies which are often used by politicians to pay lip service to anti-immigration and border control rhetoric while actually promoting other policies that lead to more immigration because that is what the labor market and the economy need.[37]

Fourthly, the U.S. government and some scholars have been referring to the expansion of the *polleros* (smugglers) networks and the death of so many immigrants as the "unintended consequences" of this border policy.[38] This "unintended" discourse is irritating because it becomes once again an excuse for those in power to avoid any responsibility for the growing casualty toll at the border. It is quite difficult to believe that the deaths of thousands of immigrants are "unintended" for at least two reasons: first, because this border strategy was designed by scholars who have studied in depth the phenomenon of Mexican immigration to the U.S. like, for instance, Robert Bach who, besides being a widely published immigration scholar, was the Executive Associate Commissioner for policy, planning, and programs of the INS at the time of the implementation of Operation Gatekeeper in 1994. To think that the planners were not expecting immigrants to risk their lives by crossing the dangerous deserts and mountains of the border region is quite naïve. Second, Claudia Smith proves this suspicion by pointedly affirming that the planners of Operation Gatekeeper were completely aware of the tragedy they were about to provoke by implementing such strategy. According to the text of the "U.S. Border Patrol Strategic Plan: 1994 and Beyond" the planners of the current border policy knew very well that they were pushing immigrants toward a terrain in which they would find themselves in "mortal danger," and they were aware that those "natural" obstacles were most probably not going to deter the migrants from crossing the border.[39] In other words, the deaths of thousands of immigrants at the U.S.-Mexico border is not an "unintended" consequence of U.S. border strategy, but part and parcel of an immigration policy that is often indifferent to the humanity of immigrants, and that does not really care if "some" of them die in the process of joining the cheap immigrant labor force that the U.S. economy badly needs. After all they are criminals who are infringing the sovereignty of the U.S., and could be potential terrorists. After all they are not really human: they are "illegal aliens." This is the "price" that the U.S. is ready to pay to protect its boundary simply because Americans are not paying it. In fact, while employers of immigrants and consumers continue to reap the benefits of this situation—without acknowledging it—the immigrants pay the real price of this policy with their very lives.[40] Once again in the history of humankind it is the most vulnerable and defenseless people who must pay the price. This leads us to the next section in which we will discuss the metaphor of the crucified peoples.

The Crucified Peoples

We can safely affirm that while it was Ignacio Ellacuría who coined the theological concept of the crucified peoples, it has been Jon Sobrino who has put it on the global Christological and theological agenda.[41] This image makes perfect sense and can be understood only within the context of theologies whose primary purpose is to deal with historical reality. Sobrino succinctly describes this particular understanding of theology: "To do theology means, in part, to face reality and raise it to a theological concept. In this task, theology should be honest with the real."[42] Starting from this insight, Ellacuría first, and Sobrino after, lay out a perceptive methodological proposal whose objective is to lead theology to honestly face reality. This proposal can be summarized in four main steps:[43] (1) *hacerse cargo de la realidad,* that is, getting to know reality by being in the midst of reality, and not just by reflecting on the idea of reality; (2) *cargar con la realidad,* which is about taking responsibility for reality by realizing the demands that reality makes on us, demands that cannot be avoided; (3) *encargarse de la realidad,* that is, to understand that the fulfillment of the process of knowing and comprehending reality is to become involved in the process of its transformation; and (4) *dejarse cargar por la realidad,* which points to the fact that reality is not just to be carried, but, thanks to its grace-filled nature, it can carry (*cargar*) the person who allows this grace to work. In other words, reality is not just negativity and sin, but also surprising and unexpected grace and hope, which have the power to carry those who entrust themselves to them.

A theology that has decided to confront honestly and responsibly historical reality cannot avoid the massive and shocking reality of the poor
and victimized majorities of our planet. It is in this context that Ellacuría
forges the image of the crucified peoples in an article entitled "El Pueblo
Crucificado: Ensayo de Soteriología Histórica,"—The Crucified People:
An Essay in Historical Soteriology—which was originally published in
1978.[44] Here Ellacuría draws an engaging parallel between the figure of
the Suffering Servant of Yahweh—found in Second Isaiah—Jesus, and the
crucified peoples, which underlines the following commonalities: they
are chosen by God; they suffer for historical reasons; they are rejected and
considered sinners even if they are not responsible for what they are
suffering; they accept carrying the sins of those who are really responsible
for their suffering; and finally, precisely because of their willingness to
carry the burden of sin, they become the "light of the nations" (Isaiah
42:6). It is in this same essay that Ellacuría offers a first definition of the
metaphor:

> What is meant by crucified people here is that collective body, which
> as the majority of humanity owes its situation of crucifixion to the
> way society is organized and maintained by a minority that exercises its
> dominion through a series of factors, which taken together and given
> their concrete impact within history, must be regarded as sin.[45]

A second definition, which Ellacuría proposes in a later article, is a very interesting one because here he identifies the crucified peoples as "the" sign
of the times:

> Among so many signs always being given, some identified and others
> hardly perceptible, there is in every age one that is primary, in whose
> light we should discern and interpret all the rest. This perennial sign is
> the historically crucified people, who link their permanence to the
> ever distinct form of their crucifixion. This crucified people represents
> the historical continuation of the servant of Yahweh, who is forever
> being stripped of his human features by the sin of the world, who is
> forever being despoiled of everything by the powerful of this world,
> who is forever being robbed of life, especially of life.[46]

Sobrino, who has repeatedly written on this theme, observes that the metaphor of the crucified peoples is "useful and necessary language" on three different, but related levels. On a factual level it refers to the reality of death that these peoples have to face, swift death caused by armed repression and conflicts, and slow death provoked by material poverty. On a historical-ethical level, because they do not just die, people are killed by unjust structures, by the so-called "institutionalized violence" that the Latin American Synod of Medellín (Colombia) condemned. This means also that if there are crucified people, there are also powerful executioners who crucify them. And finally, on a religious level, the reference to the cross reminds us of how Jesus died, and this in turn evokes the concepts of sin and death, damnation and salvation.[47]

To sum up, who are the crucified peoples for Ellacuría and Sobrino? First of all, before being a sign and a metaphor the crucified peoples are a historical reality, flesh and blood people who "live each day in the shadow of death" and "languish without adequate education, healthcare, work, or the means to change their lot."[48] Second, crucified people is a collective term. It does not refer to a single person, but to a "collective body," the poor, insignificant, and oppressed majorities of the world. Third, their suffering is neither natural nor self-inflicted. These peoples are victimized by the sin of a minority that has and exercises power as dominion in our society. In other words, the crucifixion of these peoples is the product of the oppressive and sinful use of power by a few persons. The concept of the crucified peoples contains a clear conflicting element: the crucified exist because there are crucifiers. Fourth, the crucified peoples are the historical continuation of the Servant of Yahweh portrayed in the four songs of Second Isaiah, and as such they become also the continuation of the person who incarnates, in the Christian interpretation, the dynamics of suffering and salvation of this Servant: Jesus Christ. Thus, they are the body of the crucified Christ in history.

Reflecting on the relevance of this reality/metaphor today Kevin Burke brings out its three main functions. (1) The crucified peoples unmask the sin of the world and expose its need for conversion, redemption, and renewal. (2) They embody a revelatory place. It is a language that illuminates historical reality, but does more than just that. It shows the ongoing presence of Jesus Christ in history. And (3) just as the Servant of Yahweh in Isaiah is not only the principal addressee of salvation, but also a principle of salvation, the same happens with the crucified peoples.[49] It is precisely this soteriological interpretation of the crucified peoples that stands at the center of Ellacuría's reading of this reality. He makes it very clear that the crucified peoples are both *salvados y salvadores*—saved and saviors—that they are both objects and, more importantly and scandalously, subjects of salvation. They are a principle of salvation not because of their own salvific power, but because they make present in history the Savior par excellence, the *Crucified*. In this way Ellacuría underlines a primary dimension of the dynamic of salvation in Christian theology, that is, salvation comes *desde abajo,* "from below": the stone rejected by the builders becomes the cornerstone (Ps 118:22; Mt 21:42); God chooses what is foolish, weak, and despised in the world to shame the wise and the strong (1 Cor 1:26–29).[50] In other words, as Aloysius Pieris remarks, "the powerless are chosen to confound the powerful, the poor are summoned to mediate the salvation of the rich, and the weak are called to liberate the strong."[51]

Sobrino elaborates on how the crucified peoples become a principle of salvation. (1) By their very existence the crucified peoples show the presence of the enormous and deadly reality of sin within the world. At the same time they also offer the possibility of conversion. (2) They provide values that cannot be easily encountered elsewhere, values that have an extraordinary humanizing potential like a sense of community, simplicity, spirit of service, creativity, and so on—the values that we need today to purify the contaminated air which the human spirit is forced to breathe. (3) They offer hope, which might seem senseless and absurd in their situation, and yet it is mysteriously present and active. (4) They show that selfless love is possible and are prepared to forgive even their oppressors. (5) They generate solidarity, a new and mutually supporting way of relating to human beings. (6) And finally, the crucified peoples point to a new way to be church, and a holiness that is more authentic and faithful to the "signs of our times" and to the gospel.[52]

Ellacuría and Sobrino convene on stating that the notion of the crucified peoples as a principle of salvation can and does cause scandal. If the assertion that the crucified peoples, the victims of history, are the privileged recipients of God's salvation, is still quite debatable, one can imagine how much more controversy will be caused by the designation of these people as "saviors." So it is not surprising at all to find some very influential theologians within the political and liberation traditions such as Jürgen Moltmann questioning this very idea.[53] Yet, and in spite of the reasonable objections that have been raised, I firmly believe that this proposal is to be taken very seriously for two main reasons. To begin with, the idea of the crucified peoples as "saviors" has profound biblical roots. It is grounded in the image of the Suffering Servant of Yahweh, the one whose appearance was marred "beyond human resemblance" (Is 52:14), the "man of suffering . . . from whom others hide their faces," the one who was "despised and rejected," the one who was held "of no account" (Is 53:3) who is made "the light of the nations" so that God's salvation "may reach to the end of the earth" (Is 49:6). It is rooted in the story of Jesus of Nazareth, the prophet condemned to death and crucified by the powers that be, who is the One in whom God offers us salvation. In other words, the biblical traditions clearly show that liberation and salvation happens in and through the most humble, unexpected, and unlikely circumstances, places, and people.

The other extremely important reason is that, as Sobrino affirms, theology and the church do not know what to do with the crucified peoples. These peoples, the victims of poverty and injustice, massacres and genocides, and the "war on terror," are anonymous. Unlike the U.S. victims of the Vietnam War who have their names engraved on monuments in Washington, DC, and unlike the victims of 9/11, these people from El Salvador, Rwanda, Congo, Haiti, Afghanistan, Iraq, have neither names nor dates. The Western world does not care about them because they are poor and from the Third World.[54] The Church sometimes knows what to do with the "Jesuanic martyrs," the active martyrs who have lived and died like Jesus defending the poor from their oppressors, but does not know how to deal with the crucified peoples, the victimized majorities who carry the burden of sin and death in a world characterized by inequality. Yet, it is for the sake of the latter that the Jesuanic martyrs, people such as Archbishop Oscar Romero and Bishop Juan Gerardi, gave up their lives.[55] These are two paramount and urgent reasons why the crucified peoples must become a central theme in Christian theology today. What these crucified peoples ask of us is to stand at the foot of their crosses and show respect for their profound mystery—a mystery that both hides and reveals the mystery of God—and ask them to forgive and save us. And finally to do whatever is in our power, even to give up our lives, to bring them down from their crosses.[56]

The Crucified Peoples at the Southern Border:
A Challenge to U.S. Theology

The decade of the 1990s has affected our world with profound, sudden and surprising changes. The fall of the Berlin Wall can be considered the symbol of the end of an era. The construction of another wall, much longer and mortal at the border between Mexico and the U.S. can be considered the symbol of a new era of great challenges.[57]

Benjamín González provides here a perceptive vision of our world, after the Cold War era, by comparing two infamous walls: one represented the separation between "communist" and "democratic" blocs, and the other represents the dire contradictions of a globalized planet in which the affluent nations, like the U.S., want to keep the undesirable and unwanted Third World masses out of sight. We have to read the reality of the crucified peoples at the U.S.-Mexico border in the context of this ambiguous and often dehumanizing and unequal process of globalization. This reality poses great challenges to the U.S. as a nation and to U.S. Christian churches and theologies.[58]

These challenges are taken seriously when we start asking the right questions: Who are today the crucified peoples in the U.S.? What are we doing to crucify them? What can we do to bring them down from their crosses? How do these crucified peoples bring about salvation within our community?[59] One of the main objectives of this essay is to claim that undocumented immigrants are among the different groups of disenfranchised people that are crucified today in the U.S. This is not an easy objective to achieve in a nation that refuses to admit any responsibility for the reality of crucifixion at its Southern border because to do so would damage its well-rehearsed image of defender of human rights, democracy, and freedom around the world. This point is dramatically depicted by Fitzsimmons's cartoon, which not only reveals the tragic reality of suffering and death of immigrants at the U.S.-Mexico border but also underscores its utmost theological significance. Immigrants are dying by the thousands in the dangerous deserts of Arizona, but, most importantly, they are being "crucified." This was the fate of Jesus of Nazareth, that same Jesus who said "I was hungry and you gave me no food, I was thirsty and you gave me nothing to drink, I was a stranger and you did not welcome me"(Mt 25:42−43).

While this essay emphasizes the crucified immigrants at the U.S.-Mexico border as a most explicit and unambiguous historical incarnation of the Crucified Christ, it wants also to underline the plight of many undocumented workers in the U.S. as an instance of crucifixion. It is not a secret—even if sometimes some people would like to keep it secret—that in our societies these are the women and men who perform the 3-D jobs—dirty, demanding, and dangerous—in miserable working and living conditions and with shameful salaries. César Chávez, the legendary California union labor organizer, compared the harsh work of immigrant farm workers to the experience of crucifixion: "Every time I see lettuce, that's the first thing I think of, some human being had to thin it. And it's just like being nailed to a cross." And talking about the experience of working the sugar beets he says: "That was work for an animal, not a man. Stooping and digging all day, and the beets are heavy—oh, that's brutal work. And then go home to some little place, with all those kids, and hot and dirty—that is how a man is crucified."[60] Moreover, the invisibility to which these undocumented immigrants are condemned and the process of "alienization" to which they are subjected contribute to their daily experience of crucifixion.

Now, if these are the crucified peoples, then how are we contributing to this crucifixion? Who are the crucifiers? Our earlier assessment of current border policy has clearly indicated that the U.S. government, despite a stubborn unwillingness to take any blame and responsibility, must be made accountable for the deaths of the immigrants. While this is a very significant conclusion, a more thoughtful appraisal is needed in order to understand and specify responsibility vis-à-vis this mortal border policy. Joseph Nevins provides such an appraisal in a penetrating article in which he affirms that the critique of current U.S. border policy offered by academics, policy analysts, and human rights activists while disapproving of the posture of the government, fails to critique current practice. It is the practice of border enforcement in itself, Nevins states, that causes the deaths of immigrants, and not just its recent build up. Critics of border policy, according to Nevins, fail to critique U.S. border strategy in and of itself because they base their arguments on three interrelated "ways of seeing." The first has to do with the acceptance of national territorial sovereignty as an unproblematic assumption. The second refers to a conservative view of human rights that puts the right of the state to control the border over the right of immigrants to freedom of movement and other basic rights (right to life, security, health, liberty) that they can enjoy only by migrating. The third is a narrow conception of violence that looks at violence as merely direct or personal violence where there is an identifiable actor committing it. But such a view of violence ignores the existence of an indirect and structural violence, which precisely because of lack of visible agency could easily go unnoticed and unchallenged. Nevins says that if we take this latter point into consideration then

> we realize that a death caused by a bullet is not morally more reprehensible than one caused by practices and social structures, such as those embodied by the U.S.-Mexico boundary-enforcement regime. . . . In many ways, this is not surprising as personal and direct violence *shows*. It disturbs the normal environment, whereas the structural violence *is* the normal environment—at least in part.[61]

Sadly, structural violence has become the normal environment in the U.S.-Mexico border region, to the point that the death of immigrants is not an issue. The real issue, once again, is the protection of U.S. sovereignty and the security of the U.S. population in this era of "terrorism." So, Nevins remarks:

> Just as the boundary and its associated practices and identities (such as citizen, "alien," "legal," and "illegal") have become normal, so, too, have the migrant deaths, in that most people in the United States accept them as simply a fact of life, as a perhaps sad but acceptable outcome of the perceived necessity to enforce "our" boundaries.[62]

Nevins's critical insights challenge a theology that deals with the reality of the crucified peoples at the U.S.-Mexico border in at least two ways. To begin with there is the issue of national sovereignty and border control. From a Christian perspective, is national sovereignty an absolute value? Is it more important than the right to life? The document on migration issued jointly by the U.S. and Mexican Catholic Episcopal conferences, *Strangers No Longer,* mentions among the five main principles of the teaching of the church on migration the following: "Sovereign nations have the right to control their borders."[63] And it adds:

> The Church recognizes the right of a sovereign state to control its borders in furtherance of the common good. It also recognizes the right of human persons to migrate so that they can realize their God-given rights. These teachings complement each other. While the sovereign state may impose reasonable limits on immigration, the common good is not served when the basic human rights of the individual are violated. In the current condition of the world, in which global poverty and persecution are rampant, the presumption is that persons must migrate in order to support and protect themselves and that nations who are able to receive them should do so whenever possible. It is through this lens that we assess the current migration reality between the United States and Mexico.[64]

Looking at the situation at the U.S.-Mexico border and at the mortal consequences of the current policy of border enforcement it is not that clear how the right to control the borders and the right to immigrate "complement each other." The real problem is that the affirmation of the right of a nation to control its borders as one of the main principles of church teaching on migration can be manipulated to justify the continuation of policies that cause the death of migrants. Moreover, how do we reconcile the theme of national sovereignty with the prophetic mark of "catholicity"—the all-inclusive nature of our church—which we solemnly profess as one of the primary characteristics of our Christian community? The latter is a critical theological question that needs much more attention and reflection by U.S. theology.[65]

The other issue raised by Nevins is that of violence. He rightly observes that violence is not just personal and visible violence. The worst violence is the one that is invisible and seemingly has no perpetrators. This is the violence that permeates the environment to the point that people just get used to it and accept it as a normal fact of life. It is precisely to this violence, under the name of structural violence or structural sin, that Ellacuría calls our attention with the reality/symbol of the crucified peoples. They are victims of an institutionalized violence, of a violent system that, because of its ability to cover-up, often goes unrecognized and unchallenged. In our specific case, U.S. border policy has been planned in such a way that the agent and source of its violence is almost unidentifiable: it is not border enforcement in and of itself that causes the death of countless immigrants, but it is the extreme weather of the border region, or the smugglers who abandon the immigrants, or the immigrants themselves because they do not know the terrain, and so forth. The search for the direct agent of violence covers up the structural cause of this border crucifixion, which is sinful and mortal. If U.S. Christians do not become aware of the structural nature of this contemporary crucifixion, if they consider the deaths of the immigrants "as simply a fact of life"—the "collateral damage" that necessarily comes with the "sacred" duty to protect the border from invaders and terrorists—then they are contributing, even if unwittingly, to the crucifixion at the U.S.-Mexico border.

What can we do to bring the immigrants down from their border crosses? In a country like the U.S. in which immigration and border control very often provoke negative reactions among the public opinion—thanks also to the gloomy picture painted by the mass media—it is imperative to raise the awareness of the civic and religious community about these vital issues and their consequences. The historical memory of U.S. immigration is often forgotten in the midst of unfounded fears and prejudices. Immigration is a very complex human and social phenomenon that needs to be understood in its causes and whose protagonists deserve accompaniment and solidarity, not "alienization" that leads to crucifixion. Its dynamics have global and systemic dimensions that have to be honestly explained in their entirety and complexity, otherwise people will be just left with the bleak and unfair picture of the immigrants as "invaders." And an honest assessment of reality shows that the U.S., because of its foreign and economic policies, is partly responsible for the migration of people from Third World countries. A candid evaluation of the current border strategy can be achieved only in the context of an honest assessment of the reality of U.S. immigration. Such an evaluation is more difficult now than ever because of the security concerns that are constantly raised in the political discourse about the U.S.-Mexico border. These are legitimate concerns, but it is imperative to realize that real security in our world will not be the result of border enforcement and military actions, but the fruit of equal, just, and peaceful relationships among the peoples of this planet. Christian communities, inspired by their evangelical desire for compassion, intercultural fellowship, and solidarity, have to become the countercultural heralds of this crucial truth. In times like this the churches have to rediscover their prophetic role within society and raise their voices against deceptive and unilateral readings of immigration in the U.S. They have to be reminded of the critical importance of the option for the defenseless and the vulnerable. Only a more prophetic church, a church that wants to be truly honest with the reality of immigration, and attentive to the unjust suffering and death of immigrants, will be capable of bringing the crucified peoples down from their border crosses.

Can grace and salvation be found among these crucified immigrants? Grace and salvation can be found when we take the time to stand at the foot of these border crosses and reflect on the lives of these apparently "anonymous" and "insignificant" people, lives that, as Sobrino says, both hide and reveal the mystery of God and humanity.[66] The lives of these crucified immigrants are the concrete manifestation of the incarnation of the Crucified Christ in history. They make manifest the structural sin that causes this crucifixion. They talk to us about the salvific power of crucifixion that ultimately brings about new life in the midst of death. They also reveal the values that these immigrants carry: courage in the midst of apparently insurmountable obstacles; faith that recognizes in the Crucified Christ a faithful God who understands and accompanies them, and suffers with them; hope in a better future and a new life because God is good; solidarity with those who suffer; a sense of community; hospitality in a world that is suspicious about strangers; willingness to sacrifice for the sake of their families; and so on. These immigrants are neither inferior persons coming from "uncivilized" countries, nor are they just "victims" that need our paternalistic "generosity." They are the carriers of truths and values that make them the prophets and protagonists of a better society, founded on truly Christian and human values that are slowly disappearing today in the U.S., a country that is starting to choke on the arrogance of its power and superiority which are often, and grossly, justified in the name of the God of Jesus Christ. Daniel Groody, in his interviews with immigrants at the U.S.-Mexico border, shows the depth of their spirituality, and how extraordinary faith and hope are found where we expect to find just despair, abandonment, and even death.[67]

Indeed, the crucified peoples at the U.S.-Mexico border prove once again that God's grace and salvation can be found in the most unlikely places, in today's "Golgothas."

At this point the real question becomes: can U.S. Christians accept that grace and salvation may come from the "illegal aliens"? Pride and arrogance make this quite difficult. The thought that we, the "civilized" and "developed" people who have everything, might receive anything good from the "uncivilized" and the "poor" is quite alien to the Western world in general, and might sound even preposterous. Because of this Western people are more used to think of themselves as the "givers" rather than the "recipients."[68] After all, those who have nothing or not much can offer nothing or not much. A radical change of attitude is needed here, besides an abundant dose of humility that will make people recognize that we have still much to learn about being human and being Christian, and that we can learn that from the crucified "strangers."

¡Gracias a Dios estamos vivos!

Among the countless groups of immigrants that found shelter in Casa del Migrante in Tijuana, I will never forget a group that arrived from Honduras after a long, dangerous, and grueling journey. They looked so tired and eager to find a place to rest, and yet there was a spark of joy and hope in their eyes that I could not figure out. Here I was ready to do my best to encourage and console them after what they went through, but it was they who simply surprised me with their astonishing faith and hope. When I asked them, *¿Como están?* [How are you?], their answer was: *¡Gracias a Dios estamos vivos!* [Thanks to God we are alive]. They firmly believed that God had accompanied them through their unbelievable journey, and if God had given them the faith and strength to reach Tijuana, then God was going to allow them to reach their destination in the U.S. Despite being robbed by thieves and police officers, despite going with little or no food for many days, despite the difficult problems that they had to face in their journey from Central America to the U.S.-Mexico border, their faith and hope were stronger than ever. When I thought there was little hope to offer to the immigrants coming to Casa del Migrante, abundant faith and hope appeared in a most unlikely manner precisely in the people that I thought needed it the most.

In a U.S. society that believes and is prodded to believe, especially by politicians and mass media, that immigrants are a disgrace, that they are a threat to our communities and way of life, the crucified immigrants at the U.S.-Mexico border stand out as a crucial and vital challenge. These are the people who, as Fitzsimmons reminds us, evoke our primary ethical commitment as Christians to those who are thirsty, hungry, sick, naked, and strangers (Mt 25:31–46). At the same time, and here is the "scandal" of the reality/metaphor of the crucified peoples, they are the people who can save us from the injustice, structural violence, arrogance, thirst for power, and indifference that characterizes the environment in which we live. In an era in which we are encouraged to look for heroes in the battlefields of the "war on terror," the crucified peoples at the U.S.-Mexico border represent a breath of fresh air, the unlikely heroes of a globalized world who show that the earth is not ours, but belongs to God, and that we are all here as "tenants and immigrants" (Lv 25:23). They become the privileged witnesses of the mysterious presence of the Crucified Christ who came to break down the wall of hostility that divides us in order to create a new humanity (Eph 2:14–16).

NOTES

1. This is a shelter for migrants at the Tijuana (Mexico)-San Diego (USA) border. It was founded in 1987 and it is run by the Missionaries of St. Charles (Scalabrinians). It belongs to the network Red Casas del Migrante Scalabrini, with centers in Mexico (Tijuana, Nuevo Laredo, and Tapachula) and Guatemala (Tecún Umán and Guatemala City). For more information see www.migrante.com.mx (last accessed May 2007).

2. For an account of the journey of Mexican immigrants to the U.S. see Daniel G. Groody, *Border of Death, Valley of Life: An Immigrant Journey of Heart and Spirit* (Lahnam, MD: Rowman and Littlefield, 2002), 13–39.

3. See John Annerino, *Dead in Their Tracks: Crossing America's Desert Borderlands* (New York: Four Walls Eight Windows, 1999).

4. Mensaje Jubilar de la Red Casas del Migrante Scalabrini, "El Clamor de los Indocumentados," (2000); available through www.sedos.org (last accessed May 2007).

5. See Leo R. Chavez, *Covering Immigration: Popular Images, and the Politics of the Nation* (Berkeley: University of California Press, 2001).

6. One of the main segments of the CNN news show *Lou Dobbs Tonight* is precisely entitled "Broken Borders." Another very popular news show that has

covered the border issue quite extensively, and from the same negative perspective, is the *Bill O'Reilly Factor* by Fox News.

7. See the September 20, 2004, issue of *Time* with a special investigation on "America's Border: Even After 9/11, It's Outrageously Easy to Sneak In," by Donald L. Barlett and James B. Steele.

8. Samuel P. Huntington, *Who Are We? The Challenges to America's National Identity* (New York: Simon and Schuster, 2004), 82, affirms that according to recent surveys 80 to 85 percent of U.S. people identify themselves as Christians.

9. Joseph Nevins, *Operation Gatekeeper: The Rise of the "Illegal Alien" and the Making of the U.S.-Mexico Boundary* (New York: Routledge, 2002), 61–94; Chavez, *Covering Immigration,* 215–46.

10. Néstor P. Rodríguez, "The Social Construction of the U.S.-Mexico Border," in *Immigrants Out! The New Nativism and the Anti-Immigrant Impulse in the United States,* ed. Juan F. Perea (New York: New York University Press, 1997), 227; Nevins, *Operation Gatekeeper,* 63–64.

11. Quoted in Nevins, *Operation Gatekeeper,* 67–68.

12. Douglas S. Massey, Jorge Durand, and Nolan J. Malone, *Beyond Smoke and Mirrors: Mexican Immigration in an Era of Economic Integration* (New York: Russell Sage Foundation, 2002), 84–89.

13. Peter Andreas, *Border Games: Policing the U.S.-Mexico Divide* (Ithaca, NY: Cornell University Press, 2000), 85.

14. Huntington, *Who Are We?,* 180.

15. Massey, Durand, and Malone, *Beyond Smoke and Mirrors,* 89, notes how a few years before sponsoring Proposition 187 Governor Wilson "had sponsored legislation to *relax* border controls, and indeed, he regularly employed undocumented workers himself."

16. Rodríguez, "Social Construction," 228–29.

17. See once again the important work of anthropologist Leo Chavez, *Covering Immigration.*

18. For a detailed discussion of this theme see Nevins, *Operation Gatekeeper,* 95–122.

19. Ibid., 234n85.

20. Rodríguez, "Social Construction," 232.

21. Immigration and Naturalization Service, which since March 2003 has been absorbed by the Department of Homeland Security.

22. See www.stopgatekeeper.org (last accessed May 2007) and www.nomore deaths.org (last accessed May 2007); also Karl Eschbach, Jacqueline Hagan, Néstor Rodríguez, Rubén Hernández-León, and Stanley Bailey, "Death at the Border," *International Migration Review* 33, no. 2 (1999): 430–54.

23. Andreas underlines the unfortunate link that U.S. authorities make between the fight against illegal substances and "illegal" immigrants in *Border Games.*

24. Wayne A. Cornelius, "Controlling 'Unwanted' Immigration: Lessons from the United States, 1993–2004" (working paper 92, The Center for Comparative Immigration Studies, University of California, San Diego, 2004; available at http://www.ccis-ucsd.org/publications/wrkg92.pdf, last accessed May 2007).

25. See Massey, Durand, and Malone, *Beyond Smoke and Mirrors,* 112–41; Belinda I. Reyes, Hans P. Johnson, and Richard Van Swearingen, *Holding the Line? The Effect of the Recent Border Build-up on Unauthorized Immigration* (San Francisco: Public Policy Institute of California, 2002; available through http://www.ppic.org, last accessed May 2007).

26. Huntington, *Who Are We?*; Michelle Malkin, *Invasion: How America Still Welcomes Terrorists, Criminals, and Other Foreign Menaces to Our Shores* (Washington, DC: Regnery Publishing, 2002); Patrick J. Buchanan, *The Death of the West: How Dying Populations and Immigrant Invasions Imperil Our Country and Civilization* (New York: St. Martin's Press, 2002).

27. On the structural character of the demand for cheap immigrant labor see Cornelius, "Controlling 'Unwanted' Migration."

28. Yen Le Espiritu, *Home Bound: Filipino American Lives Across Cultures, Communities, and Countries* (Berkeley: University of California Press, 2003), 207.

29. Massey, Durand, and Malone, *Beyond Smoke and Mirrors,* 105.

30. Peter Andreas, "A Tale of Two Borders: The U.S.-Mexico and U.S.-Canada Lines after 9/11" (working paper 77, The Center for Comparative Immigration Studies, University of California, San Diego, 2003; available at http://www.ccis-ucsd.org/publications/wrkg77.pdf, last accessed May 2007).

31. Ibid., 3–4.

32. Peter Andreas, "The U.S. Immigration Control Offensive: Constructing an Image of Order on the Southwest Border," in *Crossings: Mexican Immigration in Interdisciplinary Perspectives,* ed. Marcelo M. Suárez-Orozco (Cambridge, MA: David Rockefeller Center for Latin American Studies, Harvard University, 1998), 353.

33. Ibid., 352.

34. The website of this group is http://www.minutemanhq.com/ (last accessed May 2007). Its founder, Jim Gilchrist, is running for Congress in California District 48.

35. The creation of a security fence along the whole border is one of the main features of the "True Enforcement and Border Security Act" (H. R. 4313), most recently introduced by Congressman Duncan Hunter (R-CA) and Virgil Goode (R-VA). For more information see http://www.immigrationforum.org/DesktopDefault.aspx?tabid=737 (last accessed July 2007).

36. For information regarding this bill see Julia Gelatt, "House Passes Enforcement Bill Lacking Temporary Worker Program," Migration Information Source, January 1, 2006 (available at http://www.migrationinformation.org/USfocus/display.cfm?id=367 (last accessed May 2007).

37. On this subject see the insightful essay by Stephen Castles, "The Factors that Make and Unmake Migration Policies," *International Migration Review* 38, no. 3 (2004): 852–84.

38. Cornelius, "Controlling 'Unwanted' Migration."

39. See http://www.stopgatekeeper.org/English/facts.htm (last accessed July 2007). The "U.S. Border Patrol Strategic Plan: 1994 and Beyond" is referenced in this fact sheet and cited in footnotes 11 and 12.

40. Cornelius, "Controlling 'Unwanted' Migration."

41. Sturla J. Stalsett, *The crucified and the Crucified. A Study in the Liberation Christology of Jon Sobrino* (Bern: Peter Lang, 2003), 537. I will not elaborate here on the profound and well recognized influence of Ellacuría on Sobrino's theological thought, which is manifest in practically all the latter's writings.

42. Jon Sobrino, *Witnesses to the Kingdom: The Martyrs of El Salvador and the Crucified Peoples* (Maryknoll, NY: Orbis Books, 2003), 13.

43. See Ignacio Ellacuría, *Escritos Teológicos* (San Salvador, El Salvador: UCA Editores, 2000), 1:187–218. This essay was originally published in 1975 with the title "Hacia una Fundamentación del Método Teológico Latinoamericano." See also Jon Sobrino, "La Teología y el 'Principio Liberación,'" in *Revista Latinoamericana de Teología* 12 (Mayo–Agosto 1995): 115–40. The first three steps of this methodology were originally proposed by Ellacuría, while the last is Sobrino's specific contribution.

44. The article can be found in Ignacio Ellacuría, *Escritos Teológicos,* 2:137–70. Here I follow the English translation, "The Crucified People," in Ignacio Ellacuría and Jon Sobrino, eds., *Mysterium Liberationis: Fundamental Concepts of Liberation Theology* (Maryknoll, NY: Orbis Books, 1993), 580–603.

45. Ignacio Ellacuría, "The Crucified People," 590.

46. The title of this article, originally published in 1980, is "Discernir el 'Signo' de los Tiempos"; it is found in Ellacuría, *Escritos Teológicos,* 2:133–35. The English translation is from Kevin F. Burke, "The Crucified People as 'Light for the Nations': A Reflection on Ignacio Ellacuría," in *Rethinking Martyrdom,* ed. Teresa Okure, Jon Sobrino, and Felix Wilfred (London: SCM Press, 2003), 124.

47. Jon Sobrino, *Jesus the Liberator: A Historical-Theological View* (Maryknoll, NY: Orbis Books, 1993), 254–55; see also his *The Principle Mercy: Taking the Crucified People from the Cross* (Maryknoll, NY: Orbis Books, 1994) 50–51.

48. Burke, "The Crucified People," 124.

49. Ibid., 123–30.

50. José Sols Lucia, *La Teología Histórica de Ignacio Ellacuría* (Madrid: Editorial Trotta, 1999), 272–78.

51. Aloysius Pieris, "Christ Beyond Dogma. Doing Christology in the Context of the Religions and the Poor," *Louvain Studies* 25, no. 3 (2000): 200.

52. Jon Sobrino, "La Teología de la Liberación en América Latina: Relación Esencial entre Teología y Pobres," in *La Teología de la Liberación en América Latina,*

Africa y Asia, ed. Jon Sobrino, Julio Lois, and Juan Sánchez-Rivera (Madrid: PPC, 1998), 53–55; also, Sobrino, *Jesus the Liberator,* 262–64.

53. See Jürgen Moltmann, *Experiences in Theology: Ways and Forms of Christian Theology* (Minneapolis: Fortress Press, 2000), 295–97; Stalsett, *The crucified and the Crucified,* 553–58.

54. Sobrino, *Witnesses to the Kingdom,* 4.

55. Jon Sobrino, "The Kingdom of God and the Theologal Dimension of the Poor," in *Who Do You Say I Am? Confessing the Mystery of Christ,* ed., John C. Cavadini and Laura Holt (Notre Dame, IN: University of Notre Dame Press, 2004), 137–38; also, Sobrino, *Witnesses to the Kingdom,* 119–33.

56. Sobrino, "The Kingdom of God," 138.

57. Benjamín González Buelta, "Rasgos de la Experiencia Cristiana en una Iglesia que Busca Justicia," *Christus* 65 (Julio–Agosto 2000): 7.

58. See Robert Lassalle-Klein, "The Body of Christ: The Claim of the Crucified People on U.S. Theology and Ethics," *Journal of Hispanic/Latino Theology* 5, no. 4 (1998): 48–77. This interesting essay addresses the challenges that the crucified people in El Salvador present to Christian theology and ethics in the U.S.

59. Ellacuría suggests some of these questions in an article entitled "Las Iglesias de Latinoamericanas Interpelan a la Iglesia de España," originally published in 1982. See Ellacuría, *Escritos Teológicos,* 2:589–602.

60. Frederick John Dalton, *The Moral Vision of César Chávez* (Maryknoll, NY: Orbis Books, 2003), 64.

61. Joseph Nevins, "Thinking Out of Bounds: A Critical Analysis of Academic and Human Rights Writings on Migrant Deaths in the U.S.-Mexico Border Region," *Migraciones Internacionales* 2, no. 2 (2003): 171–90 (available through the journal's web site, www.colef.mx/migracionesinternacionales, last accessed May 2007).

62. Ibid.

63. Mexican Catholic Bishops' Conference and the United States Conference of Catholic Bishops, *Strangers No Longer: Together on the Journey of Hope* (Washington, DC: United States Conference of Catholic Bishops, 2003), paragraph 36.

64. Ibid., paragraph 39.

65. On the theme of catholicity see Robert J. Schreiter, *The New Catholicity: Theology between the Global and the Local* (Maryknoll, NY: Orbis Books, 1997); Orlando O. Espín, "Immigration, Territory, and Globalization: Theological Reflections," *Journal of Hispanic/Latino Theology* 7, no. 3 (2000): 46–59.

66. Sobrino, *Witnesses to the Kingdom,* 133.

67. Daniel G. Groody, "Spirituality on the Western Front," *America,* Nov. 24, 2003, 9–11.

68. See Sobrino, *The Principle Mercy,* 86–87.

CHAPTER SEVENTEEN

Fruit of the Vine and Work of Human Hands

Immigration and the Eucharist

DANIEL G. GROODY

In November 2003, I attended a mass in El Paso, Texas, along the U.S.-Mexico border. We celebrated mass outside, in the open air, in the dry, rugged, and sun-scorched terrain where the United States meets Mexico. This liturgy was a time not only to remember all the saints and all the souls of history but also the thousands of Mexican immigrants who died crossing over the border in the last ten years. Like other liturgies, a large crowd gathered to pray and worship together. Unlike other liturgies, however, a sixteen-foot iron fence divided this community in half, with one side in Mexico and the other side in the United States.

To give expression to our common solidarity as a people of God beyond political constructions, the two communities joined altars on both sides of the wall. Even while Border Patrol agents and helicopters surrounded the liturgy and kept a strict vigilance, lest any Mexicans cross over, people sang, worshiped, and prayed. People prayed for the Mexican and U.S. governments. People prayed for those who died. And people prayed to understand better their interconnectedness to each other. I remember in particular the sign of peace, when one normally shakes a hand or shares a hug with one's neighbor. Unable to touch my Mexican neighbor except through some small holes in the fence, I became painfully aware of the unity we celebrated but the divisions that we experienced. In the face of the wall between us, it struck me how we could experience concurrently our unity in Christ but our dividedness in our current reality, for no other reason than that we were born on different sides of the fence. It brought to a new level the insight of Dr. Martin Luther King Jr. who said that "Sunday at 11:00 (is) the most segregated hour in America."

As I have reflected on this Eucharist at the border, I have been reminded of the integral link between social justice and the liturgy and in particular between the option for the poor in the Eucharist. Gustavo Gutiérrez says that, in the end, the option for the poor is about the Eucharist.[1] The Eucharist is the recollection of the memory of the life, teachings, death, and resurrection of Jesus, and the option for the poor tries to make this connection between what we do in Church and how we live in society. In this brief essay, I shall look at the very complex issue of undocumented immigration in the United States and analyze it through the framework of the Eucharist. As a work of constructive theology, I seek to make the critical link between the Eucharist, immigration, and the option for the poor.

A Sociotheological Hermeneutic of a Complex Reality

For the last fifteen years I have been talking to immigrants, U.S. Border Patrol agents, *coyote* smugglers (who transport people across the border), ranchers, vigilante groups, educators, congressmen, medical personnel, social workers, human rights advocates, and others involved in the complex drama along the U.S.-Mexico border. I have spoken to ranchers who have seen their property trashed by immigrants who parade through their land and leave behind water jugs, litter, and discarded clothing. I have spoken to educators and hospital administrators who feel increasing financial pressure from the influx of newly arrived immigrants. I have listened to U.S. Border Patrol agents tell stories of being pinned down by gunfire from drug smugglers of cocaine and marijuana. I have spoken to congressional leaders charged with the responsibility of safeguarding a stable economy and protecting the common good, especially since 9/11. I have spoken to coyote smugglers who have tried to guide people across the treacherous terrain along the border and find some profit in doing so. But most of all, I have spoken to immigrants and heard hundreds of stories of what it is like to break from home, cross the border, and enter the United States as an undocumented immigrant.

In speaking with these different groups along the border, I have learned that each constituency believes they have certain rights that belong to them. Even the most fringe, radical group has a point to make, a truth to defend. Some speak of the right to "private property," "American jobs," "national security," "civil law and order," "a more dignified life," and other such rights. How does one begin to sort through such a complex issue as immigration and come to grasp what are the most important issues? Dare I even ask, what does God have to say about what is happening at the border? While I make no grandiose claims to be God's spokesperson, or even a voice for the migrants, I would like to offer a Christian framework through which to read the reality of migration. I believe the biblical option for the poor challenges us to give the first hearing to those who suffer the most, and one of the ways we might better be able to hear the voice of the immigrant is by analyzing their voices through the structure of the liturgy. I offer here then a Eucharistic hermeneutic of migration and migratory hermeneutic of the Eucharist. In other words, my approach to this essay is to offer a theological interpretation of a social reality and a social interpretation of a theological reality.

Immigration and the Eucharist

While at first glance the connection between immigration and the Eucharist is not obvious, on deeper reflection there are many critical correlations between the structure of the Eucharistic prayer and the process of migration. As one looks more closely at the dynamics of immigration and the structure of the Eucharist, one can observe many connections between the breaking of the bread and the breaking of migrants' bodies, between the pouring out of Christ's blood for his people and the pouring out of migrants' lives for their families, between Christ's death and resurrection and migrants' own. Immigrants, I believe, offer a new way of looking at the Eucharist, and the Eucharist in turn gives many immigrants a new way of understanding their struggles.

As we know, beneath the surface of the scriptures, there are often many social, political, and economic struggles.[2] The scriptures take shape within the context of these struggles, and one of the key themes that emerges in the biblical narrative is that of migration. The story of Israel and Christianity is in fact a story of a migration. Accordingly, I argue here that immigration is not simply a sociological fact but also a theological event. The people of God came into being through a migration experience when God called Abraham to leave his homeland and venture forth into new and unknown territory, where God's promises would be revealed to him (Gn 12:1–9). In times of famine, Jacob's sons migrated to Egypt in search of food (Gn 42:1–2). In times of slavery, God reached out to the Israelites and set them free (Ex 1–18). In times of persecution, Joseph, Mary, and the infant Jesus became immigrants themselves when they sought refuge in Egypt (Mt 2:13). In what some scholars consider to be one of the ancient creeds of faith and one of the cornerstones of early Israelite identity, the book of Deuteronomy also records, "My father was a wandering Aramean who went down to Egypt with a small household and lived there as an alien. But there he became a nation great, strong and numerous" (Dt 26:5).[3] Their migrations were often marked by intense periods of hardship, hunger, disorientation, poverty, need, loneliness, uncertainty, and tremendous vulnerability. In the process of movement, God revealed his covenant to His people.

In time, Jewish people would gather every year in Jerusalem to remember their oppression in Egypt, God's liberating action on their behalf, and their sojourn through the desert to the promised land as immigrants. Arguably one of the reasons why Yahweh called Israel to remember His deeds was because of the human tendency towards historical amnesia, especially as one becomes more prosperous. As such, the core of Israelite faith revolved around Yahweh's commands, "So you too must befriend the alien, for you were once aliens yourselves in the land of Egypt" (Dt 10:19).

When we forget our personal and collective immigration stories, we easily repeat the same mistakes of the past. George Santayana said, "those who do not remember the past are condemned to repeat it." This remembrance is a way of acknowledging God's saving activity. When we forget, immigrants easily become the target of social problems and are quickly typecast as a threat to the common good. Instead of hospitality and openness, many immigrants find scapegoating and rejection, hostility and fear. In contrast, the covenant opens an alternative way of viewing the stranger, perceived as "the other."[4] The covenant not only acknowledges God's goodness to Israel but also calls Israel to respond to newcomers in the same way that Yahweh responded to them.

For Christians, the Passover narrative lays one of the major foundations for Eucharist; the liturgy becomes a time to remember God's saving deeds in history. This process of remembering is an "anamnesis," an ability to recall the extraordinary events of God, especially in the death and resurrection of Jesus. The Eucharist recalls not only that we are migrating towards God but that God in the Incarnation has first migrated towards the human race.[5] Only because of God's a priori migration to us can Christians in turn "migrate" in faith into all that is the reign of God. The recalling of God's saving events in history, then, is not simply a historical exercise that recalls interesting information about the past: it is a sacramental experience that makes these events effectively present to the Christian community today. This memory is ultimately directed towards the transformation—even the transubstantiation—of the people of God through love. In light of excessive nationalism and xenophobic attitudes in American culture, such a changing of people's minds and hearts might even be more difficult than the transformation of bread and wine into the body and blood of Christ.

The Dynamics of Immigration and the Structure of the Eucharist

As we look at the relationship between the Eucharist and immigration, it is also helpful to look more closely at the underlying structure of the liturgy. The Eucharist, as we have mentioned above, has its roots in the Jewish Passover meal, when the people of Israel remembered their slavery in Egypt, their cries for deliverance, the sending of Moses, God's answer to their pleas, their wandering in the desert, the covenant at Mt. Sinai, and the passage from slavery to freedom. The story of the Israelites in Egypt is an ancient story but it is also a recurring story; as the Word of God the Passover contains an enduring metaphorical truth that speaks to all generations.

In many respects, we might say the Passover narrative is the prototypical migration story: it remembers the movement of a people from oppression to liberation, from the land of slavery to the Promised Land. Christian imagery takes the Exodus imagery to a new level by saying that the Christian life is a migration from death to life. As John Chrysostom notes,

> The Israelites saw miracles. Now you shall see greater and much more brilliant ones than those seen when the Israelites went forth from Egypt. You did not see the Pharaoh and his armies drowned, but you did see the drowning of the devil and his armies. The Israelites passed through the sea; you have passed through the sea of death. They were delivered from the Egyptians; you are set free from the demon. They put aside their servitude to barbarians; you have set aside the far more hazardous servitude to sin.[6]

Many migrants, in particular, see in the Exodus story their own stories. They experience themselves as a people who experience economic slavery in their homeland, who cry out for deliverance, and who hope for a promised land where they can live with freedom and human dignity.

Beyond the narrative foundation of the Passover in the Eucharist, Jesus also follows the rites of Israel. We see these rites in the Passover narrative and the four verbs that shape the liturgy. These verbs have their origin in the scriptures, as brought out in the Gospel of Luke, where Jesus said,

> When the hour came, he took his place at table with the apostles. He said to them, "I have eagerly desired to eat this Passover with you before I suffer, for, I tell you, I shall not eat it (again) until there is fulfillment in the kingdom of God." Then he took a cup, gave thanks, and said, "Take this and share it among yourselves; for I tell you (that) from this time on I shall not drink of the fruit of the vine until the kingdom of God comes." Then he *took the bread, said the blessing, broke it, and gave it* to them, saying, "This is my body, which will be given for you; do this in memory of me."[7]

Some have claimed that the four verbs that Jesus uses in this narrative came to form the structural core of the liturgy of the Eucharist, and many liturgists today continue to discuss the theological importance of these verbs.[8] But liturgists have also raised serious methodological questions about this.[9] Nevertheless, these four action verbs from the Last Supper narratives—

taking, blessing, breaking, giving—may still provide a hermeneutical key for assessing the process of migration: people take up the decision to leave their homeland, bless God for the gift of their lives and families (even in the midst of tremendous suffering), break themselves open so they can feed those they love, and give themselves away for the nourishment of others, even at the cost of their lives.

"He Took the Bread": Making the Difficult Decision to Migrate

It is striking that bread is at the heart of the Eucharist and also at the core of the journey for many migrants.[10] When people do not have enough bread to eat, they face the difficult choice of migrating. The bread of the Eucharist recalls the death of the Lord until he comes again. The bread the migrants seek entails undergoing death, until they can become something more than their current state, something more than their dehumanizing existence. Taking up the decision to migrate involves undergoing death on many levels. It means leaving behind a family, a culture, a way of life, a familiar language, and many other things. To relinquish these is a sacrifice, a loss, a psychological death.

For some, migration also means physical death. Since 1994, when border enforcement strategies became more extensive along the U.S.-Mexico border, migrants have been forced to travel more dangerous routes in order to enter the country. Trying to evade Border Patrol agents, infrared devices, motion sensors, aerial surveillance, impermeable walls, and other deterrent strategies, migrants now cross the most treacherous terrain to make it into the United States. They will risk freezing to death as they climb ten-thousand-foot mountains, drowning in canals and rivers, and overheating in deserts that reach daytime temperatures up to 120 degrees in the shade. They will risk all of these dangers in order to find a job in the United States that no one else wants; most will find work in the agricultural industry, where they will become disposable labor. Their low wages enable us to have cheap food prices, but often at the expense of their health and well-being.

Most of them migrate not because they want to get rich but because they want to survive. Many will take up the decision to migrate in order to put bread on the tables of their families. As Francisco said,

Sometimes my kids come to me and say, "Daddy, I'm hungry." And I don't have enough money to buy them food. And I can't tell them I don't have any money, but we don't. I can barely put bean, potatoes, and tortillas on the table with what I make. But I feel so bad that I sometimes will go into a store, even if it is two or three blocks away, or even three or four kilometers away, or even another country in order to get food for my family. I feel awful, but nothing is worse than seeing your hungry child look you in the eyes, knowing you don't have enough to give them. The reason why I'm migrating is not because I want to get rich but because my family is hungry.[11]

J. B. Scalabrini said, "For the migrant, one's country is the land that gives them bread," and for many, this country and this bread is in the United States. This struggle for the basic necessities of life has a built-in theological dimension. As John Paul II said,

The immediate reasons for the complex reality of human migration differ widely; its ultimate source, however, is the longing for a transcendent horizon of justice, freedom and peace. In short, it testifies to an anxiety which, however indirectly, refers to God, in whom alone man can find the full satisfaction of all his expectations.[12]

Like the Eucharist, the migrant journey revolves around the basic elements of life, around bread, around death, around hope, and around the longing for a promised land.

"He Said the Blessing": Praising God in the Midst of Darkness

Even amidst the trials of the immigrant, one sees not only hunger for bread but hunger for God. Not all immigrants have strong religious convictions. Not all have deep or profound insights into God. And not all pray or speak about their spiritual lives. They are vulnerable to the same seductions of life as anybody. But in my experience many immigrants experience such radical need that they come to realize they have no one else they can depend on but God. Their governments have failed them. Their economies have failed them. And their financial resources have run completely dry. For many, such need opens them up to God in a way that pushes them far beyond the comfort levels of those living in more prosperous conditions. In the midst of the trials of many immigrants, one would expect to find, more often than not, sadness, suffering, and pain. These do exist. And they exist in intense measures. But as one listens to these same immigrants one can also hear a deeper current of faith welling up in unsuspecting places.

The compelling testimony of their faith emerges in their capacity to believe in a God of life, even when they face life-threatening dangers every day. In a similar way, Israel's most sweeping claims about Yahweh's fidelity are dated to the exile, as is Jesus's most radical act of trust uttered from the cross.[13]

It is worth pausing for a moment to consider that Jesus praised God in his darkest moment. On the night before he died Jesus took the bread and he blessed God, even though he knew what lay ahead of him on the journey. He blessed God even though he was going to be betrayed, even though he knew he was going to be rejected by the chief priests and elders, even though he knew he was going to be crucified. After praising God for his goodness, he sat down at table with his friends. He thanked God when he had every reason to curse him.

Many immigrants I have spoken to show a similar capacity to draw from deep spiritual wells when they face the most "godless" of moments. As immigrants stow away in boxcars to move northward, suffer theft at the hands of *bandido* gangs or are left behind by *coyote* smugglers to die in the deserts and mountains, one would expect to see migrants cursing the darkness. Some do. But others reveal a different narrative unfolding, similar to what we see unfolding in the Eucharistic narrative.

When Consuela left home to search for bread for her family, she hired a *coyote* smuggler for $2,000 to take her across the border. She tried to cross the deadly desert four times. On her first attempt, she was caught by the U.S. Border Patrol. On her second attempt someone tried to rape her. On her third attempt she was robbed at gunpoint by border thugs. And on her fourth attempt, she ran out of food and water and almost died. After hallucinations and headaches, she started throwing up, until she could barely see straight. After she had a chance to recover, she wanted to try again, because she said her family at home depended on her. It was then that I met her, and I asked her about her life. To a great extent, I expected her to complain about how much she suffered, about how many problems she had, about all she has been through. What amazed me the most, however, was that throughout the conversation she never ceased blessing God for all He had done and for all she has received.

How does life's pain get transformed into such gratitude? We are left, really, with only two possibilities: such faith is either delusional in the Freudian sense or it is graced in the Christian sense. This phenomenon needs more sustained, critical, yet humble reflection, or else I think we easily miss or dismiss the subtle traces of the Spirit. I believe there is much more going on here than meets the eye, than can be apprehended from the surface, than can be judged and easily dismissed from a "critical distance," as is also the case in the Eucharist. From the perspective of human observation, we can only see in the immigrants' journey a struggle for the ordinary element of life, for bread, for drink. From the perspective of faith, however, one sees a far greater process going on, even, I dare say, a transubstantiation of this bread and wine of their struggles into an entirely new way of living and being in the world.

"He Broke the Bread": Broken Bodies and the Fraction Rite

At the Last Supper, after Jesus took bread and said the blessing, he broke the bread. The breaking of bread is an important part of the liturgy of the Eucharist. We do this breaking at the fraction rite, and we remember how Jesus was broken for others so that they might be reconciled with God the Father through him. For the religious leaders of his day, Jesus was put to death because they believed he was disposable. It was better that he die than the whole people perish, even though through his brokenness, sacramentalized in this bread, he would give redemptive nourishment for all who believe (Jn 11:50).

Like Jesus, in their efforts to nourish their families migrants are broken on a daily basis. They are broken to the point of death in the deserts they cross, where they die of heat exhaustion and heat stroke. They are broken to the point of death in the canals they cross, where they drown because of strong undercurrents and the inability to swim. They are broken to the point of death when they freeze to death in the mountains, where they encounter freak snowstorms along the treacherous migration routes. Since 1994 at least four hundred immigrants per year have died crossing the border, and each day an immigrant continues to die trying to cross into the United States.

In addition, an immigrant a day is broken to the point of death in the workplace. According to a recent study by the Associated Press, the jobs that lure Mexican workers to the United States are killing at alarming rates.[14] Even though the U.S. workplace grows safer overall, it has become more dangerous for the undocumented Mexican immigrant, and some have called these deaths "a worsening epidemic."[15] In the mid-1990s, Mexicans were about 30 percent more likely to die than native-born workers; now they are about 80 percent more likely to die in the workplace. In several Southern and Western states it is even worse, where a Mexican worker is four times more likely to die than the average U.S.-born worker. These accidental deaths are almost always preventable and often gruesome: workers are impaled, shredded in machinery, buried alive. Many die in the prime of their lives, and some are as young as fifteen years old. They die cutting North Carolina tobacco and processing Nebraska beef, chopping down trees in Colorado, welding a balcony in Florida, trimming grass at a Las Vegas golf course, and falling from scaffolding in Georgia.[16] Beyond those who die in the workplace, many more are maimed or disabled, and most are left without workers' compensation or health care benefits.

Why is all this happening? It is happening because undocumented Mexican labor is cheap. It is happening because immigrant workers are disposable labor. This equation has benefits for U.S. consumers, who, unlike Europeans, enjoy inexpensive food prices. Yet the cheap price of food comes at a great cost, because it comes at the expense of the lives of many undocumented immigrants. Their labor is cheap because they are desperate. And they are desperate because they have neither jobs in their homeland nor papers in the foreign land of the United States. Their socioeconomic situation thereby makes them vulnerable, and in their vulnerability they are often exploited and broken.

And if they are not physically broken, many others undergo another kind of brokenness. Ironically, taking up the decision to migrate to look for bread for the sake of the family often breaks up the family. While many begin with the intention of working in the United States for only a few years and then returning home, many end up staying in the United States, in part because of the difficulties of migrating and the challenges of returning. Many migrants make nothing short of a covenant with their families in Mexico that they will work in the north for a few years and then return home. Some manage to do so; others do not. Some maintain fidelity to their families over long periods of time and long distances; others do not. Some end up forming new families in the United States. Ironically, the desire to provide for the family, in many cases, ends up breaking up the family. Regardless, the experience of migration is an experience of brokenness: family brokenness, cultural brokenness, personal brokenness. And many other types of brokenness. The immigrant is left with a tragic irony, then: the one who brings bread to the table of the average American is the one who is broken open so that others may be nourished. What offers hope to migrants is that they recognized Jesus in "the breaking of the bread," they recognize in the narrative of Jesus their own narrative.

"And Gave It to His Disciples": Pouring Out Their Lives for the Good of Others

After Jesus took bread, blessed it, and broke it, he shared it with his disciples. It is here that he offers his body and blood so that others can be united with him in a new covenant, a new relationship. In the giving of his own life he nourished his disciples, so that they, in turn, could give themselves in a life of service to others, whatever it cost them.

When we think of the Eucharist, we think of bread, we think of wine. We reflect on the words, "this is my body, this is my blood." But less often do we reflect on the words in the Eucharistic prayer, less frequently do we think of the Eucharist in terms of "the fruit of the vine and the work of human hands." Given that the agricultural industry in the United States is sustained largely through immigrant labor, the bread and wine that even comes to the table is most certainly the result of immigrant labor. And in many parts of the country, this kind of labor is a modern day form of slavery.[17] And such slavery brings us face to face not only with the immigrant story but the Passover story all over again.

This memory of Christ is institutionalized in the Eucharist, and it tells the story of salvation, of freedom, and of liberation in ritual form. In our contemporary society we not only forget where we have come from, but we also lose sight of where we are going and who we want to become in our journey through life. If our Eucharistic celebration is not intimately connected to the larger liturgy of life, to the larger search for justice, to fighting to free those who are enslaved, then it has no meaning, and singing "alleluia" has no significance. Amos warns that worship without justice is idolatry (Am 5:21–27). If Christians hunger to receive the bread of life at liturgy but have no hunger to feed those whose lives are threatened and who are in need of bread today, they ignore Christ.

On the altar, then, we see not only the body and the blood of Christ, but we see in the bread and the wine the hands, the feet, the labor, the sweat of those who worked in the fields. We see those who tilled the land so grain could be planted under the hot sun. We see those who fumigated the vines, even while their eyes turned red, their lungs filled with pesticides, and their children were born with birth defects because of it. We see those who harvested the grapes, even for less than minimum wage, so they could send what they earned to their families in Mexico. We see those who woke up at four o'clock in the morning to bake bread or work in the wineries, those who drove trucks and finally brought the bread and wine to our doors, to our altars. In the Eucharist, we see not only bread and wine but also the footprints of the immigrant. In the Eucharist, we see in faith not only the body and blood of Christ. In the Eucharist, we also see the body and blood of the migrant, the body of the crucified, who also poured out their lives for their families so that they might eat and that we might eat, so that they might drink and we might drink, even if it cost them their lives. It is in this spirit that the bishops of the United States and Mexico write that we need to "seek to awaken our peoples to the mysterious presence of the crucified and risen Lord in the person of the migrant and to renew in them the values of the Kingdom of God that he proclaimed."[18]

"Do This in Memory of Me": Remembering the Immigrant, Opting for the Poor

In summary, then, as we look at the complex reality of migration, and we see the various voices that compete for a hearing, one of these most neglected voices is the theological perspective. I offer here this Eucharistic perspective of migration and this migratory perspective of the Eucharist precisely so that the debate might be reframed in terms of human life and human dignity rather than the socioeconomic and political forces that often govern the debate. In the narrative of Jesus we see how he "took the bread, said the blessing, broke it, and gave it to [his disciples]." In the narrative of the immigrants, we see how they take up the difficult decision to migrate, bless God in the midst of adversity, break themselves open so they can feed those they love, and give themselves away for the nourishment of others, even at the cost of their lives. Looking at migration through this Christian framework, I believe, can help us see more clearly a political dimension of spirituality and a spiritual dimension of politics and to see ultimately this integral connection between liturgy and life.[19]

The Eucharist is not an escape from reality while it immerses itself in the realm of the spiritual, but a challenge to enter more deeply into these struggles while the people of God wait in eschatological hope for the fulfillment of the reign of God in history. Politics is not an escape from the spiritual realm while it deals with the difficult affairs of "reality." A political reality that creates a society where the richest prosper while the poor suffer in want is a society in need of conversion. In our globalized world, politics cannot be concerned with the interest of the few or even the interests only of a nation, but must work for the benefit of all, and particularly the most vulnerable in society. The true moral worth of any society, as noted in Catholic social teaching, is how it treats its most vulnerable members.

Gustavo Gutiérrez says that the "Eucharist is a resume of our lives and a summary of the Christian message." He also says, "to remember Jesus is to remember his preference for the least of our brothers and sisters."[20] Benedict XVI adds that the transformation of bread and wine into the body and blood of Christ is the beginning of our own transformation, from which we are called to go forth into the world until God will be all in all (1 Cor 15:28).[21] To remember in the abstract that Jesus entered our history is not difficult. It is much more difficult to understand Jesus's memory of the poor as rooted in our own day and age and our own concrete reality.[22] Our memory of Jesus is a memory of those he had a preference for; in the end, our memory of God is intimately related to a memory of the God of life, who reaches out to everyone but especially those whose life is most threatened, such as the immigrants who risk life and death every day. One of the ongoing challenges of migration and Christian faith is to begin to see the immigrant with the eyes of Christ as we also seek to discern Christ in the eyes of the immigrant. The liturgy of the Eucharist is a place where we seek to develop a community that transcends all borders, that sees in the eyes of the immigrant stranger a brother, a sister, and a real presence of Christ.

NOTES

This article comes out of a conference on Humanities and the Option for the Poor at the University of Salzburg, Salzburg, Austria, and a conference on Immigration, Labor, and Religion at Harvard Divinity School called "Do This in Memory of Me: Anamnesis and Immigration." It has been published in the September 2006 edition of *Worship,* whose editors have gratefully given permission to republish this article.

1. See Gustavo Gutiérrez, *A Theology of Liberation,* rev. ed. with a new introduction (Maryknoll, NY: Orbis Books, 1988); and his *We Drink from Our Own Wells: The Spiritual Journey of a People,* trans. Matthew J. O'Connell (New York: Orbis Books, 1984).

2. See Norman K. Gottwald, *The Hebrew Bible: A Socio-Literary Introduction* (Minneapolis: Fortress Press, 1985), and Walter Brueggemann, *Theology of the Old Testament: Testimony, Dispute, and Advocacy* (Minneapolis: Fortress Press, 1997).

3. Deuteronomy 26:5. The notion that this is an early Israelite creed is Gerhard von Rad's thesis, even though its early origins are disputed among contemporary scholars. See his *Deuteronomy* (Philadelphia: Westminster Press, 1966).

4. For more on this subject, see J. Caputo, "Adieu—sans Dieu: Derrida and Levinas" in *The Face of the Other and the Trace of God,* ed. J. Bloechl, 276–312 (New York: Fordham University Press, 2000).

5. Teilhard de Chardin saw this "migration" as a movement towards the final consummation of humanity into what he calls "the omega point." See Pierre Teilhard de Chardin, *The Divine Milieu* (New York: Harper, 1960).

6. The translation of this text actually reads as "the Jews" rather than "the Israelites." From the time of the Babylonian captivity, "Jews" became the name for the whole nation (2 Maccabees 9:17; John 4:9; John 7:1; Acts 18:2, 24). The original designation of the Israelite people was "the Hebrews," as the descendants of Abraham, and I think the use of the word "Israelites" avoids this confusion. *St. John Chrysostom: Baptismal Instructions,* trans. and annotated by Paul W. Harkins (Westminster, MD: The Newman Press, 1963), 64.

7. Luke 22:14–20; also 1 Corinthians 11:23–25; cf. Matthew 26:26–29; Mark 14:22–25.

8. For more on this subject, see T. Talley, "From *Berakah* to *Eucharistia*: A Reopening Question," *Worship* 50, no. 2 (1976): 115–137; P. Bradshaw, "Introduction: The Evolution of Early Anaphoras," in *Essays on Early Eastern Eucharistic Prayers,* ed, P. Bradshaw, 1–18 (Collegeville, MN: Liturgical Press, 1997); Gregory Dix, *The Shape of the Liturgy* (Westminster: Dacre Press, 1945).

9. Paul F. Bradshaw, *Eucharistic Origins,* 2nd ed. (New York: Oxford University Press, 2004); Bryan Spinks, "Mis-shapen: Gregory Dix and the Four-Action Shape of the Liturgy," *Lutheran Quarterly* 4 (1990): 161–77; Andrew B. McGowan, "First Regarding the Cups: Papias and the Diversity of Early Eucharistic Practice," *Journal of Theological Studies* 46 (1995): 551–55.

10. See also Joseph A. Jesus Christ Grassi, *Broken Bread and Broken Bodies,* rev. ed. (Maryknoll, NY: Orbis Books, 2004), and Monika Hellwig, *The Eucharist and the Hunger of the World,* 2nd ed., rev. and expanded (Kansas City, MO: Sheed and Ward, 1992).

11. Francisco (immigrant man), interview by Daniel Groody, June 23, 2003, tape recording, Sasabe, Mexico.

12. John Paul II, "Message for World Migration Day," National Conference of Catholic Bishops/United States Catholic Conference, http://www.usccb.org/pope/wmde.htm (last accessed July 2007).

13. See Walter Brueggemann, *Theology of the Old Testament.*

14. Justin Pritchard, "A Mexican Worker Dies Each Day, AP Finds," via the Associated Press, March 14, 2004.

15. Ibid.

16. Ibid.

17. As John Bowe notes, "Modern slavery exists not because today's workers are immigrants or because some of them don't have papers but because agriculture has always managed to sidestep the labor rules that are imposed upon other industries. When the federal minimum-wage law was enacted, in 1938, farmworkers were excluded from its provisions, and remained so for nearly thirty years. Even today, farmworkers, unlike other hourly workers, are denied the right to overtime pay. In many states, they're excluded from workers' compensation and unemployment benefits. Farmworkers receive no medical insurance or sick leave, and are denied the right to organize. . . . [T]here's no other industry in America where employers have as much power over their employees" (John Bowe, "Nobodies: Does Slavery Exist in America?" *The New Yorker,* April 23, 2003, 122).

18. Mexican Catholic Bishops Conference and United States Conference of Catholic Bishops, *Strangers No Longer: Together on the Journey of Hope* (Washington, DC: United States Conference of Catholic Bishops, 2003), no. 3.

19. For more on constructive theology, see Clemens Sedmak, *Doing Local Theology* (New York: Orbis Books, 2002); Robert J. Schreiter, *Constructing Local Theolo-*

gies (London: SCM, 1985); Stephen B. Bevans, *Models of Contextual Theology,* rev. and expanded ed., Faith and Cultures Series (Maryknoll, NY: Orbis Books, 2002). See also Jim Wallis, *The Soul of Politics* (Maryknoll, NY: Orbis Books, 1994).

20. Gustavo Gutiérrez, personal interview at the Option for the Poor in Christian Theology conference, University of Notre Dame, November 12, 2002.

21. Benedict XVI, homily on the occasion of the twentieth World Youth Day (available at http://www.vatican.va/holy_father/benedict_xvi/homilies/2005/documents/hf_ben-xvi_hom_20050821_20th-world-youth-day_en.html, last accessed May 2007).

22. For more on reality as the foundational dimensions of liberation theology, see Ignacio Ellacuría, "Historicidad de la Salvación Cristiana," in *Mysterium Liberationis: Conceptos Fundamentales de la Teología de la Liberación,* vol. 1, ed. Ignacio Ellacuría and Jon Sobrino (Madrid: Editorial Trotta, 1990), and Xavier Zubiri, *El hombre y Dios,* ed. Ignacio Ellacuría (Madrid: Alianza Editorial Fundación Zubiri, 1984).

Contributors

Graziano Battistella, CS, is the Director of the Scalabrini International Migration Institute (SIMI) in Rome, Italy, which is an international academic institute that promotes scientific formation and professional training for scholars, researchers, and operators working in different areas of human mobility. He is also the editor of *Migrazioni e Diritti Umani.*

Stephen Bevans, SVD, is Professor of Mission and Culture at the Catholic Theological Union in Chicago. His teaching and research probe issues in faith, culture, ecclesiology, and ministry. He is the author of *Models of Contextual Theology* and co-author of *Constants in Context: A Theology of Mission for Today.*

Gioacchino Campese, CS, is a professor of theology at the Scalabrini International Migration Institute (SIMI) in Rome, Italy. He is the co-editor of *Migration, Religious Experience and Globalization,* and has worked for various years at *Casa del Migrante* in Tijuana, Mexico.

Jorge E. Castillo Guerra works as a teacher and researcher of missiology at the Radboud University of Nijmegen and for the Nijmegen Institute of Missiology. He is the author of *Iglesia: Identidad, Mision y Testimonio.* He was a consultant for the Episcopal Foundation *Cura Migratorum* and the Foundation for the Pastoral Care of Foreigners in Amsterdam.

Raúl Fornet-Betancourt teaches philosophy at the University of Aachen and the University of Bremen in Germany. He is the author of *Transformación Intercultural de la Filosofía* and editor of *Interaction and Asymmetry between Cultures in the Context of Globalization.*

Daniel G. Groody, CSC, is an assistant professor in theology and the Director of the Center for Latino Spirituality and Culture at the Institute for Latino Studies at the University of Notre Dame. He is the author of *Border of Death, Valley of Life: An Immigrant Journey of Heart and Spirit,* and *Globalization, Spirituality, and Justice: Navigating the Path to Peace;* and editor of *The Option for the Poor in Christian Theology.* He is executive producer of the film *Dying to Live: A Migrant's Journey* (see www.nd.edu/~dgroody/).

Gustavo Gutiérrez, OP, is the John Cardinal O'Hara Professor of Theology at the University of Notre Dame. He is internationally known as the father of liberation theology and is the author of various books, including *A Theology of Liberation: History, Politics, and Salvation; The Power of the Poor in History; and We Drink from Our Own Wells.*

Jacqueline Hagan is an associate professor of sociology at the University of North Carolina at Chapel Hill. She is the author of *Deciding to Be Legal: A Maya Community in Houston* and *Migration Miracle: Faith, Hope, and the Undocumented Journey,* as well as various articles and book chapters on religion and migration.

Robin Hoover serves as pastor of First Christian Church in Tucson, Arizona. He is the president and founder of Humane Borders, an organization dedicated to providing life-saving humanitarian assistance to migrants and changing U.S. immigration policies and enforcement strategies that endanger migrants. His work is known worldwide and has been featured in many television programs and documentaries.

Donald Kerwin is the executive director of Catholic Legal Immigration Network, Inc. (CLINIC), the nation's largest network of nonprofit immigration service offices and a tax-exempt subsidiary of the United States Conference of Bishops. He is the author of *Chaos on the U.S.-Mexico Border: A Report on Migrant Crossing Deaths, Immigrant Families, and Subsistence-Level Laborers* and various other works that seek to put a human face on U.S. immigration and labor laws and policies. He co-directs the migration project for the Woodstock Theological Center.

Patrick Murphy, CS, is the animator of Hispanic ministry in the archdiocese of Kansas City, Kansas. He is the vice-president of the National Catholic Association of Diocesan Directors for Hispanic Ministry and the former provincial of the Scalabrinian Missionaries (St. John the Baptist Province).

Alex Nava is an assistant professor of religious studies at the University of Arizona. He is the author of *The Mystical and Prophetic Thought of Simone Weil and Gustavo Gutiérrez*. His research interests include religion and culture in Latin America and the southwestern United States.

Peter C. Phan, a native of Vietnam, is professor in the Department of Theology and holder of the Ignacio Ellacuría Chair of Catholic Social Thought at Georgetown University. He has authored 10 books, including *Christianity with an Asian Face* and *In Our Own Tongues,* edited 20 volumes, and published over 250 essays. He is also the past president of the Catholic Theological Society of America.

Oscar Andrés Cardinal Rodríguez M, SDB, is from the Archdiocese of Tegucigalpa and served as the president of the Latin American Episcopal Conference (CELAM) from 1995 to 1999. Today, he continues to speak on issues of Third World debt and was at one time the Vatican's spokesperson with the International Monetary Fund and the World Bank.

Olivia Ruiz Marrujo is a cultural anthropologist at El Colegio de la Frontera Norte in Tijuana, Mexico. She is the author of numerous articles in specialized journals, and her main academic interests are in the field of migration, culture, and ethnicity. She has done extensive research, especially at Mexico's northern and southern borders.

Robert Schreiter, CPPS, is the Vatican II Professor of Theology at Catholic Theological Union in Chicago, and professor of theology and culture at the Radboud University, Nijmegen, the Netherlands. He is the author of numerous articles and books, including *Constructing Local Theologies, The New Catholicity,* and *The Ministry of Reconciliation*. He also serves as a theological consultant to *Caritas Internationalis,* an organization widely known for its programs in peace building and reconciliation.

Donald Senior, CP, is president of Catholic Theological Union where he is also professor of New Testament studies. In 2001 he was appointed by Pope John Paul II to the Pontifical Biblical Commission, and has written various books on biblical theology, including *The Gospel of Matthew, The Passion of Jesus in the Gospel (of Matthew, Mark, Luke and John),* and *Jesus: A Gospel Portrait.* He is also the general editor for *The Catholic Study Bible,* co-editor of *The Collegeville Pastoral Dictionary of the Bible,* and general editor of *The Bible Today.*

Giovanni Graziano Tassello, CS, is the director of an Italian Catholic mission and coordinator of the Centre for Migration Research (CSERPE) in Basel, Switzerland. He is the editor of *Enchiridion Della Chiesa per Le Migrazioni.* He is also the president of the Commission on Culture and Language of the Council of Italian Migrants Abroad and a member of the board of trustees for the organization Migrantes in Italy.

General Index

Abraham, 20, 28, 30–31, 33n1, 50–51, 95, 302
adult faith formation, 146, 156
affin, 257
Afghanistan, 286
agricultural industry, 234, 310, 314n17
alien, 29, 31, 33, 48, 51, 55, 57, 70, 193
alienation, 70, 291
al Qaeda, 202–203
American Border Patrol, 170
anamnesis, 303
Andreas, Peter, 280
Apostles' Creed, 41
Aquila and Priscilla, 25, 40
Arendt, Hannah, 219
Argentina, 132
Arizona Daily Star, 273
arms trafficking, xvi
assimilation, 213, 217, 222, 248, 250, 275
Assyrian deportation (seventh century B.C.), 21, 39
asylum seekers, 181, 186, 195–196, 199–201, 204. *See also* refugees
Australia, 179

Babylonian exile (sixth century B.C.), 21–22, 39
Bach, Robert, 281
Bañuelas, Arturo, 89–90
barbarians, 45–46, 304
Basil of Caesarea, 53

Benedict XVI, 312
Berlin Wall, 277, 287
Beta Sur, 225
birth control, 228
blasphemy, 48
Boff, Clodovis, 251
Borderlinks, 63, 163
Border Patrol, xx, 10, 160–162, 165, 167, 169–170, 197, 271, 274, 276–278, 299–300, 305, 307
border security/control, xxi, 161, 168, 194, 197, 200, 204, 274–275, 289–291, 300
  inhumane/unjust policy, 160, 162–163, 166–167, 271, 273, 279, 281, 288, 291
  "prevention through deterrence," 161, 168, 276–277
  reform, 74, 161, 163, 168, 170–172, 204, 235
Bosch, David, 94
Bracero Programs (1942–1964), 85n4, 171, 273–274
brain drain, 78
Brown, Mary, 135
Buddhism, 37, 70, 263
Burke, Kevin, 284
Bush, George W., 277
Byzantine empire, 46

Campese, Gioacchino, 100
Canada, 166, 179, 201, 203, 279

Index of Scripture Reference